BECOMING A
MASTER MANAGER

BECOMING A MASTER MANAGER

A COMPETING VALUES APPROACH

FIFTH EDITION

Robert E. Quinn
University of Michigan

Sue R. Faerman
State University of New York at Albany

Michael P. Thompson
Brigham Young University

Michael R. McGrath
Executive Education—University of Michigan Graduate School of Business

Lynda S. St. Clair
Bryant University

WILEY
John Wiley & Sons, Inc.

PUBLISHER: Jay O'Callaghan
EDITOR: Lise Johnson
ASSISTANT EDITOR: Sarah Vernon
EDITORIAL ASSISTANT: Chelsea Theis
MARKETING MANAGER: Karolina Zarychta
DESIGNER: Ngieng Seng Ping
PRODUCTION MANAGER: Janis Soo
SENIOR PRODUCTION EDITOR: Joyce Poh

This book was set in 10/12 Adobe Garamond by Laserwords Private Limited and printed and bound by Malloy Lithographics. The cover was printed by Malloy Lithographics.

This book is printed on acid free paper.

Founded in 1807, John Wiley & Sons, Inc. has been a valued source of knowledge and understanding for more than 200 years, helping people around the world meet their needs and fulfill their aspirations. Our company is built on a foundation of principles that include responsibility to the communities we serve and where we live and work. In 2008, we launched a Corporate Citizenship Initiative, a global effort to address the environmental, social, economic, and ethical challenges we face in our business. Among the issues we are addressing are carbon impact, paper specifications and procurement, ethical conduct within our business and among our vendors, and community and charitable support. For more information, please visit our website: www.wiley.com/go/citizenship.

Evaluation copies are provided to qualified academics and professionals for review purposes only, for use in their courses during the next academic year. These copies are licensed and may not be sold or transferred to a third party. Upon completion of the review period, please return the evaluation copy to Wiley. Return instructions and a free of charge return shipping label are available at www.wiley.com/go/returnlabel. Outside of the United States, please contact your local representative.

Library of Congress Cataloging-in-Publication Data

Becoming a master manager : a competing values approach / Robert E. Quinn ... [et al.]. —
   5th ed.
      p. cm.
   Includes index.
   ISBN 978-0-470-28466-7 (pbk.)
      1. Leadership. 2. Executive ability. 3. Management. 4. Organizational behavior. I. Quinn, Robert E.

HD57.7.B43 2010
658.4'092—dc22

2010021338

Printed in the United States of America
10 9 8 7 6 5 4 3 2 1

INTRODUCTION TO THE FIFTH EDITION

It is with great pleasure that we celebrate the 20th anniversary of the first edition of *Becoming a Master Manager* by publishing this enhanced fifth edition. Before the publication of *Becoming a Master Manager*, few texts emphasized the importance of developing management skills or admitted that learning *about* management concepts was not the same as learning *how to apply* those concepts in practice. In the intervening years, more attention has been paid to the knowing-doing gap (Pfeffer & Sutton, 2000) and today, the plethora of skill-focused texts available (e.g., Aldag & Kuzuhara, 2005; Baldwin, Bommer & Rubin, 2008; Caproni, 2004; de Janasz, Dowd & Schneider, 2009; Hunsaker, 2004; Whetton & Cameron, 2010) attests to the value of our original emphasis on developing management skills.

Although we are pleased to see so much more attention being paid to management skills, we remain concerned about the lack of attention that has been paid to the theory behind the identification of critical managerial and leadership competencies. Many skills texts rely on a laundry-list approach and offer little in the way of explanation of why particular competencies are important or how different competencies fit together.

In contrast, *Becoming a Master Manager* has always been built on a solid foundation of both theory and empirical evidence that provide a compelling case for why specific competencies are important. The framework offers managers an enduring foundation for analyzing what types of behaviors are most appropriate to achieve organizational goals in light of the existing environment. At the same time, the framework is flexible enough to make it suitable for identifying new competencies that may help managers adapt to changing external circumstances and internal conditions.

Most significantly, the competing values framework recognizes that management is fundamentally paradoxical. Prior to the development of the competing values framework, the main approach to coping with apparently conflicting goals was to immediately begin considering tradeoffs—do we want higher quality OR lower costs? Better conditions for our employees OR faster response times for our customers? Take-charge leaders who have their own vision for the organization OR leaders who invite participation and value the ideas of others? Today, more people have come to recognize that a sustainable competitive advantage is more likely to result if we can find ways to transcend paradoxes, rather than simply accepting the conventional wisdom that tradeoffs are necessary. We need to find ways to improve quality AND lower costs; we should look for ways to improve conditions for employees AND increase customer satisfaction; we need leaders who are visionary AND participative. Not surprisingly, if we can move from an "either-or" to a "both-and" approach to management, then we are much more likely to find solutions that support all our goals.

Going forward, we believe that even more attention needs to be paid to complex paradoxes that pull us in multiple directions at the same time. It is encouraging to hear the corporate mantra, "faster, better, cheaper" because it implies the need to achieve goals that have traditionally been seen as requiring tradeoffs. From the competing values perspective, however, this mantra is incomplete. The rational goal model tells us we need to **Compete** faster, the open systems model tells us we need to **Create** better goods and services, and the internal process model tells us that we need to **Control** costs to make things cheaper. The human relations model, however, is absent from this mantra—despite the fact that we know that the most successful organizations often point to the commitment, cohesion, and positive morale of their employees as a key factor in their success. One of the benefits of using the competing values framework to identify critical management competencies is that it includes all four of these perspectives. Drawing on the insights of the human relations model, we know that we need to **Collaborate** to ensure that employees are committed to all the organization's goals, including not just making things "faster, better, and cheaper" but also acting in a socially responsible and environmentally sustainable way.

The competing values framework presented in this text is designed to help readers understand the complex and dynamic nature of the organizational world. Since the early 1980s, the framework has been used in management education programs based in academic settings, as well as in organizationally-based management and executive development programs. Because the competing values framework is grounded in paradoxical thinking, it forces us to think about the competing tensions and demands that are placed on managers in new ways. As a result, it can help current and future managers develop their capacity to act quickly, confidently, imaginatively, and ethically when faced with the paradoxes that are ubiquitous in organizations around the world.

Our approach has grown out of nearly 30 years of research and instructional experimentation. The authors of this text have been involved in doing research that has helped to shape the metatheory. We have worked with these materials in our university classrooms with undergraduate and graduate students, as well as in management and executive development programs. We have also helped major organizations in both the public and private sectors design large-scale programs to improve the competencies of professional managers. Several thousand professional managers have completed programs that have used the competing values framework as an underlying foundation and integrating theme. The results have been gratifying and instructive—gratifying because both our students and we were transformed in the process. We hope that the use of this textbook will lead to similar outcomes for you.

CHANGES FROM THE FOURTH EDITION

In preparing this revision, we faced our own paradox—while we wanted to incorporate as much new material as possible and make a significant intellectual contribution, we also realized that for instructors who have used the book in the past, change for the sake of change was not desirable. Wrestling with our own competing goals of being innovative while at the same time retaining a sense of continuity further reinforced for us the importance of looking for ways to transcend paradox, before accepting that tradeoffs must be made. We hope that readers will find that the changes from the fourth to the fifth edition, as outlined below, are consistent with both of our goals.

Because we wish to emphasize the fundamental paradoxes that make the practice of management so complex, we have chosen to reorganize the text in terms of the theories that contribute to our understanding of why different competencies are important, rather than organizing the text by managerial roles. We selected this approach because master managers must be able to shift seamlessly between different "roles" and must apply different competencies at the same time if they are going to be successful in the long run. In fact, the 21 competencies included in this version of the text can all be used to help a manager achieve the goals of any of the four management models. Although we have placed competencies in quadrants based upon on findings from empirical research, we would never suggest that a competency such as "communicating honestly and effectively" was only important for organizations whose goal is to build and sustain employee commitment. Rather, the key point of the competing values framework is that ALL these competencies contribute to positive and sustainable organizations. We were concerned that students were not receiving sufficient reinforcement of that fact when specific roles were identified in the text. Instructors who wish to emphasize roles can still do so—the *Instructor's Manual* includes a comparison of the roles and competencies as presented in the fourth edition alongside the modules and competencies in the fifth edition and provides our rationale for the changes.

Our decision to focus more on the underlying theory rather than specific roles, resulted in several changes to the structure of the fifth edition. Rather than having eight different chapters for specific managerial roles, we now use four modules, each of which essentially combines two of the chapters from the fourth edition. Each module begins with:

- *Organizational Goals*: a reminder of the criteria of effectiveness, means-ends theory, and emphasis of the management model associated with that quadrant of the framework
- *Paradoxes*: examples of some fundamental paradoxes managers face when trying to achieve the types of goals typically associated with that management model
- *Competencies*: five key competencies that can help the manager transcend or contend with those paradoxes

To provide consistency with prior editions, we continue to use many of the same competencies and activities that have proven effective in the past. Based on student feedback, we now include a portion of the Evaluation Matrix assignment that previously appeared at the end of the last chapter at the end of each module. This allows students to begin working on their strategy for mastery much earlier in the course. Consistent with recent research, we have added some new competencies and modified some of the competencies used in earlier versions of the text. These changes are described in the following pages.

INTRODUCTION: THE COMPETING VALUES APPROACH TO MANAGEMENT

The introduction explains the competing values framework and how it integrates four contrasting perspectives on organizational effectiveness by describing the evolution of management models. In this edition, we have not identified specific managerial roles, so the material is organized into four modules instead of eight chapters. We have also associated a color with each quadrant of the framework to be consistent with how the model is presented in other sources (e.g., Cameron, Quinn, DeGraff & Thakor, 2006). Although we have retained the action imperative labels (Collaborate, Control, Compete, Create) when referring to the quadrants of the framework, we have attempted to emphasize that these terms are a shorthand convenience and thus oversimplify what managers need to do to be successful. Instead, we encourage readers to keep in mind the criteria of effectiveness and means-ends theories associated with each quadrant of the model to better appreciate the competing values embedded in the framework and the need to master and then to balance and blend competencies in each area.

We now briefly introduce the idea of using the competing values framework to analyze organizational culture in the introductory chapter (previously this was not done until Chapter 6). We have found that having information about how the competing values framework can be used to diagnose organizational culture is particularly useful for students who are currently employed. Instructors may, if they wish, have students complete an organizational culture assessment at the beginning of the course so students can think throughout the course about how their skills fit with the culture of their current employer.

Next we explain the structured approach to learning used in the text. Each competency section follows the ALAPA approach to learning that has been used in all previous editions of the text. Competencies begin with a preliminary Assessment activity followed by the Learning material. Most competencies include separate exercises for Analysis, Practice, and Application, and conclude with a Reflection. This last element, Reflection, was always included implicitly in our own understanding and use of the ALAPA framework. We discovered, however, that making this part of the process more explicit was especially helpful for those students with Activist learning styles (Rodwell, 2005) and/or those who approach tasks with Control or Compete orientations. These types of student often focus on checking assignments off their to-do lists, and do not gain as much from the activities as students who approach tasks with more flexible orientations that value introspection and creativity. To provide students with an example of the ALAPA approach, we conclude the Introduction with the Thinking Critically competency that was moved to the first chapter in the fourth edition.

MODULE 1—CREATING AND SUSTAINING COMMITMENT AND COHESION

As in the fourth edition, we begin with the human relations model, which focuses on creating and sustaining commitment, cohesion, and positive morale. This perspective is consistent with the Collaborate action imperative that was introduced in the fourth edition and focuses on the desired outcome of those collaborative efforts.

Paradoxes. From the perspective of the competing values framework, the main paradox of seeking commitment and cohesion is the need to allow for individuals to express their individuality, while needing some level of conformity in order for the organization to move forward. Whether seeking commitment and cohesion in work organizations, clubs, or voluntary organizations, leaders face a number of paradoxes. Three that are discussed in this module include:

- Increasing our self-awareness and self-knowledge also increases our capacity to change, so in the process of learning who we are, we become someone new.
- Involving people in decision-making processes can increase the effectiveness of the decision, but decrease the efficiency of the process.
- Building an effective team may (temporarily) lead to reduced productivity or effectiveness as individuals are given the opportunity to develop new skills and abilities.

Competencies. All six of the competencies included in the fourth edition for the mentor and facilitator roles have been retained, although we now combine the material from Building Teams and Participative Decision-Making into a single competency—Managing Groups and Leading Teams.

MODULE 2—ESTABLISHING AND MAINTAINING STABILITY AND CONTINUITY

Module 2 covers the internal process model and focuses on establishing and maintaining stability and continuity, consistent with the Control action imperative introduced in the fourth edition.

Paradoxes. From the perspective of the overarching competing values framework, the primary paradox of seeking stability and control is the need for adaptability and external support. Paradoxes that are especially salient in the internal process quadrant include:

- Getting the details right by measuring and monitoring performance and keeping an eye on the big picture without getting bogged down in too many rules and procedures.
- Working on cross-functional teams and special projects to help make improvements in organizational processes and still accomplishing day-to-day job objectives.
- Following corporate policies and procedures and reinventing policies and procedures to be more effective and efficient.

Competencies. Module 2 retains two of the three competencies from both the monitor and coordinator roles from the fourth edition. We have kept some of the material from the other two competencies, but included this information with other competencies. Managing Information Overload has been renamed Organizing Information Flows and expanded to cover both inflows and outflows of information. Some of the information from Chapter 4—Analyzing Core Processes has been incorporated into Module 2—Planning and Coordinating Projects (formerly Chapter 5—Managing Projects). The information on the job characteristics model formerly found in Chapter 5—Designing Work has been moved to Module 3—Motivating Self and Others. A new competency, Encouraging and Enabling Compliance, was added to the text based on recent research by Lawrence, Lenk, and Quinn (2009) that suggests managers must also serve as regulators, emphasizing and clarifying policies. Including this new competency seems particularly appropriate due to increased public scrutiny and expanded legal liability under regulations such as Sarbanes-Oxley.

MODULE 3—IMPROVING PRODUCTIVITY AND INCREASING PROFITABILITY

Module 3 builds on the assumptions of the rational goal model and the Compete action imperative. It emphasizes the importance of vision, goal setting, and execution for competing effectively.

Paradoxes.   As noted earlier, the main tension for the rational goal model occurs because of the apparent opposition between increasing productivity and profitability while creating and sustaining employee commitment. Other paradoxes that hard-driving managers face include:

- Expecting the leader to provide a clear vision for the organization while wanting the vision to be based on participative processes.
- Making decisions and moving ahead while taking enough time to ensure that all the relevant facts have been appropriately analyzed.
- Using performance measurement systems to align individual goals with organizational goals without spending too much time on setting goals and reviewing performance.

Competencies.   Five of the six competencies associated with the director and producer roles from the fourth edition have been retained in this module. Two earlier competencies, Working Productively and Fostering a Productive Work Environment have been combined under the new title—Motivating Self and Others. A new competency, Managing Execution and Driving for Results, has been added based on research by Lawrence et al. (2009). This new competency includes the topic of time management, which was previously included in a competency related to managing time and stress.

MODULE 4—PROMOTING CHANGE AND ENCOURAGING ADAPTABILITY

The final module covers the open systems model, which focuses on change, adaptability, and external support, consistent with the Create action imperative.

Paradoxes. Promoting change and encouraging adaptability seems to run directly counter to the focus on stability and control identified as so critical by the internal process model, but we also consider more subtle paradoxes in this module. For example:

- Expecting leaders to be powerful and at the same time being distrustful of powerful leaders.
- Using routines and habits to improve creativity and innovation.
- Increasing resistance to change by increasing pressures to change.

Competencies. Five of the six competencies in the fourth edition have been retained in the fifth edition. Due to space constraints, we removed Living with Change as a separate competency and incorporated some of the material from that section in Implementing and Sustaining Change (formerly called Managing Change). We have also expanded the competency on presenting ideas to include more information about different types of management communication.

CONCLUSION—INTEGRATION AND THE ROAD TO MASTERY

The conclusion returns to the overall competing values framework. We begin with a discussion of integration and behavioral complexity. We have included a discussion of "Negative Zones" to the text based on instructor feedback. Rather than including this topic in the introductory chapter as in an earlier edition of the text, we chose to include it at the end of the fifth edition. This allows students to focus on the positive aspects of the competing values framework when the model is first introduced and throughout the text. New to the conclusion is a discussion of the concept of "lift" as proposed by Quinn and Quinn (2009). Because the four psychological states that are required for "lift" to occur are consistent with the four quadrants of the competing values framework, this new model adds value without overwhelming students with a completely new approach at the end of the text. We conclude the text with a discussion of the steps in the developmental process, the importance of life-long learning, and an agenda for self improvement. Our goal is to remind students that becoming a master manager is a process that will continue as long as they open themselves to new growth experiences.

HOW TO USE THIS BOOK AND ONLINE ANCILLARIES

This book may be used in several ways. It can be employed alone as the main text in a course that is specifically designed to develop competencies, or it can be used with a more traditional text to accomplish the same objective. It can accompany more traditional texts in either an organizational behavior or a management principles course. The text has been used in schools of business, as well as in departments and programs of public and nonprofit management. In addition to the material available in the textbook, there are additional supporting materials available online:

- Competing Values Competency Questionnaire
- Test Bank
- *Instructor's Manual* and Powerpoint Slides

We encourage instructors and students to contact the authors with questions, comments, and suggestions about the text and ancillaries.

ACKNOWLEDGMENTS

Many of the ideas for this book were originally developed in 1983, and elaborated in 1985, in conjunction with two professional development programs designed for New York State. Funding for those programs and for the first edition of this book was provided by the negotiated agreements between the state of New York and the Civil Service Employees Association, Inc., and the Public Employees Federation, AFL-CIO, and made available through New York State's Governor's Office of Employee Relations, Program Planning and Employee Development Division (now Division for Development Services). We particularly thank Don Giek, former Director of the Division for Development Services. Don truly is a master manager, and we respect and appreciate the enormous efforts he made for us and for so many people in and outside of New York State. Laurie Newman DiPadova was also instrumental in the original development of the first edition of this text, coauthoring the innovator chapter and authoring the original instructor's manual. We are most appreciative of her efforts. We also would like to thank people who contributed to the Instructor's Manual with creative and novel essays on alternative teaching methods: Alan Belasen, Meg Benke, and Andrew DiNitto, SUNY-Empire State College; Dan Denison, University of Michigan; David Hart, Brigham Young University; Bill Metheny, Montana State University at Billings; Larry Michaelsen, The University of Oklahoma; and Deborah L. Wells, Creighton University.

We greatly appreciate the time and energy donated by all of the reviewers of *Becoming a Master Manager.* A number of people were asked to review earlier versions of the book, including: Vijay Mathur, San Jose State University; Michael Shaner, St. Louis University; Robert Sosna, Golden Gate University; Arnon Reichers, Ohio State University; Meg G. Birdseye, University of Alabama; John D. Bigelow, Boise State University; David E. Blevins, University of Mississippi; Allen Bluedorn, University of Missouri; Kent D. Carter, University of Maine at Orono; Paul D. Collins, Purdue University; Daniel Denison, University of Michigan; Laurie N. DiPadova, University of Utah; Dennis L. Dossett, University of Missouri–St. Louis; Stuart C. Freedman, University of Lowell; Walter Freytag, University of Washington at Bothell; Richard A. Grover, University of Southern Maine; Ester E. Hamilton, Pepperdine University; Steve Inian, California State Polytechnic University; Richard B. Ives, Tarrant County Junior College; Marcia Kassner, University of North Dakota; Kimberlee M. Keef, Alfred University; Gerald D. Klein, Rider University; Mark Lengnick-Hall, Wichita State University; David M. Leuser, Plymouth

State College; William E. McClane, Loyola College; Edward J. Morrison, University of Colorado at Boulder; Paula C. Morrow, Iowa State University; Ralph F. Mullin, Central Missouri State University; Joseph Petrick, Wright State University; Gerald Schoenfeld, James Madison University; Tim Schweizer, Luther College; Gregory Stephens, Texas Christian University; William E. Stratton, Idaho State University; David Szczerbacki, Alfred University; Fred Tesch, Western Connecticut State University; Charles N. Toftoy, Golden State University; Barry L. Wisdom, Southwest Missouri State University; Joseph Weiss, Bentley College; and Mark Wellman, Bowling Green State University. We appreciate their many helpful comments and insights.

Many others also contributed to the work of this and/or the earlier editions, and we would like to thank Debbi Berg, Bill Bywater, Chris Dammer, Rachel Ebert, Pauline Farmer, Bruce Hamm, Bill LaFleur, Warren Ilchman, Kary Jablonka, Tom Kinney, Chuck Klaer, Katherine Lawrence, Vicki Marrone, David McCaffrey, Ted Peters, Norma Riccucci, Michael Roberto, Steven Simons, Onnolee Smith, Eugene Thompson, Ben Westery, Angela Wicks, and John Zanetich. All contributed significantly and we are grateful.

Our publisher, John Wiley & Sons has been an incredible partner through all five editions of this text. The publishing team for this fifth edition has been especially patient with us as we struggled to balance the many competing demands on our time. We would like to express our sincere appreciation to Lise Johnson, Sarah Vernon, as well as Carissa Marker Doshi for their assistance. They have our heartfelt gratitude.

Finally we thank our families for their continuous support.

Robert E. Quinn
Sue R. Faerman
Michael P. Thompson
Michael R. McGrath
Lynda S. St. Clair

REFERENCES

Aldag, R. J., & Kuzuhara, L. W. (2005). *Mastering management skills: A manager's toolkit*. Mason, OH: Thomson South-Western.

Baldwin, T. T., Bommer, W. H., & Rubin, R. S. (2008). *Developing management skills: What great managers know and do*. New York: McGraw-Hill Irwin.

Cameron, K. S., Quinn, R. E., DeGraff, J., & Thakor, A. V. (2006). *Competing values leadership: Creating value in organizations*. Cheltenham, UK: Edward Elgar.

Caproni, P. (2004). *Management skills for everyday life: The practical coach* (2nd ed.). Upper Saddle River, NJ: Prentice Hall.

de Janasz, S. C., Dowd, K., & Schneider, B. Z. (2009). *Interpersonal skills in organizations* (3rd ed.). New York: McGraw-Hill Irwin.

Hunsaker, P. L. (2004). *Management: A Skills Approach* (2nd ed.). Upper Saddle River, NJ: Prentice Hall.

Lawrence, K. A., Lenk, P., & Quinn, R. E. (2009). Behavioral complexity in leadership: The psychometric properties of a new instrument to measure behavioral repertoire. *Leadership Quarterly, 20*, 87–102.

Pfeffer, J., & Sutton, R. (2000). *The knowing-doing gap.* Boston: Harvard Business School Press.

Quinn, R. W., & Quinn R. E. (2009). *Lift: Becoming a positive force in any situation.* San Francisco: Berrett-Koehler.

Rodwell, J. R. (2005). The assessment of formal management development: A method, a baseline and the need to incorporate learning styles. *Journal of Management Development, 24*, 239–252.

Whetton, D. A., & Cameron, K. S. (2010). *Developing management skills* (8th ed.). Upper Saddle River, NJ: Prentice Hall.

BRIEF CONTENTS

CONTENTS

THE COMPETING VALUES APPROACH TO MANAGEMENT

◼ FOUNDATIONS

The Evolution of Management Models

The Competing Values Framework

Organizing the Learning Process—ALAPA

Core Competency: Thinking Critically

Becoming a more effective manager and leader is a life-long process in learning to transcend paradox. A paradox exists when two seemingly inconsistent or contradictory ideas are actually both true. For example, the claim that "to be a good leader, you must be a good follower" is paradoxical because leaders and followers are generally thought to be engaged in opposite types of behaviors. It also seems paradoxical that so many books have been written about how to become a better manager when most people would agree that you cannot learn how to manage people by reading books.

The competing values approach to management outlined in this text is grounded on the idea that to be effective, managers must navigate a world filled with paradoxes. Managers are often called on to do things that at first glance appear to be mutually exclusive. For example, they must focus on the future at the same time that they pay attention to the present. Managers must meet the needs of their employees while pushing those same employees to do more with less to satisfy increasingly demanding customers ever more quickly. Managers must encourage innovation and risk-taking while ensuring the stability and continuity of the organization. In short, managers must embrace a diverse set of values that often appear to be contradictory. The competing values approach to management looks for ways to transcend paradox and redefine what is possible.

1

For most people, transcending paradox requires some serious rethinking of existing beliefs. We all have beliefs, and we all make assumptions about the right way to do things. This is certainly true when it comes to managerial leadership. Although our beliefs and assumptions can make us effective, they can sometimes make us ineffective (House & Podsakoff, 1994). When they do make us ineffective, it often is hard to understand why—particularly when those beliefs seemed to work so well in the past. We are not usually very experienced at examining our basic beliefs and assumptions. Nor are we very experienced at adopting new assumptions or learning skills and competencies that are associated with those new assumptions. Often it takes a crisis to stimulate such change. Consider the following case.

I have always seen myself as a man who gets things done. After 17 years with a major pharmaceutical company, I was promoted to general manager in the international division. I was put in charge of all Southeast Asian operations. The unit seemed pretty sloppy to me. From the beginning I established myself as a tough, no-nonsense leader. If someone came in with a problem, he or she knew to have the facts straight or risk real trouble. After three months I began to feel like I was working myself to exhaustion, yet I could point to few real improvements. After six months or so, I felt very uneasy but was not sure why.

One night I went home and my wife greeted me. She said, "I want a divorce." I was shocked and caught off balance. To make a long story short, we ended up in counseling.

Our counselor taught me how to listen and practice empathy. The results were revolutionary. I learned that communication happens at many levels and that it's a two-way process. My marriage became richer than I had ever imagined possible.

I tried to apply what I was learning to what was going on at work. I began to realize that there was a lot going on that I didn't know about. People couldn't tell me the truth because I would chop their heads off. I told everyone to come to me with any problem so that we could solve it together. Naturally, no one believed me. But after a year of proving myself, I am now known as one of the most approachable people in the entire organization. The impact on my division's operation has been impressive.

The man in the preceding case had a problem of real significance. The lives of many people, including subordinates, superiors, customers, and even his family members, were being affected by his actions. He was less successful than he might have been because of his beliefs about what a leader is supposed to do. For him, good management meant tight, well-organized operations run by tough-minded, aggressive leaders. His model was not all wrong, but it was inadequate. It limited his awareness of important alternatives and, thus, kept him from performing as effectively as he might have. Fortunately, this man was able both to rethink his beliefs and to alter his behavior to reflect a more complex and effective approach to management.

THE EVOLUTION OF MANAGEMENT MODELS

It turns out that nearly everyone has beliefs or viewpoints about what a manager should do. In the study of management, these beliefs are sometimes referred to as **models.** There are many different kinds of models. Although some are formally written or otherwise explicit, others, like the assumptions of the general manager, are informal. Because models affect what happens in organizations, we need to consider them in some depth.

Models are representations of a more complex reality. A model airplane, for example, is a physical representation of a real airplane. Models help us to represent, communicate ideas about, and better understand more complex phenomena in the real world.

A model that attempts to describe a social phenomenon represents a set of assumptions about what is happening and why. By giving us a general way of seeing and thinking about that phenomenon, the model provides us with a particular perspective about a more complex reality. Although models can help us to see some aspects of a phenomenon, they can also blind us to other aspects. The general manager mentioned previously, for example, had such strongly held beliefs about order, authority, and direction that he was unable to see some important aspects of the reality that surrounded him.

Unfortunately, our models of management are often so tied to our identity and emotions that we find it very difficult to learn about and appreciate different models. Because of the complexity of life, however, we often need to call upon more than one model. When we can see and evaluate more alternatives, our degree of choice and our potential effectiveness can be increased (Senge, 1990).

The models held by individuals often reflect models held by society at large. During the twentieth century a number of management models emerged. Understanding these models and their origins can give managers a broader understanding of behavior in organizations and a wider array of choices.

Our models and definitions of management keep evolving. As societal values change, existing viewpoints alter, and new models of management emerge (Fabian, 2000). These new models are not driven simply by the writings of academic or popular writers; or by managers who introduce an effective new practice; or by the technical, social, or political forces of the time. These models emerge from a complex interaction among all these factors. In this section, we will look at four major management models and how they evolved from the changing conditions of the twentieth century. Table I.1 at the end of this section provides a summary of all four models. The discussion below draws on the historical work of Mirvis (1985). Because exact dates are not critical for our purposes, we have used time periods of 25 years to simplify the discussion. Also keep in mind that although new models typically emerge in response to problems with earlier models, the emergence of each new model does not mean that old models were completely wrong and were forgotten. Rather, some aspects of earlier models are still very relevant. Just as important, many people continue to hold onto the beliefs and assumptions they developed using an earlier model, so their decisions continue to reflect the assumptions of that earlier model.

1900–1925: THE EMERGENCE OF THE RATIONAL GOAL MODEL AND THE INTERNAL PROCESS MODEL

The first 25 years of the twentieth century were a time of exciting growth and progress that ended in the high prosperity of the Roaring Twenties. As the period began, the economy was characterized by rich resources, cheap labor, and laissez-faire policies. In

1901, oil was discovered in Beaumont, Texas. The age of coal became the age of oil and, soon after, the age of inexpensive energy. Technologically, it was a time of invention and innovation as tremendous advances occurred in both agriculture and industry. The work force was heavily influenced by immigrants from all over the world and by people leaving the shrinking world of agriculture. The average level of education for these people was 8.2 years. Most were confronted by serious financial needs. There was little, at the outset of this period, in terms of unionism or government policy to protect workers from the demanding and primitive conditions they often faced in the factories.

One general orientation of the period was Social Darwinism: the belief in "survival of the fittest." Given this orientation, it is not surprising that *Acres of Diamonds*, by Russell Conwell, was a very popular book of the time. The book's thesis was that it was every man's Christian duty to be rich. The author amassed a personal fortune from royalties and speaking fees.

These years saw the rise of the great individual industrial leaders. Henry Ford, for example, not only implemented his vision of inexpensive transportation for everyone by producing the Model T, but he also applied the principles of Frederick Taylor to the production process. Taylor was the father of **scientific management** (see Theoretical Perspective I.1). He introduced a variety of techniques for "rationalizing" work and making it as efficient as possible. Using Taylor's ideas, Henry Ford, in 1914, introduced the assembly line and reduced car assembly time from 728 hours to 93 minutes. In six years Ford's market share went from just under 10 percent to just under 50 percent. The wealth generated by the inventions, production methods, and organizations themselves was an entirely new phenomenon.

Rational Goal Model.   It was in this historical context that the first two models of management began to emerge. The first is the **rational goal model.** The symbol that best represents this model is the dollar sign, because the ultimate criteria of organization effectiveness are productivity and profit. The basic means-ends

---

THEORETICAL PERSPECTIVE I.1

TAYLOR'S FOUR PRINCIPLES OF MANAGEMENT

1. Develop a science for every job, which replaces the old rule-of-thumb method.
2. Systematically select workers so that they fit the job, and train them effectively.
3. Offer incentives so that workers behave in accordance with the principles of the science that has been developed.
4. Support workers by carefully planning their work and smoothing the way as they do their jobs.

Adapted from Frederick W. Taylor, *The Principles of Scientific Management* (New York: Harper and Brothers, 1911), 44.

assumption in this approach is the belief that clear direction leads to productive outcomes. Hence there is a continuing emphasis on processes such as goal clarification, rational analysis, and action taking. The organizational climate is rational economic, and all decisions are driven by considerations of "the bottom line." If an employee of 20 years is only producing at 80 percent efficiency, the appropriate decision is clear: Replace the employee with a person who will contribute at 100 percent efficiency. In the rational goal model the ultimate value is achievement and profit maximization. To ensure that those goals are met, managers are expected to be decisive and task-oriented.

Stories abound about the harsh treatment that supervisors and managers inflicted on employees during this time. In one manufacturing company, for example, they still talk today about the toilet that was once located in the center of the shop floor and was surrounded by glass windows so that the supervisor could see who was inside and how long the person stayed.

Internal Process Model. The second model is called the **internal process model.** While its most basic hierarchical arrangements had been in use for centuries, during the first quarter of the twentieth century it rapidly evolved into what would become known as the "professional bureaucracy." The basic notions of this model would not be fully codified, however, until the writings of Max Weber and Henri Fayol were translated in the middle of the next quarter-century. This model is highly complementary to the rational goal model. Here the symbol is a pyramid, and the criteria of effectiveness are stability and continuity. The means-ends assumption is based on the belief that routinization leads to stability. The emphasis is on processes such as definition of responsibilities, measurement, documentation, and record keeping. The organizational climate is hierarchical, and all decisions are colored by the existing rules, structures, and traditions. If an employee's efficiency falls, control is increased through the application of various policies and procedures. In this model managers are expected to be technically expert and highly dependable, focusing on coordinating and monitoring workflows for efficiency and effectiveness.

1926–1950: THE EMERGENCE OF THE HUMAN RELATIONS MODEL

The second quarter of the century brought two events of enormous proportions. The stock market crash of 1929 and World War II would affect the lives and outlook of generations to come. During this period the economy would boom, crash, recover with the war, and then, once again, offer bright hopes. Technological advances would continue in all areas, but particularly in agriculture, transportation, and consumer goods. The rational goal model continued to flourish. With the writings of Henri Fayol, Max Weber, and others, the internal process model (see Theoretical Perspectives I.2 and I.3) would be more clearly articulated. Yet, even while this was being accomplished, it started to become clear that the rational goal and internal process models were not entirely appropriate to the demands of the times.

THEORETICAL PERSPECTIVE I.2

FAYOL'S GENERAL PRINCIPLES OF MANAGEMENT

1. *Division of work.* The object of division of work is to produce more and better work with the same effort. It is accomplished through reduction in the number of tasks to which attention and effort must be directed.

2. *Authority and responsibility.* Authority is the right to give orders, and responsibility is its essential counterpart. Whenever authority is exercised, responsibility arises.

3. *Discipline.* Discipline implies obedience and respect for the agreements between the firm and its employees. These agreements are arrived at by discussion between an owner or group of owners and worker's associations. The establishment of such agreements should remain one of the chief preoccupations of industrial heads. Discipline also involves sanctions judiciously applied.

4. *Unity of command.* An employee should receive orders from one superior only.

5. *Unity of direction.* Each group of activities having one objective should be unified by having one plan and one head.

6. *Subordination of individual interest to general interest.* The interest of one employee or group of employees should not prevail over that of the company or broader organization.

7. *Remuneration of personnel.* To maintain their loyalty and support, employees must receive a fair wage for services rendered.

8. *Centralization.* Like division of work, centralization belongs to the natural order of things. The appropriate degree of centralization, however, will vary with a particular concern, so it becomes a question of the proper proportion. It is a problem of finding the measure that will give the best overall yield.

9. *Scalar chain.* The scalar chain is the chain of superiors ranging from the ultimate authority to the lowest ranks. It is an error to depart needlessly from the line of authority, but it is an even greater one to adhere to it when detriment to the business could ensue.

10. *Order.* A place for everything, and everything in its place.

11. *Equity.* Equity is a combination of kindliness and justice.

12. *Stability of tenure of personnel.* High turnover increases inefficiency. A mediocre manager who stays is infinitely preferable to an outstanding manager who comes and goes.

13. *Initiative.* Initiative involves thinking out a plan and ensuring its success. This gives zeal and energy to an organization.

14. *Esprit de corps.* Union is strength, and it comes from the harmony of the personnel.

Abridged from Henri Fayol, *General and Industrial Administration* (New York: Pitman, 1949), 20–41.

THEORETICAL PERSPECTIVE I.3

CHARACTERISTICS OF WEBERIAN BUREAUCRACY

Elements of Bureaucracy

1. There is a division of labor with responsibilities that are clearly defined.
2. Positions are organized in a hierarchy of authority.
3. All personnel are objectively selected and promoted based on technical abilities.
4. Administrative decisions are recorded in writing, and records are maintained over time.
5. There are career managers working for a salary.
6. There are standard rules and procedures that are uniformly applied to all.

Adapted from Max Weber, *The Theory of Social and Economic Organizations*, ed. A.M. Henderson and Talcott Parsons (trans.) (New York: Free Press, 1947), 328–337.

Some fundamental changes began to appear in the fabric of society during the second quarter of the century. Unions, now a significant force, adhered to an economic agenda that brought an ever-larger paycheck into the home of the American worker. Industry placed a heavy emphasis on the production of consumer goods. By the end of this period, new labor-saving machines were beginning to appear in homes. There was a sense of prosperity and a concern with recreation as well as survival. Factory workers were not as eager as their parents had been to accept the opportunity to work overtime. Neither were they as likely to give unquestioning obedience to authority. Hence managers were finding that the rational goal and internal process models were no longer as effective as they once were.

Given the shortcomings of the first two models, it is not surprising that one of the most popular books written during this period was Dale Carnegie's *How to Win Friends and Influence People*. It provided some much-desired advice on how to relate effectively to others. In the academic world, Chester Barnard pointed to the significance of the "informal" organization and the fact that informal relationships, if managed properly, could be powerful tools for the manager. Also during this period Elton Mayo and Fritz Roethlisberger carried out their work in the famous Hawthorne studies. One well-known experiment carried out by these two researchers, concerned levels of lighting. Each time they increased the levels of lighting, employee productivity went up. However, when they decreased the lighting, productivity also went up. They eventually concluded that what was really stimulating the workers were the attention being shown them by the researchers. The results of these studies were also interpreted as evidence of a need for an increased focus on the power of relationships and informal processes in the performance of human groups.

Human Relations Model. By the end of the second quarter of the century, the emerging orientation was the **human relations model**. In this model, the key emphasis is on commitment, cohesion, and morale. The means-ends assumption is that involvement results in commitment and the key values are participation, conflict resolution, and consensus building. Because of an emphasis on equality and openness, the appropriate symbol for this model is a circle. The organization takes on a clanlike, team-oriented climate in which decision-making is characterized by deep involvement. Here, if an employee's efficiency declines, managers take a developmental perspective and look at a complex set of motivational factors. They may choose to alter the person's degree of participation or opt for a host of other social psychological variables. Managers are expected to be empathetic and open to employee opinions; key activities include mentoring individuals and facilitating group and team processes.

In 1949, this model was far from crystallized, and it ran counter to the assumptions in the rational goal and internal process models. Hence it was difficult to understand and certainly difficult to practice. Attempts often resulted in a kind of authoritarian benevolence. It would take well into the next quarter-century for research and popular writings to explore this orientation and for managerial experiments to result in meaningful outcomes in large organizations.

1951–1975: THE EMERGENCE OF THE OPEN SYSTEMS MODEL

The period 1951 to 1975 began with the United States as the unquestioned leader of the capitalist world. It ended with the leadership of the United States in serious question. During this period the economy experienced the shock of the oil embargo in 1973. Suddenly assumptions about cheap energy, and all the life patterns upon which they were based, were in danger. By the late 1970s the economy was suffering under the weight of stagnation and huge government debt. At the beginning of this period, "made in Japan" meant cheap, low-quality goods of little significance to Americans. By the end, Japanese quality could not be matched, and Japan was making rapid inroads into sectors of the economy thought to be the sacred domain of American companies. Even such traditionally American manufacturing areas as automobile production were dramatically affected. There was also a marked shift from a clear product economy to the beginnings of a service economy.

Technological advances began to occur at an ever-increasing rate. At the outset of the third quarter of the century, the television was a strange device. By the end of this period, television was the primary source of information, and the computer was entering the life of every American. At the beginning of the 1960s, NASA worked to accomplish the impossible dream of putting a man on the moon, but then Americans became bored with the seemingly commonplace accomplishments of the space program.

Societal values also shifted dramatically. The 1950s were a time of conventional values. Driven by the Vietnam War, the 1960s were a time of cynicism and upheaval. Authority and institutions were everywhere in question. By the 1970s the difficulty of bringing about social change was fully understood. A more individualistic and conservative orientation began to take root.

In the workforce, average education jumped from the 8.2 years at the beginning of the century to 12.6 years. Spurred by considerable prosperity, workers in the United States were now concerned not only with money and recreation but also with self-fulfillment. Women began to move into professions that had been closed to them previously. The agenda of labor expanded to include social and political issues. Organizations became knowledge-intense, and it was no longer possible to expect the boss to know more than every person he supervised.

By now the first two models were firmly in place, and management vocabulary was filled with rational management terms, such as management by objectives (MBO) and management information system (MIS). The human relations model, however, was also now familiar. Many books about human relations became popular during this period, further sensitizing the world to the complexities of motivation and leadership. Experiments in group dynamics, organizational development, sociotechnical systems, and participative management flourished.

In the mid-1960s, spurred by the ever-increasing rate of change and the need to understand how to manage in a fast-changing, knowledge-intense world, a variety of academics began to write about still another model. People such as Katz and Kahn at the University of Michigan, Lawrence and Lorsch at Harvard, as well as a host of others, began to develop the open systems model of organization. This model was more dynamic than others. The manager was no longer seen as a rational decision maker controlling a machinelike organization. The research of Mintzberg (1975), for example, showed that in contrast to the highly systematic pictures portrayed in the principles of administration (see Theoretical Perspective I.2), managers live in highly unpredictable environments and have little time to organize and plan. They are, instead, bombarded by constant stimuli and forced to make rapid decisions. Such observations were consistent with the movement to develop contingency theories (see Theoretical Perspective I.4). These theories recognized that the simplicity of earlier approaches went too far.

Open Systems Model. In the **open systems model**, the organization is faced with a need to compete in an ambiguous and competitive environment. The key criteria of organizational effectiveness are adaptability and external support. Because of the emphasis on organizational flexibility and responsiveness, the symbol here is the amoeba. The amoeba is a very responsive, fast-changing organism that is able to respond to its environment. The means-ends assumption is that continual adaptation and innovation lead to the acquisition and maintenance of external resources. Key processes are political adaptation, creative problem solving, innovation, and the management of change. The organization has an innovative climate and is more of an "adhocracy" than a bureaucracy. Risk is high, and decisions are made quickly. In this situation common vision and shared values are very important. Here, if an employee's efficiency declines, it may be seen as a result of long periods of intense work, an overload of stress, and perhaps a case of burnout. In addition to being creative and innovative, the manager is expected to use power and influence to initiate and sustain change in the organization.

THEORETICAL PERSPECTIVE I.4

CONTINGENCY THEORY

Appropriateness of Managerial Actions Varies with Key Variables

1. *Size.* Problems of coordination increase as the size of the organization increases. Appropriate coordination procedures for a large organization will not be efficient in a small organization, and vice versa.

2. *Technology.* The technology used to produce outputs varies. It may be very routine or very customized. The appropriateness of organizational structures, leadership styles, and control systems will vary with the type of technology.

3. *Environment.* Organizations exist within larger environments. These may be uncertain and turbulent or predictable and unchanging. Organizational structures, leadership styles, and control systems will vary accordingly.

4. *Individuals.* People are not the same. They have very different needs. Managers must adjust their styles accordingly.

1976–1999: THE EMERGENCE OF "BOTH-AND" ASSUMPTIONS

In the 1980s it became apparent that American organizations were in deep trouble. Innovation, quality, and productivity all slumped badly. Japanese products made astounding advances as talk of U.S. trade deficits became commonplace. Reaganomics and conservative social and economic values fully replaced the visions of the Great Society. In the labor force, knowledge work became commonplace and physical labor rare. Labor unions experienced major setbacks as organizations struggled to downsize their staffs and increase quality at the same time. The issue of job security became increasingly prominent in labor negotiations. Organizations faced new issues, such as takeovers and downsizing. One middle manager struggled to do the job previously done by two or three. Burnout and stress became hot topics.

Peters and Waterman published a book that would have extraordinary popularity. *In Search of Excellence* attempted to chronicle the story of those few organizations that were seemingly doing it right. It was really the first attempt to provide advice on how to revitalize a stagnant organization and move it into a congruent relationship with an environment turned upside down. Like Carnegie's book, which focused attention on the previously neglected topic of the importance of people in organizations, *In Search of Excellence* addressed and made clear the most salient unmet need of the time: how to manage in a world where nothing is stable.

In such a complex and fast-changing world, simple solutions became suspect. None of the four models, discussed earlier and summarized in Table I.1, offered a sufficient answer, not even the more complex open systems approach. It had become clear that none of the existing management models was adequate. A new approach to

TABLE I.1 Characteristics of the Four Management Models

	Rational Goal	*Internal Process*	*Human Relations*	*Open Systems*
Symbol	$	△	○	☁
Criteria of effectiveness	Productivity, profit	Stability, continuity	Commitment, cohesion, morale	Adaptability, external support
Means–ends theory	Clear direction leads to productive outcomes	Routinization leads to stability	Involvement results in commitment	Continual adaptation and innovation lead to acquiring and maintaining external resources
Action imperative	Compete	Control	Collaborate	Create
Emphasis	Goal clarification, rational analysis, and action taking	Defining responsibility, measurement, documentation	Participation, conflict resolution, and consensus building	Political adaptation, creative problem solving, innovation, change management
Climate	Rational economic: "the bottom line"	Hierarchical	Team oriented	Innovative, flexible

understanding effective management was needed. It was during this period that the competing values framework, which serves as the organizing structure for this text-book, was first developed and tested.

2000–TODAY: COMPLEXITY, AMBIGUITY, AND PARADOX

As the twentieth century drew to a close, the rate of change rose to new heights. Long-standing political and business institutions began to crumble. The Berlin Wall came tumbling down. A short time later the USSR itself disintegrated. In the United States some of the most powerful and admired corporations seemed strong one day and in deep difficulty the next. In the new global economy nothing seemed predictable. This was exacerbated by the emergence of the Internet and e-commerce. In the meantime, employees with the right mix of competencies and abilities were in short supply. In 2000, a survey of executives' concerns ("Survey of Pressing Problems," 2000) indicated that the most pressing problems were the following:

- Attracting, keeping, and developing good people
- Thinking and planning strategically
- Maintaining a high-performance climate
- Improving customer satisfaction
- Managing time and stress
- Staying ahead of the competition

- Aligning vision, strategy, and behavior
- Maintaining work and life balance
- Improving internal processes
- Stimulating innovation

During the next ten years, the world continued to change. In 2001 the attack on the World Trade Center took us into the new world of constant terrorist threats. The emergence of China shifted how we looked at global business. The disaster on Wall Street, the near collapse of the banking system and general crisis in the world economy, turned corporate life upside down. In 2010, with its high rate of unemployment, it is hard to imagine that the number one concern in 2000 was attracting and keeping people.

Today executives ask us how they can manage in a world of volatility, complexity, and ambiguity. They want to know how to get cross-boundary cooperation as they seek to continually change their organizational culture. They are looking for ways to obtain employee motivation and loyalty in an environment where they cannot promise long-term job security. These questions reflect an underlying concern—the need to achieve organizational effectiveness in a highly dynamic environment filled with complexity, ambiguity, and paradoxical demands. The competing values framework is a time-tested, powerful tool that can assist managers as they grapple with these issues.

THE COMPETING VALUES FRAMEWORK

Complex situations require complex responses. Sometimes organizations benefit from stability, and sometimes they benefit from change. Often organizations need both stability and change at the same time. In contrast to earlier approaches, the development of the competing values framework did not assume that stability and change were mutually exclusive—an either-or decision. Eliminating that assumption was the key to developing an integrated model that focused on "both-and" assumptions, where contrasting behaviors could be needed and enacted at the same time (Quinn, Kahn & Mandl, 1994). This new, apparently paradoxical assumption, is at the heart of the **competing values framework**—an approach that views each of the four models as elements of a larger, integrated model. This book is organized around that framework.

INTEGRATING IDEAS ABOUT EFFECTIVENESS

At first, the models discussed earlier seem to be four entirely different perspectives or domains. However, they can be viewed as closely related and interwoven. They are four important subdomains of a larger construct: organizational effectiveness. Each model within the construct of organizational effectiveness is related. Depending on the models and combinations of models we choose to use, we can see organizational effectiveness as simple and logical, as dynamic and synergistic, or as complex and paradoxical. Taken alone, no one of the models allows us the range of perspectives and the increased choice and potential effectiveness provided by considering them all as part of a larger framework.

The relationships among the models can be seen in terms of two axes. In Figure I.1 the vertical axis ranges from flexibility at the top to control at the bottom. The horizontal axis ranges from an internal organizational focus at the left to an external focus at the right. Each of the earlier management models fits in one of the four quadrants.

The human relations model, for example, stresses the criteria shown in the upper-left quadrant: participation, openness, commitment, and morale. The open systems model stresses the criteria shown in the upper-right quadrant: innovation, adaptation, growth, and resource acquisition. The rational goal model stresses the criteria shown in the lower-right quadrant: direction, goal clarity, productivity, and accomplishment. The internal process model, in the lower-left quadrant, stresses documentation, information management, stability, and control.

To translate these four theoretical models into management practice, we have labeled each quadrant according to the central action focus related to each model: Collaborate for the human relations model, Control for the internal process model, Compete for the rational goal model, and Create for the open systems model. We have also assigned different colors to each quadrant: yellow for Collaborate, red for Control, blue for Compete, and green for Create. Master managers do not view the world in terms of "black/white" or "either/or" and thus are able to engage in practices that support all

FIGURE I.1 *Competing values framework: effectiveness criteria.*

Each of the four models of organizing in the competing values framework assumes different criteria of effectiveness. Here we see the criteria in each model; the labels on the axes show the qualities that differentiate each model.

Source: R. E. Quinn, *Beyond Rational Management* (San Francisco: Jossey-Bass, 1988), 48. Used with permission.

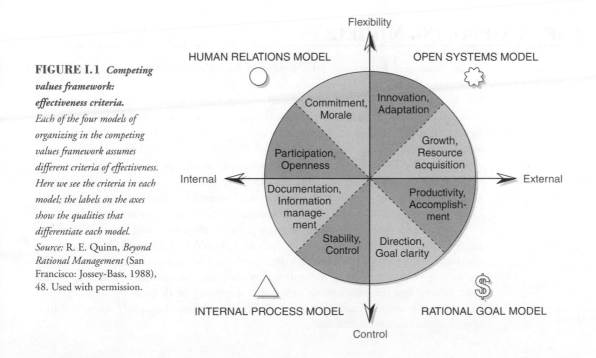

four of these foci. Throughout the text we refer to the quadrants by either their associated action imperative or the related management model. Keep in mind, however, that these labels are just a convenient shorthand for referring to a complex set of interrelated activities associated with achieving the goals associated with different effectiveness criteria.

As can be seen in Figure I.2, some general values are also reflected in the framework. These appear on the outer perimeter. Expansion and change are in the upper-right corner and contrast with consolidation and continuity in the lower-left corner. On the other hand, they complement the neighboring values focusing on decentralization and differentiation at the top and achieving a competitive position of the overall system to the right. Each general value statement can be seen in the same way.

Each model has a perceptual opposite. The human relations model, defined by flexibility and internal focus, stands in stark contrast to the rational goal model, which is defined by control and external focus. In the first, for example, people are inherently valued. In the second, people are of value only if they contribute greatly to goal attainment. The open systems model, defined by flexibility and external focus, runs counter to the internal process model, which is defined by control and internal focus. While the open systems model is concerned with adapting to the continuous change in the environment, the internal process model is concerned with maintaining stability and continuity inside the system.

Parallels among the models are also important. The human relations and open systems models share an emphasis on flexibility. The open systems and rational goal models share an emphasis on external focus. The rational goal and internal process models emphasize control. And the internal process and human relations models share an emphasis on internal focus.

THE USE OF OPPOSING MODELS

We will use this framework, which includes four different models of management, throughout the book to organize our discussion of different core competencies required for effective management. This integrated management model is called the ***competing values framework*** because the criteria within the four models seem at first to carry conflicting messages (Figure I.2). We want our organizations to be adaptable and flexible, but we also want them to be stable and controlled. We want our internal processes to be standardized and efficient, but we also want to be able to change and innovate so we can adapt operations to shifting external conditions. We want to value and respect employees as our most important resources, but we also want to establish plans and set goals that are likely to be very demanding. In any real organization all of these concerns are valid.

In contrast to earlier models of management, the competing values framework suggests that these opposing concerns can and should be addressed in real systems. Although we tend to think of these criteria, values, and assumptions as opposites, the competing values framework recognizes that they are not mutually exclusive. Rather than valuing one perspective over others and devaluing or discounting opposing perspectives, it is possible and, in fact, desirable, to perform effectively using the four opposing models simultaneously.

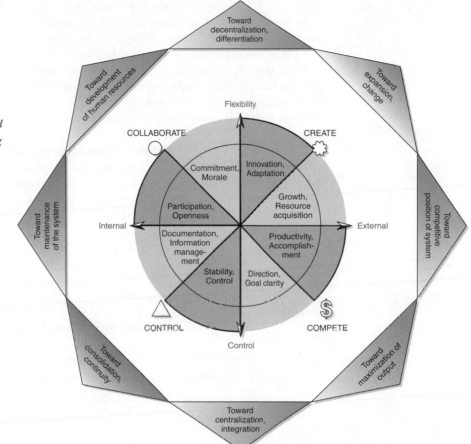

FIGURE I.2 *Eight general orientations in the competing values framework.*

The eight general values that operate in the competing values framework are shown in the triangles on the perimeter. Each value both complements the values next to it and contrasts with the one directly opposite it.

Source: R. E. Quinn, *Beyond Rational Management* (San Francisco: Jossey-Bass, 1988), 48. Used with permission.

The four models in the framework represent the unseen values over which people, programs, policies, and organizations live and die. Like the pharmaceutical executive at the outset of this introduction, we often blindly pursue values in one of the models without considering the values in the others. As a result, our choices and our potential effectiveness are reduced.

To be effective in the long run, managers must engage in a variety of types of behaviors. As a convenient shorthand, we use the labels Collaborate, Control, Compete, and Create to refer to the different quadrants of the competing values framework and to represent the types of actions managers need to engage in. Keep in mind, however, that these four action imperatives are broad categories of behaviors and that the specific practices that managers must engage in will differ depending on the specific circumstances.

One of the key strengths of the competing values framework is that the model itself is flexible enough to accommodate change and still provides enough structure to help guide behavior. For example, Lawrence, Lenk, and Quinn (2009) recently used a sample of 528 managers to re-examine the basic structure of the competing values framework. Their findings supported the fundamental structure of the competing values framework that was originally reported by Quinn and Rohrbaugh (1983). When looking at specific measures, however, Lawrence, et al., found a greater emphasis on speed in the Compete quadrant and on ensuring compliance with policies in the Control quadrant than had been reported in earlier studies. These findings are consistent with the fundamental assumptions of the competing values framework and also make sense in light of changes that have taken place in the business environment over the past 25 years.

For managers, like everyone else, the world keeps changing. It changes from hour to hour, day to day, and week to week. The strategies that are effective in one situation are not necessarily effective in another. Even worse, the strategies that were effective yesterday may not be effective in the same situation today. Managers tend to become trapped in their own style and in the organization's cultural values. They tend to employ very similar strategies in a wide variety of situations.

The overall competing values framework, based on the four models described here, can increase effectiveness by helping managers expand their perspectives. Each model in the framework suggests value in different, even opposite, strategies. The framework reflects the complexity confronted by people in real organizations. It therefore provides a tool to broaden thinking and to increase choice and effectiveness. This, however, can only happen if three challenges are met. We must:

1. Appreciate both the values and the weaknesses of each of the four models
2. Acquire and use multiple competencies associated with each model
3. Dynamically integrate competencies from each of the models with the managerial situations that we encounter

BEHAVIORAL COMPLEXITY AND THE EFFECTIVENESS OF MANAGERIAL LEADERS

When a person meets challenge 1 above and comes to understand and appreciate each of the four models, it suggests she has learned something at the conceptual level and has increased her cognitive complexity as it relates to managerial leadership. A person with high cognitive complexity regarding a given phenomenon is a person who can see that phenomenon from many perspectives. The person is able to think about the phenomenon in sophisticated, rather than simple, ways. Increased complexity at the conceptual level is the primary objective in most traditional management courses. Meeting challenge 1, however, does not mean someone has the ability to be an effective managerial leader. Knowledge is not enough.

To increase effectiveness, a managerial leader must meet challenges 2 and 3. Meeting these challenges leads to an increase in behavioral complexity. The term *behavioral complexity* was coined by Hooijberg and Quinn (1992) to reflect the capacity to draw on and use competencies and behaviors from the different models. Behavioral complexity builds on the notion of cognitive complexity and is defined as "the ability to act out a cognitively complex strategy by playing multiple, even competing, roles in a highly integrated and complementary way" (p. 164).

Several studies suggest a link between behavioral complexity and effective performance. In a study of 916 CEOs, Hart and Quinn (1993) found that the ability to play multiple and competing roles produced better firm performance. The CEOs with high behavioral complexity saw themselves as focusing on broad visions for the future (open systems model), while also providing critical evaluation of present plans (internal process model). They also saw themselves attending to relational issues (human relations model), while simultaneously emphasizing the accomplishment of tasks (rational goal model). The firms with CEOs having higher behavioral complexity produced the best firm performance, particularly with respect to business performance (growth and innovation) and organizational effectiveness. The relationships held regardless of firm size or variations in the nature of the organizational environment.

In a study of middle managers in a *Fortune* 100 company, Denison, Hooijberg, and Quinn (1995) found behavioral complexity, as assessed by the superior of the middle manager, to be related to the overall managerial effectiveness of the manager, as assessed by subordinates. In a similar study, behavioral complexity was related to managerial performance, charisma, and the likelihood of making process improvements in the organization (Quinn, Spreitzer & Hart, 1992). Lawrence et al. (2009) conducted further tests on the psychometric properties of measures of behavioral complexity in an instrument that was based on the competing values framework. They also demonstrated that higher levels of behavioral complexity as measured by a 36-item CVF Managerial Behavior Instrument were correlated with higher levels of managerial performance.

An Important Caveat about Organization Culture. Before we turn to more specific competencies for managers, it is important to note that what is considered effective performance by a manager in practice is likely to depend less on the prescriptions of management theory and research and more on the existing norms and values of that manager's particular organization. For example, if an organization has a strong culture oriented toward control, managers who seek to encourage creativity and innovation may find it difficult to be promoted, even though their ideas might be better for the organization in the long run. Fortunately, the competing values framework can be applied at the organization level to assess organization culture (Cameron & Quinn, 2006). Conducting an organizational culture assessment, which we discuss in more detail in Module 3, can be invaluable for managers trying to gain insight into their organizations.

ACTION IMPERATIVES AND COMPETENCIES FOR MANAGERS

The competing values framework integrates opposites. It is not easy to think about opposites. The failure to understand them, however, can hinder your development as a managerial leader. We will therefore begin by describing in more detail four broad action imperatives that managers face in their organization. We will then turn to the specific **competencies** that are associated with each action imperative. Finally, we will describe a process for developing each of the competencies at the behavioral level.

FOUR ACTION IMPERATIVES

The competing values framework is helpful in pointing out some of the values and criteria of effectiveness by which work units and organizations are judged. As noted above, because these values and criteria of effectiveness often appear to call for different types of action by managers, we use the terms Collaborate, Control, Compete, and Create as a shorthand labels to refer to much more complex sets of activities.

Collaborate.   The upper left quadrant of the competing values framework, reflecting the values of the human relations model, relates to the Collaborate action imperative (designated by the color yellow). Effectiveness in the collaborate quadrant depends on creating and sustaining commitment and cohesion. Collaborators are expected to encourage open and respectful communication from everyone, which requires first and foremost a deep understanding of and concern for others as well as oneself. Collaborators benefit the organization by mentoring and developing individuals as well as managing groups and leading teams. Perhaps most importantly, collaborators are expected to manage conflict in ways that encourage constructive conflict and discourage destructive conflict. Consider, for example, this description of a public manager who excels at the collaborate action imperative:

It is like any company. The finance people and the operations people are always at war. He brings people like that into a room, hardly says a word, and walks out with support from both sides. Same with subordinates—he brings us together, asks lots of questions, and we leave committed to get the job done. He has a gift for getting people to see the bigger picture, to trust each other, and to cooperate.

Control.   The bottom-left quadrant of the competing values framework is associated with the Control action imperative (designated by the color red). Effectiveness in the control quadrant is based on establishing and maintaining stability and continuity. With respect to control, managers are expected to know what is going on in the unit, to determine whether people are complying with the rules, and to see whether the unit is meeting its goals. The complex nature of most organizations also requires that managers be able to work across functions, not just within their own unit. Planning and coordinating projects requires handling data and forms, reviewing and responding to routine information, conducting inspections and tours, and authoring reviews of reports and other documents. Performance must be measured for both efficiency and effectiveness, and feedback must be provided in timely and relevant ways. Managers who excel at control are often recognized for their extensive understanding of the most minute details of the organization, as seen in the following description of one manager.

She has been here for years. Everyone checks with her before doing anything. She is a walking computer. She remembers every detail, and she tracks every transaction that occurs. From agreements made eight years ago, she knows which unit owes equipment to which other unit. Nothing gets past her. She has a sixth sense for when people are trying to hide something.

Compete.   The lower-right quadrant represents the Compete action imperative (designated by the color blue). Improving and increasing productivity and profitability is the central criteria of effectiveness for the compete quadrant. This requires that all members of the organization understand the mission of the organization and what they must to do to help achieve that mission. Managers focusing on the Compete action imperative need to have a thorough understanding of the external environment before they can develop an appropriate vision for the organization. To turn that vision into a reality, managers must communicate not only the broad vision but must also clarify expectations for employees through processes such as planning and goal setting, and designing and organizing work. Finally, the effective competitor must translate goals into actions with effective execution. Competing effectively in today's fast-paced environment requires a strong work ethic and the ability to take quick, decisive actions. Managers who excel at competing are expected to be task oriented and work focused. They are characterized as having high interest, motivation, energy, and personal drive. They are supposed to accept responsibility, complete assignments, and maintain high personal productivity. This usually involves motivating members to increase production and to accomplish stated goals. The following description exemplifies a manager who focuses on the compete action imperative:

She is everywhere. It seems as if she never goes home. But it is not just her energy; she is constantly reminding us why we are here. I have worked in a lot of organizations, but I have never been so clear about purpose. I know what I have to do to satisfy her and what the unit has to do. In some units around here, the employees really don't care; she has caused people to care about getting the job done.

Create.   Finally, the upper-right quadrant of the framework reflects the values of the open systems model and is labeled Create (designated by the color green). Effectiveness in the create quadrant is evaluated based on the ability to adapt to change and acquire external support. All managers are expected to facilitate adaptation and change, of course, but this core competency is especially relevant in the create quadrant. Paying attention to the changing environment, identifying important trends, and fueling and fostering innovation are fundamental tasks for managers in the create quadrant. In addition, managers must build their power base and negotiate agreement before they can put their ideas into action. Consider, for example, this description:

In a big organization like this, most folks do not want to rock the boat. She is always asking why, looking for new ways to do things. We used to be in an old, run-down wing. Everyone accepted it as a given. It took her two years, but she got us moved. She had a vision, and she sold it up the system. She is always open, and if a change or a new idea makes sense, she will go for it.

MANAGING AT DIFFERENT ORGANIZATIONAL LEVELS

As you think about the four action imperatives for managerial leaders described above, you may notice that these descriptions are as applicable to first-level supervisors as they are to executive-level managers of large organizations. The descriptions of the action imperatives are not tied to a particular level of organizational hierarchy or type of organization. Indeed, researchers and consultants have used the competing values framework to structure management education, development, and training programs for first-, middle-, and upper-level managers in a wide variety of public, private, and not-for-profit organizations in the United States as well as internationally (Ban & Faerman, 1988; Faerman, Quinn & Thompson, 1987; Giek & Lees, 1993; Quinn, Sendelbach & Spreitzer, 1991; Sendelbach, 1993).

Managerial responsibilities do, of course, vary across levels of organizational hierarchy. Common sense will tell you that the specific job tasks and responsibilities associated with the first-level manager related to the Create action imperative, for example, will likely be starkly different from those of the upper-level manager focusing on this same action imperative. In some cases, however, while the specific job tasks and responsibilities vary across levels of organizational hierarchy, some of the required competencies will remain the same. For example, all managers need to have good interpersonal skills and to have a high level of self-awareness (Kiechel, 1994). Similarly, all managers need to be able to develop plans and to adapt those plans when circumstances change. In this latter case, however, the scope and time frame of planning will likely differ, as will the steps of the planning process. Thus managers may need to learn different competencies to plan at different levels of the organization.

As managers are promoted from one level of the organization to the next, they need to identify which behaviors associated with the various action imperatives will generally remain the same, as well as which new behaviors need to be learned and which must be unlearned (Faerman & Peters, 1991). They must also understand how to use multiple competencies and perform in behaviorally complex ways as this may change from one managerial position to another. Similarly, human resource managers and those who are mentoring managers as they are promoted need to understand what the similarities and differences in managerial jobs across levels of organizational hierarchy are so that they can help these individuals to grow and develop as they make these transitions (DiPadova & Faerman, 1993).

IDENTIFYING MANAGERIAL COMPETENCIES

The managerial competencies covered in this text and shown in Table I.2 reflect both management practice and theory. They are derived from two principle research studies conducted with practicing managers. More than 250 initial competencies were generated by mid-level and senior managers, administrators, union representatives, and scholars (see Faerman, et al. 1987; Lawrence et al., 2009 for details). In terms of theory,

TABLE I.2 Key Competencies Associated with the Four Quadrants of the
Competing Values Framework

Collaborate: Creating and Sustaining Commitment and Cohesion
Understanding Self and Others
Communicating Honestly and Effectively
Mentoring and Developing Others
Managing Groups and Leading Teams
Managing and Encouraging Constructive Conflict

Control: Establishing and Maintaining Stability and Continuity
Organizing Information Flows
Working and Managing Across Functions
Planning and Coordinating Projects
Measuring and Monitoring Performance and Quality
Encouraging and Enabling Compliance

Compete: Improving Productivity and Increasing Profitability
Developing and Communicating a Vision
Setting Goals and Objectives
Motivating Self and Others
Designing and Organizing
Managing Execution and Driving for Results

Create: Promoting Change and Encouraging Adaptability
Using Power Ethically and Effectively
Championing and Selling New Ideas
Fueling and Fostering Innovation
Negotiating Agreement and Commitment
Implementing and Sustaining Change

when the initial lists of competencies were analyzed, they clustered into four basic categories, consistent with the structure of the competing values framework. Some competencies may be less relevant to you in your current position than others. You may have responsibilities that require competencies that we have not covered but that clearly fit within the theoretical framework. That should not be surprising. In the final analysis, master managers cannot rely on simple checklists for success. Master managers must be able to step back, see the big picture, and then modify their strategies and actions according to the demands of the current situation. The four action imperatives and underlying theoretical models help us to organize our thoughts about what is expected of a person holding a position of leadership. The ultimate goal is for you to be able to integrate a diverse set of competencies that will allow you to operate effectively in a constantly changing world of competing values.

ORGANIZING THE LEARNING PROCESS—ALAPA

A competency suggests both the possession of knowledge and the behavioral capacity to act appropriately using that knowledge. To develop competencies, you must both be introduced to knowledge and have the opportunity to practice your skills. Many textbooks and classroom lecture methods provide the knowledge but not the opportunity to develop behavioral skills and to reflect on the use of those skills.

In this book, we will provide you with both. The structure we will use is based on a five-step model developed by organizational scholars Kim Cameron and David Whetten. Rather than focusing on learning from a simple instructional approach of an expert giving a lecture, Whetten and Cameron (2010) recommend an instructional–developmental approach that includes an expert giving a lecture plus students experimenting with new behaviors. Each of the competencies covered in the text includes the five-steps of the ALAPA model, as described below.

Step 1: Assessment Helps you discover your present level of ability in and awareness of the competency. Any number of tools, such as questionnaires, role-plays, or group discussions, might be used. In this text, we generally use brief questionnaires.

Step 2: Learning Involves reading and presenting information about the topic using traditional tools, such as lectures and printed material. Here we present information from relevant research and suggest guidelines for practice.

Step 3: Analysis Explores appropriate and inappropriate behaviors by examining how others behave in a given situation. We will use cases, role-plays, or other examples of behavior. Your professor may also provide examples from popular movies, television shows, or novels for you to analyze.

Step 4: Practice Allows you to apply the competency to a work-like situation while in the classroom. It is an opportunity for experimentation and feedback. Again, exercises, simulations, and role-plays will be used.

Step 5: Application Gives you the opportunity to transfer the process to real-life situations. Usually assignments are made to facilitate short- and long-term experimentation.

When initially exposed to these components, students respond in different ways. Some appreciate the structure and invest themselves in the complete learning process. Others may feel that the Assessment exercises are unnecessary; they want to jump directly into the Learning. Still others may think that a particular Practice or Application activity isn't relevant to their current job or career aspirations. Although no textbook can perfectly meet the expectations and needs of every student, we have found that most students only fully appreciate the benefits of the activities *after* they have invested time in them. For example, after completing an exercise on assumptions about performance evaluations, one MBA student wrote, "I never realized my thoughts on performance evaluation until this exercise. [It] gave me thoughts about how I could change this process at my work." This type of reaction emphasizes the importance of reflection throughout the learning process. Reflection helps us move to a higher level of understanding. Research suggests that reflection can greatly enhance awareness of the impact of self-directed learning (Rhee, 2003) and improve skill development (Argyris, 2002). To encourage reflection, we include a brief comment after most of the exercises throughout the text.

In working with the ALAPA model, we discovered that the five components, and the methods normally associated with each component, need not be implemented separately. A lecture, for example, does not need to follow an assessment exercise and precede an analysis exercise; a lecture might be appropriately combined with a role-play in some other step. The methods can be varied and even combined in the effective teaching and learning of a given competency.

The next section uses the ALAPA model to introduce a competency that all students can immediately put into practice: *Thinking Critically*.

Core Competency Thinking Critically

ASSESSMENT Going Public with Your Reasoning

This assessment exercise has two parts. Please complete part 1 before moving to part 2.

Directions Part 1 Think of a topic or issue or situation that you find very upsetting or frustrating. Do a little "ranting" on that issue. That is, write some very strong and emotional statements about this issue or situation. You might begin with "One thing that makes me furious is _____." Try to write four or five sentences.

Part 2 Now imagine that you need to "go public" with your feelings and opinions and convince someone else to share at least some of the intensity you feel about this issue. Is there anything in your ranting that you might convert into an argument, a line of reasoning that another person might find legitimate?

Read and discuss your sentences with a classmate. Talk about why you feel that some of your statements are not good raw material for public reasoning but others might be.

LEARNING Thinking Critically

Organizations want people who can "go public" with their ideas and reactions, quickly and concisely. When you have casual conversations with your friends, you don't always have to support your opinions with evidence. You can just express an opinion. But in the workplace you have to support your claims and proposals in a more systematic and concise way. It's one thing to say that you like the color blue; it's quite another to say that you prefer one brand of cell phone over another. In the first case you are simply expressing a preference whose grounds are wholly personal. Another person can "argue" that green is the best color, but the argument cannot be resolved by recourse to external issues. The preferences here are purely and completely personal.

However, in the second example, in which you state that you prefer this cell phone over another, the grounds for the claim you are making do not depend completely on your own taste. There are external factors you can discuss with another party. There are criteria of design, cost, convenience, and so forth that can be put on the table—"I like the smaller size and lighter weight of the Nokia phone; the user interface on the Nokia makes messages easier to read; the menu has fewer steps for manipulating the functions I use most often; the sound quality is better." True, some of these are personally experienced, but they are criteria that go beyond personal taste. They are shareable, and in some cases impersonal (cost, for example), grounds for having a preference or making a recommendation.

In this section, we examine the skill of thinking critically, which is the first step in formulating clear and compelling arguments. Developing critical thinking skills will improve the quality of your evaluations and increase the credibility of your recommendations.

THINKING ABOUT THINKING

Let's think for a moment about thinking itself as a learned human activity. In what ways has your formal education helped you to "think" more effectively? We're not asking about specific knowledge you've accumulated, but how your ability to handle ideas and marshal evidence has improved. Another way to pose the question is, "How has your formal education helped you to understand the events that you observe and the information you encounter in daily life?" We have asked this question of many MBA students. Here are some of the responses we have found most interesting and helpful.

My education has helped me "complexify" my thinking. I have learned that there are seldom simple, single causes for events. There are usually complex, multiple causes that drive events. As an undergraduate, I majored in history. I wrote my senior research paper on the causes of World War I. I can't tell you in one sentence what caused that war; but I can tell you what the contributing conditions were and what "trigger events" led to the outbreak of the war. That's what I mean by complex thinking rather than simple, black-and-white thinking.

Some of the tools I've gained from school have helped me approach things in a more systematic way. For example, my study of statistics has really helped me separate the single dramatic cases, the N of 1 examples, from patterns of events. The other day, as part of preparing to write a paper on healthcare policy, I watched a person on the C-Span TV network who was testifying before a congressional committee about the quality of healthcare. This person, who couldn't get some important surgery paid for by his HMO (health maintenance organization), had a heart-rending story to tell. But I wanted to know how representative this example was. How many people have been in this situation? Is it a one-of-a-kind case, or is it typical? So often, the most dramatic data crowds out the more valid, less dramatic data.

I am a lot better at asking precise questions than I was before I went to college. Even in casual conversation with people, I can learn a lot more and contribute more to a conversation by asking good questions. When someone makes a statement like "I thought that movie was really lame," I follow up with a question like, "What makes you say that?" When someone says, "This book was stupid," I want to ask a question like "Was everything in the book stupid, or just part of it?" Sometimes people think I'm weird, but most of the time my questions make the conversations go better.

The students quoted above all realize that issues are often more complex than they at first appear, that the "facts" needed to make a rational decision are not always available to us, and that people often make decisions based on very thin or limited information. They also seem to understand that different people will not always agree on what a "fact" is in a particular case—or perhaps not agree on the meaning or significance of that fact.

The kind of attitude these students demonstrate is appropriate to the role of the manager. Managers spend a lot of time both presenting evidence to support their own ideas and evaluating evidence presented by others. Effective managers are effective thinkers. They don't have to be brilliant, but they need to approach evidence and data with both openness and some healthy skepticism.

MANAGEMENT AND SOUND REASONING: CREATING AND EVALUATING ARGUMENTS

When reasons are put together and presented to one or more people, they form an argument. We are using the term "argument" to mean a train of reasoning, not a quarrel or a disagreement you have with another person. An argument, in this sense, is a case we make for doing, or believing, or recommending something.

Effective managers are good at both framing their own arguments and reacting to the arguments of others. At any given moment, your task as a manager may be to react to someone else's recommendation or to make your own recommendation for doing something. For example, you might make the following suggestion at a weekly staff meeting: "We need to adopt this software application for tracking our financial data because . . ." What comes after that "because" is the support or the gist of your argument. Without that support, your suggestion or proposal would probably not carry much weight. Now, note that reasoning, or critical thinking, as we are describing it, is primarily a process not of creating ideas but of presenting and evaluating ideas and information. The task of the critical thinker is to make the best decision with the available information in a particular circumstance. The better you are at presenting your own cases and analyzing the cases others put in front of you, the more effective a leader you will be. We're now going to present some tools for mapping arguments and examining evidence clearly and efficiently. This approach to mapping arguments is based on *An Introduction to Reasoning* (Toulmin, Rieke, and Janik, 1984, pp. 1–59), which notes that most arguments, whether simple or complex, have three elements:

1. The **claim** or conclusion of the argument. The claim answers the question, "What's the point here?"
2. The **grounds**, or the facts and evidence that support the claim. The claim can be no stronger than the grounds that support it. The grounds answer the question, "What do you have to go on?" or "What leads you to say that?"

3. *The **warrant**,* or the bridge between the claim and the grounds. Sometimes this bridge is obvious; sometimes not. The warrant or bridge answers the question, "How does your claim connect to the grounds you've offered" (Toulmin et al., 1984, pp. 30–38). The warrant is the most subtle of the three elements of argumentation, but if you develop an understanding of it, it will prove a powerful tool for both creating and evaluating arguments.

The following example demonstrates how an implied warrant can be used. The argument is simple because only the claim and grounds are indicated:

I see smoke; there must be fire.

The claim here is "there must be fire." The grounds or evidence on which the claim is based is "I see smoke." Another way to say this is "I see smoke, so there must be fire." But the warrant or bridge that makes the connection between the claim and the evidence is not stated. The warrant is, of course, "where there's smoke there's usually fire." (Notice that the warrant has a qualifier to it: the word "usually." Sometimes there is smoke without fire.)

Now, examine the following train of reasoning. The elements in this argument are scrambled. Some of the statements below regarding a patient who was admitted to a hospital emergency room (ER) are warrants; some are grounds; one is a claim. All the other statements revolve around that claim. For each statement, indicate whether you think it is a claim, a ground, or a warrant.

_____   *The patient complains of nausea, which has lasted for over 24 hours.*

_____   *The patient's examination shows pain and tenderness in his lower-right abdomen.*

_____   *The patient has a temperature of 101°.*

_____   *Appendicitis is often triggered by a viral flu infecting the gastrointestinal tract.*

_____   *The patient's pain has migrated over the past 48 hours from the center of the belly to the lower-right abdomen.*

_____   *The pain associated with acute appendicitis often "migrates" from the left side, or the midsection, to the lower-right abdomen.*

_____   *The patient is most likely suffering from acute appendicitis and should be X-rayed and prepared for surgery.*

_____   *The patient's history shows a bad case of viral flu within the past two weeks.*

Notice that the warrants are the items that create a bridge between a factual observation and the one claim or recommended action in the list. In the list above there happens to be only one claim. Everything else is either a ground or a warrant. When experts communicate among themselves, they often leave out the warrants behind their reasoning because the warrants are understood. But when they talk to a nonexpert, they need to be more explicit. That means they have to spell out the warrants that connect the claims they are making to the grounds used to support those claims.

For example, a medical intern who had just examined the patient described above might say to the attending physician in the ER,

The patient has a temperature of 101, nausea for the past several hours, migrating pain and tenderness now settled in the lower-right abdomen. The patient says he has also had a recent case of viral stomach flu. I recommend we prep him for surgery on his appendix.

The attending physician might say, "Fine, sounds like an inflamed appendix to me." The warrants, all taken from clinical research, are already understood. But often we need to make our warrants explicit. As our colleague Allen Bluedorn says when teaching this model of reasoning, you need to "show your work" as you do on a calculus homework problem or a chemistry exam. If the attending physician wants to test the logic of the intern's diagnosis, he might ask a question such as, "How does the patient's recent case of the flu support your diagnosis?" The intern would then say that clinical research shows that a viral flu is often the triggering event in causing a person's appendix to become infected. The questions asked by the attending physician require the intern to show her work.

In argumentation, you show your work when you expose the bridges or warrants between the evidence you're presenting and the claim(s) that your evidence supports. When people have difficulty following our train of reasoning, the problem is often caused by our failure to make our warrants explicit.

Let's see how we can use this model of argumentation to map some arguments that managers encounter in reports or meetings. Here's an example from a report by a sales manager in a manufacturing company.

We conclude that the 28 percent decrease in unit sales for this quarter was caused by a dramatic deterioration in the quality of service provided during the previous quarter.

The strongest evidence that poor service is the cause of the lower sales is the fact that more than half of our large, regular accounts ordered no new units during the quarter. These are the customers who have a history with our service—some benchmarks for tracking how our service stacks up over time. Now, they apparently have a reason to be dissatisfied and feel that service quality had declined.

On the other hand, sales to new accounts were about average during this quarter. These are customers who have had little experience with the quality of our service work. Further, we suspect that the quality of our service has dropped sharply, because the number of complaint calls recorded in the log, as well as repeat calls requesting service, is about 60 percent higher than during any other quarter on record.

This argument is pretty straightforward:

1. The claim is that a 28 percent decrease in sales last quarter was caused by poor service performance during the quarter that preceded it.

2. The grounds or evidence that the quality of service declined in the previous quarter is threefold.

   ▪ Ground 1: More than half of our large-account customers ordered no new units during the past quarter.

   ▪ Ground 2: Sales to new customers were about average during the quarter.

   ▪ Ground 3: The number of logged complaint calls, as well as repeat calls requesting service, was 60 percent higher than during any previous quarter on record.

3. The warrants, or bridges, that tie the data and claim together are also threefold.

- Warrant 1: The fact that current, large-account customers ordered no new units indicates some form of dissatisfaction.

- Warrant 2: We sold an average number of units to new customers. These are people who had no basis of comparison for judging our service.

- Warrant 3: The complaint call log is our official vehicle for tracking customer satisfaction data. When the calls increase, we assume we have some kind of service problem.

Notice how the author of the report supports his statement that the quality of service has "dramatically deteriorated." He alludes to an official piece of evidence, the service department's log book. Notice that while there is only one major claim, there are several grounds, or pieces of evidence, supporting the claim and a matching number of warrants connecting each ground to the claim. We can draw or map this argument as shown in Figure I.3.

As you work through the exercises in the rest of this text, apply what you have learned about claims, grounds, and warrants. For example, when assessing whether you are a team player (Module 1), recognize that your assessment is simply a claim—what grounds do you have to support that claim? By pushing yourself to provide, not just claims, but also grounds and warrants in the exercises throughout this text, you will continue to develop your critical thinking skills. This practice will also be valuable for improving related competencies such as communicating honestly and effectively (Module 1) and negotiating agreement and commitment (Module 4).

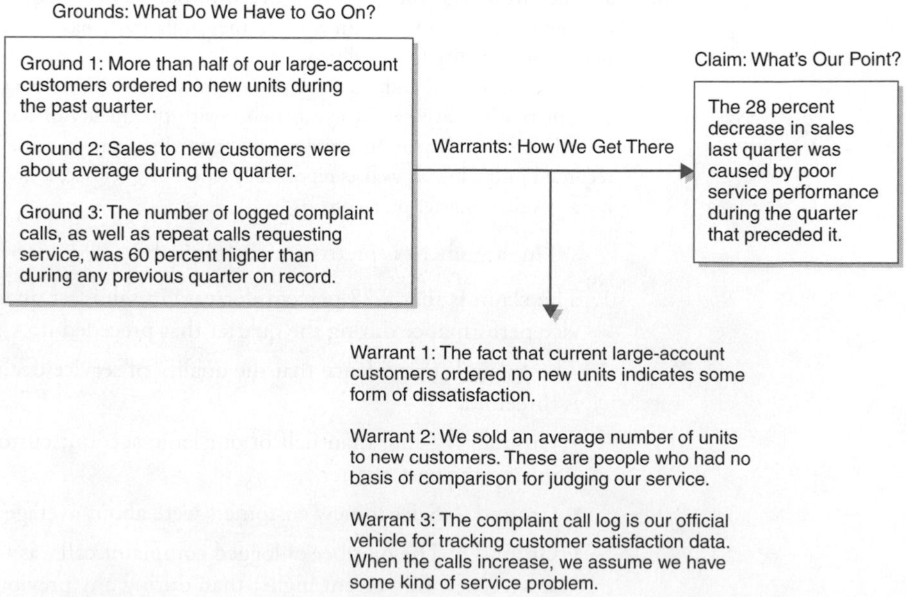

FIGURE I.3 *Basic argument map.*

Grounds: What Do We Have to Go On?

Ground 1: More than half of our large-account customers ordered no new units during the past quarter.

Ground 2: Sales to new customers were about average during the quarter.

Ground 3: The number of logged complaint calls, as well as repeat calls requesting service, was 60 percent higher than during any previous quarter on record.

Warrants: How We Get There

Claim: What's Our Point?

The 28 percent decrease in sales last quarter was caused by poor service performance during the quarter that preceded it.

Warrant 1: The fact that current large-account customers ordered no new units indicates some form of dissatisfaction.

Warrant 2: We sold an average number of units to new customers. These are people who had no basis of comparison for judging our service.

Warrant 3: The complaint call log is our official vehicle for tracking customer satisfaction data. When the calls increase, we assume we have some kind of service problem.

ANALYSIS Argument Mapping

Objective This exercise will give you more experience at analyzing arguments.

Directions The following exercise includes two arguments on the same topic. Your job is to read these arguments and analyze them in terms of their plausibility, validity, and persuasiveness.*

This can be a group exercise or an individual task. If your instructor prefers to have you work as a group, here are guidelines for the process.

Group Task Break into groups of four. Two people should analyze one argument together, and the other two people should analyze the other argument together. Take 15 minutes to read and discuss the arguments, and then present your analysis to the other pair of classmates. Evaluate the arguments using the 7-point scale and the evaluation criteria below.

Scale

| Terrible | | 1 | 2 | 3 | 4 | 5 | 6 | 7 | | Excellent |

Argument	Explicitly Stated Claims	Explicitly Stated Grounds	Quality of Grounds	Explicitly Stated Warrants	Overall Quality
1					
2					

1. Discuss in one page the strengths and weaknesses of the arguments in terms of the major claims being made as well as the grounds and warrants the authors provide to support those claims.

2. Do you find the arguments persuasive and compelling? Why? Why not? Use the 7-point scale above in writing your analysis.

Argument 1

The National Scholarship Achievement Board recently revealed the results of a five-year study on the effectiveness of comprehensive exams at Duke University. The results of the study showed that since the comprehensive exam has been introduced at Duke, the grade point average of undergraduates has increased by 31 percent. At comparable schools without the exams, grades increased by only 8 percent over the same period. The prospect of a comprehensive exam clearly seems to be effective in challenging students to work harder and faculty to teach more effectively. It is likely that the benefits observed at Duke University could also be observed at other universities that adopt the exam policy.

Graduate schools and law and medical schools are beginning to show clear and significant preferences for students who received their undergraduate degrees from institutions with comprehensive exams. As the dean of the Harvard Business School said, "Although Harvard has not and will not discriminate on the basis of race or sex, we do show a strong preference for applicants who

*From R. Petty and J. T. Cacioppo, *Communication and Persuasion: Central and Peripheral Routes to Attitude Change.* (New York: Spring-Verlag New York Inc., 1986), 54–55, 57–58. Used with permission. We wish to thank Allen Bluedorn of the University of Missouri for suggesting this exercise and for his helpful advice on teaching critical thinking.

have demonstrated their expertise in an area of study by passing a comprehensive exam at the undergraduate level." Admissions officers of law, medical, and graduate schools have also endorsed the comprehensive exam policy and indicated that students at schools without the exams would be at a significant disadvantage in the very near future. Thus, the institution of comprehensive exams will be an aid to those who seek admission to graduate and professional schools after graduation.

Argument 2

The National Scholarship Achievement Board recently revealed the results of a study they conducted on the effectiveness of comprehensive exams at Duke University. One major finding was that student anxiety had increased by 31 percent. At comparable schools without the exam, anxiety increased by only 8 percent. The board reasoned that anxiety over the exams, or fear of failure, would motivate students to study more in their courses while they were taking them. It is likely that this increase in anxiety observed at Duke University would also be observed and be of benefit at other universities that adopt the exam policy.

A member of the board of directors has stated publicly that his brother had to take a comprehensive exam while in college and is now a manager of a large restaurant. He indicated that he realized the value of the exams, since his father was a migrant worker who didn't even finish high school. He also indicated that the university has received several letters from parents in support of the exam. In fact, four of the six parents who wrote in thought that the exams were an excellent idea. Also, the prestigious National Accrediting Board of Higher Education seeks input from parents as well as students, faculty, and administrators when evaluating a university. Since most parents contribute financially to their child's education and also favor the exams, the university should institute them. This would show that the university is willing to listen to and follow the parents' wishes over those of students and faculty, who may simply fear the work involved in comprehensive exams.

Reflection   The way that information is presented can have a significant impact on how that information is perceived. When crafting persuasive arguments, having solid grounds and warrants to substantiate your claim may not be enough if you are unable to convey your thoughts in a clear, compelling way.

PRACTICE   Providing Warrants

Objective   As we noted earlier, warrants connect your grounds to your claims and are often the most difficult part to establish when you first begin develop your argumentation skills.

Directions   In groups of three to five people, practice supplying the warrant for each set of claims and grounds listed in the table below. More than one plausible warrant can be given for each set. There is no one, perfectly worded answer. The idea is to provide a bridging statement between the claim being made and the grounds provided to support that claim.

Reflection   When listening to the claims made by others, it can be very helpful to apply what you have learned about argumentation. Sometimes, positions that sound reasonable when we first hear them, fail to hold up once we analyze them more carefully.

Claims	Grounds	Warrant(s)
Southwest Airlines will have a profitable year next year.	The nation's economic growth is predicted to continue at an annual rate of at least 3 percent over the next year.	
	Southwest has enjoyed greater profits than any airline in North America for the past three years.	
I do not believe Gretchen is an ideal choice for supervisor of the customer service department.	She has worked in the department for only eight months and has been with the company for less than two years.	
	She seems to be rather reclusive—eating lunch by herself and not communicating much with other workers during breaks.	
Our firm needs to invest more resources into new product development in order to remain competitive in the future.	Our sales research shows that 80 percent of our profits over the past three years have been made from products that are more than six years old.	
	We reduced our research and development budget by 28 percent over the past three years.	
	We are living off "the fat of the land."	

APPLICATION Reflected Best-Self Portrait

Objective The objective of this exercise is to help you gather evidence about your current skills as a manager. Rather than focusing on your weaknesses at this point, however, we would like you to focus on your strengths. Researchers in the area of Positive Organizational Scholarship (Cameron, Dutton & Quinn, 2003) have developed a number of tools for improving leadership skills. This exercise will give you the opportunity to explore some of those tools.

Directions Making claims is simple: "Susan is a great manager." Substantiating claims, however, requires much more effort. What evidence are we relying on when we claim that Susan is a great manager? What assumptions do we hold about what makes a great manager in the first place? For this exercise, you will be gathering information about your own skills as a manager, from the perspective of your colleagues.

    1. Go to the webpage for Positive Organizational Scholarship (POS) at http://www.bus.umich.edu/positive/. Under the POS Teaching and Learning drop down box, select POS Tool. Click on the Purchase and Download link to obtain the Reflected Best-Self exercise. Follow the instructions in the exercise and any additional directions that your instructor may provide so that you can create your own Reflected Best-Self Portrait (Quinn, Dutton & Spreitzer, 2004).

Reflection Committing to this type of exercise takes courage. Even though the exercise asks for positive examples, it still requires that you open yourself up to hearing what other people think about your performance. Learning to think critically often requires us to let go of old ideas when we discover that the evidence supporting those ideas is weak or non-existent. People who shut down and refuse to accept new ideas and supporting evidence are not only failing their organizations, they are failing themselves.

RECAP AND PRECOURSE ASSESSMENT

People use models that sensitize them to some things and blind them to others. When we act as a managerial leader in an organizational unit, our models greatly affect our level of effectiveness. We have traced the evolution of four basic models in management thinking: rational goal, internal process, human relations, and open systems. Each model is based on assumptions that lead to different sensitivities, decisions, and behaviors.

In recent years, world conditions have made it increasingly obvious that there is a need for both–and thinking. As we increase the number of models that we can use to assess a situation, we increase our array of choices, and we increase both our cognitive and behavioral complexity.

The competing values framework suggests that the four basic models of organizational effectiveness can be integrated into a comprehensive whole. This integrated model is called the "competing values" framework because, although we tend to see the oppositions as conflicts, they are not mutually exclusive. In fact, they need to be complementary. We can use the framework to get out of a single mindset and to increase choice. In becoming a master manager, we seek to use, simultaneously, two or more seemingly opposite approaches. Think, for example, of the leader who practices "tough love." This person is effectively integrating, or making complementary, domains that we normally keep separate.

The competing values framework suggests three challenges we need to master: using multiple mindsets in viewing the organizational world; learning to use competencies associated with all four models; and, finally, integrating the diverse competencies in confronting the world of action. People who meet these three challenges are cognitively and behaviorally complex and are the most effective managerial leaders.

We use the ALAPA model in presenting these competencies. Although the book allows the instructor to follow traditional instruction methods, it also allows a second phenomenon to occur. It allows you to develop, grow, and internalize new competencies. The emphasis, then, is not on learning traditional social science theory, but on learning how to apply certain aspects of this literature to learning to perform more effectively as a managerial leader. To help gauge your personal development, you can complete an assessment of yourself on the competencies included in this text now and again when you have completed the text. Your instructor can provide you with directions on how to access the assessment survey on the student companion website for this textbook.

REFERENCES

Argyris, C. (2002). Double-loop learning, teaching, and research. *Academy of Management Learning & Education, 1*(2), 206–218.

Ban, C., & Faerman, S. R. (1988). Advanced human resources development program: Final impact report (unpublished technical report). Rockefeller College of Public Affairs and Policy, University at Albany, SUNY, Albany, NY.

Bigelow, J. D. (Ed.) (1991). *Managerial skills: Explorations in practical knowledge.* Newbury Park. CA: Sage Publications.

Cameron, K. S., Dutton, J. E., & Quinn, R. E. (2003). *Positive organizational scholarship: Foundations for a new discipline.* San Francisco: Berrett–Koehler.

Cameron, K. S., & Quinn, R. E. (2006). *Diagnosing and changing organizational culture based on the competing values framework.* San Francisco: Jossey Bass.

Denison, D., Hooijberg, R., & Quinn, R. E. (1995). Paradox and performance: Toward a theory of behavioral complexity in managerial leadership. *Organization Science, 6*(5), 524–540.

DiPadova, L. N., & Faerman, S. R. (1993). Using the competing values framework to facilitate managerial understanding across levels of organizational hierarchy. *Human Resource Management, 32*(l), 143–174.

Fabian, F. H. (2000). Keeping the tension: Pressures to Keep the Controversy in the Management Discipline. *Academy of Management Review 25*(2), 350–371.

Faerman, S. R., & Peters, T. D. (1991). A conceptual framework for examining managerial roles and transitions across levels of organizational hierarchy. *Proceedings of the National Public Management Research Conference*, Syracuse, NY.

Faerman, S. R., Quinn, R. E., & Thompson, M. P. (1987). Bridging management practice and theory. *Public Administration Review, 47*(3), 311–319.

Fayol, H, (1949). *General and industrial administration.* New York: Pitman.

Giek, D. G., & Lees, P. L. (1993). On massive change: Using the competing values framework to organize the educational efforts of the human resource function in New York state government. *Human Resource Management, 32*(1), 9–28.

Hart, S., & Quinn, R. E. (1993). Roles executives play: CEOs, behavioral complexity, and firm performance. *Human Relations, 46*, 115–142.

Hooijberg, R., & Quinn, R. E. (1992). Behavioral complexity and the development of effective managers. In R. L. Phillips & J. G. Hunt (Eds.), *Strategic Leadership: A Multiorganizational-Level Perspective* (pp. 161–176) Westport, CT: Quorum.

House, R. J., & Podsakoff, P. M.. (1992). Effectiveness: Leadership past perspectives and future directions for research. In J. Greenberg (Ed.), *Organizational behavior: The state of the science.* Hillsdale, NJ: Lawrence Erlbaum.

Kiechel, W., III. (1994, April 4). A manager's career in the new economy. *Fortune, 68*–72.

Lawrence, K. A., Lenk, P., & Quinn, R. E. (2009). Behavioral complexity in leadership: The psychometric properties of a new instrument to measure behavioral repertoire. *Leadership Quarterly, 20*, 87–102.

Mintzberg, H. (1975). The manager's job: Folklore and fact. *Harvard Business Review, 53*, 49–61.

Mirvis, P. H. (1985). *Work in the 20th century: America's trends and tracts, visions and values, economic and human developments* (rev. ed.). Cambridge, MA: Rudi Press.

Quinn, R. E. (1988). *Beyond rational management: Mastering the paradoxes and competing demands of high performance.* San Francisco: Jossey-Bass.

Quinn, R. E., Dutton, J. E., & Spreitzer, G. M. (2004). Reflected best self exercise: Assignment and instructions to participants. University of Michigan Ross School of Business, Product Number 001B. Ann Arbor, MI.

Quinn, R. E., Kahn, J. A., & Mandl, M. J. (1994). Perspectives on organizational change: Exploring movement at the interface. In J. Greenberg (Ed.), *Organizational Behavior: The state of the science* (pp. 109–134) Hillsdale, NJ: Lawrence Erlbaum Associates.

Quinn, R. E., & Rohrbaugh, J. (1983). A spatial model of effectiveness criteria: Towards a competing values approach to organizational analysis *Management Science, 29*(3), 363–377.

Quinn, R. E., Sendelbach, N. B., & Spreitzer, G. M. (1991). Education and empowerment: A transformational model of managerial skills development. In J. D. Bigelow (Ed.), *Managerial Skills: Explorations in Practical Knowledge*. Newbury Park, CA: Sage Publications.

Quinn, R. E., Spreitzer, G. M., & Hart, S. (1992). Integrating the extremes: Crucial skills for managerial effectiveness. In S. Srivastava, R. E. Fry, et al., *Executive and organizational continuity: Managing the paradoxes of stability and change*. San Francisco: Jossey-Bass.

Rhee, K. S. (2003). Self-directed learning: To be aware or not to be aware. *Journal of Management Education, 27*(5), 568–589.

Sendelbach, N. B. (1993). The competing values framework for management training and development: A tool for understanding complex issues and tasks. *Human Resource Management* 32(1): 75–99.

Senge, P. (1990). *The fifth discipline: The art and practice of the learning organization*. New York: Doubleday Currency.

"Survey of Pressing Problems 2000: Innovative Solutions to the Pressing Problems of Business." (2000). Working paper. University of Michigan, School of Business.

Taylor, F. W. (1911). *The principles of scientific management*. New York: Harper and Brothers.

Toulmin, S., Rieke, R., & Janik, A. (1984). *An introduction to reasoning*. New York: Macmillan.

Weber, M. (1947). *The theory of social and economic organizations* ed. A. M. Henderson & T. Parsons (Trans.). New York: Free Press.

Whetten, D. R., & Cameron, K. S. (2010). *Developing management skills* (8th ed.). Upper Saddle River, NJ: Prentice Hall.

MODULE

CREATING AND SUSTAINING COMMITMENT AND COHESION

1

FLEXIBILITY

COLLABORATE
Commitment & Cohesion

CREATE
Change & Adaptability

COMPETING VALUES FRAMEWORK

INTERNAL

EXTERNAL

CONTROL
Stability & Continuity

COMPETE
Productivity & Profitability

CONTROL

■ COMPETENCIES

Understanding Self and Others

Communicating Honestly and Effectively

Mentoring and Developing Others

Managing Groups and Leading Teams

Managing and Encouraging Constructive Conflict

In this first module, we look at the human relations model, which focuses on commitment and cohesion. In building commitment and cohesion, we emphasize an internal focus and flexibility. That is, we are concerned about individuals and groups within the organization and the need to allow for flexibility in order to help employees grow and develop. When employees have opportunities to develop their skills and abilities, they can contribute more effectively to the organization's performance needs.

Organizational Goals. The human relations model has as its primary goal developing committed and involved organizational members. Here we assume that the best way to develop committed and involved members is to give them an opportunity to be involved in organizational processes. In order for employees to be involved, managerial leaders need to help employees see how their work fits into the work unit. Managers must also provide employees with feedback on how well they are performing. In addition, managers need to balance the needs of individuals with the needs of the work unit and to build cohesion among employees, while encouraging employees to express their individuality.

Paradoxes. In the Introduction to this text, we noted that paradoxes exist when two seemingly inconsistent or contradictory ideas are actually both true and that the competing values framework recognizes that managerial leaders are consistently faced with paradoxical situations. Some of these paradoxes emerge from competing demands that result from competing values across quadrants. For example, as we learn about the human relations quadrant, we are, by definition, highlighting aspects of the organization that emphasize flexibility and an internal focus. An overemphasis on internal aspects of the organization, however, can lead managers and employees to lose sight of the fact that the purpose of work organizations is to produce a product or deliver a service to external customers. Similarly, an overemphasis on flexibility can lead managers and employees to forget the value of maintaining stability and continuity in an organization.

In this module, we focus more on paradoxes that emerge from expectations within the human relations quadrant. As you examine each of the competencies, you will see that overemphasis on a particular value can actually lead to poor performance. For example, we believe that one of the most important competencies of a managerial leader is understanding oneself. Increasing one's self-awareness, however, should be understood as a starting point for developing one's capacity for personal growth and development, rather than as an end in itself. Thus, a paradox associated with learning more about yourself is that you increase your capacity to change and become someone new. A second paradox associated with the human relations quadrant emerges when there is an overemphasis on building commitment and cohesion by involving people in decision-making processes. Anyone who has ever been involved in a learning group, however, knows that groups do not always make the best or most efficient decisions. And when employees have opportunities to participate in decision-making processes, it virtually always takes longer than having one person make the decision. We thus need to be careful about not overusing work groups when a quality decision could be made by an individual. Finally, a paradox emerges from the fact that it takes time to develop any skill or ability. Thus, in trying to build the team's capacity in the long run, managerial leaders need to recognize that in the short term the team will be less effective and/or less efficient as individuals are given the opportunity to learn new tasks. As you work through this module and attempt to develop your competencies, keep in mind that effective performance will require you to transcend these paradoxes.

Competencies. The competencies associated with the Collaborate quadrant focus on how managerial leaders can be more effective in their interactions with others. We begin this module by emphasizing what some would argue is one of the most important competencies a managerial leader can possess—*understanding self and others.* To be effective, a managerial leader must be able to inspire others to action and so must have an understanding of how she is seen by others. Managerial leaders must also be able to monitor how they react to situations and determine the basis for this reaction. By developing this type of self-awareness, managerial leaders also develop their capacity to understand others in their organization. Our next two competencies, *communicating honestly and effectively* and *mentoring and developing employees,* focus on interactions with individuals and introduce some important ideas about effective communication that are useful not only in the workplace, but also in your relationships outside the workplace. We then address key issues associated with *managing groups and leading teams*. Working on effective teams can be an incredibly energizing experience, but ineffective teams can destroy motivation and jeopardize organizational success. Our last competency, *managing and encouraging creative conflict*, can be applied at both the individual and the group level and challenges the idea that conflict in organizations is bad and should always be avoided.

Module 1 Competency 1   Understanding Self and Others

ASSESSMENT   Anchors and Oars

Objectives

The Anchors and Oars Assessment has two objectives. The first, addressed by Part 1 of the exercise, is to help you identify some of your personal characteristics that are most salient to your own self-image. The second, addressed by Part 2 of the exercise, is to have you learn more about how others see you, as well as to provide insights into how other people see themselves.

Directions Part 1:

Respond to statements 1a, 1b, and 1c, one at a time. Once you have started on your response to 1b and 1c, do not go back to change any of your previous responses.

1. (a) Write down 10 or more adjectives and nouns that describe who you are now. Examples of nouns that describe you might be *son/daughter, student, manager, musician,* and so on. Examples of adjectives that describe you might be *adventurous, introverted, physically active, well-organized,* and so on. Think of as many adjectives and nouns as you can; include phrases if you find this helpful.

   (b) Now write down 10 or more adjectives and nouns that describe who you were 5 to 10 years ago. Again, write down as many ideas as you have.

   (c) Now write down 10 or more adjectives and nouns that describe who you expect to be 5 to 10 years from now. Again, write down as many ideas as you have.

2. Note which items have stayed constant across your life. Note which items have changed from 5 to 10 years ago and which you expect to change over the next 5 to 10 years.

Part 2:

Find a partner and write down 10 or more adjectives and nouns that describe that person based on what you know about him. After you have finished, exchange lists and talk about the similarities and differences between the list you created for yourself and the one your partner created for you. Are there some characteristics that your partner identified for you that were absent from your own list? Did either of you make assumptions about characteristics of the other person that were not accurate?

Discussion Questions

Anchors keep a boat steady, while oars propel a boat forward. All individuals have some personal characteristics that remain constant over time and some characteristics that change. Characteristics that remain constant help keep the individuals steady; those that change allow for development over time.

1. How have your anchors helped you? Are there anchors that have kept you from making important changes?

2. How have different situations in your life encouraged you to make changes?

3. How might you use your current characteristics to help you make the changes you expect to see in yourself over the next 5 to 10 years?

4. How might some of the characteristics that your partner identified but that were not on your own list affect your ability to achieve your personal goals?

Reflection   The salience of different personal characteristics can vary greatly across individuals and even across situations. For example, a student's identity as a male may be highly salient in a class that is predominantly female, but much less salient in a class that is evenly split between males and females. Identities that derive from group status are likely to be much more salient to members of a minority group than members of the majority group. In addition, your answers should reflect that the salience of various personal characteristics may change over time. For example, you may have been actively involved in certain activities 5 to 10 years ago that are no longer central to your life now.

Researchers have examined how professional identities can create difficulties as individuals are promoted to managerial positions (Hill, 2003). In these situations, individuals not only need to learn about the knowledge, skills, and abilities expected for their new responsibilities in managerial positions, they also need to unlearn some behaviors that were central to their professional positions. For example, managerial leaders need to be more aware of their own strengths and weaknesses and how these strengths and weaknesses are complemented by others in the work unit they manage. One way to increase your effectiveness as a managerial leader is to have a firm grasp on the critical competency of understanding self and others as described in the following pages.

LEARNING   Understanding Self and Others

Unlike professionals who are only responsible for their own work, managerial leaders are responsible for bringing together the work of a number of people and creating a cohesive work unit. Being effective as a managerial leader thus not only requires individuals to be aware of their own strengths and weaknesses in terms of the specific work performed in the unit, but also to be aware of their work style and how they interact with others. It also requires individuals to become more aware that although all members of a work group have something in common, each individual is also in some way unique. Managerial leaders must learn about each employee's abilities, understand how employees' work styles may differ, and consider how each person contributes to the work of the unit and the organization as a whole. Managerial leaders must also consider how employees differ in their feelings, needs, and concerns. People react differently to different situations, and it is important for managerial leaders to be able to perceive and understand these reactions.

As a manager, you need to understand both the commonalities and differences among employees as a first step to understanding how people relate to one another in various situations. By being aware, you can better understand your own reaction to people and their reactions to each other. In the past two decades, many companies have begun to focus on helping managers develop their emotional and social intelligence (Goleman, 1995, 1998; Goleman, Boyatzis & McKee, 2002; Seal, Boyatzis & Bailey, 2006), which involves both intrapersonal competence (how we manage ourselves) and interpersonal or social competence (how we handle relationships). Research in this area has shown that emotional and social intelligence plays a particularly crucial role at higher levels of the organization, where managers spend the vast majority of their day interacting with others.

UNDERSTANDING YOURSELF

We begin this section with a focus on understanding yourself, sometimes referred to as self-awareness. The importance of having a good understanding of yourself and what motivates or influences your behaviors should be obvious. If you do not understand yourself, it is nearly impossible to understand others. Yet people often find it difficult to learn about themselves. One reason that people find it difficult to learn about themselves is because their friends and colleagues fear being honest because they think such honesty will create conflict or embarrass the other person. Jerry Hirshberg, founder of Nissan Design International, Inc., notes that people "have mixed feelings about hearing the truth." He states, "It's like a chemical reaction: Your face goes red, your temperature rises, you want to strike back." He labels this reaction "defending and debating" and argues that people need to fight back the tendency to defend and debate by "listening and learning" (Muoio, 1998).

While it may be difficult to receive negative feedback, there is strong evidence that managers with higher levels of self awareness are more likely to advance in their organizations than those with low self-awareness (Dulewicz & Higgs, 2000). There are, of course, many different dimensions of yourself that you could learn about. For example, Peter Drucker (1999), one of world's foremost authorities on management and leadership, argues that in today's economy, people must be aware of their strengths, their values, and how they best perform. Robert Staub, cofounder and president of Staub-Peterson Leadership Consultants, asserts that "the golden rule of effective leadership [is]: Don't fly blind! Know where you stand with regard to the perceptions of others" (Staub, 1997, p. 170).

Goleman and colleagues' (2000; Goleman, Boyatzis & McKee, 2002) work on emotional and social intelligence identifies self-awareness and self-management as the two key dimensions of emotional intelligence. Within self-awareness, there are three subdimensions: emotional awareness, self-assessment, and self-confidence. Emotional awareness involves recognizing your emotions and how they affect you and others. Individuals who have emotional awareness know what they are feeling and why, and they also understand the connection between their feelings and their actions. Self-assessment involves knowing your strengths and limits and being open to feedback that can help you to develop. Individuals who develop this competence are able to learn from experience and value self-development and continuous learning. Self-confidence refers to an awareness of one's self-worth and capabilities. Individuals who possess self-confidence present themselves with a strong sense of self and are willing to stand up for what they believe in, even if their perspective is unpopular.

In addition to knowing about your emotions, your strengths and limits, and how others perceive you, it is important to know what motivates your behaviors—what influences how you will react in different situations. One major influence on your behavior is your personality. While no one always reacts in the same way under all circumstances, people do have a tendency to act and react to situations with some level of consistency. An individual's personality is generally described in terms of those relatively permanent psychological and behavioral attributes that distinguish that individual from others. The notion that personality is relatively permanent stems from the idea that personality is a trait that can change in adulthood but is mostly formed in childhood and adolescence. Thus, "individuals can be characterized in terms of relatively enduring patterns of thoughts, feelings, and actions . . . [that] show some degree of cross-situational consistency" (McCrae & Costa, 2008, p. 160). The concept of personality can thus be used to differentiate among individuals as well as to describe similarities among people with similar personality traits.

TWO APPROACHES TO PERSONALITY

While there are many different approaches to understanding personality, two of these approaches stand out as being the most widely used in research and in organizational training and development seminars on individual differences in organizations. The first, the Five-Factor Model, is generally seen by psychologists as the most widely accepted taxonomy for studying personality (John, Naumann & Soto, 2008). The second, the Myers-Briggs Type Inventory, is based on the work of Carl Jung and is more popular in organizations for understanding differences in employee' work styles.

As the name would imply, the Five-Factor Model presents five factors, or basic tendencies, that researchers argue encompass most of what has been described as personality (McCrae & Costa, 2008). In the model, each factor is named for one of two ends of a continuum. Of course, most individuals do not fall at the ends of the continua, although people are likely to have a tendency toward one end or the other. As you read the description of each of the traits, you might try to place yourself on each of the continua.

The first factor is referred to as **neuroticism**. Individuals who score high on this dimension tend to worry a lot and are often anxious, insecure, and emotional. Alternatively, those who score low tend to be calm, relaxed, and self-confident. The second factor, **extraversion**, has also been referred to as urgency and assertiveness. This factor assesses the degree to which individuals are sociable, talkative, and gregarious in their interactions with others versus reserved, quiet, and sometimes even withdrawn and aloof. The third factor, **openness**, also sometimes called intellectance, focuses on the degree to which an individual is proactive in seeking out new experiences. Individuals who score high on this measure tend to be curious, imaginative, creative, and nontraditional. Those who score low tend to be more conventional, concrete, and practical. **Agreeableness**, the fourth factor, focuses on the degree to which individuals are good-natured, trusting of others, and forgiving of others' mistakes, as opposed to cynical, suspicious of others, and antagonistic. Finally, **conscientiousness** is associated with individuals' degree of organization and persistence. Those who score high on this continuum tend to be more organized, responsible, and self-disciplined; those who score low tend to be more impulsive, careless, and perceived by others as undependable.

Interestingly, researchers have found inconsistent relationships between the five factors and various aspects of leadership. For example, some researchers found extraversion and agreeableness to be positively related, and neuroticism negatively related, to some aspects of leadership, particularly emergent leadership in a leaderless group, suggesting that when a group is formed with no explicit leader, the individual who is more extraverted, agreeable, and emotionally stable will likely emerge as the informal leader (Hogan, Curphy & Hogan, 1994). Other researchers have found conscientiousness to be the strongest predictor of leadership performance (Strang & Kuhnert, 2009). Regardless of which personality factors predict leadership performance, it is important for managerial leaders to be aware of their tendencies as they perform their work.

The Myers-Briggs Type Inventory (MBTI) is one of several personality assessment instruments based on Carl Jung's theory of psychological types. Jung noticed that people behaved in somewhat predictable patterns, which he labeled types. He noted that types could be described along three dimensions: **introversion–extraversion**, **sensing–intuition**, and **thinking–feeling.** Later, Katharine Briggs and her daughter, Isabel Briggs Myers, added a fourth dimension: **judging–perceiving** (Keirsey, 1998). Their assessment instrument is widely used in organizational workshops to help people understand the different work styles of people in a work unit.

The first dimension, introversion–extraversion, is similar to the Five-Factor Model's extraversion factor. It focuses on the degree to which individuals tend to look inward or outward for ideas about decisions and actions. Individuals who are introverted tend to be reflective and value privacy. Individuals who are extraverted tend to like variety and action, and are energized by being with people. The second dimension, sensing–intuition, focuses on what we pay attention to when we gather data. Individuals who are sensing types tend to focus on facts and details; they absorb information in a concrete, literal fashion. Intuitive types, on the other hand, tend to try to see the big picture and focus more on abstract ideas.

While sensing–intuition focuses on how we gather data, thinking–feeling focuses on how we use information when making decisions. Thinking types tend to decide with their brains, whereas feeling types tend to decide with their hearts. Thinking types use analytical and objective approaches to decision-making. Feeling types tend to base decisions on more subjective criteria, taking into account individual differences. The final dimension, judging-perceiving, focuses on approaches to life and thinking styles. Judging types are task oriented and they tend to prefer closure on issues. They are good at planning and organizing. Perceptive types are more spontaneous and flexible, and they tend to be more comfortable with ambiguity.

Because the underlying management models of the competing values framework reflect different assumptions about how decisions should be made, some organizational scholars have suggested that certain personality types may be more inclined toward some approaches to management than others. For example, individuals who score high on thinking are likely to prefer the rational approach to decision-making based on goals and objectives that is the hallmark of the rational goal quadrant. In contrast, individuals who score high on feeling are likely to be more comfortable with the human relations quadrant approach, which calls for more participative approaches. With respect to the data-gathering dimension, sensing types who want to see the facts and figures are likely to fit well in the internal process quadrant with its emphasis on measurement and control. Conversely, intuitive types who are more interested in the big picture may be more comfortable with the open systems approach, which argues for paying attention to what is going on outside the organization.

The four dimensions of the MBTI can be combined to create different combinations, such as extraverted–sensing–thinking–judging or introverted–sensing–feeling–judging. When you combine all four dimensions, there are 16 different personality types that can be identified. Workshops that focus on people's work styles tend to focus on the combinations because they can help people understand why people approach work tasks in different ways. You might think back to a situation where some people in the group jumped right into the task while others wanted to analyze the nature of the problem first. Puccio, Murdock, and Mance (2007) describe these differences as psychological diversity, which they define as "differences in how people organize and process information as an expression of their cognitive styles and personality traits" (p. 205). They argue that this type of diversity can have profound effects on the workplace and note that leaders who understand this type of diversity "are in a much better position to leverage their strengths and to find ways to compensate for their deficiencies" (Puccio et al., 2007, p. 205).

INCREASING YOUR SELF-AWARENESS

As noted above, research has shown that managers with higher levels of self-awareness are more likely to advance in their organizations. It is not, however, simply important to increase your self-awareness. Rather, effective managerial leaders use their self-awareness to identify areas of potential growth, that is, areas where they can become more effective. Seal, Boyatzis, and Bailey (2006) describe a process called "intentional change theory," whereby individuals can identify desirable, sustainable changes they would like to make by asking themselves a series of questions, starting with "Who do I want to be?" (p. 201). The answer to this question gives individuals a sense of their "ideal self." By then asking questions about how one's current strengths and weaknesses (real self) differ from one's ideal self, individuals can create an action plan, or what they label as one's "learning agenda."

In the Assessment exercise, you had the opportunity to use self-reflection, as well as feedback from a partner to help you learn about yourself (real self). Here we present a simple but helpful framework that can help you to develop a more realistic picture of your real self. The framework was developed by Joseph Luft and Harry Ingham (1955), who named it after themselves, calling it the Johari window. As shown in Figure M1.1, it has four quadrants. In the upper left is the Open area, which represents the aspects of who you are that are known both to yourself and to others with whom you interact. In the upper right is the Blind area. Here are the aspects of you that others see but you do not recognize. In the lower left is the Hidden quadrant, sometimes referred to as the façade. These are the things that you know but do not reveal to others. Finally, in the lower right is the Unknown quadrant. Here are those aspects of who you are that neither you nor others are yet aware of; they exist but have not been directly observed, and neither you nor those with whom you interact are aware of their impact on the relationship. When they are discovered, often through deep self-reflection, their impact becomes an important place for personal growth.

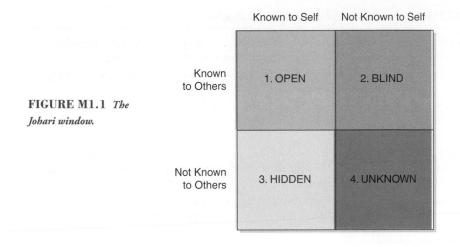

FIGURE M1.1 *The Johari window.*

The sizes of the four quadrants change over time. In a new relationship, the Open quadrant is small. As communication increases, it grows large and the Hidden quadrant begins to shrink. With growing trust, we feel less need to hide the things we value, feel, and know. It takes longer for the Blind quadrant to shrink in size because it requires openness to honest feedback. Not surprisingly, the Unknown quadrant tends to change most slowly of all because it requires people to be introspective and to explore things about themselves that are generally taken for granted. While it is can be a very large quadrant that greatly influences what we do, many people totally close off the possibility of learning about the Unknown quadrant.

As noted above, people sometimes use a great deal of energy in order to hide, deny, or avoid learning about themselves, particularly their inconsistencies and hypocrisies. When colleagues and employees sense that you are not open to feedback, they will avoid sharing important information with you. As a result, the Open quadrant begins to shrink, and the others begin to enlarge. When the Open quadrant increases in size, however, the others shrink. As a result, more energy, skills, and resources can be directed toward personal growth and development and the tasks around which the relationship is formed. This leads to more openness, trust, and learning, and positive outcomes begin to multiply. One way for you to show others that you are open to feedback is to systematically share information about yourself. Ben Dattner (2008) urges managers to provide their employees with a "Managerial User's Manual." He notes that the more you can tell your employees about what you value, what motivates you, and how you work, the more likely it is that you can create an open dialogue about how to work together. He also suggests that the manual should be an evolving document, and that managers should actively solicit input from colleagues and employees about the accuracy and usefulness of the manual. Table M1.1 provides some basic guidelines that can help you increase the size of your Open quadrant by asking for feedback.

TABLE M1.1 Guidelines for Asking for Feedback

- Before asking for feedback, make sure you are open to hearing information that may alter your perceptions. Prepare yourself to hear things that may make you uncomfortable.
- Be aware that the person giving you the feedback is describing her own perception of the situation, but realize that her feelings are real.
- Ask specific questions about your behaviors. Provide the individual with a clear sense of what types of information you are looking for and how you intend to use this information for your personal growth and development.
- Check your understanding of the feedback. Ask questions or give examples and share your reaction(s). Clarify issues, explain your actions, and correct perceptions people may have of you, but do not defend and debate.
- Express your appreciation for the person who has given you the feedback. It may have been difficult for that person to be honest with you, and it is important that you show clearly and unequivocally that you welcome the feedback.

UNDERSTANDING OTHERS

The second two dimensions of emotional and social intelligence are social awareness and relationship management. Within the area of social awareness, the three subdimensions are empathy, organizational awareness, and service orientation. Empathy lies at the heart of understanding others. It involves "sensing others' emotions, understanding their perspective, and taking active interest in their concerns" (Goleman, Boyatzis & McKee, 2002). Leaders who are able to show empathy are able to put themselves in the position of others and see the world as others see it. While employees may not always agree with managers' decisions, they are more likely to trust managers who demonstrate an understanding of their reactions to organizational decisions.

One difficult part of practicing empathy is that some people are uncomfortable with expressing negative emotions in the workplace. That is, they believe that it is unprofessional to express fear, sadness, or anger in the work setting. The fact is, however, that individuals do react emotionally to situations, and the better a leader is at reading people's emotions, the more effective the leader will be at helping to resolve difficult issues and maintaining a more cohesive work environment.

What then can managers do to demonstrate more empathy? What steps can they take to help employees feel that managers are truly interested in their ideas and opinions, even if the final decision is not the one the employee would make? First, it is important to begin practicing empathy before there is a difficult situation. That is, keep in mind that empathy is more than understanding people's emotions; it also involves understanding those individuals' perspectives and concerns. Here, it is helpful to recall the quadrants of the Johari window and to remember that others also have Blind, Hidden, and Unknown areas. Managers who appreciate that employees and colleagues also have these three covert areas and are likely be defensive about them, can begin by encouraging those individuals to move information from the Hidden quadrant to the Open quadrant. That is, in the same way that trust increases when you provide others with a user's manual to help them learn more about you, you might encourage your employees (and colleagues) to also develop a user's manual in which they tell you about

TABLE M1.2 Empathic Listening: Feeling the Experience of Others

1. *Emptying Oneself*: Before you can engage in empathic listening, you must move away from your own problems and concerns. While your personal problems and concerns may be important to you, when you are engaging in empathic listening, you must remember that you need to focus on the other person's problems and concerns.

2. *Paying Attention*: Listen carefully to what the person is saying, and remember that communication is more than words. What is behind the words? Are the words that are being expressed congruent with the individual's nonverbal signals? You can use reflective listening (see Competency 2 in this module) to see if there are things the individual is not saying.

3. *Accepting the Other Person's Reaction*: Remember that you are accepting this reaction as the other person's reaction. You do not need to agree with this reaction; you simply need to assure the other person that you accept that this is how he understands the situation. Listen carefully for the feelings beneath the statement.

4. *Avoiding Judgment or Comparison*: Once you have accepted the other person's reaction as valid, avoid comparing this reaction to your own or to other individuals' reactions. Do not try to suggest that the person should see this in another way or try to provide "the correct facts."

5. *Staying with the Feeling*: If you have followed the first four steps carefully, you will likely feel some of the same emotions the other person is feeling. Experience that feeling. Determine what you can learn from truly feeling the experience of the other person.

what they value, what motivates them, and how they work best. Of course, managers need to be sensitive and respectful of others' need for privacy and to recognize that their first reaction may be defensiveness. If, however, managers provide a role model of sensitivity, openness, and willingness to learn, and ask others for feedback, it is more likely that employees with reciprocate with the same.

Second, it is important for managers to develop their ability to engage in empathic listening. Sparrow and Knight (2006) identify empathic listening as a type of listening that involves trying to understand the situation in the same way that the other person understands it and also trying to feel what she is really feeling. They indicate that there are five requirements for engaging in empathic listening: emptying oneself, paying attention, accepting the other person's reaction, avoiding judgment or comparison, and staying with the feeling. Table M1.2 summarizes these requirements for empathic listening.

ANALYSIS   Using the Johari Window to Analyze Behavior

Objective   The objective of this analysis is to give you an opportunity to analyze the behavior of others and discuss your observations in class. Because most people are not comfortable analyzing their friends and coworkers publicly, this exercise focuses on analyzing the behavior of fictional characters.

Directions   Use the Johari window as a way to analyze the behavior of a character in a television program or movie as you watch it. You may want to watch with other classmates and compare your observations after you have developed your own ideas.

Discussion Questions 1. Were there obvious instances of Hidden, Blind, and/or Unknown areas? If so, how would the course of events change if the character's Open area was larger?

2. Did any of the other characters attempt to make something in a person's Blind area known to them? If so, were they successful? Why or why not?

Reflection Just as in real life, characters in popular television shows, movies, and books often behave in ways that either attempt to conceal their true feelings (Hidden areas) or reflect a lack of self-awareness (Blind and Unknown areas). Depending on the aims of the writers in fiction-based programs or the reactions of other cast members in reality shows, the results may be comic or tragic, and characters may end up enlightened or disbelieving.

PRACTICE   Practicing Receiving Feedback

Objective Increasing your self-awareness requires that you be open to receiving feedback. For many people, however, this is extremely difficult. Often, we tend to shut down and stop listening when someone is trying to give us constructive criticism. Defensiveness is natural, but can be costly—preventing us from learning more about ourselves and improving our personal effectiveness. The objective of this in-class role-play is to give you a chance to experience receiving negative feedback and to think about your responses to it.

Directions Your instructor will provide you with information for this role-play scenario. Working with a partner, one person should give feedback to the other person. After the first round of feedback, switch partners and have the people who previously gave the feedback receive feedback for the second round.

Discussion Questions 1. How did it feel to give negative feedback to another person? To receive negative feedback?

2. Even though you knew that this was just a role-play, did you find yourself getting defensive or angry as you listened to the negative feedback? If so, why do you think that happened?

Reflection Sometimes feedback is too vague to be helpful. Critical thinking skills can be used to develop feedback that is more effective. For example, rather than making a general claim such as "Tom has an attitude problem," describing specific examples of Tom's behaviors and demonstrating why those behaviors are causing problems in the workplace provides more clarity about what Tom needs to do to improve.

APPLICATION   Soliciting Feedback

Objective Now that you have completed the first four steps of the learning process (assessment, learning, analysis, and practice), it is time to take what you have learned and apply it in the workplace and then reflect upon the results.

Directions 1. Based on the Assessment that you completed at the beginning of this chapter and any additional insights that you have gained from the readings and exercises, write down the key aspects of yourself that you believe are in your Open area of the Johari window.

2. Choose a friend or coworker that you feel comfortable with and trust. Make sure this is a person who knows you and someone you think will be honest with you.

3. Explain the Johari window to this person and show him what you have in quadrant 1 (Open area). Explain that you would like to reduce the size of your Blind area (quadrant 3) and are looking for feedback about your work behaviors, focusing on information that will help you work better with others. Go back to Table M1.1 and try to follow the guidelines provided. For example, develop some specific questions about how you work with others. Try to assure the person that you will welcome feedback that will help you become more aware of your work behaviors. Make sure to show your appreciation to the person for taking a risk.

4. As you listen to the feedback about your Blind area, pay attention to your feelings. If you begin to feel defensive, take a deep breath, and ask yourself why the information you are hearing is upsetting you. For general comments about your attitudes, ask for behavioral examples to help you understand why you are being seen in a particular way.

Reflection   Soliciting feedback is an important step in the process of understanding yourself, as well as improving yourself. As you continue to work through the competencies in this text, pay attention to your reaction to the different readings and exercises. If something strikes you as "trivial" or "a waste of time," ask yourself why you are reacting the way that you are. Sometimes we reject ideas because they conflict with our existing beliefs, and we don't take the time to think critically about whether our beliefs or the new ideas have stronger supporting evidence.

Module 1 Competency 2   Communicating Honestly and Effectively

ASSESSMENT   Communication Skills

Objective   The objective of this assessment is to provide you with insights into how you communicate differently with different individuals. Although every interpersonal relationship is unique, we can learn a great deal about our own communication patterns by observing how we communicate with different individuals and people in different positions.

Directions   Think about the communication patterns in two of your relationships—one that is very painful and one that is very pleasant—by assessing the degree to which each item listed creates a problem for you. Next, think about how your communication behavior varies in the two relationships and what areas of communication you might need to work on. Answer the questions by using the following scale.

Scale

Minimal Problem	1	2	3	4	5	6	7	Great Problem

Painful		*Pleasant*		
Other	Self	Other	Self	
_____	_____	_____	_____	1. Expresses ideas in unclear ways.
_____	_____	_____	_____	2. Tries to dominate conversations.
_____	_____	_____	_____	3. Often has a hidden agenda.
_____	_____	_____	_____	4. Is formal and impersonal.
_____	_____	_____	_____	5. Does not listen well.
_____	_____	_____	_____	6. Is easily distracted during the conversation.

				7. Is withdrawn and uncommunicative.
___ ___		___ ___		8. Is overly sensitive, too easily hurt.
___ ___		___ ___		9. Is too abstract and hard to follow.
___ ___		___ ___		10. Is closed to the ideas of the other.
___ ___		___ ___		Total score

Now go back and reexamine your answers. What patterns do you see?

Discussion Questions   1. How does your own communication behavior vary in these two relationships?

2. As you compare your own behaviors across the two relationships, can you identify ways that you could change to be more effective in your communication in the painful relationship? What would you like the other person to change?

Reflection   Many people find it difficult to communicate with people with whom they have a negative relationship. Unfortunately, this can result in a downward spiral, as poor communication results in misunderstandings that may cause the relationship to deteriorate even further. In contrast, learning to communicate more effectively and practicing what you have learned may actually help improve negative relationships and strengthen positive ones.

LEARNING   Communicating Honestly and Effectively

Interpersonal communication is perhaps one of the most important and least understood competencies that a manager can have. Arguably, it is at the heart of all the competencies you will encounter in this textbook. Studies consistently show that managers spend the majority of their time engaging in various types of communication—face-to-face, telephone, e-mail, teleconferences, memos, and presentations; organizational researchers see communication as central to the study of both managerial and organizational effectiveness (Tourish & Hargie, 2004). Knowing when and how to share information requires a very complex understanding of people and situations (Zey, 1991).

Communication is the exchange of information, facts, ideas, and meanings. The communication process can be used to inform, coordinate, and motivate people. Unfortunately, being a good communicator is not easy. Nor is it easy to recognize your own problems in communication. In the Assessment exercise you just completed, for example, you may well have downplayed your own weaknesses in communicating and rated yourself more favorably than you rated the other person in the painful relationship.

If, however, you practiced applying the critical thinking tactic described in the Introduction, identifying the grounds and warrants that support your claim, your assessment is likely to be more accurate than if you simply responded based on your initial impression of your behavior. Although most people in organizations tend to think of themselves as excellent communicators, they consider communication a major organizational problem and generally see the other people in the organization as the source of the problem. It is very difficult to see and admit the problems in our own communication behavior.

Despite this difficulty, analyzing communication behavior is vital. Poor communication skills result in both interpersonal and organizational problems. When interpersonal problems arise, people begin to experience conflict, resist change, and avoid contact with others. Organizationally, poor communication often results in low morale and low productivity. Given that organizing *requires* that people communicate—to develop goals, channel energy, and identify and solve problems—learning to communicate effectively is key to improving work unit and organizational effectiveness.

A BASIC MODEL OF INTERPERSONAL COMMUNICATION

Whenever we attempt to communicate, the information exchanged may take a variety of forms, including ideas, facts, and feelings. Despite these many possible forms, the communication process may be seen in terms of a general model (Shannon & Weaver, 1948), which is shown in Figure M1.2. Although this model was developed over 60 years ago, it remains a useful tool for understanding how communication works and why it often fails.

The model begins with the **communicator** encoding a message. Here the person who is going to communicate **encodes** ideas into **message**, which is sent as a system of symbols, such as words or numbers. While you may not think of yourself as encoding your ideas when you plan to communicate, think about the differences between how you might convey an idea when speaking in class and how you might write that same idea in a paper, or the difference between a text message you might send to your friends to confirm when you are meeting and the e-mail you might send to your professor with the same message. The fact is, there are many things that influence how ideas are translated (encoded) into the message, including the urgency of the message, the experience and skills of the sender, the sender's perception of the receiver, and the sender's cultural expectations and experiences (Beamer & Varner, 2008). For example, in some cultures, a verbal agreement is enough to finalize a deal, while in other cultures a written contract is required. Moreover, each language has certain sayings and expressions that are

FIGURE M1.2 *A basic model of communication.*

Source: *Developed from C. Shannon and M. Weaver, The Mathematical Theory of Communication* (Urbana: University of Illinois Press, 1948). Used with permission

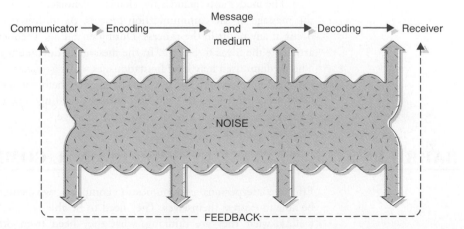

unique to that language and sometimes difficult to convey to others from a different culture.

Once the message is encoded, it must be transmitted through a **medium** (or channel) of some sort. A message, for example, might be written, oral, or even nonverbal. When choosing the appropriate medium, one consideration is the capacity of that medium to convey information, or what it often called the *richness* of that medium. Lengel and Daft (1988) developed a composite measure of richness based on how well the medium can deal with multiple pieces of information simultaneously, the degree to which the medium facilitates feedback, and the degree to which the medium allows for a personal focus. Based on this composite measure, face-to-face communication is considered the richest medium, whereas written communications, such as reports and general announcements, and formal numerical information, such as statistical reports and graphs, are considered the least rich. Lengel and Daft argue that one of the most important skills for a manager is to match the richness of the medium with the needs of the message, rather than merely using the richest medium available (see also Robert & Dennis, 2005). In recent years, newer technologies for mobile communications have been developed (e.g., Short Message Services for sending brief text messages and Multimedia Messaging Services for sending a variety of multimedia content such as photos and video) (Lee, Cheung, & Chen, 2007). As a result, managers have even more choices when selecting the most appropriate communication medium for their messages. For example, Paul F. Levy, the CEO of Beth Israel Deaconess Medical Center, a major hospital in Boston, uses Facebook, Twitter, and a blog to communicate with his employees (Miller, 2009).

Once the message is sent and received, it must be **decoded**, which means that the person who receives it must interpret the message. Like the encoding process, the decoding process is subject to influence by a wide range of factors. Finally, there is a feedback loop between the receiver and the communicator. The **feedback** can take three forms: informational, corrective, or reinforcing. Informational feedback is a nonevaluative response that simply provides additional facts to the sender. Corrective feedback involves a challenge to, or correction of, the original message. Reinforcing feedback is a clear acknowledgment of the message that was sent. It may be positive or negative.

The model also includes the element of **noise,** which is anything that can distort the message in the communication process. As indicated in Figure M1.2, noise can occur at any point in the process. During encoding, a sender may be unable to clearly articulate the ideas to be sent. In the message, a document may leave out a key word. The medium used may have limitations, as when a voicemail system allows only a limited time for recording and cuts off the message before it is complete. Even if no problems occur earlier in the process, during decoding, the receiver may make wrong assumptions about the motive behind the message.

BARRIERS TO EFFECTIVE INTERPERSONAL COMMUNICATION

Effective interpersonal communication comprises two elements. First, individuals must be able to express themselves. They need to be able to convey to others what they are feeling, what they are thinking, what they need from others, and so on. Second, individuals must be good listeners. They must be open to truly hearing the thoughts and ideas that other people are expressing (Samovar & Mills, 1998).

Even if these two conditions are met, problems can occur because of characteristics of the situation. For example, the physical setting may be too hot, cold, noisy, or it may have other distracting features. In other cases, the situation might be inappropriate for the medium chosen. For example, in the movie, *Up in the Air* (Reitman, 2009), an organization discovered that firing people using a video meeting via computer was not as appropriate as meeting with people face-to-face. In contrast, some information should not be conveyed solely through face-to-face interactions. For example, most performance evaluations should be supplemented with a written document that includes an assessment of the prior period's performance, as well as expectations for the coming performance period. Also, oral presentations that include statistical analyses should be supplemented with charts and graphs. Similarly, formal messages may be inappropriate in settings that are highly informal, and informal messages may be inappropriate in a setting that is highly formal.

Here we list some barriers that reduce the effectiveness of interpersonal communication.

- *Inarticulateness.* Communication problems may arise because the sender of the message has difficulty expressing the concept. If the receiver is not aware of the problem, completely inaccurate images may arise and result in subsequent misunderstandings.

- *Hidden agendas.* Sometimes people have motives that they prefer not to reveal. Because the sender believes that the receiver would not react in the desired way, the sender becomes deceptive. The sender seeks to maintain a competitive advantage by keeping the true purpose hidden. Over time, such behavior results in low trust and cooperation.

- *Status.* Communication is often distorted by perceptions of position. When communicating with a person in a position of authority, individuals often craft messages so as to impress and not offend. Conversely, when communicating with a person in a lower hierarchical position, individuals may be dismissive or insensitive to that person's needs. Similarly, a person may not be open to listening to the ideas and opinions of persons who are in a lower hierarchical position.

- *Hostility.* When the receiver is already angry with the person sending the message, the communication will tend to be perceived in a negative way, whether or not it was intended that way. Hostility makes it very difficult to send and receive accurate information. When trust is low and people are angry, no matter what the sender actually expresses, it is likely to be distorted.

- *Distractions.* If people believe that they can multitask while they are communicating, they may not be focused on the subject of the communication. For example, people may try to listen to a conversation while they are also listening to music or reading their e-mail. While this is especially true of the receiver, it can also be true of the sender. In addition, senders may create distractions by fidgeting while talking or looking away from their communication partner during a conversation.

- *Differences in communication styles.* People communicate in different ways. For example, some people speak loudly; others speak softly. Some people provide a great deal of context; others get right to the point and are only interested in "the bottom line." Some of the many differences in communication style are attributable to personal characteristics, such as gender or cultural background. Misunderstandings can develop if people listen less carefully because they are distracted by or uncomfortable with another person's style of communication.

- *Organizational norms and patterns of communication.* Communication barriers that stem from organizational norms and communication patterns may prevent individuals from asking questions or discussing difficult issues. For example, scheduling meetings with no time on the agenda for discussion is likely to stifle communication. Similarly, if every proposed change is routinely dismissed with "that's not the way we do things here," employees learn not to make suggestions.

When combined with the fact that individuals are often reluctant to engage in conflict, organizational norms that stifle communication can be extremely powerful barriers. As discussed in Competency 1 of this module, people have defenses that prevent them from receiving messages they fear. All people have some amount of insecurity, and there are certain things they simply do not want to know. Because people in organizations know this, they develop defensive routines (Argyris & Schön, 1996) in which they avoid saying things that might make the other person or themselves uncomfortable. Defensive routines are particularly likely to occur when discussing issues that relate to values, assumptions, and self-image.

Chris Argyris of the Harvard Business School refers to the thoughts and feelings that are relevant to a conversation but are not explicitly stated as "left-hand column issues" because of an exercise he uses to discover what they are (Senge, Roberts, Ross, Smith & Kleiner, 1994). Left-hand column issues include both the things people are thinking but not saying and the things they think the other person is thinking but not saying. You can think of left-hand column issues as things that are "left out" of the conversation. Argyris contends that organizations develop left-hand column issues that keep important issues from surfacing and being discussed. Instead of surfacing these issues, people work around them, avoid them, make things up, and say things they don't mean or believe. Often they go through these pretenses to avoid offending people or having to deal with a difficult situation. But when the list of "undiscussables" becomes larger than the list of "discussables," the organization begins to suffer. Trust erodes, and lots of covering up and avoidance make it difficult for people to improve their performance because they have no idea where they stand with one another. Important information is lost or kept concealed.

How does the left-hand-column exercise work? Imagine a conversation you have had or might have with a person at work. The person might be your boss, a coworker, or someone who reports to you. You could probably write down this conversation fairly easily, but before doing so, draw a vertical line down the middle of the paper. Now, in the right-hand column, write down the actual words spoken by you and the other person. In the left-hand column, write down the thoughts, feelings, questions, and concerns that you have but that you would not express out loud. Here's an example of such a conversation:

Left-Hand Column: What Is Thought (But Is Not Directly Communicated)	Right-Hand Column: What Is Said
Terry: I don't want to wait any longer on getting this position filled. We've already waited too long as it is.	**Terry:** Have you had a chance to look at the memo with the list of candidates? If you have any questions or hesitations about who ought to be on the list, just let me know. I want you to be comfortable with the people we bring in to interview.
Troy: I knew Terry wasn't going to add Michelle LaFleur to that list. We talked about it, and he knows I wanted her to be interviewed.	**Troy:** I think it looks pretty good. Have you gotten any feedback from the rest of the team?
Terry: I know what he's thinking: "Does anyone else agree with me that LaFleur should be interviewed?" Why doesn't he just say it? That bugs me.	**Terry:** I haven't heard from anyone yet, but we've got three people out of town until Friday. They may get back to me before then on e-mail. I'd like to interview these people next week. Do you think that's possible?
Troy: Right, another question from the guy who doesn't listen to my suggestions anyway.	**Troy:** I don't see why not. Let's move ahead with it. The last thing we want is to get stuck in a hiring freeze before we get someone in the door.
Terry: I know Troy is miffed about this process. He gets frustrated because we don't follow his proposals, but he keeps putting unqualified people in front of us because he wants to work with them. He's always looking for friends instead of someone to get the work done.	**Terry:** I agree. Thanks, Troy. I think we're making progress.

Clearly, these two people are not saying what they are thinking or feeling, but those feelings are influencing the "deep structure" of their behavior. The conversation on the surface is not as powerful as the silent conversation taking place beneath the surface, in the left-hand column. At the end of the right-hand column conversation that actually took place, both Terry and Troy feel somewhat dissatisfied, but neither one feels comfortable talking about the reason for their dissatisfaction.

People need to be trained to surface left-hand-column issues in ways that are positive and nonpunishing. They need to develop the skills to express their concerns in a

TABLE M1.3 Rules for Effective Communication

1. *Be clear on who the receiver is.* What is the receiver's state of mind? What assumptions does the receiver bring? What is she feeling in this situation?
2. *Know what your objective is.* What do you want to accomplish by sending the message?
3. *Analyze the climate.* What will be necessary to help the receiver relax and be open to the communication?
4. *Review the message in your head before you say it.* Think about the message from the point of view of the receiver. Do you need to clarify certain ideas?
5. *Communicate using words and terms that are familiar to the other person.* Use examples and illustrations that come from the world of the receiver.
6. *If the receiver seems not to understand, clarify the message.* Ask questions. If repetition is necessary, try different words and illustrations.
7. *If the response is seemingly critical, do not react defensively.* Try to understand what the receiver is thinking. Why is he reacting negatively? The receiver may be misunderstanding your message. Ask clarifying questions.

way that helps the other person want to hear what they have to say. In the next competency, we will focus on mentoring and developing employees. In order to be able to perform this competency effectively, managers need to be open and honest with their employees. Effective managers also role-model these behaviors for their employees so that they can learn to be more effective at surfacing left-hand column issues.

Of course, it is important to recognize that not all left-hand column issues should be communicated. In the conversation above, for example, it would most likely be helpful for Terry to explicitly state that he considered Michelle LaFleur but did not think that her qualifications fit the position. This might lead to a response from Troy that identified something that Troy had overlooked about Michelle. In contrast, it would not be helpful for Terry to say that he thought Michelle's only qualification was that she was a friend of Troy's, even if that was indeed how Terry felt.

Given the number and intensity of these barriers to effective communication, what should you know to help yourself to communicate effectively? First, you need to develop a few basic skills to express yourself more effectively. Table M1.3 gives seven basic rules for sharing your ideas with others. Most important, always keep in mind the old adage "Think before you speak." An effective speaker who communicates the wrong information can create far more problems than an ineffective speaker who struggles to convey the correct information.

REFLECTIVE LISTENING

Of all the skills associated with good communication, perhaps the most important is listening. The Stoic philosopher Epictetus, in *The Golden Sayings,* reportedly said, "Nature hath given men one tongue but two ears that we may hear from others twice as much as we speak." This is a good thought to keep in mind, but we should remember that listening is more than hearing what others have to say. Listening requires that we truly focus and try to understand what the other person is saying. Harris (2006) suggests that we should think of listening as having two dimensions: concentration and collaboration. Concentration involves focusing and attending to what the person is saying. Collaboration involves responding and providing feedback, letting the other person know that we are actively engaged in the conversation. When we define listening in terms of both of these dimensions, it becomes clearer that listening is a skill that we must develop, rather than one that we acquire as a by-product of how we hear.

Reflective listening is a tool that is based on empathy (recall Table M1.2), which helps us to experience the thoughts and feelings of the other person. In using empathy and reflective listening, instead of directing and controlling the thoughts of the other person, you become a helper who tries to facilitate her expression. Instead of assuming responsibility for another's problem, you help that person explore it on her own. Your job is not to talk but to keep the other person talking. You do not evaluate, judge, or advise; you simply reflect on what you hear. In fewer words, you descriptively, not evaluatively, restate the essence of the person's last thought or feeling. If the person's statement is factually inaccurate, you do not immediately point out the inaccuracy. Instead of interrupting, you keep the person's flow of expression moving. You can go back later to correct factual errors.

The reflective listener uses open-ended questions, such as "Can you tell me more?" or "How did you feel when that happened?" Evaluative questions and factual, yes-or-no questions are avoided. Sometimes, it is simply helpful to mirror what the other person has said, but to turn it into a question that indicates that you want to hear more about that idea. The key is to keep the conceptual and emotional flow of expression. Instead of telling, the reflective listener helps the other person to discover. Here is an example of reflective listening to help illustrate how it works.

Kathie is the manager of the Training and Development Office in a large public agency. The office has 13 professional employees whose primary job is to conduct training for the agency and 2 secretaries. Allen is a relatively new employee who has been asked to develop new training on "Dealing with Crisis Situations." Kathie is having her first formal meeting with Allen since he was hired two months ago.

Kathie:	Allen, I was wondering how you're doing on the new training program. I had originally hoped that during your first few months we would meet more often, but things have been very hectic. Are you moving along with the project?
Allen:	Well, at first I felt like I was making good progress, but now I'm at an impasse. I'm just feeling frustrated.
Kathie:	Can you tell me why you're feeling frustrated? Is there something about the project that isn't going right?
Allen:	I guess I'm just frustrated with the assignment. I've gathered lots of information, but when I ask the others about what should be included, some say I'm putting in too much information, and others say there isn't enough time to practice the new skills.
Kathie:	So are you feeling like you're getting different messages from different people?
Allen:	Yes, and I'm not sure how long the training program is supposed to be. Is it a half-day program, a whole-day program, or a multiday program?
Kathie:	Based on the information you have gathered, how long do you think it should be?
Allen:	Well, I think it should be a two-day program, but I didn't think that I was responsible for making that decision. That's part of my frustration!

> *Kathie:* I think I understand. Is part of your frustration that you're not sure which decisions you can make on your own and which you need to get approval from others?
>
> *Allen:* Yes, that's exactly it. I'm not sure of what the rules are around here and how decisions are made.

To the first-time reader, reflective listening sounds very strange. Experience shows, however, that it can have major payoffs. Trust and concern grow with an ever-deepening understanding of interpersonal issues. More effective and lasting problem solving takes place, and people have a greater sense that their ideas are being listened to by others. In short, communication is greatly improved.

Reflective listening is not, however, a panacea. It is time-consuming to really listen. It requires confidence in one's interpersonal skills and the courage to possibly hear things about oneself that are less than complimentary. There is also a danger that the sender will get into personal areas of life with which the listener is not comfortable and for which a professional counselor would be more appropriate. It is, nevertheless, a vital tool that is seldom understood or employed.

ANALYSIS Using the Left-Hand Column to Develop Your Communication Skills

Objective   The objective of this analysis is to help you begin to identify gaps between what you say and what you think, as well as to help you understand why those gaps occur.

Directions   1. Think back to a conversation you had with a friend or work colleague involving a problem that you tried to resolve. This may be a problem that has since been solved or one that still does not have a usable solution, but the key is to find a problem that you were unable to resolve at that time. Try to identify a difficult problem that involved interpersonal difficulties, such as a conflict about how to do an assignment or a disagreement about who should perform different parts of a task.

   Write down the approach that you initially took to resolve the problem. What did you talk about? What ideas did you have? What were the interpersonal communication barriers that hindered your ability to resolve the issue? For example, did one of you have a hidden agenda? Were there status differences that created problems? Were there distractions that kept you from being focused on the conversation?

   Using a fresh piece of paper, divide the paper in half and write down the conversation that occurred on the right-hand side of the page. If you cannot remember the conversation verbatim, try to remember the key issues that were raised.

   On the left-hand side of the page, write down your thoughts and feelings that were unexpressed during the conversation.

   2. Reflect on what you have in your left-hand column. What led you to feel that way? What kept you from expressing your thoughts and feelings? What assumptions did you make about the other person? What did you lose from keeping certain thoughts and feelings to yourself?

   3. Think about how you might move some of your thoughts and feelings from the left-hand column to the right-hand column.

Reflection Sometimes we don't express our thoughts and feelings because we don't feel that we have sufficient grounds for the claims that we would like to make—we don't trust our intuition. But often our reticence is based on a desire to avoid conflict, rather than a lack of solid arguments. Feelings that are not expressed, however, do not simply disappear. In addition to being willing to express our own thoughts and feelings, we need to encourage others to express their thoughts and feelings and we need to listen carefully when they do. Often the best way to minimize conflict is to raise potentially contentious issues early, before they escalate.

PRACTICE Using Reflective Listening to Move Thoughts and Feelings to the Right-Hand Column: The Case of Stacy Brock and Terry Lord

Objective This practice exercise is designed to help you enhance your ability to use reflective listening to surface left-hand column issues and clarify roles and expectations with another person—a boss, peer, or direct report. The two people in this case, Stacy Brock and Terry Lord, have gotten themselves into a box in their working relationship. They have already had one blowup, and they may have another if they cannot handle themselves effectively. Both need to listen to the other, both need some feedback, and both have things they need to say.

Directions Your instructor will provide you with a role description for either Stacy Brock or Terry Lord. Read the information carefully so that you are prepared to play your role from the perspective of your character. Your instructor may have some people role-play the situation in front of the class or may ask everyone to work together in dyads. After you have completed the role-play, respond to the following discussion questions.

Discussion Questions 1. How well were you and your partner (or the individuals who did the role-play in the front of the class) able to communicate?

2. Did you surface the real issues? Which issues were carefully discussed?

3. Which issues, if any, were undiscussable?

4. What types of reflective listening statements did each person make to help the issues become more discussable?

Reflection For many employees, performance evaluations are difficult conversations because they involve status differences. Both managers and employees may feel uncomfortable engaging in conflict with the other. If, however, the manager is able to use reflective listening effectively, a potentially explosive situation can turn into a very productive conversation where each can learn from the other.

APPLICATION Developing Your Reflective Listening Skills

Objective It is one thing to practice reflective listening in the classroom, but quite another to apply it in your daily life. The objective is this activity is to help you transfer what you have learned about reflective listening into a habit at work and at home.

Directions   1. Over the next week, practice your reflective listening skills. Whenever you are involved in a conversation, try to gain a better understanding of what the other person is thinking and feeling by asking questions.

2. Keep a journal of your experiences using reflective listening and assess whether, over the course of the week, you found that you were able to become a more patient listener. In your journal note what you said and how the person responded. Note what types of statements elicited strong responses from the other person, and identify ways to continue developing your reflective listening skills.

Reflection   Techniques such as reflective listening are not difficult to understand, but mastering them requires repeated practice and reflection. The idea of keeping a journal about your experiences with reflective listening may seem time consuming at first, but it can provide specific ideas about where you need to increase your effort to develop your competence as an effective listener as well as more general feedback about how you are progressing in your development as a more effective communicator. The journal will also help remind you about the importance of practicing listening, in the same way you would practice any other skill you want to develop.

Module 1 Competency 3   Mentoring and Developing Others

ASSESSMENT   Assumptions about Performance Evaluations

Objective   Often we hold unconscious assumptions that keep us from questioning the way things are done. The objective of this assessment exercise is to examine your own assumptions and learn about the assumptions that other people hold concerning performance evaluations.

Directions   Check off the statement in each of the following pairs of statements that best reflects your assumptions about performance evaluation.

Performance evaluation is:

_____ 1a. a formal process that is done annually

_____ 1b. an informal process that is done continuously

_____ 2a. a process that is planned for employees

_____ 2b. a process that is planned with employees

_____ 3a. a required organizational procedure

_____ 3b. a process done regardless of requirements

_____ 4a. a time to evaluate employee performance

_____ 4b. a time for employees to evaluate the manager

_____ 5a. a time to clarify standards

_____ 5b. a time to clarify the employee's career needs

_____ 6a. a time to confront poor performance

_____ 6b. a time to express appreciation

_____ 7a. an opportunity to clarify issues and provide direction and control

_____ 7b. an opportunity to increase enthusiasm and commitment

_____ 8a. only as good as the organization's forms

_____ 8b. only as good as the manager's coaching skills

Discussion Questions

1. As you review your eight answers, do you see any patterns in your assumptions or in the assumptions you did not choose?

2. As you review the statements, think about how the use of performance evaluation benefits the organization, the manager, and the employee. In what ways does each benefit? Are the benefits shared equally?

3. How would you design a performance evaluation process where the benefits are more equally shared?

4. What characteristics of your performance evaluation process would make it more attractive to employees? Would those characteristics increase or reduce the usefulness of the performance evaluation process for the organization?

Reflection

All performance evaluation systems are not created equal, and even the same system may be evaluated differently by different people and at different times. For example, for decades General Electric's performance evaluation system and leadership training practices have been praised for developing top-flight talent. At the same time, GE has been criticized for its requirement that managers must fire those employees who rank in the bottom 10 percent. In a cover story in *Bloomberg BusinessWeek,* Diane Brady (2010) notes that recently some people have begun to question whether GE's approach is too rigid. For example, although in the past, many other companies have looked to GE when recruiting for top positions, executive recruiter Peter Crist notes that today, companies are looking at other organizations that are seen as "decentralized, sophisticated, and young" (quoted in Brady, 2010, p. 29). Similarly, the idea of firing people just because their performance is at the bottom of the curve may not really make sense if your talent pool is exceptionally strong. As Google's Director of Talent Management, Judy Gilbert, notes "When you're killing yourself to hire the right people, it doesn't make sense to cull" (quoted in Brady, 2010, p. 31).

LEARNING Mentoring and Developing Others

Depending on your work setting, new employees may be expected to have a great deal of prior education or experience in the work performed in your organization, or they may be expected to learn much of their work on the job. Even within many work settings, some types of jobs may require individuals to have more knowledge and skills as they begin their work than others. For example, within a bank, most bank tellers do not know much about banking when they are hired, but are expected to have basic skills in communication and mathematics and to have a problem-solving orientation. On the other hand, when an individual is hired as a loan officer, he would likely be expected to be familiar with basic economic and accounting principles, understand marketing strategy and tactics, and also have good communication skills. Regardless of the knowledge and skills employees are expected to have when they are hired, your role as a managerial leader is to mentor and develop employees.

In a literal sense, *mentor* means a trusted counselor or guide—a coach. The term derives from a character in *The Odyssey,* the Greek epic poem written by Homer (Bell, 1996). In the poem, Odysseus asks a family friend, Mentor, to serve as a tutor and coach to his son, Telemachus, while he is off at war. In this section, we explore how managerial leaders can be more effective in mentoring and developing employees. We begin by examining formal organizational systems of performance evaluation and examine ways in which these can be structured to provide benefits to the employee, the manager, and the organization. We then look at mentoring and performance coaching as more informal processes that can be used to develop employees in an ongoing fashion. We conclude by looking at delegation as a means of developing employees' competencies and abilities by providing them with opportunities to take on more responsibility. While the primary focus here is on mentoring and developing employees, you should keep in mind that there are many other situations where you can apply the knowledge and skills presented here. For example, if you are a member of a club or community organization, you may have opportunities to mentor and develop others. Even outside of formal organizational settings, you may serve as a mentor to friends and family members.

CONDUCTING EFFECTIVE PERFORMANCE EVALUATIONS

In the Assessment exercise at the beginning of this competency, you chose between two options in eight pairs of assumptions about performance evaluation. In each pair of statements, answer *a* reflects traditional control values that provide the basis for most organizational performance evaluation processes. Evaluation processes that are based on these control values, however, are generally disliked by both managers and employees because they are generally associated with negative criticism (Jackman & Strober, 2003). Indeed, as you might expect based on your own experiences of being graded in school, performance evaluation is one of the most uniformly disliked processes in organizational America, as demonstrated by a survey of human resources professionals conducted in 1997 by Aon Consulting and the Society for Human Resources Management, which found that only 5 percent of the respondents were very satisfied with their organization's performance-management systems (Imperato, 1998). Since employees are not eager to hear criticism and managers fear negative reactions from employees, even to what managers see as constructive criticism, most individuals look on performance evaluation as a management process with little benefit to the organization, the manager, or the employee (Jacobs, 2009).

On the other hand, within the eight pairs, answer *b* reflects values rooted in involvement, communication, and trust. When performance evaluations are conducted within this perspective, they are not one-time, stand-alone meetings. Rather, from this perspective, performance evaluation is seen as part of an ongoing, multistage process that mixes the *a* and *b* views of the world by emphasizing both control and collaboration, and allows for regular feedback between the manager and employee.

Individual performance evaluations are a key component of an organization's comprehensive performance management system, a topic we return to in Module 3, where we will address how effective performance management systems translate the organizational vision into unit and individual goals. At the individual level, Grote (2002) presents a model of a strategy-based performance management system that includes four stages. The first stage, *performance planning*, begins a year before the actual performance review, and involves a meeting between the manager and the employee to discuss performance expectations for the next 12 months. Both the manager and the employee contribute actively to this discussion, which focuses on "the key responsibilities of the person's job and the goals and projects the person will work on" as well as "the behaviors and competencies the organization expects of its members" (p. 1). The discussion may also focus on specific development activities, such as attending a training workshop or webinar.

In the second stage, *performance execution*, the employee carries out his tasks and responsibilities, and the manager provides coaching and feedback on a regular basis. As you will see in the next section, coaching is generally seen as less formal than performance evaluation, but provides the foundation for that meeting. Grote suggests that the manager and employee should meet together midway through the year, and maybe more often, to discuss progress toward meeting goals developed at the performance planning meeting.

The third stage, *performance assessment*, involves gathering information on how well the employee has performed, and should begin a few weeks before the performance review meeting. The performance assessment should focus on how successful the employee was in reaching her goals, as well as how well the employee performed with respect to expected behaviors and competencies. Here, the manager may involve others in the organization who interact with the employee on a regular basis.

The final stage is the *performance review* meeting. At this meeting, the manager provides formal feedback on the employee's performance and suggests areas for development. During this session, you should be sure that your own objective is clear. Know what you want to accomplish. Get into an appropriate frame of mind (Krieff, 1996). Ask yourself how you really feel about the person and, most importantly, how you can really help the person. Few managers enter the process in such a frame of mind. Begin by making sure that the employee is also in an appropriate frame of mind. Remember that the performance evaluation will be most effective if the employee is ready to hear your feedback (Silberman, 2000).

Focus first on positive behaviors. If you have not already asked the employee to write a self-evaluation, ask him to list the things that he has done well; contribute to the list as much as possible. When you turn to areas that might need improvement, again ask the person to begin; in a supportive way, continue together until you agree on a list. At this point, you can use the skills discussed in the previous two competencies related to understanding self and others and communicating honestly and effectively and ask how you as a manager are contributing to this person's problems. For example, you might suggest going through the list and asking what you could do differently. As the person responds, use reflective listening to explore the person's claim in an honest way. Make commitments to change your behavior where possible. In doing so, you are modeling the behavior you would like the employee to practice and develop. After doing this, you might again go through the list and ask the employee what changes he might make.

Next, you should discuss the person's career development plan and what progress has been made with respect to the plan. If there is no such plan, one of the assignments should be to write a plan; you may need to help the person here. At the conclusion of the session, summarize what each of you might do differently during the next few months. After this, do an overall review, checking the employee's understanding of each action step. Do a final summary, and set a time for the next performance planning meeting.

While some organizations use the performance review meeting to begin the next cycle, Grote (2002) suggests that the next performance planning meeting should be held separately, but should build on the outcome of the performance review meeting. At that meeting, you should review the outcomes of the performance review meeting.

If your organization already has a system in place, you might consider its effectiveness from the perspective of employee growth and development. Does your current system consider employees' need for feedback? Does it encourage managers to engage in frequent conversations with employees during the time period from one performance evaluation to another? As noted above, managers should meet at regular intervals with each employee to provide specific feedback on employee performance and suggestions for improving performance. Table M1.4 provides some guidelines for giving feedback. While these guidelines are generally useful for both informal conversations and formal performance evaluation sessions, managers should recognize the differences between ongoing feedback and the performance review meeting. Bacal (2004) differentiates between the two by defining evaluation as focused on judging an individual's contributions, whereas feedback is more focused on "improving performance by making information available to the employee" (p. 146). To provide such information, managers need to make sure that they regularly observe the performance of employees and make notes of concrete incidents that can provide specific examples of both positive and negative behaviors.

TABLE M1.4 Guidelines for Giving Feedback

- Before giving feedback, examine your motivation and make sure the receiver is ready and open to hear you. Ask the person whether or not this is a good time to receive feedback.
- Make sure to give the person feedback in a private place that allows for further dialogue.
- Be supportive and encouraging in your feedback. Focus on behaviors you are looking for in the future rather than on your disappointment over past behaviors.
- Provide feedback on both positive and negative behaviors. No one is either all bad or all good. Managers who present only one side lose their credibility for being honest.
- Describe the other person's behavior and your perceptions of it. Present specific examples of behavior that you have observed, rather than generalized statements that describe a demeanor or an attitude. Make sure your examples are timely. Giving feedback on a behavior that has long passed is both annoying and difficult to discuss
- Try to remain calm and emotionally neutral. Be direct in your statements. Even if you are somewhat uncomfortable about giving negative feedback, don't avoid the key issues.
- Ask the other person to clarify, explain, change, or correct.
- After giving feedback, give the receiver time to respond.
- Use the opportunity to develop a joint action plan. Identify ways that you can contribute positively to improving the employee's behavior.

In considering your organization's performance management system, you may also try to identify additional techniques for increasing employees' involvement, communication, and trust. For example, Jacobs (2009) argues that performance management systems should focus more on employees' perceptions of their work and suggestions for improvement than on the managers'. Of course, this would require that employees have access to other forms of feedback, either directly based on output or from others with whom they interact, such as colleagues or customers. Jacobs suggests that such a system helps develop employees to a greater extent because it gives them greater responsibility for their success. Even if the employee's perception does not drive the performance review meeting, you can ask the employee to prepare a written evaluation of her performance for you to read in advance of this meeting. By reading the employee's self-evaluation in advance, you can develop greater empathy and gain a better understanding of how this person sees her performance. In scheduling the session, be sure to set aside enough time to fully discuss the employee's self-evaluation and make sure that you have a private setting where you will not be interrupted. By allowing enough time and space to fully discuss the employee's self-evaluation, the session can become a learning opportunity for both yourself and the employee.

COACHING AND MENTORING EMPLOYEES

In the previous section, we examined the performance evaluation process and noted that it is generally disliked in organizations. One reason why performance evaluations are generally disliked is that managers and employees both tend to see the performance evaluation process as focused on control, providing managers with an opportunity to raise concerns about employees' poor performance. In contrast, the performance evaluation process also can be seen as focused on collaboration. From this perspective, the performance evaluation process provides an opportunity to celebrate an employee's successes and identify opportunities for new achievements in the future. In making suggestions about how to improve such systems, the focus was on finding ways to personalize the process and providing employees with more opportunities for input into the process. In recent years, there has been growing emphasis on two organizational processes that are designed to help employees grow and develop—coaching and mentoring. Both of these processes emphasize the one-on-one relationships between an employee and someone who is more experienced, either a coach or a mentor, and both emphasize the use of feedback as a tool for development.

Although the terms "coaching" and "mentoring" are often used interchangeably, many differentiate between the two, emphasizing that coaches tend to be the individual's direct supervisor, whereas mentors are often one or two levels higher in the organizational hierarchy and may even be in a different department or division. In addition, many organizations have formal mentoring systems, in which an individual is assigned a mentor, whereas coaching occurs when a trusting relationship develops between an employee and his supervisor so that the individual is able to grow and develop in his career and in the organization. In organizations that have formal mentoring systems, the focus of the mentoring relationship may be to help the protégé build his network within the organization, rather to provide feedback on specific work-related behaviors (Hughes, Ginnett & Curphy, 1999).

Gilley and Gilley (2007) identify a number of benefits of coaching to the individual, the manager, and the organization. Several of these benefits also occur when the relationship is with a mentor, rather than with a coach. For individuals, the greatest benefit is having the opportunity to develop to their fullest, which generally leads to greater job and career satisfaction. In addition, in coaching situations, individuals have the opportunity to work in a positive work environment. Managers also benefit from coaching; working with a more motivated and productive workforce energizes managers, which can result in further improvements to unit performance. In addition, Boyatzis, Smith, and Blize (2006) argue that leaders who "coach with compassion" benefit because it reduces their personal level of stress. Finally, coaching benefits the organization, because there is better communication among managers and employees, as well as enhanced creativity in decision-making and problem solving, which ultimately leads to improved effectiveness and enhanced productivity.

The question then becomes: How do managers develop their skills and abilities as coaches? Gilley and Gilley (2007) identify four roles that coaches play: career advisor, trainer, performance appraiser, and strategist. Interestingly, these four roles bear some similarities to the quadrants of the competing values framework. Career advising has elements of the collaborate quadrant and focuses on being supportive and helping employees develop their self-awareness. As a trainer, the coach is more directive and takes on responsibilities associated with the control quadrant, focusing on specific information the employee needs to enhance her work performance. The performance appraiser is also directive, and takes on responsibilities associated with the compete quadrant, emphasizing goals and standards as a means to enhance performance results. Finally, the strategist focuses on developing employees using approaches associated with the create quadrant and is skilled at facilitating change. This suggests that to develop your capacity as a coach, you should develop your capacity to perform well in each of the quadrants and be flexible enough to switch between roles, depending on the needs of your employees. To better understand the needs of your employees, you especially need to build your capacity to empathize and understand your employees' perspectives. You also need to gain a strong understanding of their strengths and weaknesses so that you can encourage them to take on new tasks and responsibilities, as appropriate. In the next section, we focus on delegation as one approach to helping employees take on new tasks and responsibilities.

DEVELOPING EMPLOYEES THROUGH EFFECTIVE DELEGATION

Most often, when organizational researchers examine delegation, they do so from the perspective of how it can help managers use their time more effectively. They note, for example, that managers who learn to delegate effectively provide themselves with additional time and thus are able to focus attention on more significant issues. By delegating tasks, managers can increase efficiency and productivity by ensuring that (1) the work is being done at the appropriate level and managerial time is saved for work that requires managerial attention and (2) employees are not waiting for managers to complete tasks that could be performed by others (Hughes, Ginnett & Curphy, 1999).

Despite the potential benefits of delegation, many managers, especially new managers, resist delegating tasks to employees (Walker, 2002). Why do managers find it difficult to delegate? First, some managers associate delegation with negative managerial behaviors, such as abdicating responsibility for a task or letting someone else—typically those "lower" in the organization—do the dirty work. Some are concerned that employees will be offended if their manager asks them to take on a task previously performed by the manager. Second, many managers fear that they will lose control. They are concerned that employees will not do the job as well or exercise the same level of judgment as the manager would if she did the job herself. Third, many new managers do not fully grasp that they must make a transition from their previous role as contributor to a new role as leader (Hill, 2003; Walker, 2002), and assign tasks. Finally, and perhaps most important, is the fact that many managers have not learned how to delegate effectively; they have not learned that delegation is more than simply giving assignments to employees and hoping for the best. Rather, it is the entrusting of a particular assignment, project, task, or process by one individual to another (Schwartz, 1992). As such, it requires a good understanding of what can and cannot be delegated, careful attention to employees' current skill levels, and a good communication process that allows for questions and feedback for both the manager and the employees. It also requires managers to do more than simply tell employees what they want them to do; managers need to share with employees the reasons for the assignment, that is, why the task needs to be done (Klein, 2000). Navy Commander D. Michael Abrashoff, who commanded the USS *Benfold*, a ship that is known for getting tough assignments, argues that it is important for managers in all situations to communicate purpose. He states "getting [crew members] to contribute in a meaningful way to each life-or-death mission isn't just a matter of training and discipline. It's a matter of knowing who they are and where they are coming from—and linking that knowledge to our purpose" (quoted in LaBarre, 1999).

More important for the discussion here, however, is the fact that delegating tasks and responsibilities to employees is an effective means of developing employees. When managers delegate responsibilities to their employees and give them challenging assignments that push them to go beyond their current level of functioning, they give employees opportunities to develop new skills and abilities, as well as to learn more about the work unit and how it functions. This helps employees to be more effective in their work and strengthens the work unit, thus allowing for a better allocation of organizational resources.

Becoming a more effective delegator requires managers to remember that delegation involves three core elements: responsibility, authority, and accountability. Before delegating, the manager should be aware that while she is still ultimately *responsible* for the successful execution of the assignment, project, task, or process, effective delegation involves clarifying the difference between the managers' and the employees' responsibilities. In particular, the employee should be responsible for achieving intermediate and specific goals and milestones along the way. Managers should also make sure that those individuals to whom assignments are delegated have sufficient *authority* to allow them to carry out the task and obtain the resources and cooperation required for its successful completion. Finally, individuals who are delegated assignments should be held *accountable* for meeting established goals and objectives. While using delegation as a means to develop employees suggests that employees should have a certain level of autonomy, the manager should supervise and monitor as appropriate. Periodic reports and evaluations may be critical here. Here we suggest five steps for using delegation to develop employees. You may note that these steps are similar to the four stages of effective performance evaluation systems.

FIVE STEPS TO EFFECTIVE DELEGATION

1. *Clarify, in your own mind, what it is that you want done and why this is an appropriate assignment for the individual.* Make sure that this assignment is at the proper level of difficulty, providing the employee some challenge but not so much that he becomes frustrated with the assignment. Make sure that the employee has time to do the assignment. Also, make sure that the person has appropriate authority to carry out the task and obtain the resources and cooperation required for its successful completion. Think about how you will explain to the employee what is to be done and whether or not this assignment should be considered a high priority, relative to the other work he is doing, as well as why this assignment is important for the work unit. Writing it down can be helpful.

2. *Meet with the employee and discuss the assignment and your expectations.* Once you are certain in your own mind about the nature of the task and any expectations you have regarding the outcome, you need to communicate that information to the employee in a clear and specific manner. Make sure the employee understands how the task relates to organizational goals, when the subordinate's responsibility begins, whether or not this task is a new task or has been performed by others in the past, and what sources of help are available. If the task has been performed by others in the past, provide relevant information about problems that have been encountered. Also discuss how you will supervise and monitor (Hughes, Ginnett & Curphy, 1999). To ensure the task is fully understood and that deadlines and time horizons are clear, ask questions. You might even ask the employee to repeat or feed-back his understanding of the delegated assignment.

3. *Allow the employee to do the task the way she feels comfortable doing it.* Show some trust in the employee's abilities, but make sure the employee feels comfortable coming to you to discuss any concerns the employee has. Make sure the employee is given the authority to complete the task and the appropriate discretion in choosing the manner of completion.

4. *Check on the progress of the assignment, but do not rush to the rescue at the first sign that things may not be on track.* Hold the person responsible for the work and any difficulties that may emerge. Again, make sure the employee knows that he can discuss any concerns with you, but give the employee a chance to try solving the problem on his own. Also keep in mind that the employee may have initially felt that the assignment surpassed his ability, and so may fear being embarrassed by failure but also feel uncomfortable raising this issue. When you show confidence in your employee, the employee will likely gain the self-confidence necessary to solve the problem. You may be able to avoid this problem at the start by explicitly conveying to the employee your level of confidence in his ability to complete the assigned task and asking about any concerns he has.

5. *Recognize the employee's accomplishments.* Acknowledge what has been done, and show appropriate appreciation. Also make sure that the employee recognizes what she has accomplished and how it has contributed to the work unit's functioning, as well as to her own growth and development.

As noted above, we focus on delegation in this module as a means to develop employees. As such, the new responsibility or task should be integrated into the employee's performance appraisal, discussed earlier in this competency. While focusing here on the employee who is taking on a new assignment, it should also be clear that managers who are effective delegators benefit personally and also provide benefits to the organization. In the exercises that follow, you will have a chance to analyze how a performance evaluation was handled, practice giving feedback as part of a performance evaluation role play, and think about how the performance evaluation could have been improved. The final exercise asks you to apply what you have learned in the first three competencies in this module when delegating a task to someone else.

ANALYSIS   United Chemical Company*

Objective   When faced with our own performance evaluations or those of our subordinates, it is often difficult to separate the people from the issues. The objective of this case analysis and the practice exercise that follows it is to give you the opportunity to examine how the principles of supportive communication and reflective listening that you learned about earlier in this module can be applied to a performance review situation that is "neutral" for you so that you can gain a more in-depth understanding of how these techniques can be used in mentoring and developing employees.

Directions   Read the case and then answer the questions that follow.

The United Chemical Company is a large producer and distributor of commodity chemicals with five chemical production plants in the United States. The operations at the main plant in Baytown, Texas, include not only production equipment but also the company's research and engineering center.

The process design group consists of eight male engineers and the manager, Max Kane. The group has worked together steadily for a number of years, and good relationships have developed among all members. When the workload began to increase, Max hired a new design engineer, Sue Davis, a recent master's degree graduate from one of the foremost engineering schools in the country. Sue was assigned to a project involving expansion of the capacity of one of the existing plant facilities. Three other design engineers were assigned to the project along with Sue: Jack Keller (age 38, with 15 years with the company), Sam Sims (age 40, with 10 years with the company), and Lance Madison (age 32, with 8 years with the company).

As a new employee, Sue was enthusiastic about the opportunity to work at United. She liked her work very much because it was challenging and offered her a chance to apply much of the knowledge she had gained in her university studies. On the job, Sue kept to herself and her design work. Her relations with her fellow project members were friendly, but she did not go out of her way to have informal conversations during or after working hours.

Sue was a diligent employee who took her work seriously. On occasions when a difficult problem arose, she would stay after hours in order to come up with a solution. Because of her persistence, coupled with her more current education, Sue usually completed her portion of the various project stages a number of days before her colleagues. This was somewhat irritating to her, and on these occasions she went to Max to ask for additional work to keep her busy until her fellow workers caught up to her. Initially, she had offered to help Jack, Sam, and Lance with their parts of the project, but each time she was turned down tersely.

*Adapted from Andrew D. Szilagyi, Jr., and Marc J. Wallace, Jr., *Organizational Behavior and Performance*, 3rd ed. (Scott, Foresman and Company, 1980), Copyright © 1983. Used with permission.

About five months after Sue had joined the design group, Jack asked to see Max about a problem the group was having. The conversation between Max and Jack was as follows.

Max: Jack, I understand you wanted to discuss a problem with me.

Jack: Yes, Max. I didn't want to waste your time, but some of the other design engineers wanted me to discuss Sue with you. She's irritating everyone with her know-it-all, pompous attitude. She just isn't the kind of person that we want to work with.

Max: I can't understand that, Jack. She's an excellent worker whose design work is always well done and usually flawless. She's doing everything the company wants her to do.

Jack: The company never asked her to disturb the morale of the group or to tell us how to do our work. The animosity of the group can eventually result in lower-quality work for the whole unit.

Max: I'll tell you what I'll do. Sue has a meeting with me next week to discuss her six-month performance. I'll keep your thoughts in mind, but I can't promise an improvement in what you and the others believe is a pompous attitude.

Jack: Immediate improvement in her behavior isn't the problem—it's her coaching others when she has no right to engage in publicly showing others what to do. You'd think she was lecturing an advanced class in design with all her high-power, useless equations and formulas. She'd better back off soon, or some of us will quit or transfer.

During the next week, Max thought carefully about his meeting with Jack. He knew that Jack was the informal leader of the design engineers and generally spoke for the other group members. On Thursday of the following week, Max called Sue into his office for her midyear review. One portion of the conversation was as follows:

Max: There is one other aspect I'd like to discuss with you about your performance. As I just related to you, your technical performance has been excellent; however, there are some questions about your relationships with the other workers.

Sue: I don't understand—what questions are you talking about?

Max: Well, to be specific, certain members of the design group have complained about your apparent "know-it-all attitude" and the manner in which you try to tell them how to do their job. You're going to have to be patient with them and not publicly call them out about their performance. This is a good group of engineers, and their work over the years has been more than acceptable. I don't want any problems that will cause the group to produce less effectively.

Sue: Let me make a few comments. First of all, I have never publicly criticized their performance to them or to you. Initially, when I was finished ahead of them, I offered to help them with their work but was bluntly told to mind my own business. I took the hint and concentrated only on my part of the work. What you don't understand is that after five months of working in this group I have come to the conclusion that what is going on is a "rip-off" of the company. The other engineers are "goldbricking" and setting a work pace much slower than they're capable of. They're more interested in the music from Sam's radio, the local football team, and the bar they're going to go to for TGIF. I'm sorry, but this is just not the way I was raised or trained. And, finally, they've never looked on me as a qualified engineer, but as a woman who has broken their professional barrier.

Discussion Questions
1. What are the key problems with this portion of the performance review?

2. How would you use the knowledge and skills you have acquired thus far in this module to redesign the meeting between Max and Sue?

3. What concerns, if any, do you have with Max's conversation with Jack? What might Max have done differently?

Reflection In describing the objective of this analysis, we wrote that this was a "neutral" situation. We used quotation marks because, in reality, many people tend to identify with the characters in case studies based on their own past experiences and characteristics they might share with these characters. Discussing this case in class can be very productive for surfacing different assumptions that people are making about the characters in the case based on stereotypes rather than based on the limited facts presented in the case.

PRACTICE   What Would You Include in the Performance Evaluation?

Objective Supportive communication and reflective listening are useful tools during the performance review, but managers need to remember that the performance review is only useful if it is part of a larger performance evaluation process. This exercise gives you an opportunity to think about the role of the performance review in planning the next cycle of performance evaluation.

Directions Review the guidelines for developing an effective performance evaluation system. Then think about the suggestions you had for redesigning Max's midyear review of Sue.

1. What elements would you include in a performance review of Sue? What kind of feedback should you give her? What skills will you suggest that she develop? What other issues will you raise?

2. In dyads, role-play the conversation that occurs in Max's midyear performance evaluation review of Sue.

Discussion Questions 1. During the role-play, how successful were you conducting a successful performance evaluation?

2. Did you follow the guidelines for giving and receiving feedback?

3. To what degree did the performance review focus on Sue's technical skills, and to what degree did it focus on her role as a member of the process design group? To what degree was Max's role in helping Sue develop as an employee in the process design group part of the performance review?

4. What did you learn from this role-play?

Reflection Evaluating employees' performance is a complex task that is made more complicated when we see it as having conflicting objectives. We want to motivate our employees by giving them "positive" feedback. On the other hand, we often need to give them "negative" feedback that they may not agree with and will not be happy to hear. Similarly, we want to be supportive and provide employees the opportunity to raise concerns, but we also want them to take responsibility for problems or issues that arise. Instead of seeing these as conflicting objectives, emphasizing the goal of employee development helps us transcend this paradox. Employee development focuses our attention less on what has happened in the past and more on what we are working to achieve in the future.

APPLICATION   Developing Your Capacity to Develop Others

Objective In the introduction to this competency, we noted that while our primary focus is on mentoring and developing employees, there are many other situations where the knowledge and skills presented here can be applied. This exercise gives you an opportunity to develop your capacity to develop others by planning how you would delegate a responsibility to someone else.

Directions   1. Review the guidelines for effective delegation.

2. Identify a task that you currently perform on a regular basis that you would like to be able to delegate to someone else. If you are a manager, think about a task you would like to delegate to an employee. If you are an officer of a club or other organization, think about a task you would like to delegate to one of the other officers or a member of the club or organization. You might even think about a household chore that you would like to delegate to someone else in your household.

3. Complete the first of the "Five Steps to Effective Delegation" by writing a one-to-two-page action plan that describes the task and why the person you selected is an appropriate choice. Indicate any concerns you have about delegating this task to this individual.

4. If appropriate, carry out the second step of the delegation process, and describe your interaction with the individual.

Reflection   Managers sometimes resist delegating tasks because it is seen as time consuming. That is, effective delegation requires managers to carefully consider both the task and the individual to whom the task will be delegated. Time taken in the short run to plan the delegation process, however, should have important pay-offs for the employee, the manager, and the organization. In using delegation as a tool for developing employees, it is important for managers to consider how they and the organization will also benefit.

Module 1 Competency 4   Managing Groups and Leading Teams

ASSESSMENT   Are You a Team Player?[1]

Objective   Using the Johari window in Competency 1, Understanding Self and Others, we saw that sometimes the images that we have of ourselves are not the same as the images that others have of us. One of the objectives of all the assessments in this text is to help you develop a more accurate picture of yourself. The critical thinking technique described in the introductory chapter for identifying claims, grounds, and warrants can be an effective tool when completing the assessments in the text.

Directions   The following assessment instrument asks you to examine your behavior as a team member in organizational settings. For each pair of items, place a checkmark in the column that best identifies how you behave in a working group at school, in student or community groups, or on your job.

---

[1]*Adapted from* training material for Income Maintenance Supervisors, Special Topics Workshop: "Motivation, Teambuilding, and Enhancing Morale," Professional Development Program, Rockefeller College of Public Affairs and Policy, State University of New York at Albany. Used with permission.

	Very like me	Somewhat like me	Both describe me	Somewhat like me	Very like me	
Flexible in my own ideas	____	____	____	____	____	Set in my own ideas
Open to new ideas	____	____	____	____	____	Avoid new ideas
Listen well to others	____	____	____	____	____	Tune out others
Trusting of others	____	____	____	____	____	Not trusting of others
Prefer to raise differences and discuss them	____	____	____	____	____	Prefer to avoid discussing differences
Readily contribute in group meetings	____	____	____	____	____	Hold back from contributing in group meetings
Concerned with what happens to others	____	____	____	____	____	Not concerned with what happens to others
Fully committed to tasks	____	____	____	____	____	Have little commitment to tasks
Willing to help others to get the job done	____	____	____	____	____	Prefer to stick to my own task or job description
Share leadership with group	____	____	____	____	____	Maintain full control of group
Encourage others to participate	____	____	____	____	____	Expect others to participate without encouragement
Group needs come before my individual needs	____	____	____	____	____	My individual needs come before group needs

Discussion Questions

1. In what ways do these team behaviors agree with your concept of team membership? How do they differ?

2. What strengths do you think you have when working on a team? Weaknesses?

3. Are there times when you have performed more effectively as a team member? Alternatively, have there been times when you did not fully contribute as a team member? If so, what events or circumstances made you behave differently in these different situations?

4. In thinking about your past experiences working in groups, do you think that the people who have worked with you in the past see you as you see yourself? If not, what grounds and warrants would they use to contradict your claims?

Reflection

Two points should be made about this assessment exercise. First, it is not difficult to see that the items on the left are more reflective of team-oriented behaviors than the items on the right. As a result, there is some concern that responses may reflect social desirability bias—the tendency some people have to respond to questions based on what they think the "right" answer is, rather than based on their actual opinions or behaviors. Asking respondents to think about the grounds and warrants that they would use to justify their responses may help to increase the accuracy of their responses.

A second important point to recognize is that these assessments are intended as a starting point, rather than an end point. If you are honest with yourself and your assessment suggests that you are not a team player, you should not assume that you are doomed to fail in a team-based organization! It simply means that you may need to focus more attention on developing certain team skills such as trusting others and dealing with differences in a team setting. Remember, there is nothing to lose by being honest with yourself in an assessment exercise. This is your chance to get personal feedback, which can direct you towards new areas of personal growth and development.

LEARNING   Managing Groups and Leading Teams

In the 1980s, organizations in the United States were introduced to the notion of teams as a more effective way to organize (Parker, 2008; Thompson, 2000). While some saw teams as a way to increase workplace democracy, arguing that employees should have the opportunity to have input into decisions that affect their lives (Weisbord, 1987), most argued that that the most compelling reasons for adopting team-based arrangements are economic—that organizations that use teams to involve employees in organizational decision-making will have a competitive advantage because those closer to the actual work have more knowledge and understanding of the issues and are therefore able to make better decisions (Lawler, 1992).

Indeed, largely as a result of global competition, changes in workplace technology, and other external pressures, organizations in the public, private, and nonprofit sectors began to experiment with a variety of team-based arrangements in the 1980s and 1990s. Understanding the value of team-based arrangements, however, is rather complicated, given that there is no consensus on the definition of work teams or a single taxonomy for classifying teams. Some, for example, differentiate between work groups and work teams based on both structural and affective criteria. From this perspective, groups are generally defined as two or more individuals who interact to fulfill a common goal (Bowditch, Buono & Stewart, 2008), whereas teams not only share a common goal, but also work together interdependently. Thus, they share a sense of mutual accountability and have a sense of connection with other team members. When defining teams in this way, there is an expectation that each individual who works (or plays) on a team sees how she contributes to the common goal and is willing both to express opinions and to listen to others' ideas, with the expectation that civilized disagreement will lead to the best decision (Parker, 2008). When people define teams in this way, they often talk about the synergy that is created when the individuals interact, that is, the sense that the whole is greater than the sum of the parts.

Alternatively, many organizations define teams strictly in terms of structural criteria, whereby individuals in the work unit work together interdependently and may be involved in some of the decision-making associated with the work arrangements. From this perspective, people differentiate among different types of team-based approaches based on how much autonomy and control team members are granted in carrying out their work (Thompson, 2000). For example, in traditional manager-led teams, team members have no little or no input in deciding the team's goals, but may be involved in deciding how the work will be carried out. Alternatively, in self-managed teams (a.k.a. self-directed or empowered teams), team members are responsible for many tasks that are traditionally held by supervisors or managers, including planning, scheduling, and performance evaluation. When defining teams as structures, it is important to remember that teams may be made up of individuals from within functional work units or involve individuals from several different work units who come together to serve as a cross-functional team (Parker, 2003). In addition, bringing individuals together to form a team does not necessarily mean that team members will interact regularly on a face-to-face basis; some teams interact through computing technology and are referred to as virtual teams. And sometimes team-based arrangements involve individuals working on a short-term project or task, and sometimes team-based arrangements involve permanent organizational structures that are considered to be more formal elements of the organization's design.

Here we will use Thompson's (2000) definition: "A team is a group of people who are interdependent with respect to information, resources, and skills and who seek to combine their efforts to achieve a common goal" (p. 2). This definition recognizes that not all work groups are teams, but does focus more on the structural, rather than affective, nature of teams. Nevertheless, we will also recognize that the most effective teams develop a way of interacting that leads team members to feel a sense of "team spirit." We begin with a framework for understanding the types of factors that influence group and team effectiveness and identify some potential positive and negative consequences of using teams to make decisions. Next, we consider the topic of member roles. This competency concludes with a discussion of some ways to enhance group and team performance, including increasing the effectiveness of meetings and using techniques to facilitate the process of team development.

WHAT INFLUENCES TEAM EFFECTIVENESS?

In trying to determine how to improve group and team effectiveness, many researchers begin with a basic model that examines inputs, processes, and outcomes (Mathieu, Maynard, Rapp & Gilson, 2008). Traditionally, outcomes have included task performance and member satisfaction. That is, managers want to know whether or not the group or team has been able to accomplish its goal (what was done) and whether members were satisfied with the group process (how it was done). More recently, researchers have begun to look at team learning as an outcome that goes beyond whether or not the group or team has accomplished its goal, and considers whether the team gained a better understanding of the problem and/or developed an ability to improve its task performance (Edmondson, Dillon & Roloff, 2007).

Inputs involve an array of factors including individual team member characteristics (e.g., individual competencies and personalities), team-level factors (e.g., team size, team composition, task structure, and leadership structure), and contextual factors, which may be internal to the organization (e.g., organizational culture, reward systems, and information and communication technologies) or external to the organization (e.g., national culture, economic environment, and laws and regulations). Mathieu et al. (2008) note that, more recently, researchers have adapted this general inputs-processes-outcome (IPO) model to recognize the contextual nature of the inputs. Thus, individuals' competencies are seen as embedded within the team-level factors, which are in turn embedded within the contextual factors. While members do have influence on team-level factors, which then influence contextual factors, these influences are not as strong as the influences in the other direction.

In the Assessment exercise, you rated yourself along a variety of individual-level inputs, such as whether or not you tend to trust others in the group, the degree to which you are open to or avoid new ideas, and whether you share leadership with others or try to maintain control of the group. Inputs such as these create conditions for potential effectiveness. Whether or not the group reaches its potential depends on group processes, or how team members interact. Sometimes there is conflict in groups, which may reduce group members' willingness to trust others and to participate fully. Other times, individuals may not believe that their effort makes a difference (social loafing) or may actively believe that no one will notice if they slack off (free-riding). Such situations are referred to as "process losses" because they detract from the teams' performance (Brown, 2000). As noted above, there are also times when individuals are open to learning from others and may even be inspired by other team members' actions. In these situations, team members trust each other and are willing to exert great amounts of effort because they see themselves as working toward a common goal and so identify with the team. In these situations, there are process gains; that is, total team performance exceeds what individuals would have been able to accomplish if they were acting individually (Brown, 2000). Recent models of team effectiveness emphasize the complexity of these processes, as well the temporal nature of team functioning (Mathieu et al., 2008).

In deciding whether or not to bring individuals together to solve a problem or make a decision, managerial leaders need to consider both the potential advantages and disadvantages of team decision-making, as well as the likelihood that the inputs (team members, organizational context, and environmental context) can be brought together and structured (processes) in a way that is more likely to lead to process gains than process losses. Here we list some potential positive and negative outcomes and the conditions that lead to these outcomes.

ADVANTAGES OF TEAM DECISION-MAKING

1. Involving more individuals in the decision-making process generally leads to better decisions because greater knowledge or expertise is brought to bear on the problem.

Involving employees in the decision-making process increases the probability that important issues affecting the decision will surface.

2. Involving employees in decisions can help to generate a wider range of values and perspectives, representing the range of issues and concerns at stake in the decision. Increasingly, we are aware that neither the labor force nor the marketplace is homogeneous in background, values, or needs. Reflecting the customer profile in the decision-making group can be a competitive advantage (Cox, 1993; Loden & Rosener, 1991).

3. When employees contribute to the decision-making process, they tend to have a greater commitment to implementing a decision, because they understand the reasons behind the decision.

4. When employees are involved in the decision-making process, they will often be able to identify potential obstacles to implementing the decision as well as ways to avoid them. Kathleen Rhodes, a technical manager at U.S. West, says, "Being a technical manager helps employees to understand the overall concept of [our work]. Plus, they have to tap into every part of the organization to solve problems. People who work in the front row for long enough can do it all because they've seen it all" (quoted in Lieber, 1999).

5. Being involved in the decision-making process will enhance employees' skills and abilities, and help them to grow and develop as organizational members.

DISADVANTAGES OF TEAM DECISION-MAKING

1. Involving employees in organizational decision-making takes time. As the number of people who are involved in a decision increases, so does the time it takes to reach a decision.

2. Involving employees in organizational decision-making will likely result in a low-quality decision if the team is involved in a decision for which it does not have the proper expertise.

3. When team meetings are not well structured, individuals with the appropriate expertise may fail to contribute to the discussion, whereas those with little or no knowledge may overcontribute and dominate the discussion.

4. When team members are overly cohesive, they may also become overly concerned with gaining consensus. This is a phenomenon known as "groupthink" (Janis, 1972). When groupthink occurs, team members avoid being critical of others' ideas and so cease to think objectively about the decision at hand or critically evaluate options.

Early models of participative decision-making (Vroom & Yetton, 1973; Vroom & Jago, 1974) distinguished between true group decision-making (the group comes to a consensus decision), consultative decision-making (the group provides input but the manager makes the decision), and autocratic decision-making (the manger makes the decision without input from the group). Determining which approach to use was based on problem attributes such as the required quality of the decision, the necessity of group acceptance and commitment to the decision, and the time available to make the decision. Decision quality can also be affected by how effectively members perform different roles that are needed for effective team functioning.

ROLES OF TEAM MEMBERS

One factor that is consistently identified as an important characteristic of effective teams is that team members have specific, and sometimes very specialized, roles (Katzenbach & Smith, 1993). A *role* is a set of expectations held by the individual and relevant others about how that individual should act in a given situation. For example, in basketball, the point guard is expected to bring the ball down the court and set up the play; the center is expected to get under the basket and to rebound. In the workplace, an employee's role is defined by the specific tasks he or she is expected to perform. For example, in a factory there are production managers, machine operatives, and repair persons. In addition, there are health and personnel specialists, accountants and financial managers, maintenance staff, secretaries, and office clerks. Each of these individuals has a specialized role.

In pulling a new team together, people are often expected to perform somewhat different roles on the team. Therefore, it is important to think about the specific competencies, both technical and interpersonal, that people can bring to the task. Technical competencies refer to substantive knowledge, skills, and abilities needed to complete a task. Interpersonal competencies refer to more personal qualities, skills, and abilities that help the team work together. Some organizations, such as Context Integration, have developed web-based knowledge-management systems to help employees identify who can be a resource for solving specific technical problems (Salter, 1999). In addition to the specific or unique competencies that can be used to select team members, team leaders might also consider general characteristics that all team members should possess. At the Mayo Center, for example, teams are composed of specialists who know why they are there and what to do, but all team members are guided by the motto "The best interest of the patient is the only interest to be considered" (Roberts, 1999, p. 156). Each team is assembled and disassembled to achieve this goal, and doctors are paid a set salary to avoid incentives or penalties for referrals or consulting with colleagues. Such an example suggests that whether we focus on technical or personal competencies or unique abilities or general characteristics everyone on the team should possess, one of the important responsibilities of the manager is to provide role clarity for her employees—to make clear what is expected of each individual performing on the team.

ROLE CLARITY

Role clarity implies the absence of two stressful conditions: role ambiguity and role conflict. *Role ambiguity* occurs when an individual does not have enough information about what he should be doing, what are appropriate ways of interacting with others, or what are appropriate behaviors and attitudes. Consider the following story about four people: Everybody, Somebody, Anybody, and Nobody.

There was an important job to be done and Everybody was asked to do it. Anybody could have done it, but Nobody did it. Somebody got angry about that because it was Everybody's job. Everybody thought Anybody could do it, but Nobody realized that Everybody wouldn't do it. It ended up that Everybody blamed Somebody when actually Nobody asked Anybody.

New employees, who are not familiar with the work unit's norms and procedures, will likely experience role ambiguity if their manager does not clarify for them what is expected in their job. New managers, making the transition from worker to manager, also often experience role ambiguity because their role expectations have changed (Hill, 2003).

Role conflict occurs when an individual perceives information regarding her job to be inconsistent or contradictory. For example, if manager X tells employee Y to perform task A, and then manager X's boss tells employee Y to stop what she is doing and to perform task B, the employee is likely to experience role conflict. Role conflict can also occur when an individual's own morals and values conflict with the organization's mission or policies and procedures. For example, an environmentally minded advertising executive might find it difficult to accept a contract with a company that produces toxic or nuclear wastes as a side effect of its primary production of goods (Katz & Kahn, 1978).

Team-building efforts that focus on clarifying roles help everyone in the work unit or work team understand what others expect. Later in this section, we will discuss how team-building techniques can help with the clarification of roles. First, however, we discuss four roles that employees play in teams, each of which can facilitate or hinder team effectiveness.

FOUR TEAM PLAYER STYLES

Most often, when people talk about the roles people play in groups and teams, they differentiate between task roles and group maintenance roles (Benne & Sheats, 1948; Dyer, 1995). In a *task role*, one's behaviors are focused on *what* the team is to accomplish. Performing in a task role is sometimes referred to as having a task orientation, or being task oriented. In a *group maintenance role*, one's behaviors are focused on *how* the team will accomplish its task. Performing in a group maintenance role is sometimes referred to as having a group maintenance, or process, orientation, or being process oriented. Because many maintenance activities focus on the team members and how they interact, some texts refer to people in those roles as being relationship oriented.

More recently, Parker (2008) has proposed four roles, or team player styles: the communicator, the contributor, the collaborator, and the challenger. Most often, people are most comfortable with one or two of these roles and will tend to emphasize the behaviors associated with these roles during team meetings. As team members take on these different roles, however, they can play the roles in a positive way that aids team effectiveness or in a negative way that hinders team effectiveness. Interestingly, although Parker uses somewhat different terms from those in this book, these four roles match closely to the four quadrants of the competing values framework.

Communicator Role. According to Parker, "The Communicator gives primary emphasis to team process . . . [and] believes there is an interpersonal 'glue' that must be present for the team to be effective" (p. 85). When working on a team, the communicator displays many of the competencies associated with the Collaborate (Human Relations) quadrant such as listening carefully to concerns of team members, providing feedback to team members, and helping resolve conflicts as they arise.

Contributor Role.   The Contributor is focused on problem solving and decision-making and "sees his or her role as providing the group with the best possible information . . . freely offering all the relevant knowledge, skills and data they possess" (p. 73). When working on a team, the contributor displays many of the competencies associated with the Control (Internal Process) quadrant such as setting high standards and insisting on high-quality outputs, ensuring that tasks are appropriately distributed across team members, and providing technical training for other team members.

Collaborator Role.   The Collaborator is "goal directed . . . [and] sees the vision, goal, or current task as paramount in all interactions" (p. 79). When working on a team, the collaborator displays many of the competencies associated with the Compete (Rational Goal) quadrant such as establishing long-term goals, working hard to achieve those goals, and helping team members see how the immediate tasks fit into the long-term goals.

Challenger Role.   Finally, the Challenger is courageous and willing to question the status quo, even if it means challenging the team's leader. Challengers will also "push the team to be more creative in their problem solving" (p. 96). They are also highly ethical and expect team members to talk openly about team problems. When working on a team, the challenger displays many of the competencies associated with the Create (Open Systems) quadrant, such as encouraging team members to be innovative and to try new approaches, challenging the team to take on well-conceived risks, and insisting on high ethical standards.

   While it is expected that different people on a team will take on different roles, it is also important that individuals not overplay a role. Indeed, Parker argues that when any particular role is overplayed, the behaviors can have a negative effect on the team. Parker's description of the consequences of overplaying each role mirrors our discussion of the negative zones of the competing values framework that you will see in the concluding chapter of this text. For example, individuals who overplay the communicator role (collaborate in the CVF) may focus too much on creating harmony and cohesion in the team, and so avoid focusing on the task or, in an attempt to avoid conflict, fail to challenge or confront other team members, even when they believe the other team members are not contributing to the team in a positive way. Individuals who overplay the contributor role (control in the CVF) may focus too much providing data and technical information and thus may lose sight of overarching team goals or advocate for unrealistic performance standards. Individuals who overplay the collaborator role (compete in the CVF) may be so focused on meeting long-term goals that they become insensitive to individuals' concerns and stop encouraging active participation by all team members. In addition, they may be so focused on achieving goals that, even when environmental conditions change, they do not take the time to question whether missions and goals developed at a prior time are still relevant. Finally, individuals who overplay the challenger role (create in the CVF) may focus too much on change and innovation, and may suggest that the team take risks that are not appropriate for the team, or they may present ethical issues to the team in a way that alienates others, who see them as self-righteous.

As a manager, it is your job to ensure that the behaviors associated with each of these roles are valued in the team and that no one role is overplayed in team meetings. Two ways to accomplish this are to carefully structure team meetings and to engage in team-building activities. The next two sections provide some suggestions to help you become more effective with each of these activities.

INCREASING MEETING EFFECTIVENESS

No doubt you have attended some pretty horrible meetings in your life. You have also likely attended some good meetings. What characteristics differentiate good meetings from bad meetings? First, good meetings accomplish the desired task. Second, in good meetings there is appropriate input from group members, and everyone feels that he contributes in an important way. Third, in trying to make decisions, people feel that they have the necessary information to make decisions that need to be made. Finally, in good meetings, individuals feel safe to challenge others' ideas, and do so in a respectful way. Note the similarity of these characteristics to the four roles discussed in the previous section. Here are some guidelines for effective meeting management; the guidelines focus on preparing for the meeting, running the meeting, and following up on the meeting. (For more detailed suggestions, see Tropman, 1996.)

PREPARING FOR THE MEETING

1. *Set **objectives** for the meeting.* If you are not clear about the purpose of the meeting, it is unlikely that you will feel that you have accomplished something at the end of the meeting.

2. *Select **appropriate participants** for the meeting.* Invite individuals who are affected by, or have an important stake in, the outcome of the decision. Where appropriate, choose participants with the intent of maximizing diversity in terms of knowledge, and perspectives.

3. *Select an appropriate **time** and **place** to meet.* Choosing the appropriate time depends on individuals' work schedules, the amount of time required for the meeting, and what time of day is most appropriate: the fresh early morning or the work-focused end of day. Choosing an appropriate location depends on how large the group is, whether you will need special equipment (such as a whiteboard, computer projection screen, DVD player, or video conference equipment, etc.), and how much privacy or formality is necessary. Holding a meeting in your office will carry a very different message to your employees from holding the meeting in a conference room.

4. *Prepare and distribute an **agenda** in advance.* Like setting the objectives for the meeting, preparing and distributing an agenda in advance increases the likelihood of accomplishing the objectives of the meeting. Include the time and place of the meeting and an estimated time for dealing with each major item on the agenda. Sequence the items so that there is some logic to the flow of topics. This gives participants a better sense of direction for the meeting. It also allows individuals to gather whatever information or resources they may feel will be important for the meeting.

RUNNING THE MEETING

1. ***Start on time.*** Starting on time allows for the best use of everyone's time.

2. *Make sure that someone is taking* **minutes.** Having a record of what decisions were made or were tabled (i.e., temporarily deferred) helps ensure that future meetings do not get bogged down in repeating discussions from prior meetings. Minutes are especially valuable to keep everyone informed in case someone has to be absent from a meeting.

3. ***Review the agenda*** *and check whether there are any necessary adjustments.* Again, this provides a sense of direction for the meeting and will increase the likelihood of task accomplishment.

4. *Make sure that* ***participants know each other.*** The atmosphere in the meeting will be much more pleasant when people know the others with whom they are meeting.

5. ***Follow the agenda.*** Pace the meeting. Make sure that each topic is carefully discussed; individuals should not go off on tangents or take the focus away from the item at hand.

6. ***Minimize*** *(or eliminate)* ***interruptions and distractions.*** Show respect to others in the meeting and expect respect from them. No one should be checking messages, texting, surfing the Internet, or taking phone calls during the meeting. Treating your employees and peers as you would a customer demonstrates that you value their input.

7. ***Encourage participation by all.*** Remember, you selected the participants because you felt they had something to contribute to the decision. If some individuals dominate the discussion, politely ask them to give others an opportunity to contribute. If some are reticent to contribute, try to ask for their opinions or suggestions without embarrassing them.

8. *Conclude the meeting by reviewing or* ***restating any decisions*** *reached and* ***assignments*** *made.* In order to ensure agreement and to reinforce decisions, it is helpful to review or restate all decisions at the conclusion of the meeting. Clarification of decisions and assignments will increase the likelihood that the next meeting will be productive. You may also want to schedule the next meeting at this time.

FOLLOWING UP ON THE MEETING

1. ***Distribute minutes*** *in a timely manner.* This reminds people (or informs them, if they were unable to attend the meeting) of what happened in the meeting and what the group accomplished, as well as what their responsibilities are for the next meeting.

2. *If individuals have been given assignments, periodically* ***check on their progress***. It is best not to wait until the next meeting to find out that someone has been delayed in completing an assignment.

TEAM DEVELOPMENT AND TEAM-BUILDING

When a new work group forms, or an established work group undertakes a new task or problem, the group needs to be designed, staffed, structured, and trained before it can transform into a high performance team (Sundstrom, 1999). For example, if team members do not know one another well or have never worked together before, it is important for them to get acquainted and to discuss what competencies each person brings to the team and what types of preferences people have regarding how to approach the task. Alternatively, when an established team takes on a new project, team members are likely to have a good sense of the different competencies people have but still need to discuss various unique perspectives they have on the problem or different approaches that different team members may think are appropriate for the particular project.

Tuckman (1965) identified four stages of team development—forming, storming, norming, and performing—that many teams experience when they first form. More recently, researchers have noted that teams do not pass through these stages in a linear way (Mathieu et al., 2008). That is, when new team members are added to a team or when the team takes on a new task, the team may revert to a previous stage. In addition, researchers have added a fifth stage—adjourning. Parker (2008) notes that each team role has something to contribute in each stage.

When *forming*, the goals of the group are established and the task is defined. Group members ask themselves what the purpose of this team is and how they can contribute. As noted above, an advantage of team decision-making is that people with different expertise and different backgrounds can bring different ideas, values, and perspectives to bear on the issue being addressed. Here, people in the communicator role can help people get to know one another and create a climate where people can share ideas and feelings. Contributors will focus on what tasks need to be done and how each person can contribute. Collaborators help to ensure that everyone understands the team's overall mission and how it fits into the organizational mission. Challengers can work to ensure that all team members are comfortable with the team's mission and what is expected of the team.

In the next stage, *storming*, there is generally conflict as each team member learns more about the task and interdependencies are tested. In addition, if the group has been brought together to reflect different types of expertise and/or different backgrounds, conflict may be generated as team members try to decide how to approach the task. As a result, this is not a productive stage, except insofar as it moves the team to the next stage. To increase the productivity of the team during this stage, the communicator can listen carefully to team members' concerns and work to resolve the conflicts. Contributors can try to help people identify what data and information will help them perform the task. Collaborators might help keep people focused on the mission and might even suggest revising the goals, depending on team members' concerns. And challengers can suggest innovative approaches for performing the task, and avoid challenging the team if it appears that the team has reached consensus.

When teams enter the *norming* stage, they begin to set the ground rules for working together. It is in this stage that cohesion begins to develop, but the value of differences in individuals' expertise and backgrounds should not be lost. At this stage, it is important that communicators remind team members that disagreements are acceptable and that "getting along" does not mean that everyone must "go along." Druskat and Wolf (2001) argue that, like individuals, groups can build their emotional intelligence. To do so, communicators can encourage team members to provide each other appropriate feedback, which can help build the team's emotional intelligence. Contributors should help the group think about setting priorities and ensuring that everyone knows who is responsible for which tasks. Collaborators can help ensure that tasks are aligned with the team's and the organization's greater mission. Finally, challengers should continue to ask questions and make sure that the ground rules are not arbitrary, that they work for the team.

Finally, the team will move into its most productive stage, *performing*. In this stage, there is general agreement on both the goals and how the team should work to achieve its goals. During this stage, the communicator can make sure that positive accomplishments are celebrated. Contributors can remind team members of the standards it has set and can focus on whether the team has the necessary resources, human and otherwise, to continue performing in a positive manner. Collaborators can suggest that the team revisit its goals, based on what it has accomplished, possibly identifying new tasks that are aligned with the team's mission. Challengers can help ensure that the team is aware of external changes and adapting, as needed, as well as ensure that different opinions and perspectives are voiced.

If a team does *adjourn*, it needs to make sure that all members leave with a sense of accomplishment, positive feelings towards the team, and new knowledge that they can use and share as a result of their experience. This can be an emotional period, and communicators play an important role in making sure that everyone's contributions have been appropriately recognized. Contributors can ensure that final products are appropriately documented. Collaborators can encourage team members to stay focused on the team's task until it is clear the goal has been accomplished and help individuals see their contributions in the larger organizational context. Challengers can encourage team members to review the final product and make sure it is of the necessary quality.

In reviewing these stages of team development, one can see how the role that the team leader plays in helping the team develop is both critical and paradoxical. On the one hand, the team leader sets the climate and must be seen as someone with a strong personal vision. On the other hand, the leader must clearly demonstrate a belief in the team's purpose and in the notion that each person's contribution to the team is equally valuable. Thus, team leaders must simultaneously lead and give team members the opportunity to take a leadership role, suggest directions and listen to others' suggestions, and be appropriately involved in the day-to-day work while not micromanaging. In addition, team leaders must find ways to value differences and reward successes, while never allowing some individuals to shine at the expense of the other team members. In the next section, we suggest some formal approaches to team-building that can help increase team effectiveness.

TEAM-BUILDING

As noted above, even when a team reaches the performing stage of its development, it will likely cycle back through the earlier stages when it encounters new challenges. For example, group members may leave, new people may join the group, tasks and goals may be revised, new tasks and responsibilities may be added, and changes may occur in the group's external environment. These are often times when it is important to "stop the action" and involve the group in formal team-building activities.

You may have heard the expression, "When you are up to your hips in alligators, you forget that you came to drain the swamp." Sometimes it is important to step out of the swamp and think about what you are doing. Formal team-building activities allow the group to put aside the work of the day, evaluate how well the group is performing as a team, and make any necessary changes. Two points are important here. First, team-building activities should not be seen as isolated experiences or events. Rather, they should be part of an integrated approach to team-building that involves regularly scheduled sessions to allow the team to address whatever issues it is currently facing (Dyer, 1995). Second, team members should understand that team-building is not about getting people to like each other. As Dyer (1995) notes, "The fundamental emotional condition in a team is not liking but *trusting*. People do not need to like one another as friends to be able to work together, but they do need to trust one another" (p. 53, emphasis added). They need to trust that other team members are equally invested in accomplishing the team's goals; they need to trust that other team members will share information appropriately; and they need to trust that other team members will be willing to work out disagreements in a professional manner. At Whole Foods Market, a natural foods grocery chain, teams have clear performance goals and meet at least once a month to share information and solve problems (Fishman, 1996).

Interim Performance Reviews. A fairly simple, but effective, team-building technique involves setting aside a day or two, away from the worksite if possible, to examine three questions: (1) What do we do well? (2) What areas need improvement? (3) What are the barriers to improvement? Starting with an examination of what the team does well reminds the group that while there may be some problems or issues to deal with, the team also has strengths upon which to build. This establishes a positive climate for the team-building session and gets people involved in the discussion. Depending on how much time there is between team-building sessions, the list of areas for improvement may be short or long. This is a good reason to schedule regular team-building sessions. If the list is too long, the team may need to set priorities regarding which issues should be handled first. The last question reminds the team that team-building is more than short-term problem solving. It involves taking a larger look at the system and examining specific problems to determine whether they are isolated events or the result of an underlying structural issue. If there is an underlying structural issue, it will likely need to be dealt with before the improvement can be made. The final team product of such a session should be an action plan to deal with whatever problems or issues are raised in the session. The action plan should include a statement of objectives (what the team wants to accomplish with this improvement effort), a time frame for addressing the issue, and a clear assignment of who is responsible for organizing the improvement effort (remember Anybody, Everybody, Nobody, and Somebody!).

Role Clarification Sessions. As mentioned earlier, one key to effective team functioning is having each team member know her role and how that role fits into the larger team effort. Several techniques are available. Scearce (2007) suggests a variety of techniques to help teams clarify role expectations. She suggests that team members should meet every few months to review their roles and give others feedback. At such a session, each team member has the opportunity to share what he likes best about his job, what he likes least and what might help the individual perform better in his role. In addition to sharing this information with others, each person works with a partner to receive feedback on what he has done well, how the other person can help the focal individual perform more effectively, and one or more ideas the individual has about that role.

Whether focused on how the team as a whole can improve or on how individual team members can be more effective in their roles, team-building activities provide the team with a chance to "step out of the swamp" and look at the big picture. In addition, such activities can give team members an opportunity for informal interactions. When individuals have a chance to get to know one another, there is greater potential for building trust among team members.

The following exercises will give you an opportunity to apply the team concepts we have covered to enhance your ability to manage groups and lead teams.

ANALYSIS   Stay-Alive Inc.*

Objective   Effective managers need to master team-building techniques not only when they are creating a new team, but also when they begin working with an existing team. The objective of this case analysis is to give you an opportunity to identify ways in which the members of Stay-Alive, Inc. applied (or failed to apply) key principles concerning effective team-building.

Directions   Read the case study and respond to the questions that follow.

Stay-Alive Inc., a small not-for-profit social service agency, hired Jean Smith to design, implement, and coordinate halfway house living programs for young adults.

When Jean arrived, the agency had an informal organization with little hierarchical structure and extensive participative decision-making. The prevailing ideology that shaped virtually all decisions and interpersonal relationships was that a democratic system would be most effective and would lead to a higher level of job satisfaction for workers than would a more rigid hierarchical structure. The staff members attended at least five meetings weekly. Incredibly, the group devoted the majority of time at each one to exploring interpersonal problems.

Most staff were young and had recently finished college. They often remarked that they sought a place to belong and feel accepted. Stay-Alive met that need in many ways: The group acted as a surrogate family for many employees. Even their life outside of work revolved heavily around activities with other Stay-Alive members. Salaries were low, and so the agency hired inexperienced people. Although the employees were bright, enthusiastic, and motivated, some were just beginning to develop the skills needed for effective performance in their jobs. Organizational leaders, therefore, defined success on the job primarily in terms of the employees' ability to relate well to others at work and only secondarily in terms of their ability to work with clients.

Within three months of her arrival, Jean submitted her plan for implementing the program. Her manager praised it, calling it a remarkable piece of work. Soon after the program was implemented, however, it became clear that it was not working. Still, the agency members responded by patting her on the back and telling her what a great job she was doing. Jean soon became frustrated and angry and left the agency.

Discussion Questions   1. Is Stay-Alive Inc. an effective team? Why or why not?

2. How were the various team behaviors performed in this agency? What roles do you think have been considered the most important in the past? What roles do you think have been neglected?

*Adapted from Judith R. Gordon, A Diagnostic Approach to Organizational Behavior (Boston: Allyn & Bacon, 1983), 304–305.

3. Rather than leaving, how might Jean have helped Stay-Alive to become a more effective organization?

4. What other suggestions would you give to the management team at Stay-Alive to help them to improve?

5. If you were the director of Stay-Alive, what issues would you want to see addressed in a team-building session?

Reflection   Of all the people involved in the Stay-Alive case, it is possible that only Jean viewed the problems with the program implementation as a "failure." Look back at the scenario. What evidence is there to suggest that the members of the organization were really interested in making changes to the organization? As we shall see in the last module, which focuses on Promoting Change and Encouraging Adaptability, implementing and sustaining change in an organization can be extremely challenging, especially when the existing organizational culture is entrenched.

PRACTICE Ethics Task Force

Objective   When a group is given an assignment, the members often have a tendency to jump directly into trying to perform the task, rather than spending time in the Forming, Storming, and Norming stages described above. What may appear at first to be a way to save time, however, often turns out to result in a much less efficient process. This exercise gives you a chance to practice the activities described in the first three stages of the team development model. It also encourages you to practice your meeting skills, as well as observe how others behave in meetings. As with any meeting, you will find it helpful if someone is responsible for taking minutes to provide accurate information for the discussion about what took place during the meeting.

Directions   The class will be divided into several small groups to consider an organizational dilemma. In your meeting to discuss the dilemma, think about which participative decision-making skills you can practice.

Directions for the Small Groups   You are members of a task force that has been called in to discuss and make suggestions for policies and procedures to deal with the use of work time and computers for personal business. Recently, some employees have reported to their managers that they feel that some individuals spend a substantial amount of time doing personal business during working hours and that this affects the workload of other employees. A few managers have confronted employees about doing personal tasks during working hours. These managers learned that some employees believe that they can only do personal business with some companies during office hours; these employees argue that it is not fair to expect them to take personal leave for a few minutes here and there. Other managers have indicated that not enough time is lost to make a big deal about it. Furthermore, they argue, raising the issue will result in negative feelings toward the organization. The division director has asked you to come up with a list of recommendations in which you recognize the need for optimum employee productivity as well as the potential costs, both financial and personal, of monitoring and attempting to change such behaviors.

Discussion Questions   1. What happened during the meeting of the ethics task force?

2. Did you feel prepared for the meeting? If not, what additional information or material would have been helpful?

3. Did all task force members participate in the meeting? How well did the task force do at discussing how it could make best use of each person's abilities?

4. Think about the stages of team development. What elements of stage 1 (forming) did you accomplish in your task force? What elements of stage 2 (storming) or stage 3 (norming) were accomplished? What member behaviors provided support for the team's development?

5. Did the discussion stay on track, or was there a tendency to go off on tangents?

6. What suggestions would you make to the meeting chair about running future meetings?

7. What suggestions do you have for yourself for the next time you chair a meeting?

Reflection   Even when specifically asked to focus on team development activities, some people tend to gravitate toward trying to "solve the problem" rather than focusing on how to *approach* solving the problem. Even for individual decision-making, this can lead to jumping to conclusions, but it is especially problematic in team decision-making because it may result in decisions that do not reflect the wisdom of all the members of the team.

APPLICATION   Team-Building Action Plan

Objective   Now that you have had a chance to read about team-building and practice some team-development activities, it is time to put your learning into practice. The objective of this exercise is to give you a chance to improve the effectiveness of a team on which you are a member.

Directions   Think about a student group, a work unit, a task force, or a committee of which you are currently a member, where you could do some informal or formal team-building.

1. Consider carefully which team-building activities are most appropriate. For example, you may feel that the roles and responsibilities of group members are not clear and that you would like to focus on clarifying role expectations. Or you may decide you need to personally practice using one of the four roles—communicator, contributor, collaborator, or challenger—in group meetings. If you are a group leader, think about whether it is appropriate to meet privately with individuals who have been exhibiting negative behaviors.

2. Write a one-to-two-page memo to your team members describing your concerns about the team. Include a proposed action plan for team-building activities. Remember to use grounds and warrants to justify why you think the team would benefit from participating in these team-building activities.

Reflection   In writing your memo, did you remember to use what you learned about communicating honestly and effectively earlier in this module? Did you leave any "left-hand column" issues unmentioned? What do you think the long-term impact of that decision will be for your team's effectiveness?

Module 1 Competency 5   Managing and Encouraging Constructive Conflict

ASSESSMENT   How Do You Handle Conflict?

Objective   Conflict is present in every organization, and not all conflict is bad. Understanding how you generally approach conflict is an important first step in improving your ability to manage conflict productively. This exercise is an adaptation of the Organizational Communication Conflict Instrument (OCCI), Form B, developed by I. L. Putnam and C. Wilson. Reprinted in Steven R.

Wilson and Michael S. Waltman, "Assessing the Putnam-Wilson Organizational Communication Conflict Instrument (OCCI)," *Management Communication Quarterly* 1(3): pp. 382–384, copyright © by Sage Publications. Reprinted by permission of Sage Publications, Inc.

Directions   Think of a friend, relative, manager, or coworker with whom you have had a number of disagreements. Then indicate how frequently you engage in each of the following behaviors during disagreements with that person. For each item select the number that represents the behavior you are ***most likely*** to exhibit. There are no right or wrong answers. Please respond to all items using the scale below.

Scale

Always	Very Often	Often	Sometimes	Seldom	Very Seldom	Never
1	2	3	4	5	6	7

_____ 1. I blend my ideas to create new alternatives for resolving a disagreement.

_____ 2. I shy away from topics that are sources of disputes.

_____ 3. I make my opinion known in a disagreement.

_____ 4. I suggest solutions that combine a variety of viewpoints.

_____ 5. I steer clear of disagreeable situations.

_____ 6. I give in a little on my ideas when the other person also gives in.

_____ 7. I avoid the other person when I suspect that he or she wants to discuss a disagreement.

_____ 8. I integrate arguments into a new solution from the issues raised in a dispute.

_____ 9. I will go 50–50 to reach a settlement.

_____ 10. I raise my voice when I'm trying to get the other person to accept my position.

_____ 11. I offer creative solutions in discussions of disagreements.

_____ 12. I keep quiet about my views in order to avoid disagreements.

_____ 13. I give in if the other person will meet me halfway.

_____ 14. I downplay the importance of a disagreement.

_____ 15. I reduce disagreements by making them seem insignificant.

_____ 16. I meet the other person at a midpoint in our differences.

_____ 17. I assert my opinion forcefully.

_____ 18. I dominate arguments until the other person understands my position.

_____ 19. I suggest we work together to create solutions to disagreements.

_____ 20. I try to use the other person's ideas to generate solutions to problems.

_____ 21. I offer trade-offs to reach solutions in disagreements.

_____ 22. I argue insistently for my stance.

_____ 23. I withdraw when the other person confronts me about a controversial issue.

_____ 24. I sidestep disagreements when they arise.

_____ 25. I try to smooth over disagreements by making them appear unimportant.

_____ 26. I insist my position be accepted during a disagreement with the other person.

_____ 27. I make our differences seem less serious.

_____ 28. I hold my tongue rather than argue with the other person.

_____ 29. I ease conflict by claiming our differences are trivial.

_____ 30. I stand firm in expressing my viewpoints during a disagreement.

Scoring and Interpretation   Three categories of conflict-handling strategies are measured in this instrument: solution-oriented, nonconfrontational, and control. By comparing your scores on the following three scales, you can see which of the three is your preferred conflict-handling strategy.

     To calculate your three scores, add the individual scores for the items and divide by the number of items measuring the strategy. Then subtract each of the three mean scores from 7. The closer your score is to 0, the less likely you are to use that type of strategy; the closer your score is to 7, the more likely you are to use that type of strategy.

Solution-oriented: Items 1, 4, 6, 8, 9, 11, 13, 16, 19, 20, 21

Nonconfrontational: Items 2, 5, 7, 12, 14, 15, 23, 24, 25, 27, 28, 29

Control: Items 3, 10, 17, 18, 22, 26, 30

Solution-oriented strategies tend to focus on the problem rather than the individuals involved. Solutions reached are often mutually beneficial, where neither party defines herself as the winner and the other party as the loser.

Nonconfrontational strategies tend to focus on avoiding the conflict by either avoiding the other party or by simply allowing the other party to have his way. These strategies are used when there is more concern with avoiding a confrontation than with the actual outcome of the problem situation.

Control strategies tend to focus on winning or achieving one's goals without regard for the other party's needs or desires. Individuals using these strategies often rely on rules and regulations in order to "win the battle."

Discussion Questions   1. Which strategy do you find easiest to use? Most difficult? Which do you use most often?

2. How would your answers to these items have differed if you had considered someone different from the person you chose?

3. Would your answers differ between work-related and non–work-related situations? Between different types of work-related situations?

4. What is it about the conflict situation or strategy that tells you which strategy to use in dealing with a particular conflict situation?

Reflection   Understanding your preferred conflict-handling style is a first step toward being able to thoughtfully choose an approach to handling conflicts in the future, rather than simply falling into habitual patterns of responding to conflict.

LEARNING   Managing and Encouraging Constructive Conflict

Over the past several decades, the topics of conflict and conflict management have become increasingly important to managers in organizations of all sizes. In the 1980s, research on organizational conflict indicated that managers were spending between

20 and 50 percent of their time dealing with conflict, with managers at the lower levels of the organizational hierarchy reporting more time spent than managers at the higher levels (Lippitt, 1982). Since then, one might expect these numbers to have increased. Considering the nature of changes that are occurring in organizations as they attempt to adapt to and/or anticipate changes in their external environment, it would seem inevitable that conflict will increase as individuals disagree over how work should be organized, who should participate in various decisions, and what strategies should be used to accomplish organizational goals. In addition, as organizational workplaces become more demographically diverse, individuals with different cultural backgrounds may differ in how they approach problem solving and/or in what criteria they believe are most important to determine solutions. Although these statements may at first seem to suggest that organizational anarchy is imminent, you will see in this section that conflict over these types of decisions can potentially lead to stronger organizational performance. When managed appropriately, conflict can be a positive and productive force in decision-making.

DIFFERENT PERSPECTIVES ON CONFLICT

Although many people in U.S. society will instinctually say that they see conflict between individuals or groups as harmful and will try to avoid conflict in both work-related and non-work-related situations because they believe it will create bad feelings among people, research shows that conflict can be useful. Studies have found that there are different types of conflict—relationship conflict and task conflict—and that these different types of conflict have different consequences for effective decision-making (Simons & Peterson, 2000). In addition, researchers have found that people use different adjectives when describing these two different types of conflict. When describing relationship conflict, which focuses on differences in personalities and work styles, people typically use negative words, such as "frustrating, anger, stressful, fear and wasteful" (Runde & Flanagan, 2008, p. 22). Alternatively, when people describe task conflict, which focuses on the tasks for which the group is responsible and what alternative approaches might be taken to research the group's goals, they more often use positive words, such as "opportunity, challenge, energizing, learning, and resolution" (Runde & Flanagan, 2008, p. 24).

When individuals in organizations differentiate between these two types of conflict, they are more likely to recognize that not only is conflict in organizations inevitable, but that it should sometimes be encouraged in order to increase opportunities for innovation and change and create a climate where new ideas can surface. As William Wrigley Jr. noted, "When two [people] . . . always agree, one of them is unnecessary" (quoted in Tjosvold, 1993, p. 133). Viewing conflict from this perspective requires us to seek challenges to our thoughts and ideas, to value those challenges over unquestioning acceptance, and to trust those with whom we work (Simons & Peterson, 2000). Jerry Harvey's famous story of the Abilene Paradox (see Box M1.1) provides a clear example of when a challenge can be more valuable than acceptance.

BOX M1.1 THE ABILENE PARADOX

The July afternoon in Coleman, Texas (population 5,607) was particularly hot—104 degrees as measured by the Walgreen's Rexall Ex-Lax temperature gauge. In addition, the wind was blowing fine-grained West Texas topsoil through the house. But the afternoon was still tolerable—even potentially enjoyable. There was a fan going on the back porch; there was cold lemonade; and finally, there was entertainment. Dominoes. Perfect for the conditions. The game required little more physical exertion than an occasional mumbled comment, "Shuffle 'em," and an unhurried movement of the arm to place the spots in the appropriate perspective on the table. All in all, it had the makings of an agreeable Sunday afternoon in Coleman—that is, it was until my father-in-law suddenly said, "Let's get in the car and go to Abilene and have dinner at the cafeteria."

I thought, "What, go to Abilene? Fifty-three miles? In this dust storm and heat? And in an unairconditioned 1958 Buick?" But my wife chimed in with, "Sounds like a great idea. I'd like to go. How about you, Jerry?" Since my own preferences were obviously out of step with the rest I replied, "Sounds good to me," and added, "I just hope your mother wants to go."

"Of course I want to go," said my mother-in-law. "I haven't been to Abilene in a long time."

So into the car and off to Abilene we went. My predictions were fulfilled. The heat was brutal. We were coated with a fine layer of dust that was cemented with perspiration by the time we arrived. The food at the cafeteria provided first-rate testimonial material for antacid commercials.

Some four hours and 106 miles later we returned to Coleman, hot and exhausted. We sat in front of the fan for a long time in silence. Then, both to be sociable and to break the silence, I said, "It was a great trip, wasn't it?"

No one spoke.

Finally my mother-in-law said, with some irritation, "Well, to tell the truth, I really didn't enjoy it much and would rather have stayed here. I just went along because the three of you were so enthusiastic about going. I wouldn't have gone if you all hadn't pressured me into it."

I couldn't believe it. "What do you mean 'you all'?" Don't put me in the 'you all' group. I was delighted to be doing what we were doing. I didn't want to go. I only went to satisfy the rest of you. You're the culprits."

My wife looked shocked. "Don't call me a culprit. You and Daddy and Mama were the ones who wanted to go. I just went along to be sociable and to keep you happy. I would have to be crazy to want to go out in a heat like that."

Her father entered the conversation abruptly. "Hell!" he said.

He proceeded to expand on what was already absolutely clear. "Listen, I never wanted to go to Abilene. I just thought you might be bored. You visit so seldom I wanted to be sure you enjoyed it. I would have preferred to play another game of dominoes and eat the leftovers in the icebox."

After the outburst of recrimination we all sat back in silence. Here we were, four reasonably sensible people who, of our own volition, had just taken a 106-mile trip across a godforsaken desert in a furnace-like temperature through a cloud-like dust storm to eat unpalatable food at a hole-in-the-wall cafeteria in Abilene, when none of us really wanted to go. In fact, to be more accurate, we'd done just the opposite of what we wanted to do. The whole situation simply didn't make sense.

Source: Reprinted by permission of publisher, from *Organizational Dynamics,* summer, 1974. All rights reserved

To manage conflict more effectively, we need to understand how conflict emerges naturally, so we begin by presenting some basic definitions and frameworks for understanding the sources and progression of naturally emerging conflict. We will then look at strategies for managing these conflicts that increase the likelihood that positive outcomes will result. Finally, we will look at a technique for stimulating conflict for the purpose of encouraging innovation (and avoiding unnecessary trips to Abilene).

LEVELS, SOURCES, AND STAGES OF CONFLICT

To use conflict constructively, it is important to understand how conflicts arise and how they develop. While our primary focus here is on conflicts that arise between individuals or between groups (and, in fact, that is where most conflicts of consequence to organizations tend to arise), it is important to recognize that conflict occurs at all levels of the organization. For example, conflicts may occur between two different organizations or between units of an organization, when one of these organizations or units senses that the other is working against its particular goals or interests.

Conflicts in organizations develop for a wide variety of reasons. Often conflicts develop because of individual differences, such as differences in values, attitudes, beliefs, needs, or perceptions. Conflicts also develop between individuals when there are misunderstandings or communication errors that lead individuals to believe that there are differences in values, attitudes, beliefs, needs, or perceptions. As organizations expand their use of participative decision-making, there will be more and more situations in which conflict can arise. In addition, as the work force becomes increasingly culturally diverse, conflict may arise out of misperceptions that are related to differing worldviews held by different cultural groups (Cox, 1993). The tremendous benefits that derive from diverse people bringing differing perspectives to the decision-making process are not likely to occur without conflict over how the decision should be made, who should have input into the decision, how information about the decision should be disseminated, and what the actual decision should be.

Organizational structures may also increase the likelihood of conflict within or between groups. For example, when two or more units perceive that they are in competition with each other for scarce resources, there is likely to be conflict among the units. Similarly, conflicts can arise when two or more units see themselves as having different goals. For example, in large organizations, units associated with cost or quality control, or with setting organizational policies and procedures, often find themselves in conflict with other organizational units. Although this appears to be a natural consequence of the differing focuses of the units and of the checks and balances that organizations build into the system, Tjosvold (1993) reminds us that our assumption that conflicts arise out of opposing interests and goals is only partly true and that, most often, conflicts arise out of interdependence. That is, conflicts do not arise because two departments or work units have incompatible long-term interests or goals, but because they disagree on the path or means to accomplish the goal and, more important, one cannot accomplish the goal without the other. As Wheatley (2005) reminds us, most systems in nature "arise from two seemingly conflicting forces: the absolute need for individual freedom, and the unequivocal need for relationships" (p. 46). Not surprisingly, many conflicts in organizations emerge from the existence of these two countervailing forces.

STAGES OF THE CONFLICT PROCESS

Regardless of the level or the source of the conflict, conflicts often follow a set sequence of events or stages. In the first stage, the conflict is latent. Neither party senses the conflict, but the situation is one in which individual or group differences or organizational structures have created the potential for conflict.

When the potential conflict situation is perceived by one or more of the individuals or groups, the conflict moves into the second stage. In this stage, individuals become cognitively and emotionally aware of the differences. Here each of the two parties may attribute intentional and unjustifiable acts to the other. Emotional reactions may take the form of anger, hostility, frustration, anxiety, or pain.

In the third stage, the conflict moves from a cognitive and/or emotional awareness to action. It is in this stage that the conflict becomes overt, and the individuals or groups implicitly or explicitly choose to act to resolve the conflict or to escalate it. Actions to escalate the conflict include various forms of aggressive behaviors, such as verbally (or physically) attacking the other person or group, acting in ways that purposefully frustrate others' attainment of goals, or attempting to engage others in the conflict by getting them to take sides against the other party. Actions to resolve the conflict generally require both parties to take a positive problem-solving approach that allows both of their needs and concerns to be heard and handled. If the two parties believe that they are bound by a common long-term goal, it is more likely that they will take a positive problem-solving approach.

The fourth stage of conflict is the outcome or aftermath. Actions taken in the third stage directly affect whether the outcomes are functional or dysfunctional. Functional outcomes include a better understanding of the issues underlying the conflict, improved quality of decisions, increased attention to the use of creativity and innovation in solving and resolving future problems, and a positive approach to self-evaluation. Dysfunctional outcomes include continued anger and hostility, reduced communication, and a destruction of team spirit. More important, conflicts that result in dysfunctional outcomes often snowball, setting the stage for new conflicts that will potentially be more difficult to resolve because their source will be more complex.

CONFLICT MANAGEMENT APPROACHES

In the Assessment activity, you identified your preference among three conflict-handling strategies in a particular situation. These three strategies can be represented along two dimensions that show how individuals think and act in approaching situations in which there is conflict (Thomas, 1976). The first dimension represents cooperativeness, or the extent to which you are willing to work to meet the other party's needs and concerns. The second dimension represents assertiveness, or the extent to which you are willing to work to meet your own needs and concerns. Figure M1.3 shows how these two dimensions define five conflict management approaches. Nonconfrontational strategies are associated with avoiding and accommodating approaches, control strategies are associated with a competing approach, and solution-oriented strategies are associated with collaborating and compromising approaches.

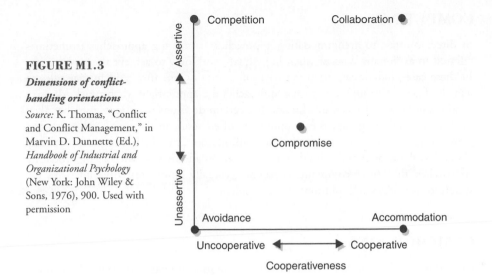

FIGURE M1.3

Dimensions of conflict-handling orientations

Source: K. Thomas, "Conflict and Conflict Management," in Marvin D. Dunnette (Ed.), *Handbook of Industrial and Organizational Psychology* (New York: John Wiley & Sons, 1976), 900. Used with permission

AVOIDING

Avoiding approaches are used when individuals recognize the existence of a conflict but do not wish to confront the issues of the conflict. In avoiding the issues, they work neither to satisfy their own goals nor to satisfy the other party's goals. Individuals may avoid by withdrawing and creating physical separation between the parties or by suppressing feelings and attempting not to discuss the issues of the conflict. This approach is often useful when some time is needed to allow two parties engaged in a conflict to cool off. In the long term, however, if the conflict is not dealt with, it is likely to surface again. Moreover, if employees avoid dealing with conflict situations because they fear that it is not safe to bring bad news to their boss, organizations risk not finding out important information about organizational problems (Bennis, Goleman, O'Toole & Biederman, 2008).

ACCOMMODATING

When individuals use accommodating approaches they do not act to achieve their own goals but rather work only to satisfy the other party's concerns. This approach has the advantage of preserving harmony and avoiding disruption. In the short term, this approach is useful when the issue is not seen as very important or when the other party is much stronger and will not give in. In the long term, however, individuals may not always be willing to sacrifice their personal needs in order to maintain the relationship. In addition, accommodating approaches generally limit creativity and stop the search for new ideas and solutions to the problem. Many unnecessary "trips to Abilene" have been taken by individuals believing that they were helping the situation by accommodating.

COMPETING

In direct contrast to accommodating approaches, competing approaches (sometimes referred to as "forcing") occur when individuals work only to achieve their own goals. In these cases, individuals often fall back on authority structures and formal rules to win the battle. Although competing approaches are appropriate when quick, decisive action is necessary or when one knows that certain decisions or actions must be taken for the good of the group, these approaches often result in dysfunctional outcomes. Competing behaviors set up a win–lose confrontation, in which one party is clearly defined as the winner and the other as the loser. In addition, as with accommodating approaches, the use of competing behaviors generally limits creativity and stops the search for new ideas and solutions to the problem.

COMPROMISING

Compromising approaches are the first of the solution-oriented strategies. Individuals using these approaches are concerned both with their own interests and goals and with those of the other party. These approaches usually involve some sort of negotiation during which each party gives up something in order to gain something else. The underlying assumption of compromising strategies is that there is a fixed resource or sum that is to be split and that, through compromise, neither party will end up the loser. The disadvantage to this approach, however, is that neither party ends up the winner, and people often remember what they had to give up in order to get what they wanted.

COLLABORATING

The second solution-oriented strategy is collaboration. Individuals using collaborating approaches are concerned with their own interests and goals as well as those of the other party. The difference is that there is no underlying assumption of a fixed resource that will force everyone to give up something in order to gain something else. Rather, the assumption is that by creatively engaging the problem, a solution can be generated that makes everyone a winner and everyone better off. Clearly these approaches have great advantages with respect to cohesion and morale; the great disadvantage is that they are time consuming and may not work when the conflict involves differences in values.

Each of the conflict management approaches has advantages and disadvantages that make it more or less appropriate for a given situation. Table M1.5 presents the five approaches and the appropriate situations for using each. Clearly your approach will also depend on your own comfort in using the various approaches. Research has shown, however, that approaches that allow for different perspectives and inputs to be integrated into the final decision are associated with such positive outcomes as decision-making productivity and organizational performance (D. Thomas, 2004; D. Thomas & Ely, 1996; K. Thomas, 1976).

TABLE M1.5 When to Use the Five Conflict Management Approaches

Conflict Management Approach	*Appropriate Situations*
Competing	1. When quick, decisive action is vital.
	2. On important issues where unpopular actions need implementing.
	3. On issues vital to the organization's welfare, when you know you are right.
	4. Against people who take advantage of noncompetitive behavior.
Collaborating	1. To find an integrative solution when both sets of concerns are too important to be compromised.
	2. When your objective is to learn.
	3. To merge insights from people with different perspectives.
	4. To gain commitment by incorporating concerns into a consensus.
	5. To work through feelings that have interfered with a relationship.
Compromising	1. When goals are important, but not worth the effort or potential disruption of more assertive approaches.
	2. When opponents with equal power are committed to mutually exclusive goals.
	3. To achieve temporary settlements to complex issues.
	4. To arrive at expedient solutions under time pressures.
	5. As a backup when collaboration or competition is unsuccessful.
Avoiding	1. When an issue is trivial, or more important issues are pressing.
	2. When you perceive no chance of satisfying your concerns.
	3. When potential disruption outweighs the benefits of resolution.
	4. To let people cool down and regain perspective.
	5. When gathering information supersedes the need for an immediate decision.
	6. When others can resolve the conflict more effectively.
	7. When issues seem tangential or symptomatic of other issues.
Accommodating	1. When you find you are wrong—to allow a better position to be heard, to learn, and to show your reasonableness.
	2. When issues are more important to others than to you—to satisfy others and maintain cooperation.
	3. To build social credits for later issues.
	4. To minimize loss when you are outmatched and losing.
	5. When harmony and stability are especially important.
	6. To allow subordinates to develop by learning from mistakes.

Source: Kenneth W. Thomas, "Toward Multi-Dimensional Values in Teaching: The Example of Conflict Behaviors." *Academy of Management Review* 2(3) (1977): 487. Used with permission.

ADVOCACY AND INQUIRY

A similar framework for thinking about managing conflict is presented in Senge's (2006) discussion of the need for balancing advocacy and inquiry. Senge argues that while many managers are initially promoted because of their advocacy skills, that is, their ability to influence others, the emphasis on advocacy can actually become counterproductive as managers move up the organizational hierarchy and problems become more complex. At this point, "they need to tap insights from other people. They need to learn" (Senge, 2006, p. 183). Learning requires genuine inquiry, asking questions about the other person's understanding of the situation and why they are taking a particular position and truly listening to that person's response.

In many ways, advocacy is similar to K. Thomas' notion of assertiveness and inquiry is similar to cooperativeness. However, unlike assertiveness, both advocacy and inquiry involve actions to develop a deeper understanding of the problem and what data and assumptions have led each party to take the position each is taking. When individuals learn to balance advocacy and inquiry, they can engage in "dialogue," which comes from the Greek "dia-logos . . . [or] a free-flowing of meaning through a group, allowing the group to discover insights not attainable individually" (Senge, 2006, p. 10).

Senge suggests a few guidelines for balancing advocacy and inquiry that use two competencies we have already covered: thinking critically and communicating honestly and effectively. First, when advocating, it is important to clarify one's own reasoning and to encourage others to ask questions that explore how you arrived at a particulate position. Second, when inquiring, ask others to explain their assumptions and how they arrived at their conclusions. Ask questions in a way that shows openness to the other person's response, rather than in a way that suggests that you already know the answer to your question. And, if you arrive at an impasse, think about what additional information or logic you and the other person might need to change your minds.

MANAGING CONFLICT CONSTRUCTIVELY

As indicated above, approaches that encourage individuals and groups to work together to engage the problem creatively and to develop integrative solutions have been found to be most effective, especially in the long run. These approaches, however, which fall under the solution-oriented strategies, may be especially difficult since, as Wheatley (2005) notes, conflict is generally associated with aggression, so individuals may be hesitant to back off their preferred solution. If individuals and organizational units can move away from associating conflict with aggression, however, they can begin to collaborate and/or engage in productive dialogue.

The first step in taking such approaches is to face the conflict. One party must recognize that a conflict exists, face her feelings about the conflict, and be willing to approach the second party to talk about that person's feelings about the conflict. People often find this to be difficult because it requires that they put aside any anger or hostility they are feeling and also that they be willing to face the anger or hostility that may be presented by the other party. Moreover, if there has been a long history of conflict, the second party might not yet be willing to try to collaborate. In a large group, Wheatley (2005) talks about the need for a process that cools down the situation. If you want to try to manage the conflict using a collaborative process, you will need to think in advance about how to handle this situation. Decide how to approach the other person. Be persistent, but give the other person whatever time and space he or she needs to agree to collaborate.

It is often a good idea to meet with the other party in a neutral environment. This will promote an atmosphere of willingness to work together on generating positive solutions. When you meet, it is important that you examine your feelings as well as the actual source of the conflict. Each person should state his views in a clear, nonthreatening way. Make use of the reflective listening techniques presented in Competency 2 of this module—Communicating Honestly and Effectively.

After both parties have had a chance to surface their personal feelings and views of the conflict, try to move to a mutual definition of the conflict in terms of needs. It is important that both parties share a definition of the conflict before attempting to resolve it; otherwise, you may be focusing on two separate and distinct issues. Again, it is important that you use reflective listening to come to a mutual definition of the conflict.

The next step is to generate potential solutions. Search for solutions that address the needs of both parties. Use creative thinking techniques (see Module 4) to increase the likelihood of finding a solution that meets everyone's needs; avoid making judgments about any of the solutions. Instead of asking yourself "What about this solution will not work?" ask "What about this solution will work?" Wheatley refers to this as "enriching through fruitful opposition" and emphasizes that this is a time to learn by "*amplify[ing] the differences* as the means to create a fuller, detailed appreciation of the situation or problem" (p. 188, emphasis in the original).

After both parties have listed all possible solutions, it is time to select an alternative. Both parties should identify their preferred solutions and think about why these solutions best meet their needs. The two parties should then see if any of the preferred solutions coincide or what sorts of compromises are required to allow them to come to a mutually acceptable agreement.

Once the solution has been identified, decide who will do what and when it will be done. That is, make sure you have an action plan that outlines the steps to carry out the solution and identifies the person responsible for each step. At the end of a meeting, everyone should be clear about what decisions have been reached and what assignments have been made. You may also want to identify steps to evaluate your success in implementing your solution. As a final step, it may be appropriate for both parties to identify what they learned from this conflict and what they will do in the future to avoid finding themselves in the same situation again.

In Module 4, we will go into more detail on negotiating agreement and commitment using a solutions-oriented approach. Ultimately, the key to managing conflict constructively is to keep in mind this maxim: Confront the conflict; confront the problem; do not confront the person. That is, if the two parties in conflict can see the problem as their enemy, rather than each other, it will be easier to come to a mutually acceptable solution.

HOW TO STIMULATE CONFLICT AND MANAGE AGREEMENT

In the beginning of this section, we discussed the notion that sometimes unquestioning or unhealthy agreement can be more harmful to the organization than overt conflict. Indeed, as was evident in the case of the Abilene Paradox, unhealthy agreement can lead organizations to "take actions in contradiction of what they really want to do and therefore defeat the very purposes they are trying to achieve" (Dyer, 1995, p. 37).

While there are a number of techniques for stimulating conflict in groups (Faerman, 1996), here we present a technique that divides the larger group into two smaller groups and assigns both groups the task of developing a set of recommendations. The assumption here is that higher-quality decisions will emerge from the juxtaposition of two (or more) opposing sets of recommendations, allowing a synthesis of the best of each set of recommendations. In fact, to stimulate creative solutions, Jerry Hirshberg, founder and president of Nissan Design International, advocates "hiring in divergent pairs"; that is, finding two people who have opposite ways of approaching a situation and thus will create abrasion (Hirshberg, 1999). The guidelines in Table M1.6 are adapted from Johnson, Johnson, and Smith (1989), who refer to these groups as advocacy groups; these authors suggest that advocacy groups provide a way for decision-making groups to structure the discussion to guarantee that differing perspectives will be presented.

Note that there are similarities between the approaches discussed above for managing existing conflicts constructively and this technique, which is designed to stimulate conflict. That is, whether you are trying to increase or decrease conflict, it is important to ensure that opportunities are created to present and advocate differing ideas, to learn about these differing ideas, and ultimately to search for a solution that is mutually beneficial to all involved parties. The implication of this similarity, of course, is that most organizational conflicts do not involve a "right" and a "wrong" side, or a "correct" and an "incorrect" way of doing something. Rather, there are numerous alternatives that can be chosen, with the best often being a synthesis of the various possibilities.

TABLE M1.6 Guidelines for Advocacy Groups

1. Groups (two or more) are assigned different positions to adopt.
2. Groups gather data and structure a case for their position and present the case to all other groups.
3. Each presentation is followed by a discussion in which the group is challenged by others who present opposing positions. (It should be noted that these discussions are referred to as controversy, rather than debate, because the goal is not to win but to hear the different ideas, information, theories, conclusions, etc.)
4. More information is sought to support and refute positions presented as well as to understand others' positions.
5. A synthesis of the different alternatives is sought. This involves creative (divergent) thinking to see new patterns and integrate the various perspectives (see Module 4).

ANALYSIS   Zack's Electrical Parts*

Objective   Conflicts often can be linked back to multiple causes, not just a single difference of opinion. In analyzing the situation at Zack's Electrical Parts, try to think about how the current conflict developed over time and escalated into a potentially serious problem for this organization.

Directions   Read the following case study and answer the questions that follow.

Bob Byrne's ear was still ringing. Bob was director of the audit staff at Zack's Electrical Parts. He had just received a phone call from Jim Whitmore, the plant manager. Jim was furious. He had just read a report prepared by the audit staff concerning cost problems in his assembly plant.

Jim, in a loud voice, said that he disagreed with several key sections of the report. He claimed that had he known more about the audit staff's work, he could have shown them facts that denied some of their conclusions. He also asked why the report was prepared before he had a chance to comment on it. But what made him particularly angry was that the report had been distributed to all the top managers at Zack's. He felt top management would get a distorted view of his assembly department, if not his whole plant.

Bob ended the call by saying that he'd check into the matter. So he called in Kim Brock, one of his subordinates who headed the audit team for the study in question. Kim admitted that she had not had a chance to talk to Jim before completing and distributing the report. Nor had she really had a chance to spend much time with Dave Wells, who headed the assembly department. But Kim claimed it wasn't her fault. She had tried to meet with Jim and Dave more than once. She had left phone messages for them. But they always seemed too busy to meet and were out of town on several occasions when she was available. So she decided she had better complete the report and get it distributed in order to meet the deadline.

That same day, Jim and Dave discussed the problem over lunch. Dave was angry, too. He said that Kim bugged him to do the study, but her timing was bad. Dave was working on an important assembly area project of his own that was top priority to Jim. He couldn't take the time that Kim needed right now. He tried to tell her this before the study began, but Kim claimed she had no choice but to do the audit. Dave remembered, with some resentment, how he couldn't get Kim's help last year when he needed it. But the staff audit group seemed to have plenty of time for the study when he couldn't give it any attention. Jim said that he'd look into the matter and agreed that they had been unnecessarily raked over the coals.

Discussion Questions   1. What were the sources of conflict between the staff audit group and the managers in the plant?

2. What were the differences between the interpersonal conflict and the intergroup conflict in this case?

3. How would you describe the conflict in terms of the stages it went through?

4. What should Bob and Jim do now to resolve this conflict?

5. What might Bob do to avoid future conflict situations between the staff audit group and other line managers?

*Reprinted from Henry L. Tosi, John R. Rizzo, and Stephen J. Carroll, Managing Organizational Behavior (New York: Harper & Row), p. 504. Copyright © 1986 Henry Carroll. Used with permission.

Reflection   The auditing function is critical to the control action imperative of the internal process quadrant (see Module 2). Not surprisingly, conflict often results when one department is charged with evaluating another.

PRACTICE   Win as Much as You Can

Objective   Conflict can emerge in many different settings for many different reasons. After completing this practice exercise, you will be given an opportunity to reflect upon any sources of conflict that emerge during the ten rounds of the activity.

This classic experiential activity is adapted from "Win As Much As You Can," by William Gellermann, Ph.D., in *A Handbook of Structured Experiences for Human Relations Training*, Vol. II, Revised, J. William Pfeiffer and John E. Jones (eds.) (San Diego: University Associates, Inc. 1974), pp. 62–67. Used with permission.

Directions   Your instructor will place you in groups of eight (or more). Each of these groups should divide into four smaller groups, trying to keep the small groups evenly balanced. If you have exactly eight, you will be in four dyads; if you have more than eight, you will have some small groups with three or four people. Once you have decided on the small groups, seat yourself so that people in each small group can talk among themselves without being heard by the other small groups.

You will play 10 rounds. In each round, your small group will tell the instructor whether you would like to say X or Y. You will win points based on the configuration of X's and Y's according to the following payoff schedule. Rounds 5, 8, and 10 are bonus rounds. In Round 5, your points are multiplied by 3; in Round 8 they are multiplied by 5; and in Round 10 they are multiplied by 10. The objective of the exercise is to win as much as you can.

PAYOFF SCHEDULE

4 X's	Each small group loses 1 point
3 X's 1 Y	Each small group that said X wins 1 point Small group that said Y loses 3 points
2 X's 2 Y's	Each small group that said X wins 2 points Each small group that said Y loses 2 points
1 X 3 Y's	Small group that said X wins 3 points Each small group that said Y loses 1 point
4 Y's	Each small group wins 1 point

In each round, confer within your small group and make a group decision. In rounds 5, 8, and 10, you may confer with the other small groups before making your decision. Use the following scorecard to keep track of your points.

SCORECARD

Round	Time Allotted	Your Choice	Pattern of Choices	Payoff	Balance
1	1½ mins.	__ X __ Y	__ X __ Y		
2	1 min.	__ X __ Y	__ X __ Y		
3	1 min.	__ X __ Y	__ X __ Y		
4	1 min.	__ X __ Y	__ X __ Y		
5	1½ mins.	__ X __ Y	__ X __ Y	× 3	
6	1 min.	__ X __ Y	__ X __ Y		
7	1 min.	__ X __ Y	__ X __ Y		
8	1½ mins.	__ X __ Y	__ X __ Y	× 5	
9	1 min.	__ X __ Y	__ X __ Y		
10	1½ mins.	__ X __ Y	__ X __ Y	× 10	

Discussion Questions

1. Who was "you" in the phrase "win as much as you can"?

2. What does "win" mean in that phrase?

3. What did you assume that your instructor did not say to you?

4. What, if any, conflicts arose within your small group? How did you resolve these conflicts?

5. Does this resemble any real-life experiences you have had? If so, how might you approach this type of conflict differently in the future?

6. Does this exercise tell you that conflict is inherently bad?

Reflection   Observing how you (and others) respond to this exercise can be a useful tool for increasing your understanding of self and others by helping to expand the Open area in people's Johari window.

APPLICATION Managing Your Own Conflicts

Objective   Managing conflict in a controlled setting is one thing. Managing conflict outside the class is another. Several of the techniques that we have covered thus far, however, will be very helpful. Perhaps most obviously, effective communication and reflective listening skills are essential to managing conflict. In addition, many of the guidelines for leading teams also come into play. For this application exercise, work on integrating all of the competencies from this module.

Directions   Select a situation in which you currently are in conflict with someone else.

1. Write a brief description of the conflict that includes
   - The nature of the situation and the underlying issues
   - Your feelings about the situation
   - Your behavior and the behavior of the other party (parties) in the situation, including any conflict management strategies that have been used thus far

2. Develop a plan for resolving that conflict. Your plan should be actionable and should identify:

  - The issues that you plan to address
  - When and where you plan to address those issues
  - What you plan to say and why you plan to say it
  - The type of responses that you anticipate from the other party
  - How you plan to reply to those responses

Reflection   It is easier to manage conflict when it does not take you by surprise. Preparation is one of the best prescriptions for managing conflict.

MODULE 1   Collaborate–Focused Competency Evaluation Matrix

Objective   The final exercise in each module is intended to give you a starting point for developing a comprehensive strategy for mastery that you can implement and monitor in the future. These competency evaluation matrices will be used at the end of this book to help you create a long-term development plan that focuses on enhancing your behavioral complexity

Review   The first competency in the Collaborate quadrant, understanding self and others, discussed different personality variables that can affect how people behave in organizations. Next, we discussed the importance of communicating honestly and effectively. We noted that there are many barriers to effective communication and offered suggestions on overcoming these barriers. In this competency we also introduced the concept of "left-hand column" issues—those things that people think and feel but that they chose not to communicate, and we discussed why it is often important to find ways to raise those hidden issues. Our third competency, mentoring and developing others, addressed formal performance evaluation processes as well as more informal coaching and mentoring activities. We also discussed the value of using delegation as a tool for developing others. We then moved from one-on-one interactions to consider managing groups and leading teams. After presenting key variables that influence team effectiveness and suggestions for increasing meeting effectiveness, we discussed the team development process and offered some suggestions for team-building activities. Our final competency focused on managing and encouraging constructive conflict. We noted that although interpersonal conflict can be dysfunctional, conflict that focuses on the task at hand can actually help improve our decisions. We identified five different ways that people tend to respond to conflict and provided examples of when each of the five ways might be appropriate.

Directions   Answer the questions in Table M1.7 for each competency in this module based on the reading material, class discussions, and your personal work (e.g., Assessment exercises, Application exercises, etc.).

Reflection   Taking time to record how you feel about your current performance for the five competencies and to identify specific actions that you can take to improve your performance helps to reinforce what you have learned. If you have questions as you are going through this exercise, you can ask for guidance from your instructor or work with your peers to ensure that you have a solid understanding of the material covered up to this point in the text.

TABLE M1.7 Module 1 Collaborate-Focused Competency Evaluation Matrix

With respect to this competency:	Understanding Self and Others	Communicating Honestly and Effectively	Mentoring and Developing Others	Managing Groups and Leading Teams	Encouraging and Containing Constructive Conflict
1. What do I know about my current performance?					
2. How could I be more effective?					
3. Who are some people I could observe?					
4. What books should I read?					
5. What objectives and deadlines should I set?					
6. With whom should I share my objectives?					
7. How will I evaluate my efforts?					

REFERENCES

Argyris, C., & Schön, D. A. (1996). *Organizational learning II: Theory, methods, and practice.* Reading, MA: Addison-Wesley.

Bacal, R. (2004). *Manager's guide to performance reviews.* New York: McGraw-Hill.

Beamer, L., & Varner, I. (2008). *Intercultural communication on the global workplace* (4th ed.). New York: McGraw–Hill.

Bell, C. R. (1996). *Managers as mentors: Building partnerships for learning.* San Francisco: Berrett-Koehler.

Benne, K. D., & Sheats, P. (1948). Functional roles of group members. *Journal of Social Issues,* 4(2), 41–49.

Bennis, W., Goleman, D., O'Toole, J., & Biederman, P. W. (2008). *Transparency: How leaders create a culture of candor.* San Francisco: Jossey-Bass.

Bowditch, J. L., Buono, A. F., & Stewart, M. M. (2008). *A Primer on organizational behavior* (7th ed.). New York: John Wiley & Sons.

Boyatzis, R. E., Smith, M. L., & Blaize, N. (2006). Developing sustainable leaders through coaching and compassion. *Academy of Management Learning and Education,* 5(1), 8-24.

Brady, D. (2010, April 25). Can GE still manage ? *Bloomberg Business Week*, 27-32.

Brown, R. (2000). *Group processes* (2nd ed.) Malden, MA: Blackwell Publishers.

Cox, T., Jr. (1993). *Cultural diversity in organizations: Theory, research and practice.* San Francisco: Berrett-Koehler.

Dattner, B. (2008). Forewarned is forearmed: Give your staff a user's manual—to you. *Business Week.* [On-line.] Available: http://www.dattnerconsulting.com/businessweek82508.

Drucker, P. F. (1999). Managing oneself. *Harvard Business Review, 77*(2), 65–74.

Druskat, V. U., & Wolff, S. B. (2001). Building the emotional intelligence of groups. *Harvard Business Review, 79*(3), 81-90.

Dulewicz, V., & Higgs, M. (2000). Emotional intelligence: A review and evaluation study. *Journal of Managerial Psychology* 15(4): 341-372.

Dyer, W. G. (1995). *Team-building,* 3d ed. Reading, MA: Addison-Wesley.

Edmondson, A. C., Dillon, J. R., & Roloff, K. S. (2007). Three perspectives on team learning: Outcome improvement, task mastery, and group process. In J. P. Walsh & A. P. Brief (Eds.), *The academy of management annals* (Vol. 1). London: Routledge.

Faerman, S. (1996). Managing Conflicts creatively. In J. L. Perry (Ed.), *The handbook of public administration* (2nd ed., pp. 632–646). San Francisco: Jossey-Bass.

Fishman, C. (1996). Whole Foods Is All Teams; and The Whole Foods Recipe for Teamwork. *Fast Company* (April–May): 103–111.

Gilley, J. W., & Gilley, A. (2007). *The manager as coach.* Westport, CT: Praeger.

Goleman, D. (1995). *Emotional intelligence.* New York: Bantam.

Goleman, D. (1998). *Working with emotional intelligence.* New York: Bantam.

Goleman, D. (2000). Leadership that gets results. *Harvard Business Review, 78*(2): 78–90.

Goleman, D., Boyatzis, R., & McKee, A. (2002). *Primal leadership: Learning to lead with emotional intelligence.* Boston: Harvard Business School Press.

Gordon, J. R. (1983). *A diagnostic approach to organizational behavior.* Newton, MA: Allyn & Bacon.

Grote, D. (2002). *The performance appraisal question and answer book: A survival guide for managers.* New York: AMACOM.

Harris, R. M. (2006). *The listening leader: Powerful new strategies for becoming an influential communicator.* Westport, CT: Praeger Publishers.

Hill, L. A. (2003). *Becoming a manager: How new managers master the challenges of leadership* (2nd ed.). Boston, MA: Harvard Business School Press.

Hirshberg, J. (1999). *The creative priority: Putting innovation to work in your business.* New York: HarperBusiness.

Hogan, R., Curphy, G. J., & Hogan, J. (1994). What we know about leadership: Effectiveness and personality. *American Psychologist, 49*(6), 493–504.

Hughes, R. L., Ginnett, R. C., & Curphy, G. J. (1999). *Leadership: Enhancing the lessons of experience.* Boston: McGraw-Hill.

Imperato, G. (1998, September). How to give good feedback. *Fast Company* [On-line], no. 17. Available: http://www.fastcompany.com/online/17/feedback.html.

Jackman, J. M., & Strober, M. H. (2003). Fear of feedback. *Harvard Business Review, 81*(4), 101–107.

Jacobs, C. S. (2009). *Management rewired: Why feedback doesn't work and other surprising lessons from the latest brain science.* New York: Penguin Group.

Janis, I. (1972). *Victims of groupthink.* Boston: Houghton Mifflin.

John, P. J., Naumann, L. P., & Soto, C. J. (2008). Paradigm shift to the integrative five-factor trait taxonomy. In O. P. John, R. W. Robins, & L. A. Pervin (Eds.), *Handbook of personality: Theory and research* (3rd ed., pp. 114–156). New York: Guilford.

Johnson, D. W., Johnson, R. T., & Smith, K. S. (1989). Controversy within decision-making situations. In M. Afzalur Rahim (Ed.), *Managing conflict: An interdisciplinary approach.* Westport, CT: Praeger.

Katz, D., & Kahn, R. L. (1978). *The social psychology of organizations* (2d ed.). New York: John Wiley & Sons.

Katzenbach, J. R., & Smith, D. K. (1993). *The wisdom of teams.* New York: HarperCollins.

Keirsey, D. (1998). *Please understand me II: Temperament character intelligence.* Del Mar, CA: Prometheus Nemesis.

Klein, G. (2000). Why won't they follow simple directions? *Across the Board, 37*(2), 14–19.

Krieff, A. (1996). *Manager's survival guide: How to avoid the 750 most common mistakes in dealing with people.* Englewood Cliffs, NJ: Prentice-Hall.

LaBarre, P. (1999, April). The agenda—grassroots leadership. *Fast Company* [On-line], no. 23 Available: http://www.fastcompany.com/online/23/grassroots.html.

Lawler, E. E., III. (1992). *The ultimate advantage: Creating the high-involvement organization.* San Francisco: Jossey-Bass.

Lee, M. K. O., Cheung, C. M. K., & Chen, Z. (2007). Understanding user acceptance of multimedia messaging services: An empirical study. *Journal of the American Society of Information Science and Technology, 58*(13), 2066–2077.

Lengel, R. H., & Daft, R. L. (1988). The selection of communication media as an executive skill. *Academy of Management Executive, 2*(3), 225–232.

Lieber, R. (1999, November). Information is everything. *Fast Company,* 246–254.

Lippitt, G. L. (1982, July). Managing conflict in today's organizations. *Training and Development Journal,* 67–74.

Loden, Marilyn, & Rosener, Judy B. (1991). *Workforce America! Managing employee diversity as a vital resource.* Homewood, IL: Business One Irwin.

Luft, J., & Ingham, H. (1955, August). The Johari Window: A graphic model of interpersonal awareness. *Proceedings of the Western Training Laboratory in Group Development.* University of California, Los Angeles Extension Office.

Mathieu, J., Maynard, M. T., Rapp, T., & Gilson, L. (2008). Team effectiveness: A review of recent advancements and a glimpse into the future. *Journal of Management, 34*(3) (2008), 410–476.

McCrae, R. R., & Costa, P. T., Jr. (2008). The five-factor theory of personality. In O. P. John, R. W. Robins, & L. A. Pervin (Eds.), *Handbook of personality: Theory and research* (3rd ed., pp. 159–181). New York: Guilford.

Miller, G. W. (2009, May 11). Tomorrow's bosses: Open and accessible. *Providence Journal.* Available: http://www.projo.com/news/content/boss_of_the_future_05-11-09_TAE3V14_v24.3998056 .html.

Muoio, A. (1998). The truth is, the truth hurts. *Fast Company* [On-line]. Available: http://www.fastcompany.com/online/14/one.html.

O'Kane, P., Hargie, O., & Tourish, D. (2004). Communication without frontiers: The impact of technology on organizations. In D. Tourish & O. Hargie (Eds.), *Key issues in organizational communication* (pp. 74–95). London: Routledge.

Parker, G. M. (2003). *Cross-functional teams: Working with allies, enemies and other strangers.* San Francisco: Jossey-Bass.

Parker, G. M. (2008). *Team players and teamwork: New strategies for developing successful collaboration.* San Francisco: Jossey-Bass.

Puccio, G. J., Murdock, M. C., & Mance, M. (2007). *Creative leadership: Skills that drive change.* Thousand Oaks, CA: Sage Publications.

Reitman, J. (Producer/Director). (2009). *Up in the air* [Motion picture]. United States: Paramount Pictures.

Robert, L. P., & Dennis, A. R. (2005). Paradox of richness: A cognitive model of media choice. *IEEE Transactions on Professional Communication, 48*(1), 10.

Roberts, P. (1999, April). The agenda: Total teamwork. *Fast Company,* 148–162.

Salter, C. (1999, September). Ideas.com. *Fast Company,* 292–307.

Runde, C. E., & Flanagan, T. A. (2008). *Building conflict competent teams.* San Francisco: Jossey-Bass.

Samovar, L. A., & Mills, J. (1998). *Oral communication: Speaking across cultures* (10th ed.). Boston: McGraw-Hill, 1998.

Schwartz, A. E. (1992). *Delegating authority.* Hauppauge, NY: Barron's Educational Series.

Seal, C. R., Boyatzis, R. E., & Bailey, J. R. (2006). Fostering emotional and social intelligence in organizations. *Organization Management Journal, 3*(3), 190–209.

Scearce, C. (2007). *123 ways to build teams* (2nd ed.). Thousand Oaks, CA: Corwin Press.

Szilagyi, Jr., A. D., & Wallace, M. J., Jr. (1983). *Organizational behavior and performance* (3rd ed.). Glenview, IL: Scott, Foresman and Company.

Senge, P. M. (2006). *The fifth discipline: The art and practice of the learning organization* (rev. ed.). New York: Currency Doubleday.

Senge, P. M., Roberts, C., Ross, R. B., Smith, B. J. & Kleiner, A. (1994). *The fifth discipline fieldbook: Strategies and tools for building a learning organization.* New York: Currency Doubleday.

Shannon, C., & Weaver, W. (1948). *The mathematical theory of communication.* Urbana: University of Illinois Press.

Silberman, M. (2000). *PeopleSmart: Developing your interpersonal intelligence.* San Francisco: Berrett-Koehler.

Simons, T. L., & Peterson, R. S. (2000, February). Task conflict and relationship conflict in top management teams: The pivotal role of intragroup trust. *Journal of Applied Psychology,* 102–111.

Sparrow, T., & Knight, A. (2006). *Applied EI: The importance of attitudes in developing emotional intelligence.* Chichester, England: John Wiley & Sons.

Staub, R. E. (1997). *The heart of leadership: 12 practices of courageous leaders.* Provo, UT: Executive Excellence Publishing.

Strang, S. E., & Kuhnert, K. W. (2009). Personality and leadership developmental levels as predictors of leader performance. *Leadership Quarterly 20*(3), 421–433.

Sundstrom, E. (Ed.). (1999). *Supporting work team effectiveness: Best management practices for fostering high performance.* San Francisco: Jossey-Bass, 1999.

Thomas, D. A. (2004). Diversity as strategy. *Harvard Business Review, 82*(9), 98–108.

Thomas, D. A., & Ely, R. J. (1996). Making differences matter: A new paradigm for managing diversity. *Harvard Business Review, 74*(5), 79–90.

Thomas, K. W. (1976). Conflict and conflict management. In M. D. Dunnette (Ed.), *Handbook of industrial and organizational psychology* (pp. 889–935). Chicago: Rand McNally.

Thomas, K. W. (1977). Toward multidimensional values in teaching: The example of conflict management. *Academy of Management Review, 2*(3), 484–490.

Thompson, L. (2000). *Making the team: A guide for managers.* Upper Saddle River, NJ: Prentice Hall.

Tjosvold, D. (1993). *Learning to manage conflict: Getting people to work together.* New York: Lexington Books.

Tourish, D., & Hargie, O. (2004). The crisis of management and the role of organizational communication. In D. Tourish and O. Hargie (Eds.), *Key issues in organizational communication* (pp. 1-16). London: Routledge.

Tropman, J. E. (1996). *Making meetings work: Achieving high quality group decisions.* Thousand Oaks, CA: Sage Publications, 1996.

Tuckman, B. W. (1965). Developmental sequence in small groups. *Psychological Bulletin, 63*(6), 384–399.

Vroom, V. H., & Jago, A. G. (1974). Decision-making as a social process: Normative and descriptive models of leader behavior. *Decision Sciences, 5*(4), 743–769.

Vroom, V. H., & Yetton, P. W. (1973). *Leadership and decision-making.* Pittsburgh: University of Pittsburgh Press.

Walker, C. A. (2002). Saving your rookie managers from themselves. *Harvard Business Review, 80*(4), 97–102.

Weisbord, M. R. (1987). *Productive workplaces: Organizing and managing for dignity, meaning, and community.* San Francisco: Jossey-Bass.

Welch, J., with Welch, S. (2005). *Winning.* New York: HarperCollins.

Wheatley, M. J. (2005). *Finding our way: Leadership for an uncertain time.* San Francisco: Berrett-Koehler Publishers, Inc.

Zey, M. (1991). *The mentor connection: Strategic alliances within corporate life.* New Brunswick, NJ: Transaction Publishers.

ESTABLISHING AND MAINTAINING STABILITY AND CONTINUITY

■ COMPETENCIES

Organizing Information Flows

Working and Managing Across Functions

Planning and Coordinating Projects

Measuring and Monitoring Performance and Quality

Encouraging and Enabling Compliance

Joining an organization gives us an opportunity to work toward significant outcomes that we could not accomplish individually. To make that opportunity a reality, members must find ways to coordinate their activities. Complete flexibility without any control would result in chaos.

Organizational Goals. Just as commitment and cohesion are important for the success of organizations, so, too, are stability and continuity—the goals associated with the internal process model. Control is the action imperative of the internal process model based on the assumption that routinization will lead to stability and continuity. Key activities tend to be focused on internal issues and include defining responsibilities and measuring and documenting performance.

Paradoxes. While these activities are important, managers who create complex control systems often discover that excessive constraints on workers can paradoxically undermine the welfare of the organization. Similarly, an overemphasis on control also can result in getting the details right but failing to accomplish broader objectives. The paradoxical need to accomplish special projects while still completing day-to-day tasks is another challenge that managers focused on control must face. Perhaps the most common paradox associated with control, however, relates to the creation of bureaucratic red-tape. Over time, rules and procedures that initially increased organizational effectiveness later become impediments to performance.

Competencies.   The five competencies included in this module are all valuable for contending with the paradoxes associated with control. They take into account the impact that people, as well as organizational processes, have on the stability and continuity of the organization. We begin with a discussion of *organizing information flows.* Information is the lifeblood of the organization, and managing information effectively is a critical aspect of a managerial leader's job. Next, we offer general guidelines for *working and managing across functions* and then go on to describe some specific tools that managers can use when *planning and coordinating projects.* Our fourth competency in this module, *measuring and monitoring performance and quality*, takes us beyond issues of process to consider the types of outcomes that organizations seek to achieve. Evaluating organizational outcomes has become even more complex in recent years, as social and political pressures have been applied to get businesses to think about more than just increasing the value of their stock. We conclude this module with the quintessential control question—how can managers *encourage and enable compliance?* We consider this question with respect to compliance with not only organizational rules and procedures, but also with legal and regulatory requirements for organizations.

Module 2 Competency 1 Organizing Information Flows

ASSESSMENT   Identifying Data Overload and Information Gaps

Objective   Before we can manage data overload, we need to recognize it. Sometimes we assume that all the data that comes to us is information that we need. This exercise will help you think about the amount and type of data that you receive and how important those data really are to you.

Directions   Listed below are some questions about the amount of data and information you routinely have to deal with. You should answer these questions individually. Your instructor also may have you discuss them in small groups or as a class.

Discussion Questions

1. Has the amount of paper and documents confronting you at school, at work, and in your personal life increased or decreased over the past two years?

2. Do you feel you have become more skillful in sorting, storing, transmitting, and using information?

3. Do you spend time on the Internet scouring through data, only to log off much later without an answer to your question?

4. What are your major sources of overload in managing information—email, paper, phone messages, verbal instructions, and requests from others? What are two or three specific things you can do to manage this overload more effectively?

5. Do you often receive information that you don't have any real use for? Do you receive the same information in multiple formats (e.g., email message, paper memo, voice mail message)?

6. How confident do you feel about the information you have on your current performance as an employee? As a student? Do you know where you stand with your supervisor or boss? With your instructors?

7. What additional information would you like to have on these roles?

Reflection   Organizational systems are not always designed to provide efficient information flows. "Better safe than sorry" appears to be the motto of much corporate communication. Emails that are sent to everyone are later followed up with paper copies, "just in case someone doesn't check their email." Memos about scholarship opportunities for children of employees are sent to everyone, regardless of whether or not they have children. Viewed individually, none of these communications is particularly problematic. However, as our recycle bins fill start to overflow and our email accounts exceed our allotted capacity, these unnecessary data inflows take their toll—when employees feel overwhelmed, organizational performance suffers.

LEARNING   Organizing Information Flows

New technologies have greatly increased the amount of information we receive and the speed at which requested information arrives. In the past we could write a letter, drop it in the mailbox, and then turn our attention to other things while we waited for a reply. Now, with fax machines, cell phones, laptops, and PDAs, responses can be immediate, pushing the work back onto our desks before we even have time to take a deep breath.

Back in 1997, David Shenk wrote, "Information overload has replaced information scarcity as an important new emotional, social, and political problem" (Shenk, 1997, p. 29). Since then, the problem has only gotten worse. In 2006 alone, the amount of digital data produced was equal to three million times the information contained in all the books ever written (Nordenson, 2008). It is no surprise then, that a recent survey of 650 professionals found that across 23 professions such as consulting, financial services, and education, 69.6 percent of respondents reported that they were overloaded by the amount of information they have to cope with related to their jobs (Davis, 2008).

Paradoxically however, even though managers have a smorgasbord of data at their fingertips, they also often claim to be starved for good information (Beard & Peterson, 2003). This apparent contradiction stems in part from our failure to distinguish between data and information. The term "data" refers to facts that have no particular context or organization and, as a result, data have no clear meaning. To make data meaningful, those facts must be organized and given context. It is in this way that data are translated into meaningful and, therefore useful, information (Beard & Peterson, 2003). To keep things simple in this text, we sometimes use the term "information" when it would be more accurate to say "data and/or information." Keep in mind, however, that if it isn't meaningful and useful, it really isn't information!

DATA INFLOWS: ARE YOU IN DATA OVERLOAD?

Russel Ackoff, an international consultant on managerial problem solving, says that a major problem confronting managers is too much irrelevant information. Managers are surrounded by data that do not tell them what they need to know but that demand attention anyway. Smart managers learn to watch the helpful data and ignore the irrelevant stuff. Less sophisticated managers drown in information anxiety. Richard Wurman, an expert on making information visually accessible, says, "Information anxiety is produced by the ever widening gap between what we understand and what we think we should understand. [It is] the black hole between data and knowledge. It happens when information doesn't tell us what we want or need to know" (Wurman, 2001, p. 14). See whether you identify with some of these symptoms of information overload as a student or employee:

1. Chronically talking about not keeping up with what's going on around you.
2. Nodding your head knowingly when someone mentions a book, an artist, or a news story that you have actually never heard of.
3. Assuming you must read every email you receive, regardless of who sent it.
4. Thinking that the person next to you understands everything and you don't.
5. Calling something that you don't understand "information." It isn't information if you don't understand it (Wurman, 1989, pp. 35–36).

The fashion of referring to virtually any kind of data as "information" emerged when we started using the word to describe anything that was transmitted over an electrical or mechanical channel (Campbell, 1982). The term "information" meant anything sent by any channel to any receiver, whether or not the receiver found it informative or interesting. "Information" has since become one of the most important terms in our society; however, much of the information we receive is really just unformed data.

We are inundated with bits and pieces of data, disconnected from any coherent picture, and yet we still feel guilty when we can't assimilate it. Information is probably best thought of as "that which reduces uncertainty." If the information we use is only adding to our uncertainty, it is probably data that have not yet been converted to information. Wurman (2002) suggests that most of us need to get beyond the anxiety of not knowing so we can begin to understand. He wants us to relax, feel less guilty about our ignorance, and begin to play with and exploit information instead of being controlled and intimidated by it. That is great advice, but how do we get to that point?

THE TRAF SYSTEM: TOSS, REFER, ACT, FILE

Today's managers are more harried than ever before, not only because of all the data coming at them from so many different sources, but also because many of them are now working without an assistant. Assistants have traditionally filtered a lot of information and transactions for managers, but many of these support positions have been eliminated from contemporary organizations. Thus, the individual manager has increasingly had to handle the channeling and managing of information. The bad news is that the problem of data overload is here to stay. The good news is that managers can become more efficient and effective if they learn and apply some tools and strategies for handling data inflows.

Good managers review all incoming data flows, but great managers are able to organize data efficiently, determine what information they need, and what information needs to be channeled to others. Great managers establish information management habits and systems that force them to do something quickly with every incoming piece of data, whether it is on paper, a digital recording, or an electronic message. Without a good system, you may not be able to wade through the insignificant stuff to find the information you need, when you need it. Managers need to set up and use a system that forces them to do something with every piece of paper that hits their desk and every email that appears in their inbox.

"Traffing," a method recommended by personal efficiency expert Stephanie Winston (Winston, 2004), is designed to end the inefficient practice of handling the same piece of paper many times. The same basic process can be applied to electronic messages, whether email or voice mail, which now make up the majority of most of the data inflows that inundate managers.

The metaphor of traffic control is wisely chosen because to control traffic, we have to give it places to go. Likewise, papers and emails have to be given a few basic routes or streams in which to flow. The list of items in front of you, all pleading for your attention, may be long; however, the number of choices you have for dealing with them is, fortunately, quite short. Winston's advice on Traffing gives you four options:

1. **Toss** papers into the wastebasket or recycling bin if they are not immediately valuable. Most of us are too conservative when deciding what to save. If you throw something out that you later discover you need, you can usually get another copy. For email, the electronic version of "tossing" is deleting.

2. **Refer** messages to other people (e.g., secretary, staff, colleagues). You should probably set up files for the people you most often refer things to. If you're not using routing slips, start immediately. You can usually save time by attaching a Post-it Note that briefly explains why you're referring the information. You can easily do the same for emailed messages and documents by forwarding them with an explanatory note.

3. **Act** by putting papers requiring your personal action (for example, writing a response letter or a brief report) in an action box or folder. These are the "hot" items you must act on before they get cold. In addition to placing documents in an "act" folder (physical or electronic). You should also record the action you need to take on your to-do list. The list is a very efficient reminder of things you need to act on. Plus, the act of putting them on the list will help you remember that you need to do them. Of course at some point, you will need to prioritize what is on your to-do list—we'll get to that topic soon.

4. **File** documents by indicating on the document itself the name of the file into which it should go. Put email that you need to save into folders. Put paper in a box or file labeled "to file." Even if you don't have an assistant who will file papers for you, it generally is more efficient to file papers on a periodic basis rather than getting up to file things while you are trying to clear your desk. Keep in mind that reading, in terms of this system, is a form of acting. If a document takes more than five minutes to read, put it in the "act" box. Don't let reading short-circuit your Traffing, or you'll

never get the papers sorted. Make a clear distinction between Traffing and acting, and schedule time for doing both.

PRIORITIZING ACTION ITEMS

Traffing helps you wrap your mind around all the paper and messages you have to deal with and is an important step for dealing with data inflows. Even after tossing, referring, and filing, however, the number of items that end up in a manager's Action file is often overwhelming. Complicating matters further for managers is the fact that that they are frequently interrupted—the phone rings, a subordinate comes by to ask a question, a colleague stops off to see if you'd like to join him for lunch. Interruptions are difficult to avoid. The research firm Basex reported that "interruptions take up nearly 30 percent of a knowledge worker's day and end up costing American businesses $650 billion annually"(Nordenson, 2008).

One approach to prioritizing suggested by Steven Covey in his book, *The 7 Habits of Highly Effective People* is the Time Management Matrix (see Figure M2.1). Covey argues that we often fail to recognize the difference between Importance and Urgency and therefore allow ourselves to become bogged down in things that seem to be urgent, and we fail to devote time to what is important. Important action items are things that we need to act on related to our mission, values, and goals. Something is urgent when it requires immediate action. Because activities that are important have great significance or value, they often take a significant amount of time to complete.

Covey argues that in addition to avoiding spending time doing things that are not important, effective people also minimize the number of things that are important and urgent by spending more time doing things that are important but not urgent. As most of us have learned the hard way, tasks that are important but not urgent today, eventually become urgent as well as important if we do not attend to them.

FIGURE M2.1 *Time management matrix.*

Source: S. R. Covey, *The 7 Habits of Highly Effective People* (New York: Free Press, 2004), 151. Copyright © Franklin Covey Co. Used with permission.

	Urgent	Not Urgent
Important	Crises Pressing problems Deadline-driven projects	Prevention Production capability activities Relationship building Recognizing new opportunities Planning, recreation
Not Important	Interruptions, some calls Some mail, some reports Some meetings Proximate, pressing matters Popular activities	Trivia, busy work Some mail Some phone calls Time wasters Pleasant activities

INFORMATION OUTFLOWS: ARE YOUR MESSAGES CLEAR, CONCISE, AND COMPLETE?

Although people most often think about information flows in terms of the information that they receive, managers also have a responsibility to think carefully about the information that they pass on to others. Because we all suffer from information overload, effective managers must confront another paradox: employees don't want to be overwhelmed by unnecessary information, but they also typically do not want to be left out of the loop and be uninformed about what is happening in the organization. Deciding what information should be shared and what information need not be shared is not easy—but then, few things in management are!

One way to help you decide whether to forward an email or copy others on a message is to think about how a recipient using the Traffing method would be likely to respond to what you send. From a practical perspective, if it will just be **T**ossed, then you may want to leave their name off the list. Similarly, if you think a colleague will just **R**efer a request to someone else to do, you may be tempted to send it directly to the person who is likely to get the job. Politically, however, this could be a mistake—your colleague might think that you are trying to work around him, rather than realizing that you were just trying to save everyone some time.

Because email is such a common method for sharing important information, we offer a tool that can be used to compose your email messages. This tool can also be used for creating brief and concise voicemail messages for work and for personal use. By using this tool effectively, you can avoid confusing your customers, clients, and coworkers with unclear messages.

THE OABC METHOD: A TEMPLATE FOR COMPOSING CONCISE MESSAGES

The OABC method was developed by William Baker, our colleague and a management communication professor at BYU's Marriott School of Management. Baker drills his MBA students on his OABC method for framing both email and voice-mail messages. This acronym stands for Opening, Agenda, Body, and Closing. The OABC method is a great antidote to the rambling and foggy messages that are sent out all over the world every day. This simple method requires you to make a very brief written or mental outline of the message. The outline of the message is usually best ordered in the following way:

1. **Opening:** A quick statement of greeting that sets a positive tone and also identifies you clearly, especially if you are a stranger to your audience. Even if you know the person well, it is often helpful to include your first and last name at the beginning of a voice mail to help the listener quickly put your message into context.

   - *Example:* "Hi, Chris, it's Karen Hooper. Great job on the presentation to the marketing group."

2. **Agenda:** An outline or map of what your message is about. Even brief messages usually need a "frame" or border to go around them.

- *Example:* "I have two things I wanted to share with you: The first is about the proposal to the Gartner Group, and the second is about a message I got from Kim Lee at the Ford Foundation."

3. **Body:** The "business" message itself, expressed in concrete and simple terms.

- *Example:* "I think the proposal is solid, but it needs more work in the staffing section where we talk about our expertise in data warehousing. I'm attaching a document that gives you more specifics of what I think it should look like.

    Second, Kim Lee at the foundation really needs us to have a representative at the awards luncheon. It's on July 17 at noon. Could you possibly attend in my place? I'll be in Toronto."

4. **Closing:** A concluding statement of what you want the person to do—who does what by when?—and a cordial and efficient ending such as a simple thank-you.

- *Example:* "Please look at the attachment and share it with the design team. I'll be back on Wednesday to discuss it with you. Also, please let me know by end of the day tomorrow if you can attend the luncheon, and I will call Kim myself from Toronto. Thanks. You've been a better teammate than I've been this week."

This message is more formal than one you might send to a coworker or friend whom you know very well. But notice that it's an easy message to "unpack." It has a pleasant tone, and it's coherent and complete. Chris knows exactly what Karen needs from him and when. Make a habit of using the OABC method in any message through any channel. We have used it with high-level managers and executives who have quickly added it to their toolkit. It can be applied to memos and business letters as well as to email and voice mail.

KNOWING YOUR AUDIENCE

In addition to thinking about what information should be shared and with whom, it also is important to think about how best to share that information. Would a phone call be better than an email? Is this something that should be discussed face-to-face? Is a formal memo necessary? The answers to these questions depend not only on the content of the message but also on the characteristics of the intended recipient. Some people, for example, are much more responsive to voice-mail messages than to email messages. Some people avoid email and voice mail, preferring to stop people in the hallways when they see them to convey important information (not a method that we recommend!).

You also may discover that some people have trouble coping with emails that contain more than one topic. If Karen Hooper, in our example above, was sending an email to Chris and realized that he tended to focus only on the first topic in a message, she might want to send two separate messages, particularly because her first issue is something Chris is likely to take some time to get to, but he should be able to respond to the question about attending the luncheon immediately.

Messages can suffer from being too long and including too many issues, but they may even be more problematic when they are too short. The development of hand-held messaging technologies has resulted in the creation of a new "chat" language better suited to small screens. For example, in December 2008, Webopedia reported that there were over 1000 chat abbreviations. Unfortunately, often the same abbreviations are used to mean different things, depending on the online group that is using the abbreviation. O might mean Over, or Opponent to an online gamer, or "hugs" when used by friends (Text Messaging & Chat Abbreviations, 2010).

Unfortunately, as people become more and more accustomed to using these types of chat abbreviations, they have begun to filter into the workplace, where they can cause confusion. Therefore, although it may seem old-fashioned and cumbersome to those experienced in instant messaging, standard spellings are more appropriate for communicating in organizations.

Although changing technology has made it much easier to communicate across distances, there is no real substitute for face-to-face meetings, especially during the early stages of group formation. Box M2.1 talks about the importance of physical presence for building relationships.

BOX M2.1 THE VANISHING HUMAN MOMENT

The electronic media we use—faxes, email, voice mail, cell phones, and PDAs (personal digital assistants)—help us communicate more efficiently, but not always more effectively. Edward Hallowell, a psychiatrist who works with business executives, considers "electronic hyperconnection" a serious problem in the workplace (Hallowell, 1999). The speed and convenience of email and voice mail are great, but when we use them continuously in high-stress settings, they can make our work lives worse, not better. The constant wash of voice mail messages left on our answering systems, the staccato email messages that blip onto our computer screens by the hour—this barrage of information can make people feel isolated, out of sorts, and defensive.

According to Hallowell, the cure for hyperconnectivity is creating a face-to-face "human moment" with other people. The human moment is more than face time—being physically present is necessary, but not sufficient. The human moment requires not only our physical presence but also our emotional and mental attention. In the human moment, your full attention is on the person in front of you—you are not checking your inbox or sending a text message. The human moment, says Hallowell, is disappearing from the workplace, largely because of so much electronic connectivity.

Many managers now lead groups of people who are dispersed geographically, such as sales teams or systems specialists who travel frequently and communicate with each other by email and cell phones. Although email is a very quick way to communicate with someone, email messages are often impersonal and too crisp to really convey the human element. In our research and consulting in organizations, we see a lot interpersonal conflicts caused by email. For example, a curt message such as "We could not access this application and need to know why" can be interpreted in many ways. If you're feeling stressed and defensive to begin with, you may read sarcasm or impatience into the message when that was not intended. If you then fire back an even more defensive or sarcastic response, a downward spiral begins.

Human conversations usually go much better in person when we can read the other person's nonverbal cues. Electronic communications, says Hallowell, "remove many of the cues that typically mitigate worry. Those cues—body language, tone of voice, and facial expression—are especially important among sophisticated people (knowledge workers) who are prone to using subtle language, irony, and wit. When all we have is a written message on our computer screen, or a quick voice mail from a coworker, we often misunderstand the other person's intentions, and then start to worry and second-guess the messenger. In person, these exchanges are often fixed before they can go off course" (p. 61).

Hallowell cites the experience of Jack, who founded a real estate development firm in Boston. Jack discovered, as the years passed and the firm grew larger, that people were less and less connected to each other. There seemed to be more friction and more misunderstanding among the managers. Most of them traveled frequently, and many of them worked out of their homes to save commuting time. Everyone was wired to the office via the Internet, and everyone had cell phones and fax machines. Still, there was a growing sense of isolation. Jack's solution was not a sophisticated one, but it did wonders for his firm: free pizza every Thursday. People would sit around a big table in Jack's office and talk. There was no agenda, and not everyone could be present every week. But there was always a core of people there who provided continuity. These sessions provided the humor, the contact, and the deeper, richer flow of information the firm needed. Pizza sessions provided the essential human moment, and according to Jack, were "largely responsible for the organization's high morale and competitive strength" (Hallowell, 1999, p. 64).

This week, why not take a break from texting on Twitter and use that time to think about how you could adapt this idea to create richer connections in your own life?

Source: Adapted from Edward M. Hallowell, "The Human Moment at Work," *Harvard Business Review* (January–February 1999), 58–64

ANALYSIS   Deciding What to Do with Data Inflows Using the Traffing Method

Objective   This in-box exercise gives you a chance to analyze a typical pile of messages and documents that might appear on a manager's desk.

Directions   Imagine that, as the afternoon shift manager in a manufacturing plant, you have received the following documents during the previous few hours. Some are waiting for you in your email inbox. Others are physical documents resting in the in-basket on the corner of your desk. Using the Traffing method, first decide whether you would Toss, Refer, Act, or File these documents.

For the items that you marked as Act, note whether they are Important and Urgent (I/U), Important but Not Urgent (I/NU), Not Important but Urgent (NI/U), or Not Important and Not Urgent (NI/NU). Then, rank the Act items in the order that you plan to do them. Don't worry, for the moment, that you lack contextual details on each of these items. Just do your best to think through how and why you would respond to each item. You may find it helpful to put your responses in a table like the one below:

Item #	TRAF	Important Act Items	Urgent Act Items	Ranking	Explanation

After you have done this task on your own, your instructor may ask you to discuss and defend your choices in a small group. See how much agreement your group has in "Traffing." Disagreement is not uncommon in this exercise. People's choices are based on their assumptions about the situation, as well as their attitudes toward delegating responsibility and their own priorities, which reflect their personal values.

1. A copy of a report from a quality assurance committee. This report is being circulated to all departments. The document looks interesting, but you're too busy to read it now. You're not even sure why it came to you, but you're intrigued enough to keep it.

2. A quarterly report from the product design unit.

3. A marketing brochure on new office equipment. Your unit will be moved to a new wing in the building, and the "relocation task force" has asked all shift managers to begin making recommendations on what new office furniture to purchase.

4. A memo from the vice president for operations on increases in shop-floor accidents. The number of reported accidents is up 13 percent over last quarter. Two of these resulted in hospitalizations.

5. An invitation to the design unit's holiday party with an RSVP.

6. A list of training films that must be previewed before the end of the month (still haunting your in-basket from last week).

7. Four signed contracts for your final approval.

8. A memo requesting agenda items for the next staff meeting.

9. A sign-up sheet for the next blood drive.

10. A request from an employee who wants to take two days of vacation next month.

Reflection   In the directions for this exercise, we told you not to worry about the contextual details. In reality, of course, context is very important for deciding the relative priorities of tasks. Taken out of context, a sign-up sheet for a blood drive might seem unimportant, but within the culture of a health organization or the Red Cross, that activity might take on much more importance as a symbolic act in support of the values of the organization. Similarly, although the shift manager may not need to do anything with the accident report, she may decide to file it rather than toss it. Why? Because symbolically, tossing the report might suggest a lack of concern for employee safety.

PRACTICE   Making Messages Clear, Concise, and Complete

Objective   Even straightforward ideas like the Opening, Agenda, Body, and Closing (OABC) approach to communicating require practice, evaluation, and reinforcement. This exercise asks you to work with others on improving your ability to compose messages that are clear, concise, and complete.

Directions   In groups of three or more, take turns composing and delivering messages using the OABC method. First, make a quick written outline of what you want to say in each section; then, share the message just as you would leave it over the phone. As a listener, give your classmates feedback on the clarity and conciseness of the message. If time permits, write out a message as you would if you were using email or texting, exchange what you have written, and give one another feedback on the quality of these messages. Consider the following questions:

Discussion Questions   1. Does the Opening set a positive climate both verbally and nonverbally?

2. Does the Agenda provide a quick roadmap of what the message is about?

3. Is the Body clear? If the parts of the body relate, is it clear how they relate? Is there any possibility for misunderstanding? Any ambiguity?

4. Does the Closing include action steps—who should do what and a deadline for acting—and conclude with a positive tone? Have you included any necessary contact information (e.g., your phone number, stated slowly, clearly, and repeated for voice-mail messages; what time zone you are in if you are trying to arrange a conference call)?

Reflection   If you have ever hung up the telephone after leaving a voice mail and then realized that you failed to leave your phone number even though you requested a call back, you'll appreciate the value of the OABC system. If you have ever called to leave a voice mail and been surprised when the other party answered the phone, you may find the OABC system even more useful! When talking on the phone, it is easy to get sidetracked by issues brought up by the other party. If you have gone through the OABC process and made notes about what you want to convey, however, you are less likely to end the conversation without getting your point across to your listener.

APPLICATION   Directing Your Own Data and Information Traffic

Objectives   Think about how you can better cope with all the data and information that comes to you at home and at work. Be sure to consider all types of information including postal mail, email, voice mail, reading assignments for your classes, messages from the media (print, visual, and audio), miscellaneous documents (e.g., housing contracts, car registrations, and warranty agreements) that you must TRAF.

Step 1   First, evaluate how well you are currently directing all that traffic not only on a daily basis but also over longer periods of time. Some questions to consider:

1. Do you use a filing method for important paper documents? How well does it work?
2. What are the five most important documents that you have in your possession? How long would it take you to find/access those documents if you needed them?
3. How do you "process" your paper mail? Is your method effective? Do you allow mail to pile up unopened? Do you sort through the same piles multiple times?
4. How much time do you think you spend each day looking for documents (including scraps of paper with phone numbers or other bits of information on them)? Do you ever lose track of important correspondence?
5. How many messages do you have in your email inbox? Do you use folders to file messages you want to keep? How often do you have to search for an old email message? How long does it typically take you to locate what you are looking for?
6. How effectively do you manage phone time? Do you always answer your phone when it rings? Do you often find that you spend more time on the phone than you realized?
7. Do you turn off your email and phone when you need to concentrate on a major project? Do you forward your phone and turn off your cell phone when you are meeting with other people?
8. At your job, what kind of information do you typically need to act on? What type of information do you need to refer to others? Could you begin to refer more things to others, rather than acting on them yourself?

Step 2   Based on how you answered the questions above, choose whichever type of data or information traffic you feel needs the most improvement. Apply the Traffing method to your data inflows and the OABC method to your information outflows. For example, if you are not currently using file folders to organize your email, take some time during the next week to create some folders for the different types of messages that you need to save. If there are more old messages in your inbox than you have time to sort, put all the old messages in a "to be filed" folder. Starting with an empty inbox will help you measure your success at keeping your email organized at the end of each day.

Reflection   Although most "personal productivity" advocates such as David Allen, author of *Getting Things Done: The Art of Stress-Free Productivity*, have urged us to clean up our clutter, not everyone agrees that we are more productive if we are perfectly organized. In their 2007 book *A Perfect Mess: The Hidden Benefits of Disorder—How Crammed Closets, Cluttered Offices, and On-the-Fly Planning Make the World a Better Place*, Eric Abrahamson and David H. Freedman state, "Though it flies in the face of almost universally accepted wisdom, moderately disorganized people, institutions, and systems frequently turn out to be more efficient, more resilient, more creative and in general more effective than highly organized ones" (Abrahamson & Freedman, 2007, p. 5). The Competing Values Framework helps explain this apparent paradox. Precisely controlled and perfectly organized information may be the ideal from the perspective of the Control quadrant with its emphasis on establishing and maintaining stability and continuity, but the Create quadrant reminds us that there also is value in flexibility, which increases our ability to adapt to new situations.

Module 2 Competency 2   Working and Managing Across Functions

ASSESSMENT   Mapping Your Organization

Objective   The purpose of this exercise is to help you identify where you fit within your organization and how you are connected to other areas. Understanding how the different parts of your organization fit together can help you more effectively apply some of the other competencies that you are studying. For example, with regard to organizing information flows, understanding the overall organization structure will help you identify where you should seek information as well as where you should send information.

Directions   1. If you are currently employed, obtain a copy of an organization chart for your employer. If you are not currently employed, find a copy of your school's organizational chart (check with the Human Resources office at your institution). Review the official chart and observe how the structure of the organization is presented. Is there anything that indicates how the different parts of the organization work together? Are differences in the relative power of different departments apparent? If you had to put together a cross-functional team to work on an important project, is it clear who would need to be on the team? Are there any divisions or units that might be in competition for customers?

2. Think about your job in the organization (as employee or student), and draw a new chart. Put yourself in the center and draw connections to all the areas in the organization that you need to be effective in your work. Which areas are you most dependent on to get your work done? Which areas depend on inputs from you to get their work done?

Reflection　The formal structure found in most organization charts is often only a modestly accurate representation of how things actually work. Effective managers need to understand not only the official roles and responsibilities in the organization, but also need to recognize the informal networks that can help (or hinder) task accomplishment.

LEARNING　Working and Managing Across Functions

More than 20 years ago, the authors of *Made in America: Regaining the Productive Edge* argued that to be successful in the global economy, U.S. companies needed to have greater functional integration and less organizational stratification because functional silos often result in inefficiencies in communication and coordination, the very functions that hierarchical structures were intended to support (Dertouzes, Lester, Solow & the MIT Commission on Industrial Productivity, 1989). Over the next 10 years, many companies attempted to heed that advice. *Reengineering the Corporation* by Michael Hammer and James Champy (1993) became a best-seller. Companies began to establish teams made up of specialists from different functional areas. These cross-functional teams became especially popular, in part because they did not require excessive disruptions to the existing organizational structure. The results of cross-functional teams, however, did not always live up to their promise. For example, a study looking at 93 research and new product development teams found that functional diversity, per se, did not improve team outcomes. It was only when external communication increased due to "having members with diverse backgrounds and areas of expertise and diverse contacts with important external networks of information" that benefits were realized (Keller, 2001).

Despite growing evidence that cross-functional teams are not a panacea, their use continues to grow, driven in part by the changing nature of work (Cross, Ehrlich, et al., 2008) New technologies that allow work to be done around the globe have become increasingly affordable. Companies have outsourced activities and depend on other organizations to do tasks that were formerly handed internally. These changes have resulted in additional flexibility and also resulted in additional costs that need to be accounted for and controlled. "Teams today are frequently formed and disbanded rapidly, distributed across multiple sites, and composed of members simultaneously working on myriad projects, with different bosses, competing for their attention. Further these teams' work increasingly demands substantial coordination and integration of specialized expertise within *and* outside of the team" (Cross, Ehrlich, et al., 2008).

As described in the next section, working in and managing these types of cross-functional teams poses new challenges compared to working in a traditional functional organization. An additional set of challenges is faced when working in organizations with potentially competing divisions, a topic we address in the subsequent section.

CROSS-FUNCTIONAL TEAMS WITHIN TRADITIONAL WORK STRUCTURES

Following the principles of Adam Smith and Henri Fayol, organizations have traditionally organized work by creating departments that handle the different functions of the organization. When departments within a single organization are structured differently so that they can each approach their own task in a way that is most efficient for that particular department, we refer to this as *differentiation*. In traditionally designed organizations, differentiation is accomplished through the creation of specialized jobs and work units that are then organized hierarchically. Within this hierarchical system, labor is divided up so that individual contributors perform the organization's work. Consistent with this approach, performance-management and reward systems focus on the individual performer. Job evaluations and job descriptions clearly specify who does what and who reports to whom. Status differentiations are made clear by labels such as "labor" and "management," "bonus eligible" and "bonus ineligible," and so on. Organizational subunits typically consist of individuals with similar expertise performing similar tasks—engineers engineering, marketers marketing, and manufacturing experts manufacturing.

Although there is no question that differentiation can result in improved efficiency in many situations, it does have some negative consequences that result from employee self-interest. For example, employees concerned about their careers often become focused on moving up the hierarchy, rather than on adding value to the output of the organization. Because budget size and the number of people one manages are symbols of position and power, managers may make decisions that are more consistent with increasing their hierarchical control than in delivering products or services to a customer (Mohrman, 1993).

Even if all employees were willing and able to subordinate their own individual interests to the general interests of the organization (as Fayol's principles of management required), there would still be costs associated with differentiation. An organization that is differentiated as a consequence of its traditional structure will eventually need to coordinate or integrate the work that is being done across units. Differentiation and integration can be likened to the flexibility and control dimension in the Competing Values Framework—both are needed even though they may appear to be diametrically opposed.

Integration is primarily accomplished by processes inherent in the organizational hierarchy. Processes and procedures are standardized and formalized, specifying how the work is to be done and the sequence by which it is to proceed through the organization. Individual contributors are managed, directed, controlled, and coordinated by middle-level managers who receive strategic guidance from senior-level executives. These types of integrative processes work fairly well for relatively simple and static situations, but it has long been known that their effectiveness is limited in complex, dynamic, and turbulent environments (Galbraith, 1973). For example, in 1993 Mohrman argued that organizations had to simultaneously:

- Achieve multiple focuses (on product, market, customer, and geography) without segmenting the organization in a dysfunctional way.

- Align individuals and groups that are task-interdependent in a manner that fosters teamwork in pursuit of shared overall objectives.

- Enable quick, low-cost, high-quality performance while responding to a highly dynamic environment that calls for ongoing change.

- Respond to ongoing increases in competitive performance standards by learning how to be more effective.

- Attract, motivate, develop, and retain employees who are able to operate effectively in such a demanding organizational environment.

Taken together, these goals pose several paradoxes for managers. How can we be focused if we are trying to address multiple sets of needs? How can we evaluate individuals when they are working in teams? How can we keep quality high while we are working faster and cheaper? How can we keep costs down if we are constantly changing standards? How can we find employees who will stay committed when the organization is constantly changing?

Because most people see paradoxes in terms of either/or decisions, it is not surprising that some organizations attempted to respond to these challenges by "throwing away their organizational charts in favor of ever-changing constellations of teams, projects, and alliances" (Dumaine, 1991, p. 36). Other organizations have attempted to manage these challenges within more traditional structures; some have gone back and forth, at times favoring cross-functional diversity and at times retreating to more specialization (Sapsed, 2005). Theoretically, incorporating cross-functional teams into a traditional structure can provide the integration solution to the need for integration in differentiated organizations, but like so many good ideas, this solution comes with its own set of challenges.

OVERCOMING THE CHALLENGES OF CROSS-FUNCTIONAL TEAMS

Parker (1994) identified a number of challenges for cross-functional teams, particularly those that are formed as a result of a need to respond quickly to competitive pressures. Lack of clear and consistent support from senior management can undermine the best efforts of any cross-functional team. One type of support that can be valuable is having a physical space for the team. Co-locating team members has symbolic, as well as substantive benefits. Cross-functional teams also suffer when all of the relevant functional areas do not become involved early in the process. Projects that start out in one functional silo and then try to add team members from other functional areas may end up with teams where there is a lack of trust. Cross-functional teams can also be hindered if the allocation of work across functions seems inequitable or is inefficient, or if decision-making processes are not clearly defined. With respect to product development teams, making sure that the team moves quickly based on customer input is often a challenge because team members are typically still engaged in working on tasks associated with their functional area. Despite all these challenges, cross-functional teams can be a valuable tool in organizations, if they are effectively managed.

What is needed is a set of processes and devices that are consistent with the complex and dynamic environment that the organization faces and that allow organizations to integrate and coordinate their efforts, regardless of the formal structure of the organization. In essence, managers today need to be able to create ad hoc structures that can both transcend and operate within a traditional organizational design. The guidelines below can be helpful in accomplishing that objective.

KEY GUIDELINES FOR MANAGING CROSS-FUNCTIONALLY

The guidelines below are derived from Dumaine (1991), Meyer (1993), and Parker (1994).

1. *Clarify goals and charter and get team buy-in.* The cross-functional team will generally take the formal charge from senior management, but the team must also feel ownership over the goals. In the *Managing Groups and Leading Teams* competency in Module 1, we discussed the importance of being committed to a common goal or purpose and indicated that this is the glue that holds the team together. Sometimes the cross-functional team will need to meet with senior management to negotiate the goal or to make sure that there is a shared understanding.

2. *Seek to create a critical mass of leadership.* While a single functional unit can generally get by with a single leader, most cross-functional teams cannot. If the ultimate purpose of cross-functional teams is to make optimal use of people from different functions, each of these functions must have a strong leadership voice. In addition, this is a good time to take advantage of team members' unique talents (Buckingham, 2005).

3. *Hold the team and its members accountable for its performance.* Once team members have bought into the goals, they must also buy into the process. Everyone must feel responsible for the team's performance. Team goals should be translated into clear short-term objectives and milestones that are constantly visible and in the forefront of everyone's thinking. While senior management should avoid micromanaging, they should hold the team to standards. When standards are not met, questions should be raised in such a way that team members feel supported rather than attacked.

4. *Keep cross-functional teams as small as possible with critical functional representation.* While the purpose of creating a team is to bring together a diverse set of perspectives, years of research on group processes shows that as group size increases, there is a loss of productivity that results from increased time devoted to coordination and communication. One estimate of productivity loss indicates that in groups with as few as five people, between 10 and 30 percent of team members' time is spent communicating with other team members about the task (Parker, 1994). Alternatively, if there is not sufficient representation of all functional areas from the very beginning, the team will not be able to perform effectively. One solution is to break up the large group into smaller groups, with each small group having representation in a central decision-making group. In addition to determining the optimal team size, finding the right mix of people is critical. If all functional areas are represented, but

one team member cannot see the value of working on a cross-functional team, size will quickly become a secondary issue.

5. *Provide the cross-functional team with constantly updated and relevant information and the authority to make decisions.* If an organization is to make heavy use of cross-functional teams, it must essentially rewire the information system so that cross-functional teams have ready access to the information they need to do their jobs. Teams also need what was formerly assumed to be the prerogative of management: the authority to make decisions.

6. *Train members in teamwork and process management.* Operating in cross-functional teams with complex and fuzzy authority and reporting relationships necessitates that members know the core skills of teamwork. In Module 1, Competency 4, "Managing Groups and Leading Teams," we presented some of these core skills, including defining roles and responsibilities, using participative decision-making, and managing meetings. As was noted in that competency, teamwork does not develop naturally. There needs to be a conscious effort to develop as a team, and organizations must often be willing to make the investment to give people training in interpersonal skills.

7. *Clarify expectations within and between teams.* Each individual who is part of a cross-functional team has three responsibility perspectives: the team, the function, and the larger organization. Each of these should be clearly articulated before the start of the project. Moreover, leaders of cross-functional teams must have the ability to develop effective relationships with key stakeholders, including leaders of functional departments, senior management sponsors, and other resource people in the organization. The next competency in this module, Planning and Coordinating Projects, presents the notion of internal and external integration and suggests that regular communication with key project stakeholders is an important element of managing projects. This is even more true if the project is being carried out by a cross-functional team, where the definition of who is internal and who is external can become somewhat blurred. While it is clear that all organizations have multiple and often competing goals, these competing goals must not become a barrier to effective cross-functional team management. An organization will be able to use cross-functional teams effectively only if team members and others in the organization identify primarily with the larger organization and only secondarily with their functional units.

    One step that is often useful here is the co-location of team members. That is, whenever possible, cross-functional team members should be located as close as possible, "in the same building, on the same floor, and in the same area" (Parker, 1994, p. 78). Physical proximity allows for more regular and more informal interactions. Co-locating team project members also sends a very clear message regarding the importance of the project.

8. *Encourage team members to step out of their roles.* As a corollary to the previous guideline, we suggest that people must not only be willing to step out of their functional identity to "put on an organizational hat," they must also be willing to step out of their status or rank identity to allow for more optimal use of everyone's unique skills and abilities. As noted in the second guideline, the increasing use of cross-functional teams suggests that more and more, "leaders" on one project will be "followers" on

the next. In sum, the most successful teams are ones that are able to manage the paradoxes that are associated with having clearly defined roles and responsibilities, while simultaneously expecting that everyone will step up when necessary to ensure that everything that needs to be done, is done.

PICKING THE RIGHT PEOPLE—ADDITIONAL INSIGHTS

Identifying the right members for a cross-functional team depends on a number of variables, as noted in the guidelines above. In addition to considering the technical skills of team members, however, it is also wise to consider their interpersonal skills. As we have seen, working effectively on a cross-functional team can be very challenging. The complexity of the task itself often pales in comparison to the political issues that tend to emerge when managing across functions. In these types of situations, it is helpful to have individuals on the team who are not only energetic themselves, but who tend to energize the people around them. Empirical research from the field of network analysis has identified a key variable "energizing relationships" (Baker, Cross & Wooten, 2003) that is worth considering when creating cross functional teams.

Most people have had the experience with working with someone whose enthusiasm, optimism, and vitality seem to charge up everyone around them. Intuitively, we know that these are the kinds of people whom we want working on important projects. Network analysis research confirms that intuition and goes further to suggest that the ability to develop energizing relationships "may be more important than occupying certain positions in an information or communication network" (Baker et al., 2003, p. 339).

Recent work on the concept of "*lift*" provides additional insights into the characteristics of individuals who may be likely to create energizing relationship. In their book *Lift: Becoming a Positive Force in Any Situation*, R. W. Quinn and R. E. Quinn define "*lift*" as "influence, an uplifting effect we have on others." This definition is consistent with Baker et al.'s concept of energizing relationships. The authors go on to identify four key thoughts and feelings that, when present, cause individuals to feel uplifted and to lift the people around them. Specifically, individuals feel uplifted and lift the people around them when they are:

1. purpose-centered — they have a purpose that is not weighted down by needless expectations [Compete];

2. internally-directed — they have a story of how their personal values will guide their actions [Control];

3. other-focused — they feel empathy for the feelings and needs of others [Collaborate]; and

4. externally-open — they believe that they can improve at whatever it is they are trying to do [Create] (Quinn & Quinn, 2009, p. 3).

As noted in the brackets after each factor above, these four key thoughts and feelings map directly onto the action imperatives in the competing values framework, a point we address in more detail in the concluding chapter of this text. Further information on the concept of "lift" also can be found at http://www.leadingwithlift.com.

Unfortunately, like the manager in the Analysis that follows, you will not always be able to choose the members of the teams with which you work. Fortunately, you can have much more control over your own thoughts and feelings.

ANALYSIS   Errors in the Design?*

Directions   Read the paragraph below. It comes from a real situation encountered in one of the Big Three U.S. automobile manufacturers. Diagnose the errors that might have been made in managing across the various functional areas that were involved in designing the automobile.

The total amount of electrical power in a vehicle is determined by the capacity of the alternator. The power must serve over twenty subsystems, such as the stereo, the engine, the instrument panel, and so on. These subsystems are developed and controlled by separate "chimney" organizations, and power allocations must be made for each subsystem. The problem was, in this vehicle program, when the requirements of all the chimneys and teams were added up, they equaled 125 percent of the capacity of the alternator. Keith, who had recently taken over as head of this vehicle program (which had made changes in direction and was behind schedule to begin with), called a meeting of the Program Steering Committee designed to resolve this conflict and reach a compromise. However, many of the chimney representatives who were members of the team came to this meeting with instructions from their bosses [who, incidentally, did their performance appraisals] *not* to make any compromises, but to make certain that their chimney "got what it needed" and "didn't lose out." After Keith presented the group with the problem and the need to reach a compromise solution, their response surprised him: "It's not our problem," they replied, "it's *your* problem."

Questions   1. What advice would you give Keith for dealing with the Program Steering Committee?

2. Which other key stakeholders should Keith deal with? What advice would you give him for dealing with these other key stakeholders?

3. If Keith could "turn back the hands of time," what advice would you have given him at the beginning of this project? Be as specific as possible in your advice.

Reflection   For people who have not experienced the type of situation described above, the story seems almost unbelievable—How could members of the same organization not recognize the importance of coming up with a vehicle design that would actually work? For far too many employees, however, this type of situation rings all too true. Consistent with a sociotechnical systems perspective, organizational structures and processes can result in inefficiency and even divisiveness if people do not understand and respect the interconnections among all functions in the organization.

PRACTICE   Student Orientation

Objective   Many events require cooperation across different groups, but special issues often come into play when the groups involved are made up of volunteers. In this exercise you need to think not only about the task issues, but also the people issues given the volunteer nature of the groups who will be participating in the event.

Source: Dan Denison, Stuart Hart, and Joel Kahn, "From Chimneys to Cross-Functional Teams: Developing and Validating a Diagnostic Model." Working Paper, University of Michigan, 1993. Used with permission.

Directions   You are president of the University Students Services Association (USSA). USSA is a student-run organization that coordinates the activities of all other student-run organizations on campus. USSA monitors scheduling of all extracurricular activities, tracks consistency of student organization activities with university policy, and attempts to provide resource support whenever possible.

In the past, each major university organization—such as Academic Support Services, the USSA, the Student Health Services, the Honor Society, and so on—conducted its own new-student orientation during the general orientation prior to the beginning of the fall semester. These orientations typically lasted anywhere from one to three hours and included speeches, presentations, videotapes, and workshop-type activities. For most organizational units, these orientations were seen as an opportunity to publicize the way in which they contributed to students' experience of university life. Organizational units spent a great deal of time, effort, and attention in preparing their individual orientations, because they felt it was important for students to learn about how they might take advantage of the services provided. Organizational units took great pride in conducting a professional presentation and paid close attention to the evaluations that students completed. In fact, there was something of an informal competition among the units, with each trying to be the most innovative in its presentation.

This year the provost has decided to try a new approach, declaring that all student orientation sessions will be centrally coordinated and run over a three-day period during the first week of classes. You have been asked to head the team that coordinates this orientation.

Your first task is to prepare a one-page outline of how you will approach this new responsibility. After you have completed the outline, respond to the process questions below.

Process Questions   1. What work- or task-related issues need to be addressed in order to carry out the provost's request?

2. What people-related issues do you foresee?

3. What issues of internal and external integration will need to be addressed in carrying out this task?

4. What was better about the previous format for student orientations? What is better about the new format?

Reflection   Planning, of course, is only the beginning. Before any plan can be implemented, people will need to be convinced to go along with the plan. This is where the competencies such as Championing and Selling New Ideas and Negotiating Agreement and Commitment (see Module 4) come into play.

APPLICATION   Examining a Cross-Functional Team

Objectives   Use what you have learned about managing across functions to improve your own work situation.

Directions   Identify a situation that you are currently in at school, at work, or in some other formal organization that has cross-functional elements to it.

1. Analyze the situation in terms of the guidelines presented in this section. In analyzing the situation, find specific ways in which the situation is being managed well, as well as problems. When you identify a problem, try to determine its specific source(s). That is, don't just say, "Meetings do not accomplish anything," try to determine the cause of the problem. Are goals unclear? Are the wrong people attending the meeting? Was an agenda distributed in advance?

As you work on your analysis, keep in mind the importance of providing evidence to support your claims about problems and making connections to theory to support any recommendations you might make.

2. Once you are confident that you have identified the root causes of the problem, write a memo suggesting how the operations of the cross-functional team could be improved.

Reflection Managing cross-functional teams is complicated by the fact that there are often political, as well as practical, reasons why certain individuals are on the team. Because being left off a team may be considered a slight, cross-functional teams sometimes balloon into large groups. Novices who attempt to reduce the group to a more efficient size, however, may end up making the situation worse rather than better.

Module 2 Competency 3   Planning and Coordinating Projects

ASSESSMENT   Project Planning

Objective This exercise is intended to prime your thinking about effective project management by encouraging you to reflect on your past project experiences.

Directions Think about a project or event you have worked on, preferably one in which you had some leadership responsibility. (Note that having leadership responsibility does not necessarily mean that you were the sole project leader.) Think about the planning and coordination, and respond to the questions below.

1. To what extent were goals and objectives made explicit? What role did you play in clarifying goals and objectives?

2. To what extent was the project explicitly segmented into smaller, more manageable activities? Describe the process by which the project was divided up. What role did you play in dividing the project into the smaller activities?

3. To what extent was there a clear understanding regarding a schedule or time line? What role did you play in devising the schedule?

4. To what extent was there a need to coordinate resources (money, equipment, supplies) as well as people? What role did you play in the coordination of resources?

5. Overall, how well was this project or event coordinated? What were the key successes? Where were some needed details overlooked?

Reflection As we noted in Module 1 in the Managing Groups and Leading Teams competency, when a project is assigned there is often a tendency to try to skip over the planning and coordination tasks, and to dive directly into working on the project. Effective managers recognize that this is a mistake. Looking back at your prior experiences with project work gives you an opportunity to identify any points where planning and coordination broke down. As you read the Learning material for this competency, think about whether the tools and techniques described would have helped you to avoid those problems.

LEARNING Planning and Coordinating Projects

World-class organizations must be adaptable and flexible to succeed. What worked yesterday may not work today. As we have seen in the competing values framework, flexibility needs to be balanced with stability. To be more flexible, improve performance, and prepare for the future, many organizations are coming to rely on nonroutine projects (Anatatmula, 2008). To balance that flexibility, projects are assigned specific objectives, starting and ending times, and a predetermined budget. In the end, financial stability depends both on identifying the correct projects from a strategic perspective (a topic we take up in Module 3) as well as on effective and efficient project management (Schmid & Adams, 2008). In this competency we discuss some tools that can be used when planning, directing, and controlling resources to meet the technical requirements, cost targets, and time constraints of a project.

Although projects were originally used primarily in the military and construction industries (Baltzan & Phillips, 2008), changes in the economy, heightened competition, increased complexity in organizational environments, and rapid technological changes have created ideal conditions for project teams to spread to other organizational areas. For example, human resource managers benefitted from using project management tools when Life Technologies Corp, a biotechnology tools company, was created as the result of a merger of two smaller organizations (Robb, 2009). Today, project management concepts are being applied in a diverse array of industries, including pharmaceuticals, banking, hospitals, law, state and local governments, and the United Nations (Kerzner, 2009).

Project teams are seen as an ideal approach to deal with the need to respond more quickly to changes in the turbulent business environment for several reasons. First, project teams are task focused, thus complementing the way many organizations allocate work—through tasks. Project teams also enable companies to engage the work through the use of cross-functional teams, as discussed in the previous competency in this module. Lastly, because project teams make use of resources borrowed from within the firm, and perhaps also from outside the firm, they are flexible and able to act and react quickly to change (Frame, 1999).

PROJECT MANAGEMENT PROCESSES AND TOOLS

Harold Kerzner, one of the leading authorities on project management, summarizes the five different process groups included in the PMBOK® Guide from the Project Management Institutes as follows:

1. Project initiation
   - Selection of the best project given resource limits
   - Recognizing the benefits of the project

- Preparation of the documents to sanction the project
- Assigning of the project manager

2. Project planning
   - Definition of work requirements
   - Definition of the quality and quantity of work
   - Definition of resources needed
   - Scheduling the activities
   - Evaluation of the various risks

3. Project execution
   - Negotiating for the project team members
   - Directing and managing the work
   - Working with the team members to help them improve
   - Making adjustments

4. Project monitoring and control
   - Tracking progress
   - Comparing actual outcome to predicted outcome
   - Analyzing variance and impacts
   - Making adjustments

5. Project closure
   - Verifying that all of the work has been accomplished
   - Contractual closure of the contract
   - Financial closure of the charge numbers
   - Administrative closure of the paperwork

(Kerzner, 2009, p. 3)

In this competency, we focus on planning and monitoring; activities associated with the other three categories (initiation, execution, and closure) are addressed in other competencies in this text. For example, communication skills are considered one of the most critical skills for project managers (Henderson, 2008).

The various tools of project planning and project monitoring that we focus on for this competency are closely tied. Planning clarifies the work to be accomplished and sets priorities for task completion. Planning involves scheduling—establishing time-tables and milestones for completion—and resource allocation—developing a budget that forecasts the amount of labor and equipment that will be needed. Alternatively, monitoring tracks progress to see whether the project is proceeding as planned. Is the schedule being adhered to? Are milestones being met? How likely is the project to be completed within, or even under, the projected budget? In the next two sections, we will present several key planning and monitoring tools. It should, however, be noted that the monitoring tools will be useful only if the planning has been conducted carefully, with sufficient attention to detail.

PLANNING TOOLS

Project planning is not simply deciding on an outcome to be achieved. Project planning should make clear the path the project is expected to take as well as the destination. Consequently, the planning process should focus attention not only on the goals and objectives of the project but also on such issues as the technical and managerial approach, resource availability, the project schedule, contingency planning and replanning assumptions, project policies and procedures, performance standards, and methods of tracking, reporting, and auditing (Badiru, 1993). It is thus evident that planning is far more complex than scheduling. Indeed, while scheduling is considered a key element of coordination, it is actually the last step of the planning process and depends on the existence of a precise statement of goals and objectives, accompanied by a detailed description of the scope of work. Below we present some of the key planning tools available to the project manager, with the order of presentation based on the order in which they are likely to be used.

Today, many of these tools can be found in project management software programs such as Microsoft Office's Standard Project 2007 and Enterprise Project Management (EPM) Solution. These types of products incorporate the basic planning tools discussed below and simplify planning, monitoring, and coordinating processes by integrating all data relevant to the project. For example, data associated with the Statement of Work and Work Breakdown Structure (discussed below) related to specific tasks, working times, schedules, deadlines, people, materials, machines, and so on can be entered into computerized templates. During the data entry process, the software can also provide prompts to help establish the order in which work needs to be completed if two tasks are dependent. As data on tasks, times, and schedule are entered, the computer can generate PERT and Gantt charts, as well as other types of reports. Because not every organization requires a full-blown project management software system, a variety of other programs have been developed to address users with different needs. One example is Basecamp, a web-based program available by subscription from 37signals. The program's "to-do list" feature is used to enter information traditionally found in the Statement of Work. Milestones and a time tracking feature are available to help monitor progress. Although Basecamp lacks the capacity to produce PERT and Gantt charts, its ease of use appeals to its clients. Because new project management software and features are constantly being developed, we do not attempt to provide instruction on how any particular program works. Rather, we focus on explaining the fundamental concepts upon which those programs are based.

STATEMENT OF WORK

The statement of work (SOW) is a written description of the scope of work required to complete the project. It should include a statement regarding the objectives of the project, brief descriptions of the services to be performed and the products and documents to be delivered, an explanation of funding constraints, specifications, and an overall schedule. Specifications should be included for all aspects of the project. They will be used to provide standards for determining the cost of the project. The overall schedule should be more general, including only start and end dates and key milestones.

The statement of work may also include brief descriptions of the tasks necessary for project completion as well as a description, where appropriate, of how individual tasks will be integrated into the whole. Alternatively, this information may be included in the work breakdown structure.

WORK BREAKDOWN STRUCTURE

The work breakdown structure (WBS) shows the total project divided into components that can be measured in terms of time and cost. It may be presented in tabular or graphical form, or both (see Figures M2.2A and M2.2B). Whether in tabular or graphical form, the WBS divides the project into a series of hierarchical levels; in graphical form it resembles an organizational chart of tasks (rather than positions). The complexity of the

PROJECT: ORGANIZING THE OFFICE PICNIC

	TASK	ESTIMATED TIME (DAYS)	RESPONSIBLE PERSON
TASK 1:	Do invitations and determine number of guests	5	Sam
	Activity 1.1: Get material from last year's picnic		
	Activity 1.2: Edit last year's invitation	.5	Sam
	Activity 1.3: Set up invitation log	.5	Sam
	•		
	•		
	•		
	Activity 1.X: Do final estimate on number of guests	.5	Sam
TASK 2:	Plan and purchase food		
	Activity 2.1: Plan snack food	.5	Marty
	Activity 2.2: Plan main meal	2	Pat
	Activity 2.3: Plan beverages	.5	Chris
	•		
	•		
	•		
	Activity 2.X: Purchase beverages	.5	Chris
TASK 3:	Plan picnic activities		
	Activity 3.1: Do informal poll of activities enjoyed at last year's picnic	5	Linda
	Activity 3.2: Find out where sports equipment is held	.5	Marty
	•		
	•		
	•		
	Activity 3.X: Buy new equipment, as necessary	1	Linda
TASK 4:	Plan and purchase supplies		
	Activity 4.1: Plan food supplies (plates, cups, plasticware, etc.)	.5	Marty
	Activity 4.2: Plan decorations	.5	Chris
	•		
	•		
	•		
	Activity 4.X: Pick up decorations from Picnic Store	.5	Marty

FIGURE M2.2A *Work breakdown structure: tabular form.*

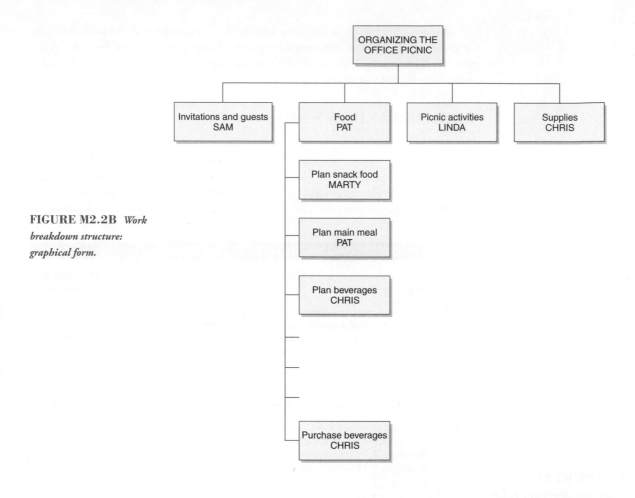

FIGURE M2.2B *Work breakdown structure: graphical form.*

project and the degree of control desired during project monitoring will determine the number of levels. Badiru (1993) suggests starting with three levels, with level 1 being the final or total project, level 2 being the major tasks or subsections of the project, and level 3 containing definable tasks or subcomponents of level 2. Again, if the project is very complex, the WBS should include additional levels, until the final level specifies discrete activities that can be examined in terms of the time and cost required to complete the activity.

At the final level, the work breakdown structure should include at least two pieces of information that are needed for coordination of effort: the estimated time to complete the activity and the name of an individual who is responsible for seeing that the activity is completed. Often a third piece of information, the estimated cost of completing the activity, is also included. This allows for better integration of cost and schedule information needed to monitor the project. When cost information is included, people refer to the work breakdown structure as a *costed WBS*. Time and cost estimates should be developed by the persons most knowledgeable about those specific activities. Thus, if project team members come from different functional areas, the project manager should likely consult with managers from those different functional areas before making time and cost estimates.

PROGRAM EVALUATION AND REVIEW TECHNIQUE AND CRITICAL PATH METHOD

The WBS provides information on the estimated time of completion for each individual activity, but it does not indicate the order in which the activities can or will take place. It does not indicate whether Activity A must be completed before Activity B can proceed, or whether the two can proceed concurrently. When a project is fairly simple, these interrelationships are not difficult to discern, and a schedule can be constructed directly from the WBS by laying out the activities in the order in which they are to be carried out (see the section on Gantt charts, later in this competency). Alternatively, when a project is complex, it is almost impossible to construct a schedule before the interrelationships among the various activities are made explicit. Network diagrams are graphical tools for making these interrelationships explicit.

In the late 1950s, *Program Evaluation and Review Technique* (PERT) and *Critical Path Method* (CPM), were developed to help with project planning. PERT was introduced by the Special Projects Office of the United States Navy in 1958 as an aid in planning (and controlling) its Polaris Weapon System, a project that involved approximately 3,000 contractors. At virtually the same time, a similar technique, CPM, was introduced by the DuPont Company. The methods are very similar and essentially show the flow of activities from start to finish. Over the years, the two methods have essentially merged and people often refer to PERT/CPM diagrams and/or analysis. As project management computer software has become more sophisticated, other similar approaches have been developed that provide more accurate time estimates, but PERT and CPM are still traditionally used to introduce the basic network diagramming concepts (Dodin, 2006).

PERT/CPM diagrams allow the project manager to see the flow of tasks associated with a project by showing the interrelationships between activities. These diagrams allow the project manager to estimate the time necessary to complete the overall project given the interdependencies among tasks and to identify those critical points where a delay in task completion can have a major effect on overall project completion. In performing the PERT/CPM analysis, one assumes that all tasks or activities can be clearly identified and sequenced and that the time necessary for completing each task or activity can be estimated.

Figure M2.3 shows a simple PERT/CPM diagram. In the diagram, arrows designate activities. The circles at the beginning and end of the arrows are referred to as nodes; they designate starting and ending points for activities. These points in time, called events, consume no time in and of themselves. An activity is referred to as Activity *i,j* or Activity *i-j*, where *i* is the start node and *j* is the end node. Because of the way the diagram is constructed, the PERT/CPM diagram is sometimes referred to as an arrow or activity-on-arrow network diagram. Alternatively, activity-in-node network diagrams, as the name implies, place the activities within the node (usually drawn in

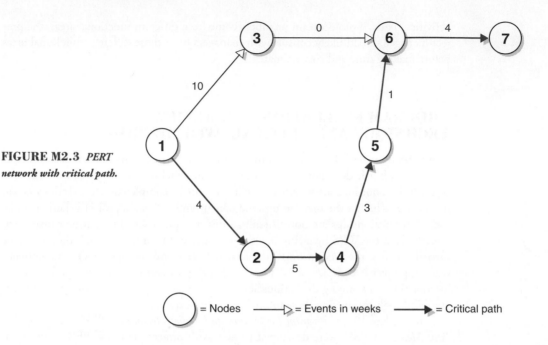

FIGURE M2.3 *PERT network with critical path.*

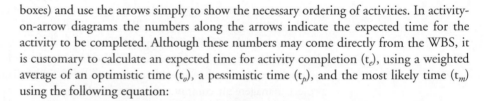

boxes) and use the arrows simply to show the necessary ordering of activities. In activity-on-arrow diagrams the numbers along the arrows indicate the expected time for the activity to be completed. Although these numbers may come directly from the WBS, it is customary to calculate an expected time for activity completion (t_e), using a weighted average of an optimistic time (t_o), a pessimistic time (t_p), and the most likely time (t_m) using the following equation:

$$t_e = (t_o + 4t_m + t_p)/6$$

Note that Activity 3,6 has an expected time of zero weeks. This type of activity, called a dummy activity, is used to indicate that Activity 6,7 cannot begin until Activity 1,3 is complete.

The critical path is that chain of activities that takes the **LONGEST** time to proceed through the network. It indicates the least possible time in which the overall project can be completed, and it is the path that needs to be watched most carefully to ensure that the project stays "on track."

To identify the critical path, it is necessary to understand the concept of *slack* or *float*. In Figure M2.3, the critical path, 1-2-4-5-6-7, takes 17 weeks from start to finish. Note, however, that there is another path, 1-3-6-7, which only takes 14 weeks from start to finish. This means that Activity 1,3 could begin three weeks later than Activity 1,2 and the project would still be completed on time, assuming, of course, that the time estimates are fairly accurate. We then say that Activity 1,3 has a total float or slack of 3 weeks. While this is easy to see in Figure M2.3, it requires more effort when the diagram is more complex.

The first step in identifying the critical path is to identify the earliest start and finish times. Start at the first node of the diagram; this has an earliest start time of zero.

TABLE M2.1 Identifying the Critical Path

Activity	Latest Finish Time (−)	Earliest Start Time (−)	Time Estimate	(=) Float
1, 2	4	0	0	0*
1, 3	13	0	10	3
2, 4	9	4	5	0*
3, 6#	13	10	0	3
4, 5	12	9	3	0*
5, 6	13	12	1	0*
6, 7	17	13	4	0*

*Critical path
#Dummy activity—has no time duration

For the other nodes, the earliest start time equals the earliest finish time of the previous activity. For all activities, the earliest finish time is the sum of the earliest start time plus the estimated time of the activity.

Next, take the largest finish time for the last node and calculate the latest start and finish times by starting at the last node and subtracting the estimated time for completion of that activity from the latest finish time of the previous activity. To identify the critical path, make a list of latest finish times and earliest start times. Time available is then calculated as the difference between the earliest start time and the latest finish time. If available time is equal to the estimated time for completing the activity, there is no float, and that activity is on the critical path. Table M2.1 shows the calculations.

As indicated above, the critical path is important because it is that path that must be most closely monitored. It is the path for which there is no slack, and activities must begin and end on time in order for the project schedule to be met. Activities that are not on the critical path can begin any time between the earliest and latest start dates. The determination is usually made in accordance with the availability of resources, primarily human resources.

Because projects typically require trade-offs among cost, time, and quality, project managers often need to estimate different approaches to the project. Project-crashing analysis can be used to help estimate the trade-offs associated with expediting a particular project by reviewing the costs associated with reducing the amount of time to complete the tasks on the critical path by adding additional resources.

RESOURCE LEVELING

The ultimate purpose of project management is to obtain the most efficient use of resources while still achieving project objectives (being effective). Efficient use of resources can be a problem, however, if there are wide swings in resource needs. Even on carefully planned projects, there may be times when team members feel they can't get enough done as well as times when team members find they do not have enough to do (House, 1988).

Resource leveling is "the process of scheduling work on noncritical activities so that resource requirement on peak days will be reduced" (Kimmons, 1990, p. 79). *Resources* here refers to all project resources that are limited within a specified time period, including personnel, equipment, and materials; resource leveling is most often used to allocate personnel to different project activities. One approach to maximizing the use of people is to use the information from the WBS, together with the information regarding the amount of float, to schedule activities that are not on the critical path.

To determine the optimal use of resources, the project manager needs to begin by assuming that all activities will begin at their earliest start dates. Based on this assumption, the project manager can then draw a graph showing the required personnel, by job type (title), over time. This graph will show peaks, times when there is a great amount of work to be done, and valleys, times when there is less work to be done. Using the PERT/CPM diagram and the table that gives the float associated with each activity, the project manager can then level the resources by moving the start dates for some of the activities that have float to a later time (but prior to the latest start date). The process continues until the changes in personnel requirements from one time period to the next are minimized, that is, until the peaks and valleys are evened. Of course, this type of manual resource leveling is extremely difficult on large, complex projects. Fortunately, in 1986, the resource-leveling paradigm was revolutionized when Primavera Software, Inc. developed an automatic resource leveling tool (Nosbisch & Winter, 2006). Since that time, other automatic resource leveling tools have greatly improved the ability of project managers to deploy resources more efficiently.

GANTT CHARTS

The most popular tool for visually displaying project activities across time is the Gantt chart, developed by Henry L. Gantt in the early part of the twentieth century. These charts are essentially bar charts that allow you to see at a glance how the different activities fit into the overall schedule.

A Gantt chart includes a timeline and a list of each of the major activities, grouped as they are in the work breakdown structure and sequenced as they are expected to occur as a result of the PERT/CPM and resource leveling analyses. The time line for the project is shown along the horizontal axis; the list of activities along the vertical axis. For each activity, a bar shows the time commitment (see Figure M2.4). The Gantt chart is most useful when each activity time is commensurate with the units of time drawn on the horizontal axis. That is, if the horizontal axis is drawn in terms of months, most activities should take at least two months. You can also identify specific milestones, or points of accomplishment, within each task by using a circled number within the bar. In Figure M2.4 the milestones could represent first drafts of status reports due at the end of the activity. While advanced project management software can be used to create Gantt charts, they can also be created in spreadsheet programs such as Microsoft Excel by using a stacked bar chart (Baltzan & Phillips, 2008).

Specialized Gantt Charts.   Once the Gantt chart is constructed, it can be used to integrate information about projected use of time with information about projected use of other resources. Two types of integrated Gantt charts are commonly

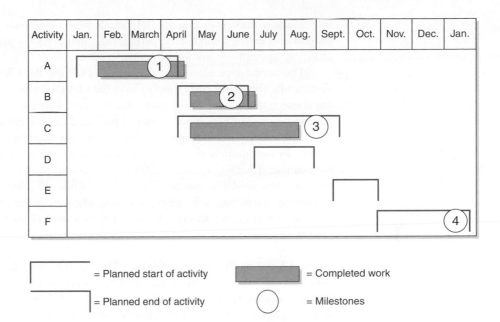

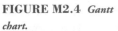

FIGURE M2.4 *Gantt chart.*

used. The first shows personnel task assignments. By listing each individual along the vertical axis, followed by all of the tasks/activities to which that individual is assigned, the project manager can see at a glance which tasks/activities each person is assigned to at each time period of the project (see Figure M2.5). If the task distribution across

FIGURE M2.5 *Personnel task assignments.*

individuals is uneven or if some individuals were mistakenly given too many work assignments during a single time period, this chart gives the project manager another chance to redistribute task assignments.

The second type of integrated Gantt chart is the Bar Chart Cost Schedule (not illustrated). This Gantt chart simply shows the projected cost of each activity below the bar showing that activity in the overall Gantt chart. This allows the project manager to have some sense of how much money is projected to be spent in each time period. It also allows the project manager to calculate the cost slope by dividing the cost of the activity by the duration of that activity (in whatever unit of time is being used). Thus, for example, if Activity A costs $4,500 and is expected to take three weeks to complete, the cost slope in dollars per week is $1,500. While this piece of information is not interesting in isolation, it becomes interesting when the project manager compares it to the cost slopes of other activities because it gives a sense of the relative cost of activities per time period.

Gantt Charts as Monitoring Tools.   The Gantt chart is also a useful project monitoring tool. By using different colors or different symbols, the Gantt chart can help the project manager track how closely the project is keeping to the planned schedule. When a given task runs over the allotted time, the Gantt chart can be used to determine whether or not the schedule needs to be rethought. Figure M2.4 shows that Activities A and B ran over schedule approximately one week each, whereas Activity C was completed almost one month ahead of schedule.

HUMAN RESOURCE MATRIX

One final planning tool is the human resource matrix. As with the Gantt chart used to show the personnel task assignments, this matrix can be used to see whether workload is evenly distributed across individuals. The human resource matrix lists the tasks/activities along the vertical axis and the names across the top of the matrix (see Figure M2.6). For each task/activity one person is designated as having primary responsibility (P), and others may be designated as having secondary responsibility (S). Other designations can be also be added as needed. For example, one can label an individual as (C) if that individual needs to be consulted, or (B) if a person can provide backup, and so on. Project teams need to be able to adapt the project management tools to best meet their needs.

FIGURE M2.6 *Human resource matrix.*

TASK	CHRIS	LINDA	MARTY	PAT	SAM
1				P	
2	S		S	C	P
3		P	S	C	
4	P		S	C	

One advantage of this chart over the personnel task assignment chart is that it is clear whether or not time spent on the project is time in a leadership capacity. Further, it makes it clear at a glance whether someone has too many leadership (primary) assignments. Alternatively, while it tells who is assigned to which task/activity, it is not as informative as the personnel task assignment chart with respect to how much time is being spent during each time period by each person. Therefore, it is probably wise to use the two charts together for keeping track of how human resources are being utilized.

PROJECT MONITORING

As indicated in the beginning of this section, monitoring is essentially keeping track of progress over the life of the project. There are four primary resources that need to be monitored: time, money, people, and materials. Monitoring involves looking at actual expenditures of resources, comparing actual with estimated, and, where necessary, deciding what adjustments need to be made in the work plan to accommodate discrepancies between actual and estimated.

COST/SCHEDULE INTEGRATION GRAPHS

In the previous section, we gave examples of planning tools that can be used in monitoring the use of human resources and time. Here we will focus on the project budget and time. Note that the tools provided here can be used to look at the total budget or at specific components of the budget, and so they are applicable to monitoring the use of human resources and materials as well.

Cost Variances. In monitoring the budget, the project manager is concerned with two types of information. The first involves the amount of money budgeted for the work to be performed (budgeted cost of work performed—BCWP) versus the actual cost of performing the work (actual cost of work performed—ACWP). The difference between the two quantities (BCWP—ACWP), called the cost variance, is an indication of how close the estimated costs were to actual costs, with a positive number indicating monetary savings and a negative number indicating a budget overrun. (Again, note that these variances can be calculated for the total budget or by category of expenditure.)

Schedule Variances. The second type of information involves the amount of money projected to be spent on the actual work performed during the time period (budgeted cost of work performed—BCWP) versus the amount scheduled to be spent during the time period (budgeted cost of work scheduled—BCWS). The difference between the two quantities (BCWP—BCWS), called the schedule variance, is an indication of whether the money is being spent according to the projected schedule. Here a positive number is an indication that the project is running ahead of schedule—that is, more work is being performed than was originally scheduled—whereas a negative number is an indication that the project is running behind schedule—less work is being performed than was actually scheduled. Alternatively, a negative number could be an indication that some work is being performed out of its scheduled sequence. Harrison (1992) suggests that schedule variance should not be looked at separately from the formal scheduling system; that is, this information should be examined in conjunction with the Gantt chart or PERT/CPM network diagram to determine the actual status of specific activities or milestones.

Cost and schedule variances can be examined graphically or in a table. To examine these variances graphically, the project manager needs to calculate at each time period a cumulative BCWS, BCWP, and ACWP. That is, for each reporting period (usually monthly) the project manager needs to calculate the total scheduled budget up to that time period (cumulative BCWS), the total projected budget for the work that has actually been performed up to that time period (cumulative BCWP), and the total budget actually spent up to that time period (cumulative ACWP). The three amounts are plotted at each time period along the vertical axis, with time across the horizontal axis. The points are then connected to make a smooth curve (see Figure M2.7). Note that the cumulative BCWS curve extends from the lower-left corner, where no money has been budgeted to be spent before the beginning of the project, to the upper-right corner, where all the money is budgeted to be spent by the end of the project. When the cumulative BCWP curve lies above the cumulative ACWP curve, then the project is running under budget. Alternatively, if the cumulative ACWP lies above the cumulative BCWP curve, the project is running over budget, and the project manager needs to understand why. Similarly, if the cumulative BCWS lies below the BCWP, then the project may well be running ahead of schedule. Alternatively, if the BCWS lies above the BCWP, then the amount that the project manager expected to spend up to that time period is less than the amount actually being spent, and the project may be behind schedule. In Figure M2.7, the project was initially running under budget but is now running considerably over budget. It was also initially behind schedule, but is catching up.

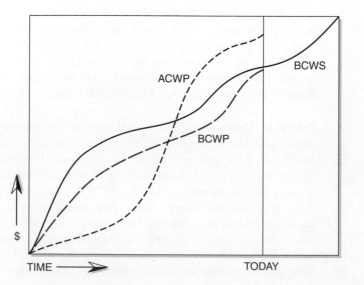

FIGURE M2.7 *Schedule integration chart.*

A *performance analysis report* presents cost and schedule variance in a tabular form. This report is usually generated on a monthly basis, although, depending on the complexity of the project, it could be done more or less often. The report includes two tables, one with information about performance in the current time period and the second with information about cumulative performance. The first table presents five pieces of information for each category of expenditure: the amount budgeted for this time period (BCWS), the amount budgeted for the work performed (BCWP), the amount actually spent in the current time period (ACWP), and the schedule and cost variance. The second table repeats this format, providing cumulative information.

Again, the project manager should be concerned when the performance analysis report indicates negative cost or schedule variances. In some cases, project variances may be related to scope creep—the expansion of the project requirements beyond the original plan due to small changes that are made over the course of time. Those seemingly small changes can add up to big differences in the scope of a project, so keeping track of them is essential. In some cases, it may be appropriate to renegotiate the terms of the project, so it is critical for project managers to have solid data to justify any request for changes in resource allocations or deadlines.

ANALYSIS Planning a Training Course

Objective This exercise asks you to analyze the tasks in a project using the tools that we have discussed.

Directions Read the following scenario and respond to the questions that follow. Your instructor may have you work individually or in small groups.

Congratulations! You have your first project manager assignment. You were asked to be the project team leader for the team that is going to design a new management training course in your organization. Here is the background information:

Last week your boss found your copy of *Becoming a Master Manager* sitting on your shelf and decided to borrow it. After reading through the book, your boss shared it with the head of the Training and Development (T&D) Unit, and they both agreed that it would provide an ideal foundation for the new management training course that was being discussed. Even though you do not know much about training, they decided that you would be an ideal project manager for the team designing the training since you are familiar with the framework. After receiving the assignment, you met with the head of T&D and agreed on a few basic concepts regarding the training program: (1) The program should run either one week or two; (2) the curriculum should be accompanied by two types of evaluation, one based on participant reaction and one based on the actual changes in work behavior when the participants return to the job; (3) the project team should conduct a needs assessment (i.e., you should interview managers) in the three divisions that will be the heaviest users of the training program to determine what they would like to see included in the curriculum; (4) you should develop some new cases or exercises based on the outcomes of the needs assessment; and (5) you should set up an advisory committee of upper-level managers from across the organization to approve the curriculum and the evaluation instruments.

Fortunately, you have some good people on your team from the training unit, and after meeting with them a few times, they volunteered to put together an initial schedule. This morning you found a memo on your desk explaining that they had developed a schedule based on a proposed list of activities with estimated times and a PERT/CPM analysis. The memo indicated that the list of activities, the PERT/CPM network diagram, and a proposed schedule were all attached to the memo, but all you could find was the following list of activities with time estimates:

Activity	Description	Estimated time (in weeks)
1,2	Track literature on evaluation	4
1,4	Set up steering committee	1
1,5	Develop needs assessment questionnaire	2
2,3	Develop reaction evaluation instrument	1
2,10	Dummy activity	0
3,11	Dummy activity	0
4,9	Meet with advisory committee to discuss curriculum	1
5,6	Conduct needs assessment in first division	4
5,7	Conduct needs assessment in second division	2
5,8	Conduct needs assessment in third division	2
6,9	Analyze data and develop cases and exercise	3
7,9	Analyze data and develop cases and exercise	2
8,9	Analyze data and develop cases and exercise	2
9,10	Develop first draft of curriculum	10
10,11	Develop behavior evaluation instrument	3
10,12	Advisory committee reviews curriculum	2
11,13	Advisory committee reviews evaluation instruments	2
12,14	Curriculum revisions based on advisory committee input	2
13,14	Evaluation revisions based on advisory committee input	1
14,15	Conduct two pilot training courses	4

When you tried calling the team members who drafted the memo, you were told that they were away for the next two days at a training conference and no one else knew anything about what they were working on. You have a breakfast meeting scheduled with your boss and the head of the training unit tomorrow morning to discuss the schedule.

1. Based on the list of activities, prepare a PERT/CPM network diagram. What is the critical path?

2. Create a chart of earliest and latest start and finish times. Determine the critical path. What is the shortest time from start to finish?

3. What are your current scheduling concerns? Assuming that you do not have unlimited resources, make a few suggestions for resource leveling and set up a Gantt chart.

4. What concerns do you have about internal and/or external integration? How do you think you should handle these concerns?

Reflection   Manually working through examples may seem unnecessary, given the availability of computer software for project management, but working through problems helps project managers develop a clear understanding of the fundamental planning and scheduling concepts on which the software is based. That conceptual understanding is critical for managers, particularly those who wish to obtain credentials in the area of project management from the Project Management Institute (PMI). Five different credentials can be earned from PMI. For each credential, applicants must meet the education and experience requirements and pass an examination.

PRACTICE   The Job Fair

Objective   The previous exercise gave you the chance to apply some of the tools of project management, but often it is coming up with the list of tasks that is the most daunting part of the project manager's responsibilities. This exercise asks you to take a step back and figure out on your own what tasks would be required to complete a complex project.

Directions   The president of the student association has asked for volunteers to organize a job fair, to be held in conjunction with the annual meeting of the Regional Management Association, and you think this is a great opportunity to try out your project management skills. The job fair was discussed during the last meeting of the student association, and there was a general consensus that:

- The job fair should take place during the first morning of the annual meeting.
- It should provide an opportunity for graduating students to meet potential employers and vice versa. Therefore, potential employers in the private, public, and nonprofit sectors will be invited.
- Organizations (potential employers) will be expected to "rent" a table so that they can advertise their organization.
- Students (potential employees) will be expected to submit an updated résumé to be placed in a résumé book that will be distributed at the job fair to all organizations that rent a table.

The job fair is three months away.

1. Start by thinking about all the activities that need to occur in order to make the job fair a success. (Here are some major tasks to keep in mind: advertising the job fair, contacting potential employers, organizing the résumé book and getting it printed in advance, arranging for the setup of tables. You may think of others.)
2. Create a work breakdown structure.
3. Propose a Gantt chart.

Reflection   In addition to the project planning and scheduling tools discussed in this module, don't forget to take advantage of other resources—particularly existing knowledge. Although planning a job fair might be a brand new task for you, staff members in the Career Services Office at a college or university are likely to be well versed in organizing these types of events and may be happy to share their knowledge with you over a cup of tea. We will talk more about the value of personal networks for gathering information and assistance in Module 4.

APPLICATION   Managing Your Own Project

Objective   Now that you have some experience using project management tools and coming up with task lists, it is time for you to tackle your own project.

Directions Choose a complex project or a program in which you are involved at school or work, or in a community organization to which you belong. If you cannot think of any such projects, think about a complex project you would like to undertake, such as organizing a fund-raising event for a nonprofit organization that you think does good work.

Write a proposal designed to convince other people to support your project. Start with a brief description of the project and what you consider to be the most challenging aspects of its planning. Then, using the planning tools presented in this competency (SOW, WBS, PERT/CPM, Gantt charts), show how you would plan to complete the project on time and within cost. If there are important issues of internal and external integration that will affect the success of the project, discuss how these issues will be handled.

Reflection Planning a complex project is typically not something that is done in a single session and then cast in stone. Many issues may arise that cause implementation activities to deviate from the original plan. The more complex the project, the more opportunities there are for problems to emerge. The fact that many projects fail to meet their objectives (Anatatmula, 2008) serves to emphasize the importance of project management skills in organizations today.

Module 2 Competency 4   Measuring and Monitoring Performance and Quality

ASSESSMENT   Identifying Appropriate Performance Criteria

Objective The first three competencies in this module focused primarily on different ways to accomplish tasks. For this competency, we turn our attention to the metrics that are used to evaluate your performance toward achieving critical outcomes.

Directions 1. Consider your current job, or if you are not currently employed, think about your job as a student. What are the most critical *outcomes* of your job—what are you actually trying to accomplish (e.g., sell 1,000 cases of wine; create an award-winning advertising campaign; learn how to analyze financial statements; earn an MBA, etc.).

2. Next, think about the tasks that you are asked to perform as part of your job. Are those tasks clearly linked to the outcome that you are trying to achieve? Are there some activities that seem to be unnecessary, or even counterproductive, for your outcome goals?

3. Finally, identify the points at which you receive feedback about your performance, as well as the types of feedback that you receive. You may find it helpful to construct a simple diagram that incorporates a time line to show when you perform different tasks and when you receive feedback.

Discussion Questions 1. How satisfied were you with your performance feedback prior to completing this exercise?

2. When considered in more detail, is the feedback that you receive specific and relevant to your tasks and critical outcomes? Do you receive the feedback on a timely basis?

3. Did any of the feedback that you receive seem irrelevant to your critical outcomes?

4. Are there any things that you would like to receive feedback about that you currently do not?

Reflection   Although providing feedback has been linked to better motivation and performance (as we shall see in Module 3, Competency 3—Motivating Self and Others), lack of timely feedback is still a common complaint in organizations. (One of us once submitted an annual self-evaluation in September and did not receive feedback from the Dean until the following July!) One solution to the challenge of providing timely feedback is to make performance criteria explicit and provide employees with methods to monitor their own performance. For example, rather than waiting until after the semester is over to get formal student evaluation feedback, some faculty take advantage of web-mediated survey systems to gather student perceptions early in the semester so they can respond to concerns when they arise, rather than after the students have completed the course. Monitoring progress and providing feedback at frequent intervals may add slightly to short-term costs, but the long-term benefits can be very worthwhile.

LEARNING   Measuring and Monitoring Performance and Quality

Establishing and maintaining stability and control depends upon having effective measurement and monitoring systems. For example, we count inventory to be sure there is enough on hand to meet anticipated demand and to identify losses from spoilage or theft. We review medical charts to see if patients have been given appropriate treatments. We record the number and length of telephone calls a customer service representative handles in a day to evaluate his productivity. We observe employees to be sure their appearance and behavior fit with our professional norms. All these measures are relevant, but are they the most important things to measure and monitor? This competency is designed to help managers find answers to that surprisingly complex question.

DECIDING WHAT TO MONITOR AND HOW TO MEASURE IT

What happens when organizations fail to monitor the right processes and outcomes? Steven Kerr (1975) addressed this question in his classic article, "On the Folly of Rewarding A While Hoping for B." Kerr provided multiple examples of situations where organizations were measuring the wrong things, resulting in reward systems that actually discouraged employees from achieving their stated goals! For example, telephone service representatives may be told that their goal is to satisfy the customer. If, however, their compensation is based solely on how many calls they handle in an hour, then they have an incentive to get customers off the phone as quickly as possible.

In explaining why reward systems sometimes use measures that are inappropriate for maximizing organizational efficiency, Kerr identified four causes. Two causes relate to the characteristics of the measurement itself. First, organizations tend to be fascinated with "objective" criteria, rather than more qualitative subjective measures. Second, organizations tend to overemphasize highly visible behavior. Both these causes are consistent with the idea that organizations tend to measure what is easy, rather than trying to measure what is most relevant. A third cause of inappropriate measurement, according to Kerr, is hypocrisy—where the stated "goals" are not actually the true goals. Finally, Kerr suggested that sometimes reward systems are designed to emphasize something other than efficiency, such as morality or equity.

More than 30 years after Kerr's classic article appeared, organizations still make serious errors when it comes to monitoring and measuring organizational processes and outcomes and rewarding employees. The potential magnitude of this problem should not be underestimated, as the recent near collapse of the global financial system can attest. Three of Kerr's four causes are relevant to that crisis.

In analyzing the events leading up to the beginning of the global financial crisis in mid-2007, Taub (2009) describes an environment in which it had become much easier for originators to sell loans in the secondary market. These sales effectively transferred risk from the loan originator to a third party. As a result, it became more common to write loans without appropriately measuring debtors' ability to repay loans. In addition, because repayments were now going to another entity, it was easier to reward people based on the amount of loans originated, rather than based on whether the loan was actually repaid. These incentives, when combined with the elimination of regulations requiring documentation, led to an upsurge in so-called liar loans—loans that did not require any documentation to verify income. The only measures that mattered were the number and amounts of loans originated, which were easy to measure because they were objective and visible. Hypocrisy also came into play because the true goals were focused on increasing the amount of fees generated by originating and selling loans, rather than on making loans only to clients who could afford to repay them.

Not surprisingly, the profound lack of control in the financial industry had major negative repercussions that are still being felt, and new regulations are being formulated to avoid these types of problems in the future. In the United States, critics of banking deregulation have pointed to the 1999 repeal of portions of the Glass-Steagall Act of 1933 (enacted following the Great Depression to reform the banking system) as a key factor in the crisis and now are seeking new banking regulation. In the U.K., the Financial Services Authority issued new rules in October 2009 to eliminate self-certified ("liar") loans (Collinson & Jones, 2009).

DEVELOPING A HIERARCHY OF MEASURES

By honing their understanding of measuring performance and quality, managers can play an important role helping to identify measures that are most closely linked with the critical outcomes for the organization. Walsh (2005) notes that companies often substitute surrogate measures for exact measures of achievement because of the costs associated with the measurement process. For example, surveying customers to learn whether they feel that service quality has improved is more costly than inferring improvements in service quality based on decreasing numbers of customer complaints. Because not all customers who are dissatisfied complain, however, this proxy measure may miss important information.

To help organizations develop a comprehensive set of indicators that measure progress and achievement, Walsh (2005) outlines a measurement hierarchy. Following Simons (2000), Walsh first classifies measures based on the characteristics of objectivity, completeness, and responsiveness.

- **Objective** measures can be verified independently, in contrast to subjective measures that are dependent on personal judgment.

- Measures that capture *all* of the attributes that are relevant in defining performance are classified as **Complete;** the fewer attributes captured, the less complete the measure.

- Measures are considered **Responsive** if the manager can act to influence the measure; the more direct and powerful that influence, the more responsive the measure.

As an example, share price is an objective measure, but because other factors such as interest rates and investor sentiment also affect share price, it is not a fully responsive measure (Walsh, 2005). Ideally, organizations would define measures that were objective, complete, and responsive. In reality, objective measures often are not complete because they fail to capture important information, particularly for intangibles such as "service quality." To measure service quality, subjective measures drawn from a customer satisfaction survey are likely to convey more useful and accurate information than objective measures of sales volume.

In addition to distinguishing between objectivity, completeness, and responsiveness, Walsh (2005) also considers whether measures focus on outcomes, processes, or initiatives. At the top of Walsh's hierarchy are **Exact Measures of Outcomes.** These are complete measures that cover all the key attributes for the outcome under consideration. Exact measures of outcomes may be objective or subjective and may have different levels of responsiveness.

Next are **Proxy Measures of Outcomes;** proxy measures are used to make inferences about exact measures. For example, an increase in customer referrals may be used to infer that service quality has improved. Proxy measures are incomplete but are often used because they are easier and less expensive to obtain. Both exact measures of outcomes and proxy measures of outcomes are intended to reflect *achievement of strategic objectives* (in the example above, for instance, improving service quality).

Simply measuring achievement/outcomes, however, may not be sufficient. For an organization to improve outcomes, it also needs to understand and measure the processes and initiatives that lead up to those outcomes. Thus, **Process Measures** of **Outputs**, **Activities**, and **Inputs** make up the third level. Process measures reflect the *degree of effort being exerted.* Effort alone is not sufficient to guarantee desired outcomes, of course, but it can be an important lever for improvement. The fourth and final level of the hierarchy includes **Measures of Initiative Progress.** These measures provide information on the *changes being made* by the organization (Walsh, 2005). As with effort exerted, simply making changes may not result in the desired outcomes. Reviewing measures that are currently being used in light of this hierarchy can help to ensure that no important indicators are being omitted.

For many organizations, the choice of measures used is affected by external factors such as accrediting organizations, and in some cases, that data is made available to the public. For example the Centers for Medicare and Medicaid Services (CMS) post data on process and outcome measures for U.S. hospitals on the Hospital Compare web site (http://www.hospitalcompare.hhs.gov). With respect to cardiac care, the CMS initially focused on process measures that can improve the quality of care; in 2007 the CMS proposed adding 30-day mortality outcomes to these measures (Krumholz, Normand, Spertus, Shahian & Bradley, 2007). In July 2009, the CMC announced that in addition to process measures and mortality rates, data on readmissions were also being added.

TAILORING MEASURES TO THE ORGANIZATION AND ITS MISSION

The hierarchy of measures presented above is general enough to be used in any type of organization. The identification of specific measures that should be collected and analyzed will depend on the mission and strategic objectives of the organization. Measuring items for which there are common industry benchmarks can provide a sound basis for comparison, but these measures may not be sufficient, depending on the mission of the organization.

In recent years, many companies have attempted to expand the way they measure performance. For example, the popular balanced scorecard approach (Kaplan & Norton, 1992) includes not only the financial perspective, but also the customer perspective, internal business perspective, and innovation and learning perspective. Incorporating these four perspectives helps to guard against suboptimization (Kaplan & Norton, 1992). More recently, Kaplan (2005) has suggested that the balanced scorecard is the contemporary manifestation of the McKinsey 7-S model (strategy, structure, systems, staff, skills, style/culture, shared values), which gained popularity as a result of Peters and Waterman's (1982) bestseller, *In Search of Excellence.* The balanced scorecard and similar approaches to measuring organizational performance still focus primarily on what is good for the company and ultimately the shareholder. Recently Wicks and St. Clair (2007) argued that more attention was needed on measures related to employee well being. For some, however, even that focus is still too narrow.

In recent years there has been a growing interest in measuring organizational performance on more than just operational and financial outcomes. The concept of the "triple bottom line" gained currency in the late 1990s after the publication of John Elkington's *Cannibals with Forks: The Triple Bottom Line of 21st Century Business* (Norman & MacDonald, 2004). Supporters of the triple bottom line approach argue that organizational success should be measured not only in terms of financial performance, but also with respect to social/ethical performance and environmental performance. Waddock, Bodwell, and Graves (2002) go so far as to suggest that the pressure that stakeholders have put on corporations to be more socially and environmentally responsible has created a new business imperative. Box M2.2 discusses one such effort by Better World Shopping and highlights the reporting of Seventh Generation, which leads the list of best companies identified by Better World Shopping.

BOX M2.2 BEYOND SHAREHOLDER RETURNS

The brainchild of Ellis Jones, Better World Shopper is a web site that is "dedicated to providing people with a comprehensive, up-to-date, reliable account of the social and environmental responsibility of every company on the planet AND making it available in practical forms that individuals can use in their everyday lives."

With a Ph.D. in sociology and an urge to build connections among academics, activists, and everyday citizens, Dr. Jones uses his research skills to analyze the performance records of companies on five different dimensions: (1) the environment, (2) human rights, (3) animal protection, (4) community involvement, and (5) social justice. Company rankings have been developed as part of a five-year research project that resulted in an extensive database. The database includes information on over 1,000 companies and was built using more than 25 different sources, some going back as far as 20 years.

The Top 10 companies as ranked by Better World Shopper are: Seventh Generation, Working Assets, Eden Foods, Organic Valley, Clif Bar, Honest Tea, Patagonia, Tom's of Maine, Ben & Jerry's, and Aveda. Given its emphasis on environmentally-friendly products, it isn't surprising that Seventh Generation tops the list. The name comes from "the Great Law of the Iroquois: In our every deliberation, we must consider the impact of our decisions on the next seven generations." In addition to its focus on environmentally-friendly products, transparency also is important to the company. Seventh Generation measures and reports on its social performance in areas such as charitable giving and diversity of employees. The company also pays close attention to the needs of its employees. For example, in its 2008 report, Seventh Generation publicly recognized that it had allowed its rapid growth to negatively affect the work/home balance that it strives to support.

Sources: Based on information presented on the Better World Shopper web site (http://www.betterworldshopper.com), the Seventh Generation web site (http://www.seventhgeneration.com/), and Seventh Generation's (2008) Corporate Consciousness Report: Crossroads: Reinventing the purpose and possibility of business.

Even for people who support the idea of evaluating organizations based on corporate social responsibility, there remains the problem of how these activities should be measured and monitored. For example, Norman and MacDonald (2004) argue that because no clear, standardized measures exist for social and environmental bottom lines, companies may benefit by adopting the rhetoric of the triple bottom line without actually changing their actions. Efforts such as the United Nations Global Compact are one attempt to move toward more standardization for social and environmental reporting. The UN Global Compact has established 10 principles for socially responsible corporate behavior related to issues of human rights, labor, the environment, and anticorruption. The voluntary organization encourages reporting in the belief that transparency about corporate activities will help lead to more socially responsible behavior. You can read more about this organization and its principles at http://www.unglobalcompact.org. While a step in the right direction, Chen and Bouvain (2009) found that although membership in the UN Global Compact had some impact in the areas of the environment and workers, there were still significant variations in how much corporate social responsibility was promoted in different countries.

Despite the substantial growth of interest in corporate social responsibility, not all business observers and academic researchers are convinced that changing business models to improve the social and environmental bottom lines is a good trade-off (Hayward, 2003). This brings us back to the key concern for every organization, no matter how it defines its mission: What drives organizational effectiveness?

IDENTIFYING DRIVERS OF ORGANIZATIONAL EFFECTIVENESS

As organizations continue to increase in complexity, it becomes more and more complicated to identify the key drivers of organizational effectiveness. Beginning in the mid-1980s, research on enhancing organizational effectiveness began focusing on three main approaches: total quality management (TQM), downsizing, and reengineering (Cameron & Thompson, 2000). Of these three approaches to enhancing organizational effectiveness, TQM devotes the most attention to diverse measures of performance and quality. Despite that fact, in their review of research on TQM, Cameron and Thompson (2000) concluded that "the studies that have attempted to evaluate the success of TQM efforts according to some standardized indicators of success do not inspire enthusiasm" (p. 216). Part of the problem appears to be due to inconsistency in applying TQM throughout the organization. One system that takes a comprehensive approach to quality is the Baldrige Criteria for Performance Excellence.

BALDRIGE CRITERIA FOR PERFORMANCE EXCELLENCE

Since 1987, the Baldrige Criteria (the Criteria) have been used by thousands of U.S. organizations to stay abreast of ever-increasing competition and to improve organizational performance practices, capabilities, and results; to facilitate communication and sharing of best practices information for organizations of all types; and to serve as a working tool for understanding and managing performance and for guiding organizational planning and opportunities for learning. The core values and concepts upon which the Criteria are built include "visionary leadership, customer-driven excellence, organizational and personal learning, valuing employees and partners, agility, focus on the future, managing for innovation, management by fact, social responsibility, focus on results and creating value, systems perspective" (NIST, 2005, p. 1).

The Baldrige Criteria go beyond measuring financial performance and incorporate a broad range of constituents. Outcomes continue to be important, but the Criteria also emphasize developing, deploying, and integrating processes that are aligned with the organization's strategic planning process. Outcome measures serve to complete the feedback loop in the strategic planning process.

The connection between quality processes associated with the Baldrige Criteria and outcome measures has been evaluated by the U.S. General Accounting Office (GAO). Looking at data from the 1988 and 1989 Malcolm Baldrige National Quality Awards (MBNQA), the U.S. GAO found that those companies that had been selected as finalists for the quality of their processes also showed improvements in specific outcome measures. Table M2.2 shows the annual percentage improvement for specific outcome measures.

Stock market analyses prepared by the National Institute of Standards and Technology (NIST) from 1994 through 2001 showed that Baldrige winners generally outperformed the S&P 500 (NIST, 2010). The studies were discontinued in 2004 because "the vast majority of Award recipients since then [2004] are either business units of larger publicly traded companies, privately held companies, or nonprofit organizations" (NIST, 2010).

OTHER APPROACHES TO IMPROVING PERFORMANCE

The literature on improving performance and quality is extensive, and many organizations have learned from a variety of techniques over the years, including the zero defects and quality is free approaches, TQM, quality circles, kaizen, ISO 9000, the Baldrige

TABLE M2.2 Results of a U.S. General Accounting Office Study of the Relationships between Quality Processes and Desired Outcomes

Outcome Category Measures	Reported Annual Improvement (%)
Employee-related indicators	
Employee satisfaction	1.4
Attendance	0.1
Turnover (decrease)	6.0
Safety and health	1.8
Suggestions	16.6
Operating indicators	
Reliability	11.3
On-time delivery	4.7
Order-processing time	12.0
Errors or defects	10.3
Product lead time	5.8
Inventory turnover	7.2
Costs of quality	9.0
Customer satisfaction indicators	
Overall customer satisfaction	2.5
Customer complaints (decrease)	11.6
Customer retention	1.0
Financial performance indicators	
Market share	13.7
Sales per employee	8.6
Return on assets	1.3
Return on sales	0.4

Criteria, and Six Sigma (Bisgaard & DeMast, 2006). Recent writings on using enterprise resource planning (ERP) software (Laframboise & Reyes, 2005) with TQM, implementing formal business performance measurement (BPM) approaches (Marr, 2005), applying quality assurance techniques to global supply chain management (Bandyopadhyar, 2005), and conducting self-assessments with the European Foundation for Quality Management (EFQM) Excellence Model (Benavent, 2006) continue to expand approaches for improving organizational performance. As technology continues to advance and societal expectations for corporations are constantly revisited, the skills and knowledge associated with monitoring and measuring performance and quality will be critical for organizational success. As Heras (2005, p. 54) notes, "A strategy with no indicators is wishful thinking, and indicators not aligned with strategy are a waste of time and effort."

ANALYSIS   Improving Performance in the Health Care Industry

Objective   The objective of this exercise is to develop a set of performance metrics for a hospital according to the measurement hierarchy outlined by Walsh (2005) and described in this competency. This will hone your ability to distinguish different types of measures.

Directions   St. Angela's Hospital has decided to adopt the Baldrige Criteria for Performance Excellence to help it meet its mission: providing the highest quality health care in a caring, community setting. You have been asked to head up a taskforce to address Criteria 3.2, part b, related to customer satisfaction and loyalty. Use the abbreviated version of instructions from *2006 Health Care Criteria for Performance Excellence* instrument shown below to prepare a brief report that proposes a set of measures you think are needed to give the hospital the data needed to improve performance with respect to patient satisfaction. (For more detailed information, you can find the entire Criteria at http://www.baldrige.nist.gov/HealthCare_Criteria.htm.)

In that report you need to:

1. Identify where each measure fits in terms of Walsh's (2005) hierarchy (e.g., Exact Outcome, Proxy Outcome, Process, or Initiative Measure).

2. Describe each measure in terms of its Objectivity, Completeness, and Responsiveness.

3. Justify that the combination of measures being recommended will capture the data necessary to meet this Criteria without imposing too high a cost on St. Angela's Hospital.

3.2 b. PATIENT Satisfaction Determination (abridged from the Criteria, see NIST, 2006).

1. HOW do you determine PATIENT satisfaction and dissatisfaction? HOW do you ensure that your measurements capture actionable information for use in securing your PATIENTS' future interactions with your organization, and gaining positive referrals, as appropriate? HOW do you use PATIENT satisfaction and dissatisfaction information for improvement?

2. HOW do you follow up with PATIENTS on the quality of HEALTH CARE SERVICES and transactions to receive prompt and actionable feedback?

3. HOW do you obtain and use information on PATIENTS' satisfaction relative to their satisfaction with your competitors, other organizations providing similar HEALTH CARE SERVICES, and/or health care industry BENCHMARKS?

4. HOW do you keep your APPROACHES to determining satisfaction current with HEALTH CARE SERVICE needs and directions?

Reflection   The type of measures that organizations choose to collect and the ways in which data are categorized can convey important messages about organizational values. But often organizations send mixed messages. In health care, high standards of performance are expected, but beliefs that perfection is attainable can result in pressure to cover up mistakes, particularly when investigations of errors focus on blaming individuals rather than identifying problems with organizational systems (Jones, 2002).

PRACTICE   Developing Education Performance Metrics

Objective   This exercise will give you a chance to develop a set of performance metrics for your own education. Try to identify measures that you think are most critical for meeting your future goals.

Directions   1. Think about what your strategic objectives are for getting an education at this point in your life. As you work on developing a list of objectives, try to think about more than just getting a degree (although that may be one of your strategic objectives) and think about WHY you want to get that degree.

2. For each of the strategic objectives that you listed, identify some key measures that will help you determine whether or not you are on track to achieve that objective. Remember, one objective may require several different measures to adequately capture whether or not that objective has been achieved.

3. Compare the objectives and measures that you have developed. Do you see any objectives that appear to be contradictory? Are there any measures that show up for multiple objectives? How much control do you have over achieving your objectives?

4. Now, consider what the instructor can do to help you achieve your objectives. What measures would be appropriate for assessing the instructor's performance relative to your objectives?

5. Finally, reconsider the situation from the perspective of your instructor. Do you think your instructor has the same objectives that you do? Why or why not? If there are differences between your objectives and the objectives of your instructor, how can those differences be reconciled?

Reflection   In many jobs, outcomes are not entirely controllable by the person who is tasked with getting the job accomplished. Doctors who treat patients often must depend on patients to take medications, participate in physical therapy, or avoid certain activities. The desired outcome of a healthy patient is not solely in the hands of the doctor. Likewise, the outcome of an educated student depends not only on the actions of the teacher, but also on the actions of the students, as well as on circumstances beyond the control of either the teacher or students. In situations where there is mutual responsibility, it may be tempting to focus on the performance of the other party, rather than on our own responsibilities. Finding the best balance of performance metrics in these types of situations is doubly difficult, but it is also doubly important.

APPLICATION   Developing Performance Metrics for Your Job

Objective   In the Assessment for this competency, we asked you to think about the type of performance feedback you receive in your current position. This exercise gives you an opportunity to use the tools we have discussed to develop enhanced performance metrics for your job.

Directions   Develop a new performance evaluation form for your job. Be sure that you include measures for Outcomes, as well as Processes and Initiatives. Think about how Objective, Complete, and Responsive the measures are, individually and as a set. Discuss your new evaluation form with your supervisor, and then revise them as needed.

Reflection   Thinking about how you are being evaluated can help you identify ways to improve your performance in your current job. Just as important, however, is thinking about where you would like to see yourself in the future. Are there some tasks that you could begin to delegate? As we discussed in Module 1, Competency 3—Mentoring and Developing Others, delegating can both help you improve your supervisory skills and free up time for developing skills in new areas. Perhaps you can incorporate some metrics for leading new initiatives into your performance evaluation to demonstrate your ability to manage change in your organization, a topic that we address in Module 4, Competency 5—Implementing and Sustaining Change.

Module 2 Competency 5   Encouraging and Enabling Compliance

ASSESSMENT   Reactions to Methods of Encouraging Compliance

Objective   This exercise is designed to help you assess your attitudes about complying with rules and how you tend to respond to different methods used to encourage compliance.

Directions   First, think about how frequently you engage in the following behaviors, and rate yourself using the following scale: 0 = Never; 1 = Rarely; 2 = Sometimes; 3 = Often

1. Drive faster than the posted speed limit
2. Skip classes
3. Arrive late to meetings
4. Submit assignments that don't reflect your best effort

Next, think about why you behave as you do.

1. What factors are influencing your behavior in each of these situations?
2. What assumptions are you making about the "rule" associated with each situation?

Finally, consider how you would feel and whether your behavior would change under the following circumstances.

1. a. The cost of speeding tickets was doubled.
   b. People caught speeding had to attend an automobile safety class.
   c. People with no speeding tickets during a calendar year received a check for $25 in January of the following year.
2. a. Students earned extra-credit points for each class attended.
   b. Students lost points from their overall average for each class missed.
   c. Students were required to write a paper for each missed class.
3. a. Your boss drew attention to your lateness when you arrived at the meeting.
   b. Your boss spoke to you after the meeting about being on time in the future.
   c. You discovered that before you arrived a task you really wanted to work on had been assigned to someone else.
4. a. Your instructor recorded a low grade on the assignment you submitted.
   b. Your instructor asked you to revise and resubmit the assignment.
   c. Your instructor asked you to come to office hours to discuss the assignment.

Reflection   It is critical for managers to understand that individuals may respond differently to different methods of encouraging compliance. For example, some people may resent what they perceive to be "bribes" for good behavior. Others may feel that "threats" are demeaning to their professionalism. Unintended consequences often result when strategies for encouraging compliance are not carefully thought through and explained to employees.

LEARNING   Encouraging and Enabling Compliance

Although in theory organizational members may be expected to comply with formal rules, policies, and procedures, as well as more informal norms about behavior, we know that in practice, there are myriad instances, both small and large, of noncompliance.

In this section we first consider reasons why individuals may not comply with organizational rules, policies, procedures, and norms. Next, we outline basic strategies for encouraging compliance. We also consider the sometimes paradoxical consequences of attempts to increase individual-level compliance. For simplicity, we generally do not distinguish among rules, policies, procedures, and norms. Instead we use the term "rule" to refer to these different concepts more generically.

We conclude this competency with a discussion of issues related to organizational-level compliance. In particular, we consider compliance with U.S. federal laws prohibiting criminal conduct such as perpetrating fraud, discharging environmentally hazardous waste, evading taxes, and engaging in anticompetitive activities.

UNDERSTANDING NONCOMPLIANCE

At the core of all sport lies a fundamental tension between the desire for rules and the desire to break them.

Mitchell, Crosset, and Barr, 1999, p. 216

Using sports metaphors when talking about other types of organizations sometimes can be misleading, but when it comes to understanding how people react to rules, the quote above seems quite apt. It highlights a key paradox—we all seem to have a love-hate relationship with rules. We need rules to keep order, but we resent them when rules prevent us from doing what we would like to do.

Although it may be human nature for us all to prefer rules that work to our benefit, in practice, responses to specific rules can differ substantially based on situational variables as well as individual characteristics. Consider, for example, how people respond to speed limits. The speed limit posted on a road states the maximum legal driving speed, but some individuals are comfortable driving faster than the speed limit while others are not. The ways that different people *typically* respond to speed limits are based on individual-level variables. In contrast, even people who typically are comfortable driving faster than the speed limit are inclined to slow down if they see a police car. Similarly, people who believe it is important not to drive faster than the posted speed limit may decide to speed in an emergency, such as taking an injured friend to the hospital. In these examples, situational variables influence individuals to change their typical behavior.

Because managers typically have much less influence over individual-level personality variables (e.g., conscientiousness, emotional stability, agreeableness, cynicism, locus of control) that might help predict noncompliant behavior (Kidder, 2005; Litzky, Eddleston & Kidder, 2006), we will focus on different types of situational variables that managers can directly affect to encourage compliance.

MANAGEMENT MISTAKES—EMPLOYEE MISBEHAVIOR

Noncompliance. Misbehavior. Wrongdoing. Deviance. All these terms have been used to refer to voluntary actions by employees that violate the norms or rules of an organization. Although many researchers use the term "deviance" (e.g., Robinson & Bennett, 1995; Litzky et al., 2006), we prefer the less loaded term "noncompliance," when violations are relatively minor. In cases where the violations are more significant, we use the terms positive deviance and destructive deviance to emphasize both the direction and the magnitude of the deviance (Quinn, 1996; Warren, 2003).

In their research focusing on noncompliance, Litzky et al. (2006) identified six different triggers for employee misbehavior: (1) ambiguity about job performance; (2) social pressures to conform; (3) compensation/reward structures; (4) negative/untrusting attitudes by managers; (5) rules that are perceived as unfair; and (6) violating employee trust. Below we organize these triggers based on how the employee is likely to explain their behavior.

"I DIDN'T KNOW"

Although not included in Litzky et al's (2006) typology, it is important to recognize that not every failure to comply with a rule is intentional. In some cases, people fail to comply with rules because they are unaware that the rule exists. For example, a new employee may not know that she is required to submit expense reports within one week after returning from a business trip. Another employee may not have read an email announcing that, in the future, all expense reports must have original receipts attached, so he may continue to submit expense reports without receipts, as he has in the past. In these types of situations, the organization can enable compliance by communicating the rules to employees and making sure that employees understand the rules.

"I WASN'T SURE"

In some cases, organizations send mixed messages about complying with rules. Mixed messages can be the result of ambiguity about job performance, the failure of managers to respond to instances of noncompliance, or inconsistency in responses to noncompliance. Finally, when a subgroup in the organization fails to follow rules, there is social pressure to conform to those subgroup norms rather than the official rules of the organization.

Employees suffer ambiguity about job performance when they are unsure of their roles, their responsibilities, and the behavior they are expected to exhibit. Employees in boundary-spanning roles, such as salespeople and service providers, bridge the boundary between the organization and its customers and are especially likely to experience this type of ambiguity (Eddleston, Kidder & Litzky, 2002). Satisfying the customer may require violating a company policy. Violations may be small or large. For example, a bus driver may wish to let a regular customer ride on a day when he has forgotten his bus pass, but that would be a violation of company policy (Litzky et al., 2006). A salesperson who is constantly told "the customer is always right" may be hesitant to refuse to pay for an expensive dinner, even though she knows that it exceeds the limits set by her organization for entertaining customers.

Organizations send mixed messages when a rule exists, but there are no consequences associated with complying with that rule. In this type of situation, once people realize that there are no consequences when the rule is ignored, some may begin to disregard the rule. Alternatively, an organization may have sanctions for failing to comply with certain rules, but at the same time may have procedures that make compliance difficult. One organization that we are familiar with, for example, requires that employees include comparative data to have their requests for salary increases considered. At the same time, the organization refuses to provide any information related to the performance and compensation of other employees in similar positions, making meaningful comparisons difficult, if not impossible. This kind of mixed message can lead to frustration, anger, and acting out.

Responding inconsistently to acts of noncompliance also sends a mixed message. Perceptions of inconsistency can result when some employees are allowed to engage in certain behaviors, but other employees are prohibited from engaging in that behavior. In some cases, this may simply be the result of failing to clarify to whom the rule applies. For example, employees may not understand that the reason some employees are allowed to take office supplies home, while others are not, is based on whether the employee is officially participating in a telecommuting option offered by the organization.

In contrast to situations where there might be some misunderstanding about what the rules are and to whom they apply, in some organizations there is social pressure to engage in inappropriate behavior because the norms of a subgroup are inconsistent with organizational rules. For example, a study of bartenders found that at an establishment where tips were pooled and divided among employees, when new employees were first hired, senior employees taught them that the amount of tip money reported for tax purposes should be considerably less than the actual amount (Litzky et al., 2006). Employees are likely to feel especially pressured if it is the managers who are encouraging or engaging in inappropriate behaviors.

"I HAD TO LOOK OUT FOR MYSELF"

In contrast to situations where there is some confusion about a rule and/or to whom it applies, individuals may also choose not to comply when they believe that they will personally benefit from noncompliance. Sometimes ignoring a rule may save a little time or inconvenience. For example, a worker may prefer not to put on safety goggles and a helmet when entering a construction site. Other times rules may be ignored in the belief that following the rules may be financially costly. For example, a sales representative may ignore a company rule forbidding expensive gifts to prospective clients in an attempt to secure a large sales commission. When compensation/reward structures are based on commissions and/or quotas, research shows that employees may find it easier to rationalize inappropriate behaviors (Litzky et al., 2006).

Special issues related to compliance may emerge in associations and voluntary organizations because of the nature of the relationship between the organization and its members. Most employees feel dependent upon their employer, especially in economic hard times, and may fear losing their jobs if they fail to comply with organizational rules. In contrast, members of voluntary organizations may feel less compelled to comply because they have less of a vested interest in retaining their membership in the organization. For example, an individual who would never consider intentionally being late to a meeting at work might feel comfortable arriving late or even skipping a committee meeting for the local food bank where she volunteers.

"THEY HAD IT COMING"

Three of the triggers identified by Litzky et al. (2006) relate to how employees feel they have been treated. When managers exhibit negative and untrusting attitudes, treat people unfairly, and/or violate their employees' trust, employees are likely to feel that noncompliance or even destructive deviance is an appropriate response (see, for example, Eddleston, et al., 2002; Harris & Obgonna, 2002; Kidder, 2005; Robinson, 1996; Robinson & Bennett, 1995). Such retaliation is viewed as appropriate because the manager (and/or organization) "had it coming." In a study of service workers, for example, one employee remarked, ". . . Managers have always asked for more than's fair and customers have always wanted something for nothing. Getting back at them is natural—it's always happened, nothing new in that" (Harris & Ogbonna, 2002).

Employees who are publically reprimanded in front of customers and peers may react very quickly and negatively to such a breach of trust. "In these types of situations, one of the most common responses by the employees was for them to do exactly what the managers told them not to do once the manager left the room. This type of behavior was often accompanied with much gusto, so that other employees and on-looking customers could play party to the unacceptable act" (Litzky et al., 2006, p. 96).

"IT WAS THE RIGHT THING TO DO"

Finally, some individuals may choose not to comply with a rule that they disagree with, not for their personal benefit, but because they believe that their actions are aligned with the overall interests of the organization or society. Researchers have used a variety of labels to refer to this type of behavior. We use positive deviance (Quinn, 1996; Spreitzer & Sonenshein, 2003). Other terms, including constructive deviance (Warren, 2003), functional or creative disobedience (Brief, Buttram & Dukerich, 2001), and tempered radicalism (Meyerson & Scully, 1995), all refer to the same basic idea—that in the particular situation in question, *not* complying was the right thing to do.

Positive deviance often includes speaking up to protest something being done in the organization. Although such "whistle-blowing" violates informal rules about accepting the status quo and not exposing information that might harm the organization, the motivation for positive deviance often is based on a desire to improve the organization and thereby improve the long-term outcomes for organizational stakeholders.

STRATEGIES FOR ENCOURAGING COMPLIANCE

Organizations use a variety of tactics to encourage compliance. For example, cities that wish to reduce accidents at intersections may install cameras and issue automated tickets to vehicles that fail to stop when the light turns red. Hospitals that wish to reduce the spread of infections may provide checklists to be followed along with information about the benefits of activities such as frequent hand washing (Gawande, 2009). Corporations that wish to reduce travel and entertainment expenditures may require itemized receipts for reimbursements. A list of specific tactics could go on and on. To help managers improve compliance, a more general strategic framework is needed.

Traditionally, tactics for encouraging compliance have been captured in the metaphor of the carrot (compensation when compliance is observed) and the stick (sanctions for noncompliance). This type of dichotomous framework, however, is antithetical to the competing values approach because it encourages either/or thinking. More recently, Mitchell et al. (1999) described a more comprehensive framework that identifies six basic strategies to encourage compliance. Table M2.3 provides a summary of that framework and includes a set of metaphors that we think help explain the key differences between these strategies.

TABLE M2.3 Compliance Strategies (Strategies and Explanations Adapted from Mitchell, et al., 1999)

Strategy	*Explanation*	*Metaphor*
Punitive	Increase negative consequences when people **do not** comply	Sticks
Remunerative	Increase positive consequences when people **do** comply	Carrots
Preventative	Make it harder for people to avoid complying	Hurdles
Generative	Make it easier for people to comply	Fast Tracks
Cognitive	Explain why complying is in a person's best interests	Enlightenment
Normative	Convince people that complying is the morally right thing to do	Conversion

STICKS AND CARROTS

Mitchell et al. (1999) begin with traditional "stick" and "carrot" approaches, which they relabel "punitive" and "remunerative" strategies, respectively. Sticks are the punishments that are imposed when individuals fail to comply with a rule. Carrots are the rewards people receive when they are observed complying with a rule. It is important to note that both sticks and carrots assume that the individual is able but unwilling (unmotivated) to comply with the existing rules. If the problem is lack of ability to comply, rather than lack of motivation to comply, sticks and carrots will be ineffective.

To be effective, stick and carrot strategies depend on the ability of the organization to provide a clear description of prohibited (undesired) or required (desired) behaviors. It is also important to have some method of monitoring behavior. In the example of the city that wanted to reduce traffic accidents, the addition of traffic cameras at intersections was an important feature when implementing that punitive strategy. The city could have just raised the cost of a ticket (also a punitive strategy), but just getting a bigger stick would not be effective without sufficient monitoring of behavior.

HURDLES AND FAST TRACKS

In contrast to attempting to alter employee motivation by focusing on consequences, the next two strategies identified by Mitchell et al. (1999), preventative and generative strategies, focus on changing the opportunities to avoid compliance. Preventative strategies are hurdles—they make it more difficult for individuals to avoid complying with rules. For example, one of our former employers wanted to reduce expenses and requested that employees not stockpile office supplies at their desks. When that request went unheeded, the managing partner had the supply cabinet locked and employees had to go through his assistant to obtain office supplies. Putting this hurdle in place made it more difficult for people to violate the no stockpiling rule.

In contrast to hurdles, which focus on decreasing opportunities to engage in undesired behaviors, fast tracks (generative strategies) attempt to increase opportunities for desired behaviors. A key assumption here is that people have not been engaging in a desired behavior because of a problem with the system, not a problem with the individual. For example, a company that wants to encourage employees to recycle might increase the number of recycling bins available to employees, perhaps placing a bin in each office. By giving employees a fast, easy way to comply with the recycling rule, the organization is able to generate a higher level of compliance.

ENLIGHTENMENT AND CONVERSION

The final two strategies identified by Mitchell et al. (1999), cognitive and normative strategies, focus on the rationale for particular behaviors. Cognitive strategies take advantage of the concept of enlightened self-interest, so we refer to these as enlightenment strategies. Enlightenment strategies assume that people mistakenly believe that following the rules is unnecessary and/or not in their best interests. Once information has been provided to correct that mistaken impression, there is no need for any additional monitoring because enlightened self-interest will result in the desired behavior. For example, workers may not realize how important wearing safety glasses is for reducing injuries. By providing information on the number and severity of injuries when safety glasses are worn versus when they are not worn, the organization may be able to change how workers think about and comply with these types of safety regulations.

In contrast to enlightenment (cognitive) strategies, normative strategies require a deeper change to the individual's values—hence our use of the term "conversion." Normative strategies assume that people need to be taught to do the right thing—they need to be converted. Once converted, these individuals will behave appropriately without any sticks or carrots and regardless of whether they are facing hurdles or have a fast track to the appropriate behavior. Because assumptions, beliefs, and values are often very deeply held, however, conversion strategies are especially challenging.

One situation when conversion strategies are likely to be used is when top executives attempt to change the values and norms of the organization as a whole. For example, an organization that has operated with monopoly power in the past may need to significantly change its attitudes about quality and customer service when competitors enter the market. It is important to recognize that changing organizational culture is a long-term project. For example, Mitchell et al. (1999) describe efforts by the NCAA beginning in the late 1950s to differentiate between professional athletes and students who participated in athletics programs. Recognizing that changes in language and rhetoric play an important role in changing values and beliefs, the NCAA insisted that the term "student-athlete" be used, rather than the terms "player" or "athlete" to reinforce the fact that these individuals were, first and foremost, students. When it comes to changing deeply held beliefs and values, however, rhetoric alone is rarely sufficient. Sustaining new values requires that structural changes be made to performance evaluation and reward systems to reinforce that rhetoric.

COSTS AND PARADOXES OF COMPLIANCE STRATEGIES

As noted above, managers can use different strategies to encourage compliance, but each strategy comes with a cost. In addition to concerns about direct financial costs, trying to force compliance may result, paradoxically, in less compliance and reduced effectiveness. Tight controls that result in a high degree of compliance can also result in missed opportunities and, in some cases, destructive deviance.

DIRECT FINANCIAL COSTS

Punitive strategies for encouraging compliance depend heavily on an effective monitoring system—employees cannot be punished unless there is evidence that they have violated some rule.

Theoretically, remunerative strategies can rely on self-disclosure (thereby eliminating monitoring costs) because employees will want to report behaviors that are rewarded. However, if there is a risk that employees may claim to have engaged in behaviors when they actually have not, then a monitoring system may be needed. To have an impact, remunerative strategies must include rewards that are sufficiently valuable to induce employees to behave as desired and to avoid behaving in undesirable ways. Depending on the difficulty of the desired behavior and the perceived benefit of violating rules, the costs of rewarding compliance can be substantial.

REDUCED COMPLIANCE AND EFFECTIVENESS

In addition to the financial costs associated with punitive strategies, the use of monitoring systems and punishments signals a lack of trust in employees, which can be a trigger for noncompliance. Even if employees continue to comply with rules, they may choose to "work to rule," doing exactly what is required and nothing more. Research on organizational effectiveness has found that organizations depend on employees going above and beyond what is explicitly required by their job descriptions. When employees chose to "work to rule," they stop performing these types of extra-role or organizational citizenship behaviors, and organizational performance suffers.

While remunerative strategies may avoid the appearance of negative attitudes about employees, they may also result in motivation problems once they have been in use for some time. Research shows that the impact of extrinsic rewards often diminishes over time, as employees begin to feel entitled to the reward, rather than motivated by it. In addition, research summarized by Gagne and Deci (2005) suggests that in some cases providing extrinsic rewards to individuals for doing a task may actually reduce their initial intrinsic motivation. Finally, if the company attempts to eliminate remunerative strategies to save money, employees may feel that they are being treated unfairly and retaliate.

MISSED OPPORTUNITIES

Sometimes organizations need members to challenge or even break rules, as in the case of positive deviance. In the Competing Values Framework, the Internal Process (Control) quadrant is directly opposite the Open Systems (Create) quadrant, indicating the tension between maintaining the status quo and encouraging change. So it should be no surprise that one of the costs of standardization and control is stifled creativity and missed opportunities. In organizations where the phrase, "That's how we've always done it," is regularly repeated, it can be difficult to convince people to consider new ideas and to implement and sustain change (two competencies we address in depth in Module 4).

DESTRUCTIVE DEVIANCE

Many examples of destructive deviant behavior are likely to be triggered when employees feel that the organization "had it coming." Research by Green and Alge (1998) suggests that acts of deviance are often preceded by perceptions of unfairness. Employees who feel that they are underpaid may feel they have the right to take organizational property or to use organizational resources for their personal benefit. Employees who feel that performance expectations are too high may look for ways to cut corners or hide poor performance from their supervisors.

It is important to keep in mind that even if destructive deviance is not targeted directly at the organization, the organization can suffer serious consequences. For example, even though the direct target of sexual harassment may be a coworker, supplier, or customer, that behavior deviates from both legal requirements and ethical standards. Organizations should also recognize that sexual harassment is not dependent only on the personality of the harasser; the organizational culture and specific circumstances also play a role. For example, when Krings and Facchin (2009) studied the sexual harassment of women by men, they found that men who felt they had been treated unfairly were more likely to engage in the sexual harassment of women than men who did not feel that they were treated unfairly. Workplace deviance has been estimated to collectively cost organizations billions of dollars per year (Ferris, Brown, Lian & Keeping, 2009). Although individual differences play a part in predicting destructive behavior by employees, situational triggers such as poorly designed compensation/reward systems, ambiguous performance expectations, and disrespectful or unfair treatment by managers form an important part of the equation.

Up to this point, we have focused our attention on compliance at the individual level. Now we turn our attention to the emerging field of organizational compliance.

ORGANIZATIONAL COMPLIANCE

In the vernacular, "compliance" means acting in accordance with a request or a rule—something that organizations have always needed members to do. Over the past 20 years, however, the term "compliance" has taken on another, more specific meaning as the United States and other countries have attempted to create incentives for organizations to behave more responsibly.

As a manager, it is important to understand that organizations can be penalized for failing to comply with countless laws and regulations. Although our focus will be on organizational compliance initiatives in the United States at the federal level, you should recognize that the United States is not alone in its quest to encourage organizational accountability and good global citizenship. Australia and the European Union have been active in developing systems that encourage organizations to institute compliance programs, while leaders in Japan, Europe, and the United States have come together to emphasize the importance of developing a set of international ethical standards (Izraeli & Schwartz, n.d.).

FEDERAL SENTENCING GUIDELINES FOR ORGANIZATIONS

In 1991 federal sentencing guidelines for organizations (referred to hereafter as "the Guidelines" were issued by the United States Sentencing Commission (USSC) and began to influence the internal mechanisms organizations use to reduce the likelihood of criminal activity. Although organizations are intangible entities and cannot be imprisoned, they can be found guilty of criminal conduct and punished (Desio, n.d.).

It is important to understand that the federal sentencing guidelines do not just apply to large corporations. According to the Guidelines:

"Organization" means "a person other than an individual." 18 U.S.C. § 18. The term includes corporations, partnerships, associations, joint-stock companies, unions, trusts, pension funds, unincorporated organizations, governments and political subdivisions thereof, and non-profit organizations (U.S. Sentencing Commission, 2007, p. 488).

Although organizations were prosecuted for criminal activity before 1991, research by the U. S. Sentencing Commission found problems with both the severity and the consistency of punishments. For example, average fines often were less expensive than the costs associated with obeying the law—suggesting "that corporate crime did in fact 'pay'" (U. S. Sentencing Commission, 1995, p. 26). In addition, there were large inconsistencies in how different organizations were being treated, even when the facts of specific cases were nearly identical (U. S. Sentencing Commission, 1995).

The Guidelines were created as a manual for judges to use when determining the appropriate sentence for organizations convicted of a federal crime (Izraeli & Schwartz, n.d.). Just as important, they also attempted to reduce organizational wrongdoing by incorporating multiple strategies for encouraging voluntary compliance.

2004 REVISION AND EXPANSION

Although the original 1991 Guidelines did appear to have a positive impact on consistency in sentencing, as the many accounting scandals in the early 2000s demonstrated, there was still much room for improvement with respect to the goal of actually reducing inappropriate activities by organizations. As a consequence, the USSC voted to make the standards under the Guidelines more stringent (U.S. Sentencing Commission, 2004).

One key aspect of the original Guidelines was the provision for a reduction in punishment for companies that had "meaningful compliance programs" in place at the time the criminal activity occurred (Kaplan, 2004). A compliance program requires substantially more than a code of conduct—it is an operational program that includes "policies, procedures and actions within a process to help prevent and detect violations of laws and regulations" (Kral, 2009, p. 1).

Not surprisingly, however, some organizations were found to have followed the letter, but not the spirit of the 1991 Guidelines, creating compliance programs that appeared to be good on paper but that were ineffective because of a bad organizational culture (Kaplan, July/Aug 2004).

To increase accountability, more responsibility was put on boards of directors and top executives for managing and overseeing compliance programs. Specifically, the revised Guidelines mandate that organizations periodically conduct risk analyses to estimate the likelihood of criminal conduct and use the findings of these analyses when designing, implementing, and/or modifying their compliance and ethics programs (Kaplan, July/August 2004).

At a more general level, the revised Guidelines call for organizations to "promote an organization culture that encourages ethical conduct and a commitment to compliance with the law" (U. S. Sentencing Commission, 2007) An April 13, 2004, press release announcing the new requirements noted, "The Commission's focus on ethical corporate behavior is a unique development in the 13-year history of the organizational sentencing guidelines" (U. S. Sentencing Commission, 2004, p. 1).

GUIDELINES FOR COMPLIANCE AND ETHICS PROGRAMS

According to Paula Desio, Deputy General Counsel of the U.S. Sentencing Commission, "The organizational guidelines criteria embody broad principles that, taken together, describe a corporate "good Citizenship" model, but do not offer precise details for implementation. This approach was deliberately selected in order to encourage flexibility and independence by organizations in designing programs that are best suited to their particular circumstances" (Desio, n.d., p. 1).

As stated in the Overview of the Organizational Guidelines (Desio, n.d., p. 1), the six key criteria for effective compliance and ethics programs include:

1. Oversight by high-level personnel

2. Due care in delegating substantial discretionary authority

3. Effective communication to all levels of employees

4. Reasonable steps to achieve compliance, which include systems for monitoring, auditing, and reporting suspected wrongdoing without fear of reprisal

5. Consistent enforcement and compliance standards including disciplinary mechanism

6. Reasonable steps to respond to and prevent further similar offenses upon detection of a violation

Not surprisingly, career opportunities focused on compliance and ethics have grown substantially since 1991. Only about 20 ethics officers attended the first meeting of the Ethics Officer Association in 1992; renamed the Ethics and Compliance Officers Association in 2005, the organization had 1,116 members as of March 2010 (E. M. L. Hebert, personal communication, 2010, March 4). Many consulting firms offer services to organizations seeking assistance meeting compliance standards. Some firms focus on industry-specific compliance (e.g., banking, health care, insurance), while other firms focus more broadly, providing training, software, and other services to a variety of organizations.

Regardless of the type or size of an organization, it is important to recognize that one-time training sessions on the importance of compliance are not sufficient. An organizational culture of encouraging and enabling compliance and ethical conduct requires that appropriate values and behaviors be integrated into the daily activities of the organization (Teicheira, 2008). As a manager you may be able to make a great contribution by playing your part in building a culture of integrity.

ANALYSIS Strategies used by the United States to Increase Compliance

Objective   This analysis exercise will give you the opportunity to test your understanding of different strategies for encouraging compliance as well as to learn more about the U.S. Federal organizational sentencing guidelines.

Directions   The United States Sentencing Commission has posted the current version of the Federal Sentencing Guidelines Manual on their web site. Download a copy of Chapter 8 (the organizational sentencing guidelines—a version is available at http://www.ussc.gov/2007guid/CHAP8.pdf), and briefly review the guidelines looking for evidence of different strategies for encouraging compliance.

1. How many different strategies did you find?
2. Which strategies do you think have the most impact in reducing illegal and unethical behavior? Why?
3. Do you feel that some strategies were not used that should have been used? Why or why not?

Reflection   If you have never read any federal regulations before, you may have been surprised at the length and complexity of Chapter 8 of the U.S. Sentencing Guidelines. Creating laws and regulations to help ensure fair competition is an extremely complicated task. It is also a highly political task. In some cases, exclusions are created for specific industries or even specific organizations. For example, states often attempt to attract new business by offering tax breaks that are not available to existing businesses.

PRACTICE   Moving Compliance Outside the Workplace

Objective   This exercise is designed to give you the opportunity to practice analyzing and developing policies to encourage and enable compliance.

Directions   Assume that you work for a university that wants to reduce health care costs. The President, a marathon runner, is especially interested in getting employees to exercise more. One of your colleagues in HR has proposed a program to reward employees who exercise. Review the program description below and then write a memo that identifies the strengths and weaknesses of the program as proposed and offers suggestions for improving the program.

GET HEALTHY, GET CREDIT!

As part of the University's "Get Healthy, Get Credit" program, faculty and staff are encouraged to maintain a healthy lifestyle including physical activity. Faculty and Staff are encouraged to be physically active a minimum of 30 minutes each day. A form has been provided to keep track of your daily or weekly hours of physical activity, excluding classes or programs sponsored by the University. Eligible faculty and staff may earn a $25 incentive credit for completing 25 hours of physical activity hours between February 1 and June 11 (20 weeks). Please note this form should only be completed for physical activity outside of University programs (i.e., if you participate in a group exercise class, you will get one point per class, and hours should NOT be tracked on this form.) Hours of physical activity must be tracked in increments of 30 minutes (= .5) OR 60 minutes (= 1).

Reflection   Not everyone is comfortable with the idea of organizations creating programs like the one described above, which focus on personal behavior outside the workplace. In addition to programs aimed at changing lifestyle behaviors that might affect health (e.g., exercise, smoking), many organizations have created programs to track employees' community service, even when that service takes place outside of work hours. Although some employees appreciate being recognized for their community activities, others feel that these types of behaviors are private and should not be tracked and used by the company to burnish its public image (Tschirhart & St. Clair, 2008).

APPLICATION Your Organization's Compliance Policies and Practices

Objective This exercise is designed to help you assess how your organization attempts to encourage and enable compliance.

Directions If you are currently employed, use the questions below to evaluate how your organization attempts to obtain compliance with rules, policies, and regulations.

If you are not currently employed, you can use the questions when interviewing potential employers or answer the questions with respect to your school or even how different teachers attempt to obtain compliance from students in the classes you are taking.

1. Does your organization have a Compliance and Ethics Office?

2. What is covered in your organization's Code of Conduct? Are copies readily available to employees? How often is the code of conduct reviewed?

3. What types of strategies does your organization use to encourage compliance?

4. Have you come across any situations where company policies made it difficult to actually comply with some requirements? If so, what can be done to improve the situation?

Reflection Encouraging and enabling compliance is not just the job of compliance officers and top managers. Every member has the opportunity to set a good example by learning about organizational policies and procedures, role modeling appropriate behavior, and, if necessary, challenging the status quo.

MODULE 2 Control-Focused Competency Evaluation Matrix

Objective The final exercise in each module is intended to give you a starting point for developing a comprehensive strategy for mastery that you can implement and monitor in the future. These competency evaluation matrices will be used at the end of this book to help you develop a long-term development plan that focuses on enhancing your behavioral complexity

Review The first competency in the Control quadrant focused on organizing information flows for the individual manager, with an emphasis on increasing the efficiency of handling information inflows and improving the effectiveness of information outflows. Next, we expanded our view of the manager's job to consider how managers can work and manage across functions. The third competency focused on planning and coordinating activities in general, while the fourth competency focused on monitoring and measuring performance to ensure that actual outcomes were aligned with goals established in the planning phase. Finally, we considered control and stability in light of pressures from the external context, particularly issues of compliance with U.S. federal guidelines for corporate accountability.

Directions Answer the questions in Table M2.4 for each of the competencies covered in this module based on the reading material, class discussions, and your personal work (e.g., Assessment exercises, Application exercises, etc.).

Reflection Completing the matrix in Table M2.4 should give you some ideas about how you can continue to improve on competencies that focus on establishing and maintaining stability and continuity, consistent with the goals of the internal process quadrant.

TABLE M2.4 Module 2 Control-Focused Competency Evaluation Matrix

With respect to this competency:	*Organizing Information Flows*	*Working and Managing Across Functions*	*Planning and Coordinating Projects*	*Measuring and Monitoring Performance and Quality*	*Encouraging and Enabling Compliance*
1. What do I know about my current performance?					
2. How could I be more effective?					
3. Who are some people I could observe?					
4. What books should I read?					
5. What objectives and deadlines should I set?					
6. With whom should I share my objectives?					
7. How will I evaluate my efforts?					

REFERENCES

Abrahamson, E., & Freedman, D. H. (2007). *A perfect mess: The hidden benefits of disorder—how crammed closets, cluttered offices, and on-the-fly planning make the world a better place.* New York: Little, Brown and Company.

Alesandrini, K. (1992). *Survive information overload: 7 best ways to manage your workload by seeing the big picture.* Homewood, Ill.: Business One Irwin.

Ali, A., Bani, S., Anbari, F. T., & Money, W. H. (2008). Impact of organizational and project factors on acceptance and usage of project management software and perceived project success. *Project Management Journal, 39*(2), 5–33.

Allen, D. (2001). *Getting things done: The art of stress-free productivity.* New York: Penguin Books.

Alster, N. (1989, February 13). What flexible workers can do." *Fortune,* 62–66.

Anantatmula, V. S. (2008). The role of technology in the project manager performance model. *Project Management Journal, 39*(1), 34–47.

Ashford, S. J., & Tsui, A. S. (1991). Self-regulation for managerial effectiveness: The role of active feedback seeking." *Academy of Management Journal. 34*(2), 251–280.

Badiru, A. B. (1993). *Quantitative models for project planning, scheduling and control.* Westport, CT: Quorum.

Baker, W., R. Cross, & Wooten, M. (2003). Positive organizational network analysis and energizing relationships. In K. S. Cameron, J. E. Dutton, and R. E. Quinn (Eds.), *Positive organizational scholarship: Foundations of a new discipline* (pp. 328–342). San Francisco, Berrett-Koehler.

Baltzan P., & Phillips, A. (2008). *Business driven information systems* (2nd ed.). New York: McGraw/Hill Irwin.

Bandyopadhyay, J. K. (2005). A model framework for developing industry specific quality standards for effective quality assurance in global supply chains in the new millennium." *International Journal of Management, 22*(2), 294–299.

Beard, J. W., & Peterson, T. O. (2003). Coming to grips with the management of information: A classroom exercise. *Journal of Information Systems Education, 14*(1), 15–30.

Benavent, F. B. (2006). TQM application through self-assessment and learning: Some experiences from Two EQA applicants. *Quality Management Journal, 13*(1), 7–25.

Berrger, W. (1999, August). Life sucks and then you fly. *Wired,* 156–163.

Better World Shopping. (n. d.). Top ten companies. Available: http://www.betterworldshopper.com/topten.html.

Bisgaard, S., & De Mast, J. (2006). After Six Sigma—What's next ? *Quality Progress, 39*(1), 30–35.

Bowen, H. K., Clark, K. B., Holloway, C. A., & Wheelwright, S. C. (Eds.). (1994). *The perpetual enterprise machine.* New York: Oxford University Press.

Bridges, W. (1994, September 19). The end of the job. *Fortune,* 62–74.

Brief, A P., Buttram, R. T., & Dukerich, J. M. (2001). Collective corruption in the corporate world: Toward a process model. In M. E. Turner (Ed.), *Groups at work: Theory and research* (pp. 471–499). Mahwah, NJ: Lawrence Erlbaum Associates.

Bunin, R. B. (2009). *New perspectives on Microsoft® Office Project 2007 introductory.* Boston: Cengage Learning, Course Technology.

Buckingham, M. (2005). What great managers do. *Harvard Business Review, 83*(3), 70–79.

Butler, T., & Waldrop, J. (1999). Job sculpting, the art of retaining your best people. *Harvard Business Review, 77*(5), 144–152.

Cabana, Ronald E., & Purser, S. (1998). *The self-managing organization: How leading companies are transforming the work of teams for real impact.* New York: Free Press.

Cameron, K. S., & Thompson, M. (2000). The problems and promises of Total Quality Management: Implications for organizational performance. In R. E. Quinn, R. M. O'Neill, and L. St. Clair (Eds.). *Pressing Problems in Modern Organizations* (pp. 215–242). New York: AMACOM,.

Campbell, J. (1982). *Grammatical man: Information, entropy, language and life.* New York: Simon & Schuster.

Carlzon, J. (1989). *Moments of truth.* New York: Perennial Library.

Champy, J. (1995). *Reengineering management: The mandate for new leadership.* New York: HarperBusiness.

Chen, P., & Bouvain, P. (2009). Is corporate responsibility converging? A comparison of corporate responsibility, reporting in the USA, UK, Australia and Germany. *Journal of Business Ethics, 87,* 299–317.

CMS Office of Public Affairs. (2009; July 9). New ratings for America's hospitals now available on hospital compare web site. Available: http://www.cms.hhs.gov/apps/media/press/release .asp?Counter=3477&intNumPerPage=10&checkDate=&checkKey=&srchType=1&numDays=3500 &srchOpt=0&srchData=&keywordType=All&chkNewsType=1%2C+2%2C+3%2C+4%2C+5 &intPage=&showAll=&pYear=&year=&desc=&cboOrder=date.

Collinson, P. & Jones, R. (2009). "Liar loans" banned as watchdog clamps down on risky mortgages. *Guardian* [On-line.] Available: http://www.guardian.co.uk/money/2009/oct/19/fsa-clampdown-on-risky-mortgages.

Covey, S. R. (2004). *The 7 habits of highly effective people.* New York: Free Press.

Cox, A. (1990). *Straight talk for a Monday morning: Creative values, vision and vitality at work.* New York: John Wiley & Sons.

Cross, R., Ehrlich, K., Dawson, R. & Helferich, J. (2008) Managing collaboration: Improving team effectiveness through a network perspective. *California Management Review, 50*(4), 74–98.

Davenport, T. H., & Prusak, L. (1998). *Working knowledge: How organizations manage what they know.* Boston: Harvard Business School Press.

Davis, J. B. (2008). Information overload. *ABA Journal, 94*(7), 14.

Denison, D., Hart, S., & Kahn, J. (1993). From chimneys to cross-functional teams: Developing and validating a diagnostic model. University of Michigan, working paper.

Dertouzes, M. L., Lester, R. K., Solow, R. M., & the MIT Commission on Industrial Productivity. (1989). *Made in America: Regaining the productive edge.* Cambridge, MA.: MIT Press.

Desio, P. (n.d.). *An overview of the organizational guidelines.* Available: http://www.ussc.gov/corp/ ORGOVERVIEW.pdf.

Dodin, B. (2006). A practical and accurate alternative to PERT. In J. Józefowska and J. Weglarz (Eds.), *International series in operations research and management science:* (Vol. 92). *Perspectives in modern project scheduling* (pp. 3–23) New York: Springer.

Drucker, Peter. (1999). Managing oneself. *Harvard Business Review, 77*(2), 64–74.

Dumaine, Brian. (1991, June 17). The bureaucracy busters. *Fortune,* 36–50.

Eddleston, K. A., Kidder, D. L., & Litzky, B. E. (2002). Who's the boss? Contending with competing expectations from customers and management. *Academy of Management Executive, 16*(4), 85–95.

Elkington, J. (1998). *Cannibals with forks: The triple bottom line of 21st century business.* Gabriola Island BC, Canada: New Society Publishers.

Ferris, D. L., Brown, D. J., Lian, H., & Keeping, L. M. (2009). When does self-esteem relate to deviant behavior: The role of contingencies of self-worth. *Journal of Applied Psychology, 94*(5), 1345–1353.

Frame, J. D. (1999). *Building project management competence.* San Francisco: Jossey-Bass.

Galbraith, J. R. (1973). *Designing complex organizations.* Reading, MA.: Addison-Wesley.

Gates, B. (1999). *Business @ the speed of thought: Using a digital nervous system.* New York: Warner Books.

Gawande, A. (2009). *The checklist manifesto.* New York: Metropolitan Books.

Gilovich, Thomas. (1991). *How we know what isn't so: The fallibility of human reason in everyday life.* New York: Free Press.

Greenberg, J., & Alge, B. J. (1998). Aggressive reactions to workplace injustice. In R. W. Griffin, A. O'Leary-Kelly, & J. M. Collins (Eds.), *Dysfunctional behavior in organizations: Violent and deviant behaviors* (pp. 43–117). Stamford, CT: JAI Press.

Grove, A. S. (1995). *High output management.* New York: Vintage Books.

Guenther, K. (2001). Creating cross-functional web teams. *Online, 25*(3), 79–81.

Gundry, L. K., Kickul, J. R., & Prather, C. (1994). Building the creative organization. *Organizational Dynamics, 22,* 22–37.

Hackman, J. R., & Oldham, G. (1975). Development of the job diagnostic survey. *Journal of Applied Psychology, 60,* 159–170.

Hackman, J. R., Oldham, G., Janson, R., & Purdy, K. (1975). A new strategy for job enrichment. *California Management Review, 17*(4), 57–71.

Hallowell, Edward M. (1999). The human moment at work. *Harvard Business Review, 77*(1), 58–66.

Hammer, M., & Champy, J. (1993). *Reengineering the corporation: A manifesto for business revolution.* New York: HarperCollins.

Harris, L. C., & Ogbonna, E. (2002). Exploring service sabotage: The antecedents, types and consequences of frontline, deviant, anti-service behaviors. *Journal of Service Research, 4*(3), 163–183.

Harrison, F. L. (1992). *Advanced project management: A structured approach.* New York: Halsted.

Hayward, S. F. (2003, March 17). The triple bottom line. *Forbes,* 42.

Henderson, L. S. (2008). The impact of project managers' communication competencies: Validation and extension of a research model for virtuality, satisfaction, and productivity on project teams. *Project Management Journal, 39*(2), 48–59.

Henkoff, R. (1994, October 3). Finding, training and keeping the best service workers. *Fortune,* 110–122.

Heras, M. (2005). The state-of-the-art in performance measurement in Spain. *Measuring Business Excellence 9*(3), 53.

Herzberg, F. (1968). One more time: How do you motivate employees ? *Harvard Business Review, 46,* 53–62.

House, R. S. (1988). *The human side of project management.* Reading, MA.: Addison-Wesley.

Izraeli,, D., & Schwartz, M. S. (n.d.) What can we learn from the U.S. Federal Sentencing Guidelines for Organizational Ethics? *European Institute for Business Ethics.* Available: http://actrav.itcilo.org/actrav-english/telearn/global/ilo/code/whatcan.htm.

Jones, B. (2002). Nurses and the "code of silence." In M. M. Rosenthal and K. M. Sutcliffe (Eds.). *Medical error: What do we know? What Do We Do?* (pp. 84–100). San Francisco: Jossey-Bass.

Kanter, R. M., Stein, B., & Jick, T. D. (1992). *The challenge of organizational change: How companies experience it and leaders guide it.* New York: Free Press.

Kaplan, J. M. (2004). Sentencing Guidelines 2.0: The next generation in compliance programs. *Corporate Governance Advisor, 12*(6), 10–12.

Kaplan, J. M. (2004, July-August). The New Corporate Sentencing Guidelines. *Ethikos and Corporate Conduct Quarterly* [On-line.] Available: http://www.singerpubs.com/ethikos/html/guidelines2004.html.

Kaplan, R. S. (2005). How the balanced scorecard complements the McKinsey 7-S Model. *Strategy & Leadership, 33*(3), 41–45.

Kaplan, R. S., & Norton, D. P. (1992). The balanced scorecard: Measures that drive performance. *Harvard Business Review, 70*(1), 71–79.

Keller, R. T. (2001). Cross-functional project groups in research and new product development: Diversity, communications, job stress, and outcomes. *Academy of Management Journal, 44*(3), 547–555.

Kerr, S. (1975). On the folly of rewarding A, while hoping for B. *Academy of Management Journal, 18*(4), 769–783.

Kerzner, H. (2009). *Project management: A systems approach to planning, scheduling, and controlling* (10th ed.). New York: John Wiley & Sons.

Kidder, D. L. (2005). Is it "who I am," "what I can get away with," or "what you've done to me"? A Multi-theory examination of employee misconduct. *Journal of Business Ethics, 57,* 389–398.

Kim, D. H. (1994). *System archetypes: Diagnosing systemic issues and designing high-leverage interventions.* Waltham, MA: Pegasus Communications.

Kimmons, R. L. (1990). *Project management basics: A step by step approach.* New York: Marcel Dekker.

Kral, R. (2009). Effective corporate compliance programs. *Corporate Compliance Insights.* Available: http://www.corporatecomplianceinsights.com/2009/effective-corporate-compliance-programs-ron-kral-candela.

Krings, F., & Facchin, S. (2009). Organizational justice and men's likelihood to sexually harass: The moderating role of sexism and personality. *Journal of Applied Psychology, 94*(2), 501–510.

Krumholz, H. M., Normand, S. T., Spertus, J. A., Shahian, D. M., & Bradley, E. H. (2007). Measuring performance for treating heart attacks and heart failure: The case for outcome measurement. *Health Affairs, 26*(1), 75–85 [On-line.].

Laframboise, K., & Reyes, F. (2005). Gaining competitive advantage from integrating enterprise resource planning and total quality management. *Journal of Supply Chain Management, 41*(2), 49–64.

Lawler, E. E., III. (1992). *The ultimate advantage: Creating the high-involvement organization.* San Francisco: Jossey-Bass.

Lawler, E. E., III, & Finegold, D. (2000). Individualizing the organization: Past, present, and future. *Organizational Dynamics, 29*(1), 1–15.

Layne, A. (2000, November). He's navigating the dotcom dustbowl. *Fast Company.* Available: http://www.fastcompany.com.

Litzky B. E, Eddleston, K. A., & Kidder, D. L. (2006). The good, the bad, and the misguided: How managers inadvertently encourage deviant behavior. *Academy of Management Perspectives, 20*(1), 91–103.

Marr, B. (2005). Business performance measurement: An overview of the current state of use in the USA. *Measuring Business Excellence, 9*(3), 56–62.

Message Overload: Employees Work to Stay Afloat as Message Volume Booms. (1999). *Knowledge Management, 34.*

Meyer, C. (1993). *Fast cycle time.* New York: Free Press.

Meyerson, D., & Scully, M. (1995). Tempered radicalism and the politics of ambivalence and change. *Organizational Science, 6,* 585–600.

Mitchell, R. B., Crosset, T., & Barr, C. A. (1999). Encouraging compliance without real power: Sports associations regulating teams. *Journal of Sport Management, 13,* 216–236.

Mitroff, I. & Killman, R. (1984). *Corporate tragedies: Product tampering, sabotage, and other catastrophes.* New York: Praeger.

Mohrman, S. A. (1993). Integrating roles and structures in the lateral organization. In Jay R. Galbraith, Edward E. Lawler III, et al. (Eds.), *Organizing for the Future* (pp. 109–141). San Francisco: Jossey-Bass.

NIST 2010. Baldrige Stock Studies. [On-line] Available: http://www.nist.gov/baldrige/publications/archive/stock_studies.cfm.

NIST 2006. National Institute of Standards and Technology. *Baldrige national quality program: Health care criteria for performance excellence (brochure).* Available: http://www.baldrige.nist.gov/HealthCare_Criteria.htm.

NIST 2005. National Institute of Standards and Technology. *Baldrige national quality program: criteria for performance excellence* (brochure).

Nosbisch, M. R., & Winter R. M. (2006). Managing resource leveling. *Cost Engineering, 48*(7), 24–34.

Nordenson, B. (2008) Overload! Journalism's battle for relevance in an age of too much information. *Columbia Journalism Review, 47*(4), 30–42.

Norman, W., & MacDonald. C. (2004). Getting to the bottom of "Triple Bottom Line." *Business Ethics Quarterly, 14*(2), 243–262.

O'Dell, C., & Grayson, C. J., Jr. (1998a). *If only we knew what we know.* New York: Free Press.

O'Dell, C., & Grayson, C. J. Jr. (1998b). If only we knew what we know, identification and transfer of best practices. *California Management Review, 40*(3), 154–174.

Parker, G. M. (1994). *Cross-functional teams: Working with allies, enemies, and other strangers.* San Francisco: Jossey-Bass.

Perry, L. & Denna, E. (1993). *Retrofitting process reengineering.* Unpublished manuscript, Brigham Young University.

Peters, T. J., & Waterman, R. H., Jr. (1982). *In search of excellence.* New York: Harper & Row.

Peters, T. (1994). *The Tom Peters seminar: Crazy times call for crazy organizations.* New York: Vintage Books.

Peters, T. (1999, May). The Wow Project. *Fast Company.* Available: http://www.fastcompany.com.

Pfeffer, J., & Sutton, R. I. (2000). *The knowing–doing gap.* Boston: Harvard Business School Press.

Porter, M. E. (1985). *Competitive advantage.* New York: Free Press.

Quinn, R. E. (1996). *Deep change: Discovering the leader within.* San Francisco: Jossey-Bass.

Quinn, R. W., & Quinn, R. E. (2009). *Lift: Becoming a positive force in any situation.* San Francisco, Berrett-Koehler.

Rethinking Work. (1994, October 17). *Business Week,* 74–117.

Robb, D. (2009). Perfecting project management. *HR Magazine, 54*(6), 115-118.

Robinson, S. L. (1996). Trust and breach of the psychological contract. *Administrative Science Quarterly, 41*(4), 574–599.

Robinson, S. L., & Bennett R. J. (1995). A typology of deviant workplace behaviors: A multi-dimensional scaling study. *Academy of Management Journal, 38*(2), 555–572.

Roman, D. D. (1986). *Managing projects: A systems approach.* New York: Elsevier Science.

Rummler, G. A., & Brache, A. P. (1990). *Improving performance: How to manage the white space on the organization chart.* San Francisco: Jossey-Bass.

Sapsed, J. D. (2005). How should "Knowledge Bases" be organized in multi-technology corporations ? *International Journal of Innovation Management, 9*(1), 75–102.

Sasser, W. E., Olson, P. R., & Wyckoff, D. D. (1978). *Management of services operations: Text, cases, and readings.* Boston: Allyn & Bacon.

Schmid, B., & Adams, J. (2008). Motivation in project management: The project manager's perspective. *Project Management Journal, 39*(2), 60–71.

Schueler, J. (2000). Customer service through leadership: The Disney way. *Training and Development, 54*(10), 26–31.

Sellen, A. J., & Harper, R. H. R. (2002). *The myth of the paperless office.* Cambridge, MA: MIT Press.

Senge, P. (1990). *The fifth discipline: The art and practice of the learning organization.* New York: Doubleday.

Senge, P., Roberts, C., Ross, R., Smith, B., & Keller, A. (1994). *The Fifth Discipline fieldbook: Strategies and tools for building a learning organization.* New York: Doubleday.

Seventh Generation. (2008). Crossroads: Reinventing the purpose and possibility of business. Corporate consciousness report. Available: http://www.seventhgeneration.com/corporateresponsibility/2007.

Shapiro, E. C. (1991). *How corporate truths become competitive traps.* New York: John Wiley & Sons.

Shenk, D. (1997). *Data smog: Surviving the information glut.* New York: HarperCollins.

Simons, R. (2000). *Performance measurement & control systems for implementing strategy: Text and cases.* Englewood Cliffs, NJ: Prentice-Hall.

Smith, A. (1937). *The Wealth of nations.* New York: Random House, 1937. (Original work published 1776).

Soames, M. (1988). *The biography of a marriage: Clementine and Churchill.* New York: Paragon House.

Spinner, M. P. (1989). *Improving project management skills and techniques.* Englewood Cliffs, NJ: Prentice-Hall.

Spreitzer, G. M., & Sonenshein, S. (2003). Positive deviance and extraordinary organizing. In K. S. Cameron, J. E. Dutton, and R. E. Quinn (Eds.) *Positive organizational scholarship: Foundations of a new discipline.* San Francisco: Berrett-Koehler Publishers.

Stewart, T. A. (1994, July 11). Managing in a wired company. *Fortune, 44*–56.

Skok, W., & Kobayashi, S. (2007). An international taxicab evaluation: Comparing Tokyo with London, New York and Paris. *Knowledge and Process Management, 14*(2), 117-130 [On-line.].

Taub, J. S. (2009). Enablers of exuberance: Legal acts and omissions that facilitated the global financial crisis. Available: http://ssrn.com/abstract=1472190.

Taylor, F. W. (1911). *The principles of scientific management.* New York: Harper & Row.

Teicheira, D. (2008, Nov.-Dec.). Compliance and ethics training: Event versus process. *Journal of Health Care Compliance, 61*–72.

Tetzeli, R. (1994, July 11). Surviving information overload. *Fortune, 60*–64.

Text Messaging Chat Abbreviations. (2010). *Webopedia.* Available: http://www.webopedia.com/quick_ref/textmessageabbreviations.asp.

Thornberry, N. E. (1987, October). Training the engineer as project manager: How to turn technical types into top-notch project managers. *Training and Development Journal, 60*–62.

Tschirhart, M., & St. Clair, L. (2008). Fine lines: Design and implementation challenges in employee volunteer programs. In M. Liao-Troth (Ed.), *Challenges in volunteer management—A volume of research in public management* (pp. 205–225). Charlotte, NC: Information Age Publishing.

Toulmin, S., Rieke, R., & Janik, A. (1984). *An introduction to reasoning.* New York: Macmillan.

U. S. Sentencing Commission. (1995, September 7-8). Corporate crime in America: Strengthening the "good citizen" corporation. Proceedings of the Second Symposium on Crime and Punishment in the United States, Washington, D. C. Available: http://www.ussc.gov.

U. S. Sentencing Commission. (2004). Sentencing commission toughens requirements for corporate compliance and ethics programs. Available: http://www.ussc.gov/PRESS/rel10404.htm accessed 8 December 2009.

U. S. Sentencing Commission. (2007). Chapter 8, Sentencing of organizations. In *Guidelines manual.* Available: http://www.ussc.gov/2007guid/CHAP8.pdf.

Waddock, S. A., Bodwell, C., & Graves, S. B. (2002). Responsibility: The new business imperative. *Academy of Management Executive, 16*(3), 132–178.

Walsh, P. (2005). Dumbing down performance measures. *Measuring Business Excellence, 9*(4), 37–45.

Warren, D. E. (2003). Constructive and destructive deviance in organizations. *Academy of Management Review, 28*(4), 622–632.

Wenger, E. C., & Snyder, W. M. (2000). Communities of practice: The Organizational frontier. *Harvard Business Review, 78,* 139–145.

Wicks, A. & St. Clair, L. (2007). Competing values in heath care: Balancing the (un)balanced scorecard. *Journal of Healthcare Management, 52*(5), 305–232.

Winston, S. (2001). *The organized executive: New ways to manage time, paper and people.* New York: Warner.

Winston, S. (2004). *Organized for success: Top executives and CEOs reveal the organizing principles that helped them reach the top.* New York: Crown Business.

Wurman, R. S. (1989). *Information anxiety.* New York: Doubleday.

Wurman, R. S. (2001). *Information anxiety 2.* Indiana: QUE.

■ COMPETENCIES

Developing and Communicating a Vision

Setting Goals and Objectives

Motivating Self and Others

Designing and Organizing

Managing Execution and Driving for Results

I n contrast to the human relations and internal process models, which take an internal focus, the rational goal model takes an external focus. It is similar to the internal process quadrant, however, in its emphasis on control and its connection to early management theories. This module in many ways reflects the more traditional definitions and purposes of leadership and organization.

Organizational Goals. The primary goals of the rational goal model are improving productivity and increasing profitability. Consistent with the assumptions of the rational goal model, the competencies in this module focus on providing clear direction as a means of achieving productive and profitable outcomes. Reflecting the external focus of this quadrant, Compete is the action imperative. Key activities focus on goal clarification, rational analysis, and action taking.

Paradoxes. Despite its emphasis on logic and rationality, paradoxes are also evident in the Compete quadrant. For example, at the same time that people want a leader to provide a clear vision for the organization, people are unwilling to embrace a vision unless they see the vision as their own. For their part, good managers want to take the lead and move ahead, but they also want to take time to be sure that they have all the relevant facts and are making the best possible decision. In terms of goal setting, we often discover that performance management systems, which are needed to ensure that individual goals are aligned with organizational goals, can become so complex that we feel that too much time is spent setting goals and not enough is spent working to achieve those goals.

Competencies.   In organizing the five competencies in this module, we begin at the highest level of abstraction with the importance of *developing and communicating a vision.* A vision communicates answers to the basic and timeless questions: Who are we? Where are we going? and Why are we going there? These are the bedrock questions that help us understand and justify the reason for the organization's existence. For individual leaders, the root questions are: What do I care most about? and How do I want to spend my life in pursuit of what is most important to me? A vision provides us with a destination, a desired future. To support that vision, our discussion of *setting goals and objectives* addresses the question: How will we get to our destination? Our next competency, *motivating self and others,* brings us to the question of energy— Where does it come from and how can we best use it? Energy relates to concepts such as inspiration, commitment, and perseverance in pursuit of our vision. Our next competency, *designing and organizing,* addresses organizational structure and culture, and their impact on our ability to achieve our vision. Lastly, we address organizational-level processes, leader behaviors, and individual-level issues associated with *managing execution and driving for results.* We explore each of the competencies in turn to see how they support individual and organizational efforts to compete in dynamic, complex environments.

Module 3 Competency 1   Developing and Communicating a Vision

ASSESSMENT   Your Experiences with Communicating a Vision

Objective   Developing and communicating a vision is a skill that is important for managers. The exercise below is designed to help you assess your prior experience with some of the key issues associated with the effective communication of a compelling vision.

Directions   Think about situations where you have made suggestions for taking some action. This could be while working with a team (e.g., project, work group, or committee) or individually (e.g., making suggestions to a supervisor, coworker, subordinate, family member, or friend). With these examples in mind, please respond to each of the items below using the following scale:

Rarely	Seldom	Sometimes	Often	Very often
1	2	3	4	5

When making suggestions for taking action, I . . .

_____ 1. explain how my idea fits in with the "big picture" of what we want to accomplish.

_____ 2. justify my suggestion and explain why it would be the right thing to do.

_____ 3. emphasize the rational arguments for taking that action.

_____ 4. try to connect the needs and interests of others to the action I'm suggesting.

_____ 5. talk about my suggestion in terms of what we would ideally like to accomplish.

_____ 6. try to make my suggestion as vivid as possible.

_____ 7. offer compelling examples of how my approach will make a difference to people.

_____ 8. avoid getting into too many details until others have agreed to my basic idea.

_____ 9. try to explain how my suggestion will benefit us all in the future.

_____ 10. look for ways to connect what I want to do with what others want to do.

Reflection　Each of the items above relates to some aspect of developing and communicating a vision. The higher your score, the more practice you have already had at using this important competency.

LEARNING　Developing and Communicating a Vision

Why is vision so important for individual leaders and for organizations? When Kouzes and Posner (1995, p. 21) asked thousands of people on many continents over a 20-year period what they expected of their leaders—what was required to generate respect and commitment in followers—the first answer was vision. These researchers argue that vision is what people want most from a leader. Vision is crucial to organizational success.

As we begin to look back on the first decade of the twenty-first century, there are additional reasons for the increasing importance of vision in organizational life. The demographics of the workforce have undergone monumental change, with increasing diversity on almost every dimension imaginable. As the baby-boom generation begins to cycle out of the workforce (or, in some cases, cut back on time spent in paid employment), the next generation of workers is already fomenting changes in the nature of work. Expectations about careers and psychological contracts (beliefs about the obligations of employers and employees to each other) are very different today from what they were when the rational goal model was initially proposed. For example, a recent *Fortune* magazine cover story on Generation Y in the workplace is very telling. A young man and woman stand next to the headline: "'Manage' Us? Puh-leeze" (2007). Many of the individuals in this new generation entering the workplace do not want to be "managed"; don't even think of it, much less try it! In addition to wanting a big say in where, when, and how they work, they also want more than a pay check. They want to ply their talents in ways that bring them meaning and fulfillment. Merely "motivating" this generation will not suffice. They want and demand inspiration.

In this Learning section, we consider both the mechanics of crafting an inspiring vision and the impact that a visionary leader can have on an organization. In terms of mechanics, the formulation of a vision includes three key processes. First, a vision must be *framed and defined*. Second, a vision must have the right *components and content*. Finally, a vision must be *effectively articulated and communicated*. We will consider each of these issues in turn.

PROCESSES FOR FORMULATING A VISION

Vision does not arise in a mysterious manner. Research suggests that vision emerges as a leader surveys the situation and finds ideas that await a champion (Nanus, 1992). The story of Charles Schwab and Company, as reported by Morris (2005) and summarized in Box M3.1, provides an example of how visions can emerge from a combination of changes in the environment and long-standing personal values.

BOX M3.1 A STOCKBROKER'S MAVERICK VISION

In 1975, on May 1—the day the U.S. Securities and Exchange Commission (SEC) deregulated brokerage commissions—Charles Schwab started his own company built on what was a unique and quite unconventional idea—that there might be a profitable business in selling stock to the middle class. Charles Schwab and Company was based in San Francisco (not Wall Street), and on that day when the SEC deregulated—every other brokerage firm increased fees on individual investors—Schwab lowered its commissions by more than 50 percent. Schwab's "rogue" status continued when it became the first firm to bundle mutual funds together and to force the funds—not individual investors—to absorb the cost of trading fees. Schwab was also the first discount brokerage to add a network of hundreds of branch offices across the United States. The company grew fast (long before the dot-com bubble) and became the biggest, most successful discount brokerage firm in the industry, and Charles Schwab became a multibillionaire and a household name.

In May 2010, Charles Schwab operates in a vastly different environment but is still committed to the same vision of helping individual investors. As in 1975, Schwab is once again trying to encourage people to invest in the stock market, maintain a broadly diversified portfolio, and hold stocks for the long term. Unlike 1975, however, far more people have personal experience with the stock market's rollercoaster ride and are afraid to get back on. Many individuals who watched their investments fall dramatically in 2008 failed to heed Schwab's advice to "just hang on" and fled from the stock market as it neared its March 2009 bottom. As a result, Schwab now faces the difficult task of coaxing people to return to investing so they don't miss out as the market rebounds.

Charles Schwab saw an opportunity in changing circumstances. Suddenly the industry was being deregulated. He anticipated a need in the middle class. His concern for the middle class was genuine, not just a business gimmick. His vision led him to a unique path; it took his organization to places other organizations could not go. When market conditions change, Schwab adjusts its business model and its tactics. What remains constant is Charles Schwab's original vision—to build a company driven by the best interests of its clients and their long term financial security.

Sources: Adapted from Morris (2005, 2010).

FRAMING AND DEFINING A VISION

Just as we can use a camera to create a focal point for a photograph, framing and defining a vision create a focus for organizational attention. Having a clear focus helps identify what the organization should be doing, as well as what the organization does not need to do. For example, Charles Schwab's decision to focus on middle-class clients meant that the company could concentrate its marketing efforts, rather than trying to appeal to clients at all income levels.

Kouzes and Posner (1995) use the metaphors of "doorman" and "jigsaw puzzle" when talking about the leader's role with respect to framing and defining a vision. As a "doorman," the leader opens the door to the future, helping people see what is ahead and what needs to be done. With respect to the "jigsaw puzzle" metaphor, it is much easier to put a puzzle together if you can see the picture on the cover of the box. No matter how many individuals are involved in the shaping of a vision, followers expect the leader to have the "big picture." In a typical organizational setting, many individuals have different pieces of the organizational puzzle. Employees may have detailed descriptions of their roles and responsibilities, but in many cases they lack the "big picture," the overall purpose or vision of the organization. Being aware of a vision and being inspired by that vision, however, are two different things. To a large extent, inspiration comes from the components and contents of the vision.

IDENTIFYING KEY COMPONENTS AND CONTENT

What is it about a vision—"a realistic, credible, attractive future" (Nanus, 1992)—that makes it impactful and effective? Three components need to be identified for a vision to capture the attention of others. First, a case needs to be made to justify changing from the status quo. Second, ideal goals need to be identified to show how the future will differ from the past. Third, the vision needs to recognize the people whose actions are necessary if the vision is to be achieved.

Making a Case for Change. In making a case for change, leaders need to clearly explain why their vision for the future is better than the status quo. The case for change may be based on a variety of factors such as changing economic conditions, new customer/market demands, the threat of rival products, or advances in technology. Regardless of the specific reason given, when deciding whether or not to accept the leader's vision, people must be convinced that change is needed. This often proves to be a difficult task and is addressed in more detail in the competency Implementing and Sustaining Change in Module 4.

Identifying Ideal Goals. A powerful vision offers followers an ideal goal or goals toward which to strive. Ideal goals establish a standard for excellence. They are not so specific as to define final outcomes or end-states, but rather relate to ideal conditions or processes.

Focusing on People. Making a case for change and establishing lofty goals set the stage for the third component of an effective vision—a focus on people. Who are the stakeholders who will be required to act to make the vision a reality? Who will benefit if the vision is realized?

ARTICULATING AND COMMUNICATING A VISION

By definition, leaders are constantly communicating since they operate in the largest of fishbowls. Everything they do and say (as well as how they do it and how they say it) is closely examined. Likewise, people pay attention to what is not done and what is not said. Given this high level of scrutiny, leaders must choose carefully what to communicate and how to most effectively communicate it, particularly when it comes to vision. Whatever medium a leader chooses (e.g., dialogue, speeches, written communications, etc.), the most important attributes of the message must be consistency and authenticity. Leaders communicate the vision through their words and their actions. Sashkin (1989) suggests that these words and actions take one of three forms: strategic, tactical, and personal. Similarly, Nicholls (1994) argues that transformational leaders address the heads, hands, and hearts of followers.

Heads—Strategic Communication of the Vision.   At a strategic level, many organizations attempt to articulate a clear organizational philosophy centered on the specific elements of their visions. Johnson & Johnson, for example, has its well-known credo or philosophy. The credo proved particularly important in 1982 when seven people died because some Tylenol bottles were laced with cyanide. The media coverage was extensive; all over the world the company faced crisis-level pressures. Later, the CEO indicated that during a crisis, a company cannot be managed. Too many things are happening at once. Johnson & Johnson's CEO had to trust the people to live the company values. They did. In thousands of decisions, the employees knew they needed to do the right thing, to live the values. They put the public interest first and made hard decision after hard decision. Decisions that led to the recall over $100 million in products and a national advertising campaign to alert customers. The result was impressive. The company saved the brand because the public believed they could trust what was being done. The people of Johnson & Johnson lived the vision (Collins & Porras, 1994, p. 69).

A vision and philosophy make a difference when they are clear enough to allow individuals to make decisions when acting autonomously. Such a vision is necessary, but not sufficient, to ensure that the ideals of the organization are upheld. For example, despite its vaunted credo, culture, and history, Johnson & Johnson was recently accused of paying kickbacks to Omnicare, a pharmacy company that primarily dispenses drugs to nursing homes, to increase sales of several J&J medications (Singer, 2010). In addition to having a clear vision, organizations must also have specific tactical policies and practices to ensure that the actions taken by employees are consistent with the vision.

Hands—Tactical Policies and Practices.   For the power of a vision to be realized, it must not only be communicated persuasively, but it also must be translated into practices that can be implemented to support the vision. The heads and hands must work together—followers must know what they need to *do* to make the vision a reality.

One example of a company that has excelled at moving from vision to implementation is Southwest Airlines. Southwest's record of profitability in the intensely competitive airline industry is often linked with the leadership of founder and former CEO, Herb Kelleher. Kelleher would be the first to insist, however, that one person does not make a successful company. Successful companies depend on "a tremendous mosaic made up of thousands of people" (quoted in Gittell, 2005, p. 56). In her book, *The Southwest Airlines Way,* Jody Gittell explores 10 organizational practices (see Table M3.1) that Southwest has developed to support the company's vision. These 10 practices help to create an environment of "relational coordination" that is characterized by shared goals, shared knowledge, mutual respect, and communication that is frequent, timely, and focused on problem-solving (Gittell, 2005, p. 198).

Hearts—Communicating at the Personal Level. Perhaps the most critical and most challenging aspect of communicating a vision is touching the hearts and connecting with the personal values and aspirations of followers. The vision must inspire followers to want to pursue it—it must be compelling and challenging. It must pique the curiosity of followers, tap into their essential motivations, and build a commitment that will bind them for the long-term in pursuit of the vision. The leader can exert incredible influence with the clear and compelling communication of the vision. Ultimately, visions are about creating the future. The more direct and authentic the plea to the heart of the follower, the better. For example, when Beth-Israel Deaconess Medical Center hired Paul Levy in 2002, the institution was "heading toward collapse" (Gray, 2005, p. 36). Levy was able to turn the organization around by connecting with the heads, hands, and hearts of employees. (Garvin & Roberto, 2005). In particular, Levy's honesty and openness with employees played a major role in establishing the trust necessary to gain the commitment and energy of employees (Garvin & Roberto, 2002).

Through his repeated and consistent messages about the vision in every medium of communication used, Paul Levy has been able to frame the vision for Beth-Israel Deaconess Medical Center so people can see a clear picture of the future. Tactical policies and practices are in place that let people know what they need to do to help achieve

TABLE M3.1 Ten Southwest Airlines Organizational Practices for Building High Performance Relationships (Gittell, 2005, p. 198)

1. Leading with credibility and caring
2. Invest in frontline leadership
3. Hire and train for relational competence
4. Use conflicts to build relationships
5. Bridge the work/family divide
6. Create boundary spanners
7. Measure performance broadly
8. Keep jobs flexible at the boundaries
9. Make unions your partners
10. Build relationships with suppliers

that vision. Most important, Levy has articulated a vision that is compelling enough to continue to inspire employees to meet any challenges they face. In an email he sent to all employees during the turnaround, Levy reminded everyone where they were headed: ". . . our target is not just survival: It is to thrive and set an example for what a unique academic medical center like ours means for this region" (quoted in Garvin & Roberto, 2005, p. 111). Finally, because he recognizes that future success is never guaranteed, Levy continues to communicate regularly with employees, using both traditional media and newer options such as Twitter (Miller, 2009).

Levy and other leaders like him are examples of individuals who are not simply leaders who have developed and communicated a vision, they are visionary leaders in the truest sense of the term.

VISIONARY LEADERS

The process described above is designed to result in a vision that is consistent with what we know about expectations for visionary leaders. To be perceived as visionary, leaders need to use powerful imagery to provide a sense of mission or purpose that challenges the status quo (Bass & Avolio, 1997). In this way, every individual leader has the ability to develop and communicate a vision that positively impacts the organization.

Research also has shown that the impact of the visionary leader goes beyond defining the direction for the organization; it also positively influences employees and inspires them to engage in extra effort; and, as a result, firm performance is likely to be improved (de Luque, Washburn, Waldman & House, 2008). In their study of CEOs in 520 firms in 17 countries, de Luque et al. (2008) also found that followers identified CEOs who emphasized stakeholder values as being visionary leaders. In contrast, these researchers found that leaders who focused more narrowly on economic values were more likely to be seen as being autocratic leaders.

Visionary leaders can be found in all types of settings, including families being led by a single parent, not-for-profit organizations, governmental units, business start ups, and multinational corporations. Our ideas about visionary leaders are drawn from media reports on people like Charles Schwab, Herb Kelleher, and Paul Levy. They are also drawn from our own experiences with parents, teachers, coaches, and friends who have inspired us to work toward a new future in our own personal sphere of influence. All these visionary leaders have lessons to teach us, so it is important to listen to their stories. In the next section, we highlight two visionary leaders who exemplify the ability to embrace competing values and transcend paradox.

FROM PARADOX TO INFINITY (AND BEYOND)

Steve Jobs (Apple Computer and Pixar) and Jeff Bezos (Amazon.com and Blue Origin) have both been hailed as visionary leaders. Their visions have truly changed the world. One of the things that sets them apart from many other leaders is their comfort with paradox. For example, in writing about Steve Jobs, Fry (2010, p. 43) uses descriptors that reflect concern for both flexibility and control and an emphasis on external focus:

[Steve Jobs] exists somewhere between showman, perfectionist overseer, visionary, enthusiast and opportunist, and his insistence upon design, detail, finish, quality, ease of use and reliability are a huge part of Apple's success" *(Fry, 2010, p. 43)*.

Create, Compete, Control—the only action imperative not reflected above is Collaborate. With respect to the Collaborate action imperative, Steve Jobs has had notable failures as well as major successes. Described both as charming and as arrogant and intolerant (Booth, Jackson & Marchant, 1997), Jobs' ouster in 1985 from Apple (the company he co-founded) might suggest a lack of skill at handling conflicts. However, it was Jobs, in 1997, who encouraged dispirited designer, Jonathan Ive, to stay with Apple. As a result, the re-energized Ive went on to develop the iMac, the iPod, and the iPhone at Apple (Fry, 2010). And it was Jobs who negotiated a strategic alliance with rival Bill Gates at Microsoft (a.k.a. the evil empire to Macintosh users) that was to be Apple's salvation (Booth, et al., 1997).

In contrast to Steve Jobs, who has been on the cover of *Time* magazine six times, Jeff Bezos, with only one *Time* cover to his credit so far, might seem a bit overmatched, but both men share the kind of passion that can be leveraged to turn threats into opportunities. They also share a willingness to embrace paradox, rather than compromise their values, a point emphasized by Alan Deutschman (2004) in his profile of Bezos for *Fast Company:*

[Jeff Bezos] Amazon.com's founder is a study in contradictions—analytical and intuitive, careful and audacious, playful and determined. . . . The seeming contradictions are what make Bezos so unusual—and so formidable. . . . He's the rare leader who obsesses over finding small improvements in efficiency at Amazon's huge warehouses right now while sustaining an entrepreneur's grand vision of changing the world over decades. Depending on the situation, he can be hyperrational or full of faith, left- or right-brained, short or long term. That's why he endured even after other 1990s dotcom founders handed over power.

Bezos himself has said, "The thing about inventing is you have to be both stubborn and flexible. The hard part is figuring out when to be which!" (quoted in Deutschman, 2004).

Although not every visionary leader attains the visibility and impact achieved by Steve Jobs or Jeff Bezos, we all can make a difference within our own sphere of influence. You can get started now, by understanding your personal passion and crafting your own leadership story.

FROM PERSONAL PASSION TO LEADERSHIP STORY

As we suggested at the beginning of this Learning segment, the fundamental questions that must be answered in an organizational vision also need to be addressed by the leader individually—Who am I? Where am I going? Why am I going there? Being able to answer these questions on a personal level can help individuals sustain the passion they need to persevere as leaders in challenging times. This is an ongoing process, one that we introduced in the Module 1 competency, Understanding Self and Others. In *Leading Out Loud*, Terry Pearce, the founder and president of Leadership Communication, a company that coaches high-profile corporate, political and community leaders, states:

As a leader, you can inspire commitment by looking inward first, by becoming aware of what you want to say, and by communicating a much more personal vision of the future, based on much more personal knowledge of the past and realistic experience in the present. Such a focus means initially ignoring potential followers in favor of personal passion. Leaders who develop their message only on the basis of what others might want invariably play to others and only try to please them. Focusing on the themes of your own consciousness is the real driver of what you have to say. Others' reaction to you will be different, depending on which focus of communication you choose. If you only perform to other's standards, they may be entertained, but if you start the communication process with **your own passion**, they will be excited, and they will grasp a new and real possibility from your own authentic experience" *(Pearce, 2003, p. 16)*.

Bennis and Nanus (1985) also stress the need for self-knowledge as a prerequisite to leadership effectiveness. Their work suggests that leaders are most successful when they "know what they want" because knowing that depends upon being clear about your individual core values.

Leadership scholars often refer to the leader's personal story or personal point of view. It is this story or point of view that makes the leader an original—an authentic leader who can effectively inspire others to pursue the organization's visions because she is clear and in touch with her personal vision and values and that in turn makes her a more effective proponent and communicator of the organization's vision. This fundamental dynamic requires the leader to be inspired by his own personal/core values and vision for self before he can most effectively inspire others to the organization's vision. The following exercises will give you an opportunity to analyze a successful manager's vision, work on creating your own personal leadership story, and consider how your story fits with your current career objectives.

ANALYSIS   S. K. Ko: The Reluctant Visionary

Objective   This exercise will give you a chance to analyze a successful leader's vision and process for developing that vision.

Directions   Read the following case study on S. K. Ko (adapted from *Motorola Penang* by J. Stewart Black, 2005 – used with permission), and answer the questions that follow.

S. K. Ko was appointed Managing Director of Motorola's Penang, Malaysia, facility in 1990. S. K. was the first native Malaysian to occupy the Managing Director position in Penang. Up until her appointment, Motorola Penang had four Managing Directors all of whom were Americans on expatriate assignment. Prior to joining Motorola, S. K. had been the first female engineer at Intel's Penang facility and later held a position as a systems engineer at IBM. Ko joined Motorola in 1982 as an MIS group leader and later she was appointed the materials manager. During the 1980s, Motorola Penang saw many of its processes automated and found itself producing more and more complex products. During the time period before she became Managing Director, "sales" for Motorola Penang went from $112 million to $155 million over a five-year period. While this was quite a significant increase, Ko still felt that both the physical and intellectual capabilities at the Penang operation were being underutilized.

S. K. Ko had a very aggressive and challenging vision for the future of the Motorola Penang facility, and she struggled with the most effective way of making that vision a reality. Ko once stated: "Ideally a vision is something that will both inspire and direct people. However, there is always the tension for a leader when it comes to giving and receiving a vision. As a leader you are expected to give the vision. But as the leader you know people will embrace visions best that they see with their own eyes—visions that they feel are their own—and not just imposed on them" (Black, 2005, p. 1). For Ko, how to approach the vision process was a dilemma. She engaged many of her top team in discussions about the challenges of the future of the facility, but they still looked to her as the leader and wanted to hear her vision of the future. Ko had many specific and concrete ideas but did not want to seem to be imposing them on the group—and, she was not totally convinced that her ideas were the appropriate and best ones. She very much wanted to get the most involvement possible from her team to ensure all relevant information was considered and to ensure buy-in and commitment from the team that would be tasked with making the vision a reality. But, she was also anxious to move forward; at the same time she was getting ever more pressure from her team to "take the lead" and share her vision.

S. K. Ko prepared a statement summarizing her management philosophy.

My Thoughts on Management by S. K. Ko

Treat your people with respect, as you would treat your own family. No yelling, no shouting, no finger pointing. Give visible rewards for achievers. Create enthusiasm. Share every success story. Minimize use of money as rewards and recognition. Preach the importance of knowledge, and advances in technology. Learning is a must. Encourage people to work in teams, to teach each other, to think about how to do better. Get to know your people. Constantly share your vision and thoughts with them. Encourage people to recommend new ideas. Give your managers challenges and let them rise to these challenges. Always be fair—irrespective of race and sex. Remember, it is the people who make the difference, no matter how automated you are. Be a visible, responsible corporate citizen in the community. Have good press relations. Concentrate on good image, high profile. Make this place the company of choice for new university graduates. Learn to always look for the positive qualities of a person.

Clearly, Ko's philosophy very much reflects a positive, familial, celebrate-every-accomplishment kind of work environment. At the same time, she took a very hard-nosed approach to Motorola Penang's viability and business model. She saw technology as a two-sided coin that would eliminate low-skill jobs at the same time that it brought new opportunities. She knew that other countries had lower labor costs. She was committed to rapidly moving Motorola Penang to produce more complex systems products, creating an increased demand for technicians and engineers and potentially less demand for unskilled operators. She had never had to do a lay-off, and she was worried about lower-skilled operators' ability to adjust to the new reality—she feared that in many cases they only knew how to do one thing and that they might not survive unless they learn to do other things.

In December 1993, as part of a management retreat for the top 40 Motorola Penang managers, Ko addressed the future vision for the facility. She tried to engage and get the input of the 40 by asking them to envision the factory in the year 2000 and then identify what needed to be done then, in 1994 to move closer to that vision. Her senior HR leader pressed her to share her vision. She pressed back once again and said she wanted to hear from them first. She finally relented.

Today we have nearly 3,000 employees but in six years, I believe that we will need only 1,500 people to produce over three times the sales turnover. Now we have islands of automation, but in six years I envision a factory that is integrated and automated from front to back—a lights out factory. Rather than simply producing components for products designed in the States for sale in Asia, I envision an Asian Design Center. Whereas now we produce many components for products, I envision us producing entire products and whole systems—maybe 50% of the total *(adapted from S. K. Ko vision statement as reported in Black, 2005).*

Ko chose to focus on five major activities to help build capability of Motorola Penang and its employees to achieve this very ambitious vision. First, external relationships—Motorola Penang had built up a very good reputation for all that it had accomplished thus far. Ko knew she had to maintain and expand those relationships—including bringing in "corporate" to the visioning process she had commenced at the management off-site. Second, management development—Ko knew she had to groom managers for the new roles that the future facility would require. Examples of how she did this include the establishment of a Master of Industrial Management program with the University of East Asia. Third, maintaining state of the art manufacturing and administrative technologies—Ko knew she had to nudge the evolution from low technology infrastructure, to robotics, to islands of automation, and finally to a fully automated factory to keep Motorola Penang competitive against the lowest cost producers in the world. Fourth, participative management processes—consistent with her own personal leadership values, Ko did everything possible to make Motorola Penang a high-involvement work place. Fifth and last, technical skills development—Ko was successful in establishing a Masters of Mechanical Engineering degree program with the University of Malaysia with classes held right on the Motorola Penang grounds.

Discussion Questions

1. How effective was Ko in defining and framing a vision for Motorola Penang? In what ways were her efforts similar to and different from the example of Charles Schwab cited earlier?

   - How did Ko resolve the dilemma of where visions come from? Where did she find her vision?

   - We cited doorman and jigsaw puzzle metaphors when describing how different leaders see themselves. Do either of these metaphors seem relevant to Ko?

2. Evaluate the content dimensions of Ko's vision work at Motorola Penang. How did she do with:

   - Making the Case for Change
   - Identifying an Ideal Goal
   - Addressing the People dimension

3. With respect to the Articulating and Communicating the Vision, how effectively did Ko address the three different levels of:

   - Strategic—"HEAD"
   - Tactical—"HANDS"
   - Personal—"HEART"

Reflection

S. K. Ko provided visionary direction. What do you think was the single most valuable aspect of what she did? With this in mind, think about your own orientation to the future. Do you have visions for your education, career, and life? What are they? How do these guide you? Have you ever articulated a vision for others? What worked and why?

PRACTICE Crafting Your Leadership Story

Objective

This exercise is adapted from *Leading Out Loud* by T. Pearce (2003); it is designed to give you an opportunity to begin or revisit your work on your personal leadership story.

Directions   Please take one hour, in a quiet place where you can do some reflection in solitude and write a draft of your leadership story. Consider the following chapter "headings":

- Chapter 1: The Early Years. Recall your formative years. How did your early personal experiences and family circumstances shape who you are today?
  What early messages, lessons, or values were inculcated during this life phase?

- Chapter 2: Angels and Heroes. Describe two people who have made a difference in your life— one from your personal life and one from your work life. What "leadership lessons" did you acquire from each person?

- Chapter 3: Leadership Courage. Think of a time in your life when your values were significantly challenged. How did you resolve or work through this situation?

- Chapter 4: Your Legacy. Everyone says it differently, but what do you think is the "true joy of life"? What personal values or wisdom would you want to pass on to those you care most deeply about?

Your instructor may construct discussion groups within which you can share your draft stories.

Reflection   Everyone has a story—leaders just use their stories better. Leaders recognize the defining moments in their lives and communicate those lessons in words and actions. Everyone's life is filled with experiences—traumatic, frustrating, or exhilarating—that can be the source of valuable learning. Stories create real human connections by allowing others to get inside our minds and our lives. With their human protagonists, dramas, and climaxes, they engage listeners on an emotional and intuitive level that is rarely touched by purely rational argument.

Presenting your leadership story to someone else takes courage, but inevitably, someone will want to hear about who you are and the story behind what is important to you. It may not come out in exactly those words, but that will be the reality of the experience. It may be during a job interview; it may come from a counselor or family member during a conversation about your career and future; or it may be part of an early conversation you have with someone with whom you are establishing a new relationship. But it will come, so be prepared.

APPLICATION   Envisioning Your Career

Objective   This application exercise will allow you to link your job search and career planning activities to your own personal vision and values (e.g., your personal leadership story as part of your leadership "point of view").

Directions   Identify three organizations where you might like to work someday. Starting with their company website, locate and print a copy of the organization's vision, mission, values, or whatever label the organization gives these types of statements.

Take each in turn, and lay it side-by-side with your personal leadership story draft. Begin to think about how you would answer the following questions, if asked by potential employers in each of the organizations you identified:

- What about this organization makes you want to be a part of it?

- Why this company and not (insert names of two most obvious competitors)?

- What do you want most from an organization/career?

- What is it about you that makes you think you would be a good fit for us and that we would be a good fit for you?

- What do you see as the most important values that define who you are as an individual?
- How aligned do you think those values will be with our organization? Why?

To help you refine your answers, your instructor may have you role play these conversations in dyads.

Reflection   Career planning should not be something that you do only when you are actively seeking a job. With demanding workloads and busy lives outside of work, however, it is easy to let career planning get pushed to the back burner. Regularly updating your career plan ensures that you are prepared if an unexpected opportunity arises. It can also help you recognize early that you are no longer on a path you feel passionate about pursuing. That knowledge gives you the opportunity to make changes that will lead to a more satisfying future.

Some people may feel that they have too much invested in their careers to make a change, but those past investments are "sunk costs." Rather than looking at past investments, you should consider only the future costs and benefits of making a career change. Consider the example of H. Edward (Ed) Roberts. Although known to many people primarily for his first career in the computer industry, Roberts's second career, as a doctor in rural Georgia, was perhaps even more important to others.

Roberts invented the Altair 8800, the first affordable home computer, which sold for $397 back in 1975. It was the Altair 8800 that led Bill Gates and Paul Allen to write Microsoft Basic. And it was Ed Roberts' company, Micro Information and Telemetry Systems in Albuquerque, New Mexico, that first distributed software for what would become the largest software company in the world. Despite his investment of time and money in the nascent computer hardware industry, Roberts had a different vision for himself. In 1977 he sold his company and moved to Georgia where he had a farm and wrote software. Later, Roberts revived his dream of becoming a doctor, attending medical school and practicing medicine until his death in 2010. In Roberts' obituary, Paul Allen noted, " . . . until he got sick, Ed was seeing up to 30 patients a day as a country doctor in Cochran, Ga. I'm sure they are all glad he didn't rest on his laurels" (Allen, 2010; "Ed Roberts (computer engineer), 2010; Lohr, 2010; "The tinkerer who helped spark the PC revolution," 2010).

Module 3 Competency 2   Setting Goals and Objectives

ASSESSMENT   Identifying Your Personal Goals

Objective   In this assessment, our intent is to get you thinking about goal setting as it relates to your academic, personal, and professional life as a prelude to discussing goal and objective setting in organizations. The questions for consideration that follow will help you focus on basic aspects of goal-setting processes. There are several keys to making *any* goal-setting process effective, and we discuss those throughout the Learning section that follows as we explore some of the connections, relationships, and challenges involved in setting goals and objectives that help us achieve our personal visions.

Directions   List *at least* one goal (but do not restrict yourself to one) that you have in each of the following four categories. You will be referring back to these goals throughout discussions and activities in this and other sections of the textbook.

1. Personal relationships
2. Academic/scholastic accomplishments

3. Career/job interests

4. Your financial future

Questions for Consideration

1. Are these goals consistent with your story/vision from the Practice segment in Developing and Communicating a Vision?

2. How do you know that the goals you identified will bring you closer to the realization of your personal vision?

3. How difficult and challenging are each of these goals?

4. Do the various goals support and complement one another, or might there be some potential conflict and competition among some of the goals?

5. How will you measure progress and success on each of the various goals?

6. How would you go about resolving any questions, inconsistencies, or problems you have, based on your answers to the questions above?

Reflection

The goals and objectives we set for ourselves in our lives ideally flow directly from the visions and personal stories we craft for ourselves, as we did in the Practice for Developing and Communicating a Vision. Sometimes, however, we set goals that don't align very well with our vision. Such goals can take us off course if we don't occasionally take the time to step back and thoughtfully review them.

LEARNING   Setting Goals and Objectives

Moving forward logically from the development and communication of vision, we come to the formulation of specific organizational plans, goals, and objectives aimed at realizing the vision. Broader organizational goals ideally get translated into various sub-goals at the divisional, functional, or other business-unit level and then ultimately cascade down the organization to relevant departments, units, teams, and individuals. Again, this is an ideal—in practice, things are rarely so tidy!

Goal setting is a critical tool both for individual achievement and for directing the efforts of individuals and groups of individuals toward a common end. When Frederick W. Taylor, the father of scientific management, was defining the appropriate amount of pig iron to be handled by a single man in a single day, he was engaging in classic goal setting for blue-collar workers. This was a fine-grained process that clearly defined and delineated every aspect of the task: how it was to be performed, expected outcomes, and rewards for accomplishing it.

In the 1960s, "management by objectives" (MBO), a white-collar, managerially-focused version of goal-setting introduced by Peter Drucker (1954), emerged and became popular. Research, theory, and practice on goal setting continued unabated through the turn of the century. While much has changed about individuals—the work they do, the settings in which they work, and their attitudes towards work—goal setting continues to be a popular tool for managers today. Our plan in this section is to review the key lessons learned about goal setting from the past, get a clear understanding of how work environments in the new economy impact goal-setting effectiveness, and gain a fuller appreciation of the relationship between developing and communicating a vision and setting goals and objectives.

GOAL SETTING—THE BASIC BUILDING BLOCKS

What is goal setting, and why should managers be concerned about it? Goal-setting theory and research emerged when the rational goal model—the theoretical forerunner of the Compete quadrant of the competing values framework—held sway as the dominant model of organizational effectiveness. The rational goal model assumes an organization is effective if it successfully achieves the goals it is pursuing. For most businesses, then as now, a primary goal is profitability. For other organizations such as nonprofits and governmental agencies, goals typically focus on a accomplishing a mission, rather than achieving a profit. From a purely rational and logical perspective, goals define the results that people should aim to accomplish in pursuit of the organization's strategy and vision. Goals serve as the foundation for performance planning, review, rewards, and improvement efforts. Without goals, time and effort would be wasted on activities not specifically focused on the organization's success—as defined by its goals.

Goal setting takes place at all levels in an organization. The focus, purpose, and kinds of activities that are part of the process, however, vary with the level of the organization in which they take place. At the most senior levels of managerial leadership—at the enterprise level, for example, goal setting tends to be focused primarily around what Latham and Wexley (1994) refer to as the organization's superordinate goal—namely its *vision.* That focus tends to be strategic and directional. It involves an organization's most basic and fundamental decision: the choice of missions, strategies, and major allocations of resources. These strategic/visionary choices, taken together, will generally shape the organization's overall future.

As the goal-setting process cascades down throughout the organization to operating unit levels and ultimately to individual employees, goal setting should stay aligned with superordinate goals set by the most senior organization leaders. At these lower levels, goal setting tends to be more tactical, with a primary emphasis on *implementing* and carrying out decisions made as part of the vision development and strategic planning process. At the tactical level, the process involves the following:

1. Formulating specific objectives, targets, or quotas that need to be achieved by a certain time.
2. Developing an action plan to be followed and identifying specific steps to be taken to meet or exceed those objectives.
3. Creating a schedule showing when specific activities will be started and/or completed.
4. Developing a "budget" (including any type of necessary resources).
5. Estimating or projecting what will have happened at certain points during the life span of the plan.
6. Establishing an organization to implement decisions.
7. Setting standards against which performance will be evaluated.

Some parts of this list should look familiar—the Module 2 competencies of Planning and Coordinating Projects and Measuring and Monitoring Performance and Quality both require that tactical goals have been set to help the organization achieve its vision.

GOAL-SETTING AS THE FOUNDATION FOR A PERFORMANCE MANAGEMENT SYSTEM

The seven-step goal-setting process above seems very logical, rational, and straightforward. As one begins to unpack each of these steps, the challenges and complexities of goals setting in twenty-first century organizations become apparent very quickly. Complex organizational designs (discussed later in this module) often contain structures that are differentiated horizontally, vertically, geographically, and culturally (e.g. global organizations). Translating the vision and strategy into a set of goals and objectives for the entire organization becomes an enormous exercise in direction setting to ensure that goals are aligned with the vision, as well as with information distribution, communication, and decision-making processes.

As we suggested above, the focus of goal setting typically varies with the relative level of the organization—with the more senior executives and leaders emphasizing superordinate (strategic) goals and mid-level and first line managers and supervisors focusing more on tactical goals for implementation and execution. Merely identifying and articulating superordinate goals at the top of an organization does not guarantee that they will be known, understood and accepted by the rest of the organization. Even when they are known, understood, and accepted by those throughout the organization, it remains a challenge to ensure that the goal-setting process that cascades down throughout the organization is vertically and horizontally aligned and results in goals and objectives that every individual in the organization owns and sees as directly connected to the vision of the organization. We will take each of these two major challenges—gaining knowledge, understanding, and acceptance of superordinate goals and translating and cascading them into individual goals clearly linked to the organization's vision—in turn and discuss how their successful resolution can result in a system of performance management for the organization.

GAINING STRATEGIC UNITY AND ALIGNMENT

One example of how organizations address the challenges of formulating high-level goals consistent with vision and strategy and ensuring that there is the necessary alignment across all of the various differentiated parts of an organization is described as "strategic unity and alignment" (Bolt, McGrath & Dulworth, 2005, p. 36). Those authors suggest that no team, function, business unit or organization could optimize its performance without a high degree of strategic unity. Strategic unity and alignment exist in organizations when four conditions are in place:

1. The unit or organization possesses a motivating and compelling vision, inspiring values, and a clear strategic intent.
2. Throughout the organization, the vision, values, and strategic intent are deeply understood and there is widespread ownership and commitment to them.
3. Across all units, teams, and individuals, goals and actions are aligned.
4. The unit or organization possesses the knowledge, skills, and mindset required to achieve the vision, live the values, and execute the strategy.

A striking example of trying to achieve strategic unity and alignment can be found in Microsoft's recent history, as described in Box M3.2.

BOX M3.2 PERFORMANCE MANAGEMENT AT MICROSOFT

In 2004, Microsoft Corporation, as part of its ongoing efforts to ensure that its structures and processes were in tune with its continuing growth and the complex business environment that all organizations were confronting, conducted a thorough review of its performance management system (we discuss the fundamentals of performance management in detail below). Microsoft wanted to ensure that its "culture based on business focus, disciplined execution, and accountability" would endure (Shaw, 2004, p. 140). Among the results of their review were findings suggesting that the rate of change was so great that setting specific goals for an entire year was becoming more difficult; there was no consistent process for aligning and cascading goals throughout the company, and in some groups, goals were assigned from the top with little or no discussion or explanation from managers. It was also concluded from the results of the review that goals were being seen more as aspirations than as a concrete commitments.

To address the concerns raised in the review, Microsoft executives changed the terminology of the performance management system from "goals" to "commitments" in the belief that a greater level of accountability is gained with a commitment versus a goal. Among other changes, the company combined that wording change with the institution of a process of commitment setting that started at the top and cascaded down and across the entire firm so that all commitments would be aligned. The process commenced with Microsoft's most senior executives gaining clarity on overall business focus so as to identify company-wide commitments. Those company-wide commitments focused on "driving shareholder value through innovation, customer responsiveness, and the development of talent" (Shaw, 2004, p.140). These company-wide commitments then drive the commitment setting process of the various organization, teams and individual's within the company.

Source: K. N. Shaw (2004), Change the goal-setting process at Microsoft. *Academy of Management Executive, 18*(4), 139–142.

Strategic unity and alignment, within the context of goal and objective setting, is by and large a top-down process. While most of the applications of it thus far have been within the context of executive development programs (Bolt, McGrath & Dulworth, 2005), the Microsoft example points out that it can be very useful in making the translation from vision/strategy to goals and objectives within the reality of large, multidifferentiated, complex global organizations. We will now turn to the second major challenge of using goal setting as a foundation for a system of performance management—translating the high-level goals (e.g., Microsoft's company-wide commitments) into individual goals clearly linked to the organization's vision.

TRANSLATING STRATEGY INTO INDIVIDUAL GOALS

Individual goals are one of the most critical elements of what organizations broadly refer to as performance management systems. In general, these systems are a series of processes and interactions between supervisors and their individual employees aimed at optimizing the performance of individual employees in achieving the organization's goals. Ideally, performance management systems accomplish the following in organizational settings:

▪ Connect the organizational vision and strategy to what individual employees do every day

▪ Promote accountability, effectiveness, and productivity

▪ Create focus and facilitate priority setting

▪ Create a shared commitment to performance between managers and employees

▪ Ensure that the organization realizes its core purposes as well as the growth and development of individual employees

Most performance management systems have four steps or phases including:

1. *Translation of vision to organizational unit goals.* Once the vision, strategy, and broad organizational goals are set, they are used to identify appropriately aligned goals for lower-level organizational, functional, departmental, and/or work team units.

2. *Joint establishment of individual goals.* Supervisors and employees agree on a specific set of goals and objectives for the individual to accomplish over a specific period of time.

3. *Ongoing coaching and feedback.* The individual is supported, guided and tracked during the specified performance period on her individual goals, receiving feedback, coaching and periodic assessments from the supervisor.

4. *Evaluation of performance.* The individual's performance is formally assessed relative to the goals established with the supervisor at the beginning of the performance period.

Translating Vision to Organizational Unit Goals. The Microsoft application of strategic unity and alignment provides us with an example of the first phase of the performance management cycle. The primary intent in this phase is to ensure that individual goals flow directly from organizational goals. The more individuals can see a direct connection between what they do every day at work and the organization's vision and strategy, the greater the likelihood that the vision will have the compelling, motivational, and inspirational qualities we discussed in the Developing and Communicating a Vision competency. This is a good example of the very important part that goal setting plays in the maximization of not only the Compete quadrant, but also the Collaborate quadrant. Connected, aligned cascading goals with clear links to the vision and strategy make the organization more effective in the Compete quadrant while at the same time enhancing the Collaborate quadrant's ability to connect and develop the human capital inside the organization.

Jointly Establishing Individual Goals. Individual goal setting, the second phase of most performance management processes, ideally begins with a discussion between the individual and her supervisor aimed at reaching agreement on what the individual's *goals* will be and what target *level of performance* will be for each of those goals.

The period of performance varies, but typically, organizations use a one-year cycle for formal annual reviews of individual performance, which often are related to base salary and incentive compensation changes. In addition, periodic less-formal reviews (twice or four times per year) may be used. Just as the reality of today's organizations makes top-down goal setting challenging, so too is the bottom-up process of individual goal setting. Peter Drucker (1954) used the term "management by objectives" (MBO) in his classic book *The Practice of Management*. Succeeding versions and generations of MBO have emphasized the rational and analytical precision required in the creation of goals and objectives that organizations can use to track and monitor the progress of employees. A paradox emerges, however, if the process becomes too mechanical and time consuming, because, as you will see in the Analysis section below, setting goals and objectives for individuals is as much about relationships, communication, and ambiguity as it is about rationality and analysis. This phase of the performance management cycle is a conversation, or series of conversations, focused not just on planning and defining performance but also on getting mutual agreement and buy-in from both parties. The process and how it is conducted is as important as the ultimate outcomes.

Ongoing Coaching and Feedback. In the third phase of performance management, ideally the supervisor supports, guides, and tracks the individual's performance during the specified performance period, providing feedback and coaching. This phase of the performance management cycle involves many of the skills and competencies we discuss throughout this textbook, including Motivating Self and Others and Managing Execution and Driving for Results in this module. In many ways, this part of the performance management cycle is where supervisors do the heavy lifting of their job: communicating, encouraging performance, making sure they are appropriately delegating, coaching, supporting, correcting, and training.

Evaluation of Performance. The fourth phase of the performance management cycle is what is usually referred to as the annual performance review or appraisal. This review ideally provides an opportunity for supervisors and individual employees to formally review their performance against the agreed-upon goals that were set at the beginning of the period. This review typically addresses outcomes attained—what actually got done/accomplished? What were the enablers and barriers? What skills, strengths, and development opportunities did the year's efforts surface? This phase of the cycle provides the opportunity to set goals and objectives for the next performance period. Just as the strategic unity and alignment process helps with creating consistency from the top down, effective organizations have a process for doing the same with the performance management cycle from the bottom up. Typically, an individual completes a self-appraisal of his performance for the prior year and submits it to the supervisor. The supervisor also completes the appraisal for the individual and usually must get it approved by one level of supervision above and/or the human resources department before discussing it with the individual. Most organizations also have a process for rolling up reviews and looking at the distribution of performance up, down, and across the organization.

SETTING "S.M.A.R.T." GOALS AND OBJECTIVES

Thirty years ago a management scholar named George Doran published an article entitled: "There's a S.M.A.R.T Way to Write Management's Goals and Objectives" (1981). In that article Doran unpacked his SMART acronym as a framework and guideline for use in formulating goals and objectives. The SMART framework is still widely used today, albeit in many slightly different adaptations. The version that we use requires SMART goals to be **S**pecific, **M**easurable, **A**ttainable, **R**elevant, and **T**ime-bound. We have found this approach to goal setting helpful at the individual- and organizational-level as well as with both the top-down and bottom-up dimensions that we have discussed. SMART goals ideally answer important, specific questions, as shown below. It may take you a few iterations to make your goals SMART, but this is time well spent.

SPECIFIC

The SMART goal describes an observable action or behavior, answering the question: What has to be done?

- Is the goal clearly stated?
- Does it describe a function to be performed?
- Does the wording connote action?

For example, if a student wants to improve his grade in a course, stating that goal as "get a better grade in calculus" or "earn an 85 average in calculus" doesn't really help much because it doesn't provide any guidance on what needs to be done to attain that higher grade. Specific goals don't just identify the desired end result, they include specific actions that will help you attain that desired outcome, like spending an hour each day working calculus problems.

MEASURABLE

A SMART goal defines the end result in qualitative or quantitative terms (e.g., quantities, frequencies, rates, etc.), answering the question: How much has to be done?

- Is the behavior quantifiable?
- Are limits and parameters defined?
- Can results be observed?

Our calculus student can easily measure how many hours he spends working problems and, because working more problems generally improves how well students understand calculus, that specific and measurable goal is well aligned with the more general goal of earning a better grade.

You may recall from our discussion of Measuring and Monitoring Performance in Module 2 that we criticized the use of some easily quantifiable measures. The situations, however, were quite different. There, we were referring to situations where the organization was allowing ease of measurement to drive the selection of goals. In the case of our calculus student, we are using strategically aligned goals to drive the choice of the appropriate measure to use. Measures should be connected to goals, and it is the goals that should drive our choice of measures.

ATTAINABLE

Can individuals be expected to achieve their SMART goals? Is the goal within reach or does it seem impossible?

- Does the person have the required experience and necessary skills and knowledge?
- Are the resources required to carry out the work available?
- Is the goal realistic under the circumstances?

As we'll explain in more detail in the next competency, Motivating Self and Others, one of the surest ways to undermine your success is by setting goals that are unattainable. For example, if our calculus student has been working an hour a day on problems for two weeks but then scores only 73 percent on the exam, he may conclude that an 85 average is out of reach and decide to go out for pizza rather than spend more time working calculus problems.

RELEVANT

Is the goal relevant to the person—does the individual have a reason to care about achieving the goal?

- Is the goal relevant to the work actually being done by the individual?
- Is there a clear link to organizational, departmental, team goals?
- Is there a clear link to the individual's key job tasks?
- Will this goal help in achievement of the person's development objectives/career plans?

Relevance generally comes into play when someone else is setting goals for you. If you don't see the relevance of doing well in calculus, you are unlikely to be motivated to spend time working problems, even if your advisor has given you advice about how to improve your grade.

TIME-BOUND

By when does the goal need to be achieved?

- Is there a clearly defined completion date?
- Is the duration for the goal set out?
- Is the frequency with which work must be performed clearly defined?

Last, but certainly not least, goals should have time frames. Research on organizational transformation by Gersick (1991) and Romanelli and Tushman (1994) suggests that the old adage, "If it weren't for deadlines, nothing would ever get done" has a great deal of truth in it.

ANALYSIS Objectives Don't Work for Me*

Objectives The following case can be analyzed in a number of different ways. Although we have included it within the Setting Goals and Objectives competency, it can also be used for analyzing the mentoring and communication skills of the manager and the communication skills of the employee.

Directions Assume that you are Nancy Stuart, plant personnel manager for Countrywide Manufacturing Company's local plant in Jamestown, Ohio, a city of about 17,000 people. The plant is the principal employer in the area. Read the following case* about one of your employees, Don Smith, and then answer the questions that follow.

During the past two years, the personnel division (see Figure M3.1 for the organization chart) in the central headquarters of Countrywide has been quite successful in helping line managers learn and implement a new management by objectives (MBO) program throughout the company. The vice president for personnel of Countrywide was recently embarrassed when the company president asked him, "If MBO is improving effectiveness in the line divisions throughout all the plants, why haven't you used it more in your own personnel area?" This resulted in a directive to you and all plant personnel officers to come up immediately with a five-year plan applying the MBO approach. You wrote a memorandum to your branch chiefs asking them to submit a first draft of a plan to include objectives and how they are to be implemented and evaluated. This would provide data for a planning conference of your branch chiefs.

Don Smith is the chief of your counseling branch. He was hired two years ago to replace an employee who was retiring. Don was right out of college, having completed a master's in counseling. He has proved himself to be highly successful in getting the line managers in the plant to use counseling services. The quality of his branch's service is recognized throughout the plant. Last year, Don recruited Donna Maire, who had just completed her graduate work. Don has trained her well, and the two of them are a great team. In addition, Don employs on a part-time basis three counselors (they work full time for the public health office, but are allowed to work for Countrywide in their free time). Don and Donna are the only regular employees in the branch.

The following is an informal memorandum you received from Don in answer to yours:

MEMORANDUM

TO: Nancy Stuart   FROM: Don Smith
RE: MBOs

I am scheduled to leave on my two-week vacation tonight, so I am writing you about my views on MBO. I am sure you will understand when I say MBO seems to apply to production areas very well and to areas of personnel such as wage and salary administration, but it really does not apply to counseling services. Last week, Donna and I saw a total of 25 employees for counseling and had 8 interviews with managers about problem people. The three part-time counselors each worked two hours last week, and their caseload was 4 each, for a total of 12. Compare this with the situation two years ago when I came aboard and the one-person counseling service was handling only 4 to 5 cases a week.

Our business is so pressing that the obvious objective is to get another full-time counselor. We find that more and more we have to book appointments for a week or two ahead. The people who need several sessions with a counselor because of the seriousness of their cases are being assigned whenever possible to the part-timers from Public Health. We are getting more and more calls from managers asking for help in handling nonproductive employees. One has asked us to work with him on a motivation program for his section that would help raise the production of all eight of his people. We have been able to do nothing so far on the

*Source: Don Smith's objection to objectives. In J. B. Lau and A. B. Shani, (1992). *Behavior in organizations: An experiential approach* (5th ed.; pp. 356–357). Reprinted by permission of Richard D. Irwin Inc. and the authors.

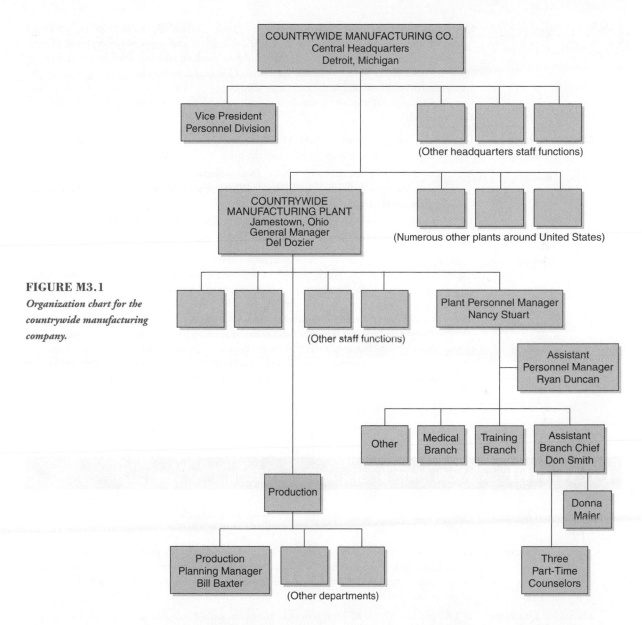

FIGURE M3.1

Organization chart for the countrywide manufacturing company.

program to help alcoholics and problem drinkers, which central headquarters thinks we should be doing. I am really not sure this is a problem here; we have had no referrals. Managers seem more interested in problems of pregnant women than social drinkers. We ought to also get started on a policy guidance statement for work-related stress illness.

Do you agree with me when I say that in a service area like counseling the main objective is to get enough qualified counselors to handle employee problems that already exist? So the objectives of my branch are (1) more personnel and (2) a bigger budget. If you need anything else on MBO for our branch, ask Donna. She knows our work as well as I do.

See you in two weeks,

Don Smith

Don's answer is the first you receive from your branch chiefs. You are a little taken aback and wonder if the rest of your team is going to be as flippant, and apparently perplexed, in trying to formulate their objectives. The chiefs of your medical training branches were making snide remarks about MBO at lunch yesterday. This could prove embarrassing because the vice president of personnel is the executive who brought MBO programs into the organization. You become vaguely aware that you are not sure how Don should go about defining his objectives.

Discussion Questions

1. Why did Nancy's approach to the MBO program generate such a negative reaction? What should she have done differently, based on the principles of effective MBO systems?

2. Assume that Nancy decides to try writing Don's objectives herself because he is on vacation. What can she do to help get herself started? What are some objectives that you think would be appropriate for Don?

3. What does the fact that neither Don nor Nancy seem to have a clear idea of what Don's objectives should be tell you about the vision for the organization?

Reflection

Depending on the culture of the organization where you work, you may never receive a response from an employee that is as brash as the one provided by Don Smith. In many organizations, most of Don's comments would have remained hidden in his "left-hand column" as something that is thought, but not said. People who have concerns or criticisms but do not openly voice those concerns often take an avoidant approach to managing conflict. Avoidant strategies might include just ignoring the request or sending back a polite memo saying "I'll get to this after vacation" but then never follow up. Because effective MBO systems depend on consistency throughout the organization as well as commitment to the objectives that are identified, it is critical that collaboration or at least compromise be used to come to agreement on what objectives should be.

PRACTICE Creating an Implementation Plan

Objective

This exercise gives you an opportunity to practice developing an implementation plan for a specific goal.

Directions

In the Assessment for this competency, you were asked to identify goals in four categories (personal relationships, academic/scholastic accomplishments, career/job interests, and financial future). Select whichever of these goals is the most important to you and begin to draft a plan for achieving that goal.

Discussion Questions

1. Did you include SMART objectives in your plan and identify the specific steps necessary to achieve your goal?

2. Are there any outside factors that might affect your ability to achieve your goal?

3. How confident do you feel about achieving this goal now that you have identified the steps you need to take to reach it?

Reflection

We all sometimes set goals that are unrealistic. By identifying the specific steps required to accomplish our goals, we may find that we need to modify our goals, perhaps by extending our timeline for achieving a particular goal or by reducing its scope.

APPLICATION   Evaluating the Use of Goal Setting In Your Organization

Objective   The objective of this exercise is to provide you with an opportunity to apply what you have learned about setting goals and objectives in an organizational setting.

Directions   1. Conduct an evaluation of the process that your organization uses for setting goals and objectives. (If you are not currently employed, use your college/university as your organization.) To gather information, you should interview not only people at the top of the organization who set the strategic direction, but also people at lower levels to see how effectively the vision and strategic goals have been cascaded throughout the organization.

2. Prepare a written summary of your analysis and be prepared to present and/or discuss in class.

Discussion Questions   1. Does the organization have some way to ensure "strategic unity and alignment" as it addresses goals top-down?

2. Do the organization-wide goals seem aligned and connected to organization's vision/strategy?

3. Does the organization's performance management system seem to make good use of goal and objective setting?

4. How do the organization-wide goals stack up against the SMART criteria?

Reflection   Aligning goals throughout an organization is not an easy task, particularly in highly turbulent environments where change seems like an everyday occurrence. One of the paradoxes of goal setting is that more time we spend setting goals and making plans, the less time we have for actually accomplishing anything!

Module 3 Competency 3   Motivating Self and Others

ASSESSMENT   When Are You the Most Motivated and Productive?

Objective   The objective of this assessment activity is to introduce the central themes we will focus on in this section as part of our treatment of Motivating Self and Others. It is an opportunity for you to reflect on a real experience you have had and "look in the mirror" to gain a clearer and deeper understanding of what really motivates you.

Directions   Take a few minutes to think about a situation during the last few months when you felt really motivated and as a result were productive and high performing. Write a short description of that situation. In your description be sure to explain:

- *Why* you were so motivated and able to work so productively

- Which of your reasons (if any) were under your *direct and personal* control

- Which of your reasons (if any) were not under your control

Conclude your paragraph with a statement about whether the situation you described is an exceptional one or a typical one for you.

Reflection   In the situation you described, your high level of productivity and motivation was very likely a consequence of a large number of factors. The ones you identified as being under your direct and personal control likely reflect your own underlying sources or catalysts for being motivated and working productively—these are the focus of the "motivating self" component of this competency. Those factors that were not under your direct and personal control are often very much a function of the context (i.e., situational factors). Many aspects of the context that affect motivation are a consequence of managerial and supervisory actions and behaviors. We address these issues in the Motivating Others component of this competency.

LEARNING   Motivating Self and Others

Competitve people want to win. For organizations, winning has traditionally been thought of in terms of productivity and profitability, the emphasis of the Compete action imperative and the rational goal quadrant of the competing values framework. Winning in today's environment requires setting lofty goals, working intensely with a focus on quality, and responding quickly to challenges that may arise. This requires each and every individual in the organization to be performing at her best. Individuals must be personally productive—possessing an appetite for hard work and demonstrating full exertion on the job. Individuals who are motivated, empowered, and committed are more productive and thus are essential components of winning organizations.

Productivity is a key concept for measuring individual, group, and organizational effectiveness. In today's economy, however, where intellectual capital has superseded natural resources and other forms of capital and technology as the primary source of competitive advantage, measuring "productivity" is complicated and often controversial. While tangible assets such as factories and other forms of capital easily lend themselves to evaluation according to established accounting and economic metrics, human capital presents challenges both in terms of measuring employee productivity as well as keeping employees productive in today's turbocharged workplaces.

The nature of organizations and the competitive environment within which they operate have made high productivity and superior performance imperative at all levels in the organization. Consequently, managers must create an environment where such productivity, empowerment, and commitment are possible, probable, and likely. Effective enactment of the Motivating Self and Others competency requires individual managerial leaders to achieve and maintain a balance between push for effort and productivity and maintenance of overall health and effectiveness for themselves individually and for their people.

We will examine the competency of motivating self and others through the lenses of three related frameworks: motivation, empowerment, and employee engagement. All three frameworks have similar foundations and their contributions to what we know about motivation complement one another. Together they provide a diagnostic and analytical approach that managers can use to improve their own motivation and to motivate others in the workplace.

MOTIVATION THEORY

We have already discussed in some detail one of the most important and widely used approaches to motivation—goal setting. Goal setting is a practical application of expectancy theory, one of the most comprehensive and practically useful theories of motivation. Before going into the details of expectancy theory, we need to set the stage by providing a brief overview of other motivation theories and how they relate to expectancy theory. Below, we organize different theories of motivation into two broad categories. Content theories focus on different needs that may motivate behavior; process theories focus on a sequence of steps (often considered to be thoughts) from some stimulus to motivation (Schermerhorn, Hunt & Osborn, 2008).

CONTENT THEORIES: WHAT IS VALUABLE ENOUGH TO MOTIVATE PEOPLE?

In the assessment for this competency, we asked you to think about when you really felt motivated and then to describe *why* you were so motivated. When we drill down into the question "why were you motivated" to try to find the source of your motivation, we are likely to discover that it was related to something that you valued, either because you needed it or you wanted it for some reason. It is also likely that different people identified different things that motivated them. So we should not be surprised to learn that psychologists and organizational scholars who have studied motivation in the work place for the better part of the last century have come up with different theories and conflicting research results. There is no single answer to what motivates people, but we have learned a great deal about different things that may motivate people.

Extrinsic and Intrinsic Motivators.   First, research has taught us that people may respond to both *extrinsic* and *intrinsic* sources of motivation. Extrinsic sources are forces that are external to the person. Extrinsic sources can be either tangible (e.g., food, money) or intangible (e.g., praise from the boss). Intrinsic sources are internally generated by the individual herself and are always intangible (e.g., a sense of accomplishment). As managers, we can directly provide extrinsic motivators to employees. For example, we can give a person a cash bonus for doing a good job or offer a "thanks for a job well done." Although managers cannot directly provide intrinsic motivation, they can try to create situations that will make it more likely that an employee will be intrinsically motivated. For example, assigning an employee a challenging task and coaching her to ensure she is successful may lead to intrinsic feeling of accomplishment on the part of the employee.

Innate and Learned Needs.   A second fundamental theme that has emerged in the study of motivation is that human behavior is motivated by "needs." Motivation theorists have debated whether needs are innate (e.g., Alderfer, 1972; Lawrence & Nohria, 2002; Maslow, 1954) or learned (e.g., McClelland, 1961), but for our purposes that distinction is not important. It is important for managers to have an understanding of what types of needs motivate behavior. Not surprisingly, theorists also disagree on that issue. McClelland (1961) suggested that there were three categories of learned needs (achievement, power, and affiliation). Of the three main proponents of innate needs, Maslow (1954) proposed five categories (physiological, safety, belongingness, esteem, self-actualization); Alderfer (1972) focused on three needs (existence, relatedness, and growth); and Lawrence and Nohria (2002) identified four drives (to bond, to learn, to acquire, and to defend). Cameron, Quinn, DeGraff, and Thakor (2006, p. 8) note that those four drives are perfectly aligned with the four quadrants of the competing values framework (i.e., collaborate—bond; create—learn; compete—acquire; and control—defend).

Fortunately, there is enough overlap across the categories identified by different motivation theorists to provide managers with useful information about the basic categories of motivators. For example:

- Physiological, safety, existence, and acquisition needs may be met using extrinsic sources such as wages that can be exchanged for food, shelter, and other things we wish to acquire.

- Belongingness, affiliation, relatedness, and bonding needs are primarily intrinsic feelings that may be met through opportunities for interpersonal and social interaction.

- Esteem and power needs may be met with promotions and decision-making authority.

- Self-actualization, achievement, growth, and learning needs may be met when we have opportunities to engage in activities that are intrinsically rewarding, where we can stretch ourselves and excel at what we do.

For managers, content theories of motivation provide useful information about broad categories of needs/wants that individuals seek to fulfill. To take advantage of content theories of motivation, managers also need to have an understanding of the process of motivation.

PROCESS THEORIES: HOW DO WE GET FROM STIMULUS TO MOTIVATION?

Process theories complement content theories by focusing our attention on *how* motivation happens—what are the steps in the process? Several different motivation theories can be classified as process theories including equity theory, the job characteristics model, goal-setting theory, and our main focus for this competency, expectancy theory. Some process theories incorporate specific needs identified by content theories while others specify only the steps in the process and make no assumptions about the specific needs that are being met. Below we present the highlights of three process theories: equity theory, the job characteristics model, and goal-setting theory. The full theories are more complex, of course, but what is presented here provides the gist of what managers need to know to translate these theories into effective practice.

Equity Theory. In contrast to other theories, which focus only on the outcomes that an individual receives for his own effort, equity theory (Adams, 1963) suggests that people also consider what other individuals' outcomes are relative to those other individuals' inputs. Equity theory assumes that people want these ratios to be equal and that if an inequity is perceived, they will try to "balance" the equation. For example, if you and I are both doing the same job for 8 hours a day and you discover that I am earning $100 for a day's work while you are only earning $80 for a day's work, equity theory predicts that you will try to find some way to bring the ratio of our outcomes to our inputs back into balance. You may respond in several ways, such as asking for a raise to increase your outcomes, or taking more breaks to reduce your inputs. To balance the equation ($100/8 = $80/?), you would need to reduce your work time (inputs) from 8 hours to 6.4 hours. ($100/8 = $12.50; $80/6.4 = $12.50). Alternatively, you could decide that because I had more experience than you, I was actually contributing more during my 8 hours than you were during your 8 hours. If you felt that my extra experience was the equivalent of an extra two hours ($100/10 = $80/8), then you would no longer have any feeling of inequity.

While there are many different responses to perceived inequity, for managers the most critical thing to understand is that if people feel under-rewarded for their efforts relative to others, their motivation is likely to decrease. This is one reason why companies do not like to make information about pay public. Of course, employees may still make assumptions about what others are being paid, so pay secrecy does not necessarily solve the problem of perceived inequity. Equity theory focuses on extrinsic outcomes; in contrast, the job characteristics model focuses on intrinsic outcomes.

Job Characteristics Model.   Although Hackman and Oldham's (1980) job characteristics model does include variables that are assumed to reflect different "needs" that employees have, we classify it as a process model because it goes beyond identifying a list of needs and describes a multistep process that is believed to result in motivation. In the model, five dimensions of a job's design (*skill variety, task identity, task significance, autonomy,* and *feedback)* are assumed to influence the psychological states (*experienced meaningfulness, experienced responsibility for outcomes of the work,* and *knowledge of actual results of the work*) experienced by the employee. Hackman and Oldham argue that intrinsic motivation occurs when these three psychological states are present. Individual differences, of course, can affect how much value employees place of different job characteristics. For example, some people may prefer to have less autonomy while others may want a great deal of autonomy. Managers wishing to apply Hackman and Oldham's model would first seek to learn more about how employees feel about the five job characteristics; then they could design jobs that had appropriately high levels of those job characteristics, which would theoretically make the work more intrinsically motivating to the employee.

Goal Setting Theory.   In our earlier discussion of setting goals and objectives, we focused on aligning individual and organizational goals and on developing goals that had SMART characteristics. Both of these recommendations are based on the findings of extensive research on goal-setting theory. The following five guidelines for managers are summarized based on the work of Locke and Latham (1990). We have italicized terms that are included in the SMART acronym and bolded two additional findings from goal setting research that managers should know.

1. *Specific* goals lead to higher performance than vague or no goals; specific goals are generally *Measurable* and **Time-bound**.

2. *Attainable* goals are more likely to lead to higher performance than unrealistic goals; people need both ability and self-efficacy to be motivated to achieve the goal.

3. *Relevant g*oals are important because goals are more likely to lead to higher performance when they are accepted and there is commitment to them.

4. **Challenging** goals lead to higher performance than easy goals.

5. **Feedback** about the task (knowledge of results) is likely to increase motivation and may encourage setting higher performance goals.

The first idea not found in the SMART acronym is that it is helpful to set challenging goals. Although goals should be attainable, they are generally more motivating if they are seen as challenging. When people are given what appears to be a simple task, they are often not very motivated to do it. Why? Think back to our discussion about intrinsic rewards and achievement/growth/learning needs. Most people do not get a sense of achievement when they do a simple task; accomplishing challenging tasks, however, often does result in a sense of achievement. The second important concept not found in the SMART acronym relates to task feedback. People like to know how they are doing relative to their goals, particularly on long-term projects. Without feedback, it is easy to become discouraged and lose motivation.

THE EXPECTANCY APPROACH TO MOTIVATION

One of the most comprehensive theories of motivation in use today is **expectancy theory**, which was originally proposed by Vroom (1964) and later expanded by Nadler and Lawler (1977) to take into account multiple outcomes. Expectancy theory attempts to answer the question of why people exert effort, not with reference to specific needs, but with respect to the process that people go through when making the decision to exert effort. The theory focuses on the employee's beliefs about the relationships between the amount of effort exerted on a job, actual performance on the job, and outcomes that may be received as a result of that performance. For our purposes, we have translated the traditional language of expectancy theory into terms more reflective of the variables that managers can influence when attempting to motivate others.

Figure M3.2 graphically depicts a simplified version of expectancy theory. In sum, the theory says individuals will be motivated to exert effort only if three conditions are met:

1. They believe that by exerting effort they will be able to perform the task in a satisfactory way.

2. They believe that if they perform the task in a satisfactory way, they will receive some outcome(s) as a result.

3. The outcome(s) that they will receive are valuable to them.

Let's consider the three conditions required for motivation under expectancy theory by looking at an example that takes you through the basic ideas behind the theory. First, we explain the theory based on the employee's perspective. We then focus on how your actions as a manager can impact motivation by altering the three key conditions identified in expectancy theory.

**Expectancy Theory
from Employee and Manager Perspectives**

	E to P Condition	P to O Condition	Valued Outcomes Condition
Employee perspective	Do I believe that my Effort will result in a satisfactory level of Performance?	Do I believe that my satisfactory Performance will result in certain Outcomes?	How much do I Value these Outcomes?
	Effort ⟶	Performance ⟶	Outcomes
Manager perspective	Set SMART goals Pick the right person Provide the necessary resources & training Offer coaching & support Provide timely, specific feedback	Use performance-contingent rewards Specify rewards for performance Build trust by always following through on commitments	Determine what resources are available to offer as outcomes Identify employee's Valued Outcomes (e.g., needs) and preferences Offer outcomes based on employee preferences

FIGURE M3.2
Expectancy theory from employee and manager perspectives (© 2010 L. St. Clair, used with permission).

THE EMPLOYEE'S PERSPECTIVE

Anne Johnson is the project leader of a group of computer programmers and systems analysts who have been charged with the task of creating a new management information system (MIS) for one of her company's largest divisions. Johnson is a little disappointed at the rate at which progress has been made. She is considering working on the project during the entire holiday weekend that is coming up. Will she be motivated to do this?

Applying the multiple outcomes version of the expectancy theory, we can analyze Anne's level of motivation regarding working over the holiday weekend. Let's begin with the Effort-to-Performance (E to P) link. Here, the consideration is whether or not working over the holiday weekend (the "effort" to be expended) will result in Anne completing the new MIS more quickly. The theory suggests that Anne will estimate the probability that her effort will lead to satisfactory performance. If she believes that she personally can be productive and move the project along over the holiday weekend, then she will be more likely to be motivated to go into work, assuming the other two conditions of the theory are met. The second condition relates to the Performance-to-Outcome link. Here, the question is, what is the probability that if Anne does complete the project more quickly, that this performance will lead to certain outcomes? The answer to this question depends on several variables that we will discuss in more detail below when we discuss the manager's perspective. The third condition relates to the value of the outcomes to Anne. Those outcomes could include a promotion, increased responsibility, a special recognition award, a spat with her husband and family about not being at home over the holiday, exhaustion, fatigue, and so on.

In theory, Anne would estimate a probability for both the E to P condition (i.e., What is the probability that if I work this weekend, I will complete this project quickly?) and the P to O condition (What is the probability that if I work this weekend, my husband will be angry? and What is the probability that if I complete this project more quickly, I will get a promotion and a pay increase?). Then she would determine how much she values each of these outcomes. Finally, she would calculate, based on the mathematical formulation of expectancy theory, a motivation score. The higher Anne's motivation score, the more likely it is that she would decide to go into work over the weekend. In practice, of course, these calculations are made much more unconsciously from Anne's perspective. For the manager, however, it is very useful to be able to identify the three conditions required for motivation according to expectancy theory.

THE MANAGER'S PERSPECTIVE

When applying expectancy theory, managers need to address all three of the conditions required for motivation. The E to P condition is addressed by tying effort to performance. The P to O condition is addressed by linking performance to outcome(s). Finally, the Valued Outcomes condition is addressed by knowing what employees want.

E to P Condition—Tying Effort to Performance.   At its most basic, the E to P condition is really about an employee's self-efficacy—his belief that he can perform satisfactorily in a given situation. We have already covered many of the things managers can do to help convince employees that their efforts will lead to satisfactory performance in our discussion of goal-setting and performance management systems. Although managers need to have some idea about project goals before selecting the right employee, once the employee is chosen, including the employee in defining "performance" and coming up with SMART goals can be very useful. Providing the necessary resources and training is also important. Coaching, support, and timely feedback all help convince the employee that effort will result in satisfactory performance. Research on the concept of "self-fulfilling prophecy" (Merton, 1968) also supports the idea that the manager's own expectations have an important impact on the employee's behavior, as described in Box M3.3.

BOX M3.3 BE A POSITIVE PYGMALION

Pygmalion was a sculptor in Greek mythology who created a gorgeous woman who was subsequently brought to life. George Bernard Shaw's play of the same name and the musical *My Fair Lady* are built on the same theme—that through the power of sheer self-effort and will, an individual can transform another person. J. Sterling Livingston's (1969) article "Pygmalion in Management", which was published in *Harvard Business Review*, popularized the idea that supervisors, managers, and executives at all levels in organizations can also play Pygmalion-type roles. His argued that:

1. What managers expect of their subordinates and the way they treat them largely determine subordinates' performance and career progress.

2. A unique characteristic of superior managers is their ability to create high performance expectations that their subordinates fulfill.

3. Less effective managers fail to develop similar expectations, so, as a consequence, the productivity of their subordinates suffers.

4. Subordinates, more often than not, do what they believe they are expected to do.

Think about your own boss. Does she expect you to be successful and encourage you to learn new things? If so, you are fortunate to be working for a positive Pygmalion and you are likely to feel highly motivated. If, instead, your boss treats you as though you cannot be trusted and are not capable of learning to improve, you are likely to feel frustrated and unmotivated, perhaps even to the point of wanting to leave the organization.

Being a positive Pygmalion is one of the single most important ways in which you can motivate others. It doesn't require money or other extrinsic rewards. It doesn't require dealing with the complexities and contingencies of job design. Most importantly, it is completely under your control. But it is not easy. Being a positive Pygmalion for your subordinates goes to the very heart of your assumptions about people and your own managerial style. It also requires that you be a positive Pygmalion for yourself—trusting in your own competencies as a manager.

P to O Condition—Linking Performance to Outcomes. Even if employees think that they can perform at a satisfactory level, they may not be convinced that satisfactory performance will result in receiving any valued outcomes. In some cases, managers can address this concern by using performance-contingent rewards and making certain that employees are aware of all the possible outcomes that will result from satisfactory performance. Regular and consistent use of goal setting, as discussed above, goes a long way in helping to clarify many performance-to-outcome linkages. One of the most important things managers can do to address the P-to-O condition is build trust by always following through on commitments. Managers who make promises and fail to keep them seriously undermine the motivation of their employees. And once trust has been lost, it is very difficult to rebuild.

Valued Outcome Condition—Understanding What Employees Want. Expectancy theory assumes that employees want to receive some valued outcome or outcomes in return for their effort. Basic categories of outcomes can be identified by referring to the content theories of motivation we discussed earlier. To be most effective, however, managers should make certain that they know what outcomes are important to their employees. There's no substitute for knowing your employees. Depending on the size of your group, you can obtain this information either through one-on-one conversations or, if the group is too large, through employee attitude surveys.

Motivation theories provide us with an important foundation upon which to build and deepen our understanding of motivating self and others. They help us as individuals understand some of what determines our personal feelings of motivation and help us as managers begin to understand the process and dynamics by which motivation actually occurs. Empowerment will provide us with another frame that helps us practically apply many of the lessons from motivation theory.

EMPOWERMENT

Our label for the competency Motivating Self and Others in many ways reflects two different schools of thought on what empowerment is and how it comes about. Some who have studied the psychology of empowerment define it as *intrinsic motivation* reflected in several psychological states related to an individual's orientation to her work role (e.g., Thomas & Velthouse, 1990; Quinn & Spreitzer, 1997; Spreitzer, 2008). Others suggest that managers can empower employees when they engage in various behaviors including sharing more rather than less information, providing appropriate structure, developing team-based alternatives to traditional hierarchy—giving employees power to make decisions that influence organizational direction and performance, providing access to relevant training, and adequately rewarding employees for risks they are expected to take (Randolph, 1995; Bowen & Lawler, 1992). These two schools of thought raise the question: from whence empowerment? Is it internally generated by the individual, or is it externally bestowed by the organization and its managers and supervisors?

Quinn and Spreitzer (1997) conducted an intensive research program that empirically examined the antecedents, consequences, and processes of implementing empowerment in large organizational settings. One finding from their study suggested that there were, in fact, two different mindsets or paradigms about empowerment.

Some people have a more top-down, "mechanistic" perspective and believe that empowerment originates at the top of an organization's hierarchy. This group feels that empowerment is reflected in an organization's mission, vision, and values and in how tasks, roles, and rewards for employees are defined. Empowerment to them means that responsibility is delegated and people are held accountable for their results.

Other people have a more bottom-up, "organic" perspective. This group feels that empowerment starts at the bottom of the organization and requires understanding employees' needs, role modeling empowered behavior for employees, and building teams where cooperative behavior and intelligent risk taking are encouraged. Empowerment to this second group is seen as less about delegation and accountability and more about trusting people to perform and supporting their efforts to take intelligent risks, grow, and change.

Quinn and Spreitzer conclude from their research that empowerment is not something that management "does" to employees—rather, it is a mindset that employees have about their job in the organization. The four psychological states that Quinn and Spreitzer (1997) identified as being required for empowerment are consistent with those identified by Thomas and Velthouse (1990):

1. *A Sense of Meaning.* The innate worthiness of the task or pursuit. Employees feel their work is important and care about what they are doing.

2. *A Sense of Competence.* Confidence in one's ability to perform the task skillfully. Employees feel that they can do the job, and they can do it well.

3. *A Sense of Self-Determination.* The discretion, autonomy, and choice involved in initiating, maintaining, and regulating one's actions in the pursuit of the task. Employees may be told what needs to be done, but not how to do it.

4. *A Sense of Impact.* The degree to which an individual can influence strategic, administrative, or other outcomes at work. Employees feel that other people listen to their ideas.

Note that these four characteristics are consistent with intrinsic motivation and align with the achievement/growth/esteem needs identified in content theories of motivation. Taken together, these four characteristics reflect the psychological experience of empowerment rather than a specific set of managerial behaviors and practices. These psychological states cannot be bestowed or mandated by management—they must be genuinely experienced by the employee. Although employees must choose to be empowered, there are things that managers can do to create environments that are more likely to cause employees to empower themselves. In sum, empowerment fits our emphasis on thinking in terms of "both/and" rather than either/or. Both the individual and the situation have a role to play in creating empowerment in the workplace.

EMPLOYEE ENGAGEMENT

The last decade has seen an increasing interest in the topic of employee engagement. Much of the work has appeared in the practitioner literature; recently the academic literature has focused on defining the parameters of the construct (Saks, 2006). Kahn (1990, p. 694) defines personal engagement as "the harnessing of organization members' selves to their work roles; in engagement, people employ and express themselves physically, cognitively, and emotionally during role performances." Conversely, Kahn defines disengagement as "the uncoupling of selves from work roles; in disengagement, people withdraw and defend themselves physically, cognitively, or emotionally during role performances" (p. 694). Much like definitions of empowerment, Kahn sees engagement as meaning the level of psychological presence while performing organizational roles.

Not surprisingly, engagement has been found to be the exact opposite of burnout. Where engagement is characterized by energy, involvement, efficacy, vigor, and dedication, burnout is characterized by exhaustion, cynicism, and inefficacy (Gonzalez-Roma, Schaufelli, Bakker & Lloret, 2006; Maslach, Schaufelli & Leiter, 2001). Other researchers have looked at various other linkages and overlaps that engagement has with organizational behavioral constructs such as organizational commitment and organizational citizenship behavior.

With respect to practice, the Gallup organization and the Corporate Leadership Council have both conducted extensive studies on employee engagement over the last decade. The Gallup organization has one of the most widely used surveys for gauging just how engaged employees are. Among the questions the survey asks are:

- Do you know what your manager and colleagues expect of you at work?
- Do you have the opportunity to do what you do best every day there?
- Does your supervisor, or someone else at work, seem to care about you as a person?
- Does the mission or purpose of your company make you feel that your job is important?

- Do you have a best friend at work?
- In the last year, did you have an opportunity at work to learn and grow? (Gallup Management Journal, 2006)

The Corporate Leadership Council (2004) defines engagement as the extent to which employees commit to something or someone in their organization, how hard they work, and how long they stay as a result of that commitment. They suggest that engagement entails two types of commitment: rational and emotional. Rational commitment results when employees believe that managers, teams, or organizations have employees' self-interest in mind (e.g., financial, developmental, and professional). Emotional commitment is the extent to which employees value, enjoy, and believe in their jobs, managers, teams, or organizations.

These two types of commitment are influenced by the nature of the day-to-day work that employees perform in the organization, the work teams that they are a part of, their direct manager, and the overall organization itself. Ideally, when these two types of commitment occur, employees will increase their efforts, go above and beyond what is required, and remain with the organization.

To measure how engaged employees actually are, the Gallup organization does periodic surveys in organizations of all kinds. Gallup's research (2010) has identified three "types" of employees:

1. *Engaged* employees are those who work with passion and feel a deep and profound connection to their company. These engaged individuals drive innovation and make the organization successful.

2. *Not-Engaged* employees are essentially going through the motions at work—they are "checked out," sleepwalking through their workday, marking time but with no passion or vigor.

3. *Actively Disengaged* employees aren't merely unhappy at work, they act out their unhappiness by doing things that undermine what their engaged coworkers are trying to accomplish.

Over the first decade of the twenty-first century, Gallup's research found that between 26 and 30 per cent of the workforce was "engaged" and between 15 and 20 percent was "actively disengaged." As late as 2009, even after nearly two years of global recession, Gallup found 30 percent engaged, 52 percent not engaged, and 18 percent actively disengaged. Various other studies yield similar patterns of results.

For managers, the topic of employee engagement continues to be of great interest because of the increasingly competitive and global nature of the talent market and continuing pressures to cut costs. Globally, the workforce is aging, due to declining birthrates and increasing numbers of older individuals choosing to remain in the workforce. However, as baby boomers leave the workforce, a very valuable source of talent and experience leaves with them. Experts predict that in the future, there will be more critical jobs to be filled than there will be available talent to fill them. In addition, as we mentioned in our discussion of vision earlier, younger generations of workers are seeking more than a paycheck and some sense of security from work organizations. These factors combined make the retention and engagement of key talent increasingly important and urgent for managers, even in periods of high unemployment.

ANALYSIS From Motivated to Demotivated in 60 Seconds

Objective   This exercise gives you the opportunity to analyze a common human resource management issue, salary compression/inversion, which occurs when market forces push salaries for new hires up faster than salary increases for existing employees. Salary compression refers to a shrinking differential in the pay received by continuing employees relative to new hires. Salary inversion occurs when the salaries of new hires exceed the salaries of current employees. This exercise also provided a fertile opportunity to test your recent learning about motivation, empowerment and employee engagement.

Directions   Read the case of Michael Simpson*, and answer the questions that follow.

Michael Simpson is one of the most outstanding managers in the management consulting division of Avery McNeil and Co. He is a highly qualified individual with a deep sense of responsibility.

Simpson obtained his MBA two years ago from one of the leading northeastern schools. Before being graduated from business school, Simpson had interviewed with a number of consulting firms and decided that the consulting division of Avery McNeil offered the greatest potential for rapid advancement.

Simpson was recently promoted to manager, making him the youngest manager at the consulting group. Two years with the firm was an exceptionally short period of time in which to achieve this promotion. Although the promotion was announced, Simpson had not yet been informed of his new salary. Despite the fact that his career had progressed well, he was concerned that his salary would be somewhat lower than the current market value that a headhunter had recently quoted him.

Simpson's wife, Diane, soon would be receiving her MBA. One night over dinner Simpson was amazed to hear the salaries being offered to new MBAs. Simpson commented to Diane, "I certainly hope I get a substantial raise this time. I mean, it just wouldn't be fair to be making the same amount as recent graduates when I've been at the company now for over two years! I'd like to buy a house soon, but with housing costs rising and inflation following, that will depend on my pay raise."

Several days later, Simpson was working at his desk when Dave Barton, a friend and a colleague, came across to Simpson's office. Barton was hired at the same time as Simpson, and had also been promoted recently. Barton told Simpson, "Hey, Mike, look at this! I was walking past Jane's desk and saw this memo from the personnel manager lying there. She obviously forgot to put it away. Her boss would kill her if he found out!"

The memo showed the proposed salaries for all the individuals in the consulting group that year. Simpson looked at the list and was amazed by what he saw. He said, "I can't believe this, Dave! Walt and Rich are getting $2000 more than I am."

Walt Gresham and Rich Watson had been hired within the past year. Before coming to Avery McNeil, they had both worked one year at another consulting firm.

Barton spoke angrily, "Mike, I knew the firm had to pay them an awful lot to attract them, but to pay them more than people above them is ridiculous!"

"You know," replied Simpson, "if I hadn't seen Walt and Rich's salaries, I would think I was getting a reasonable raise. Hey listen, Dave, let's get out of here. I've had enough of this place for one day."

"Okay, Mike, just let me return this memo. Look, it's not that bad; after all, you are getting the largest raise."

*From David Nadler, M. Tushman, and N. Hatvany (eds.), *Managing Organizations*. Boston, Little, Brown, 1982. Used with permission from the authors.

On his way home, Simpson tried to think about the situation more objectively. He knew that there were a number of pressures on the compensation structure in the consulting division. If the division wished to continue attracting MBAs from top schools, it would have to offer competitive salaries. Starting salaries had increased about $3500 during the last two years. As a result, some of the less-experienced MBAs were earning nearly the same amounts as others who had been with the firm several years but who had come in at lower starting salaries, even though their pay had been gradually increased over time.

Furthermore, because of expanding business, the division had found it necessary to hire consultants from other firms. In order to do so effectively, Avery McNeil found it necessary to upgrade the salaries they offered.

The firm as a whole was having problems meeting the federally regulated Equal Opportunity Employment goals and was trying especially hard to recruit women and minorities.

One of Simpson's colleagues, Martha Lohman, had been working in the consulting division of Avery McNeil until three months ago, when she was offered a job at another consulting firm. She had become disappointed with her new job and, on returning to her previous position at Avery McNeil, was rehired at a salary considerably higher than her former level. Simpson had noticed on the memo that she was earning more than he was, even though she was not given nearly the same level of responsibility. Simpson also realized that the firm attempted to maintain some parity between salaries in the auditing and consulting divisions.

When Simpson arrived home, he discussed the situation with his wife. "Diane, I know I'm getting a good raise, but I am still earning below my market value—$3000 less than the headhunter told me last week. And the fact that those two guys from the other consulting firm are getting more than me shows that the firm is prepared to pay competitive rates."

"I know it's unfair, Mike," Diane replied, "but what can you do? You know your boss won't negotiate salaries after they have been approved by the compensation committee, but it wouldn't hurt to at least talk to him about your dissatisfaction. I don't think you should let a few thousand dollars a year bother you. You will catch up eventually, and the main thing is that you really enjoy what you are doing."

"Yes, I do enjoy what I'm doing, but that is not to say that I wouldn't enjoy it elsewhere. I really just have to sit down and think about all the pros and cons in my working for Avery McNeil. First of all, I took this job because I felt that I could work my way up quickly. I think that I have demonstrated this, and the firm has also shown that they are willing to help me achieve this goal. If I left this job for a better paying one, I might not get the opportunity to work on the exciting jobs that I am currently working on. Furthermore, this company has time and money invested in me. I'm the only one at Avery that can work on certain jobs, and the company has several lined up. If I left the company now, they would not only lose me, but they would probably lose some of their billings as well. I really don't know what to do at this point, Diane. I can either stay with Avery McNeil or look for a higher-paying job elsewhere; however, there is no guarantee that my new job would be a fast-track one like it is at Avery. One big plus at Avery is that the people there already know me and the kind of work I produce. If I went elsewhere, I'd essentially have to start all over again. What do you think I should do, Diane?"

Discussion Questions

1. What do you think are the most important motivational drivers of Simpson's dilemma?

2. Use expectancy theory to explain how Simpson might analyze the situation. Contrast your analysis using expectancy theory with an analysis using equity theory.

3. Given the limited information in the case, what evidence do you see that Avery McNeil has a robust approach to creating an empowering work environment for its employees? How would you rate their efforts at engaging their employees?

4. If you were Simpson's manager and he approached you with this problem, how would you respond? Could you use this opportunity to apply any of the principles of the job characteristics model? Expectancy theory? Empowerment? Employee Engagement?

Reflections Although being paid less than a new hire may be unpleasant and de-motivating, is certainly not the worst problem that employees encounter. Pay compression tends to become a problem when the economy is growing and demand for talent is strong. When the economy is struggling and unemployment is high, however, employees run the risk of losing their jobs to new hires who are willing to accept lower salaries.

PRACTICE Empowerment and Engagement

Objective The two exercises below are intended to help you become more knowledgeable about what an empowering and engaging workplace is for you now or might be in the future. The first exercise, the Personal Empowerment Assessment instrument (Spreitzer, 1995) will provide you with a self-assessment of how empowered you feel in your current role in an organization. The second exercise asks you to think about organizations in general and to try to identify the reasons why people would choose to stay with an organization they currently work in versus choosing to leave for another organization or opportunity.

Directions **Personal Empowerment Assessment**

This instrument helps identify the extent to which you are empowered in your own work. You should respond to the items based on your own job. The items listed below describe different orientations people can have with respect to their work roles. Using the following scale, indicate the extent to which you believe each is true of you.

Very strongly disagree	Strongly disagree	Disagree	Neutral	Agree	Strongly agree	Very strongly agree
1	2	3	4	5	6	7

Rating

_____ 1. The work that I do is very important to me.

_____ 2. I am confident about my ability to do my work.

_____ 3. I have significant autonomy in determining how I do my job.

_____ 4. I have significant impact on what happens in my work unit.

_____ 5. I trust my coworkers to be completely honest with me.

_____ 6. My work activities are personally meaningful to me.

_____ 7. My work is within the scope of my competence and capabilities.

_____ 8. I can decide how to go about doing my own work.

_____ 9. I have a great deal of control over what happens in my work unit.

_____ 10. I trust my coworkers to share important information with me.

_____ 11. I care about what I do in my work.

_____ 12. I am confident in my capabilities to successfully perform my work.

_____ 13. I have considerable opportunity for independence and freedom in how I do my work.

_____ 14. I have significant influence over what happens in my work unit.

_____ 15. I trust my coworkers to keep the promises they make.

_____ 16. The work I do has special meaning and importance to me.

_____ 17. I have mastered the skills necessary to do my work.

_____ 18. I have a chance to use my personal initiative in carrying out my work.

_____ 19. My opinion counts in my work unit's decision-making.

_____ 20. I believe that my coworkers care about my well-being.

Personal Empowerment Assessment Scoring Key

EMPOWERMENT DIMENSION	ITEMS	MEAN (total/4)
Self-Efficacy (competence)	2,7,12,17	_____
Self-Determination (choice)	3,8,13,18	_____
Personal Control (impact)	4,9,14,19	_____
Meaningfulness (value)	1,6,11,16	_____
Trust (security)	5,10,15,20	_____

Based on the scores of approximately 3000 mid-level managers in manufacturing and service organizations, the following are comparison means.

DIMENSION	MEAN	TOP THIRD	BOTTOM THIRD
Self-Efficacy	5.37	> 6.52	<5.00
Self-Determination	5.50	> 6.28	<4.72
Personal Control	5.49	> 6.34	<4.64
Meaningfulness	5.88	> 6.65	<5.12
Trust	5.33	> 6.03	<4.73

Discussion Questions

1. On which of the five dimensions did you score yourself highest? Lowest?

2. Are you surprised by either score? Why or why not?

3. Why do you think the high and low turned out as they did?

4. If your immediate coworkers or teammates completed this self-assessment, do you think their results would be similar to yours? Why or why not?

5. Are you happy with your overall sense of how empowered you are now?

6. If not, what might you do to address the situation?

Reflection

People who have a high need for growth and autonomy may find it especially difficult to work in organizations where acting in an empowered way is not encouraged. Similarly, people who are not comfortable making decisions and taking charge may be very uncomfortable in a workplace where empowerment is the norm. If you have an employee who does not seem comfortable with being empowered, what can you do as a manager to help that person see the value of empowerment and learn to be more comfortable acting in an empowered way?

Directions

Employee Engagement: Why People to Choose to Stay with an Organization

Individually first, and then with your group (if assigned), identify **10 reasons** why individuals choose to stay with a particular organization as opposed to leaving for another organization/job. As best you can, please rank them in priority order from most important (1) to last (10).

	Reasons to Stay	**Rankings**
1.	_____	_____
2.	_____	_____
3.	_____	_____
4.	_____	_____
5.	_____	_____
6.	_____	_____
7.	_____	_____
8.	_____	_____
9.	_____	_____
10.	_____	_____

Discussion Questions

1. Compare your list to the one below. Are there any items on that list that you do not consider important? If so, why not?

2. These data are from a survey of employees in the tech sector. To what extent do you think that the reasons identified or the order of importance of those reasons are influenced by the type of people who choose to work in that industry? Can you think of examples of other industries where the rankings or reasons would be significantly different?

Top 10 Reasons Why People Stay (based on data from a tech sector population of 7,600 surveyed in 2004 by Career Systems International)

1. Exciting Work & Challenge
2. Working with Great People & Relationships
3. Career Growth, Learning & Development
4. Fair Pay
5. Management Support/Great Boss
6. Being Recognized, Valued & Respected
7. Meaningful Work, Making a Difference & Contribution
8. Pride in Organization, Mission & Products
9. Benefits
10. Great Work Environment

Reflection

People who are empowered and engaged can add tremendous value to the workplace, not only through their own contributions, but by inspiring others. What can you do as a manager to be sure that you are serving as a positive role model of empowerment and engagement?

APPLICATION   When Are You and Your Colleagues the Most Motivated and Productive?

Objective

Now that you have read about different theoretical approaches to motivation, empowerment, and employee engagement, you are in a better position to analyze how closely the situations described by you and others in the Assessment segment of this competency match some of the key themes from the learning segment.

Directions   Refer back to your description in the Assessment activity of the situation in which you were most motivated and productive. In groups formed by your instructor, consider and respond to the following questions. Appoint a spokesperson in your group to present a five-minute summary to the class.

Discussion Questions   1. What common factors exist across your descriptions of personal motivation and productivity?

2. Do you see any patterns? For example, are more of the factors listed within the control of individuals versus outside of their control? Are there any surprising or unexpected themes or relationships?

3. Which of the four psychological aspects of empowerment (meaning, competence, self-determination, and impact) seem most related to motivation and productivity in your examples?

4. Can you make any inferences about how your examples might connect to the 10 Reasons Why People to Choose to Stay with an organization?

5. Brainstorm a list of "principles" or lessons learned from the examples discussed in your group. How might these principles and lessons help you with future job searches and career planning?

Reflection   As you continue to reflect on what motivates you and makes you more productive, you may find clues that help you improve your actions in the future. Just recognizing why you are feeling unmotivated can often help you break out of your inertia. For example, although equity theory predicts that people who feel under-rewarded will try to "balance the equation" in some way, keep in mind that you still can choose not to do the predictable thing. Like all social science theories, equity theory is not an unbreakable law of nature—it is a statement about what commonly happens under certain conditions. Just as we can use knowledge to find ways to overcome the force of gravity, so too can we use knowledge to overcome the force of human nature!

Module 3 Competency 4   Designing and Organizing

ASSESSMENT   Assessing Organizational Culture

Objective   Organizational culture is a critical element of an organization's overall design. This exercise is designed to give you some insight into the culture of your work, university, or other organization. It is drawn from the Organizational Culture Assessment Instrument* (Cameron & Quinn, 2006). The interpretation is included later in this competency.

Directions   Review the following four statements and indicate how well each statement reflects your organization by dividing 100 points across the four statements.

_____   *The organization is a very personal place. It is like extended family. People seem to share a lot of themselves.*

_____   *The organization is a very dynamic and entrepreneurial place. People are willing to stick their necks out and take risks.*

Adapted from K. S. Cameron and R. E. Quinn, Diagnosing and Changing Organizational Culture Based on the Competing Values Framework (San Francisco: Jossey-Bass, 2006). Used with permission.

_____ *The organization is very results-oriented. A major concern is with getting the job done. People are very competitive and achievement oriented.*

_____ *The organization is a very controlled and structured place. Formal procedures generally govern what people do.*

__100__ *Total Points to Be Allocated*

Reflection This simplified assessment of organizational culture only taps the surface of the many ways that organizations differ. Research suggests that there is no one "best" organizational culture. Similarly, different individuals may feel more comfortable in different organizational cultures.

LEARNING Designing and Organizing

Once organizational and work unit plans are set, a manager must decide how to allocate and coordinate organizational resources to accomplish goals. As you will see in this Learning section, designing the organization structure and organizing work are intimately connected. In terms of basic management functions, organizing is required to translate our plans into action. Organizing is the process of dividing work into manageable components and assigning activities to most effectively achieve the desired results. Said in another way, if planning provides the tools for deciding where you want to go and how best to get there, organizing provides the tools to actually get you there.

In this Learning section we begin by introducing some basic concepts and principles related to organizational structure. We then describe some common options for "departmentalizing" (i.e., different ways to group work activities in the organization). The final section discusses two different models that can be used to connect an organization's strategy, structural design, and culture.

CORE CONCEPTS AND PRINCIPLES OF STRUCTURE

At the organizational level, organizing involves designing the organizational structure so that work can be efficiently and effectively allocated across different departments and work units. At the work unit level, organizing involves designing jobs and allocating tasks so that the work unit can effectively accomplish its goals in support of the overall organizational mission and vision. Although current management thought on how to design organizations and jobs no longer focuses exclusively on efficiency, efficiency remains an important building block in the process of organizing. To know what type of structure is most appropriate for an organization, we first need to understand a bit about the history of structure and organizing principles, what elements make up the structure of the organization, and how those elements work together.

DIVISION OF LABOR AND SPECIALIZATION

Many of the ideas that we discussed in the introductory chapter related to early management theories such as the rational goal model and the internal process model are related to organizational structure and evolved out of ideas first written about in *The*

Wealth of Nations, by Adam Smith (1937). Originally written in 1776, Smith established two management principles that still stand today as guiding principles for organizations. Writing about the manufacture of straight pins, Smith noted that if (1) the work were divided into its component tasks and (2) workers were specialized so that each individual had responsibility for completing only one of the component tasks, the overall job would be accomplished far more efficiently than if each worker performed all tasks associated with the job. As you may recall from the introductory chapter, Frederick W. Taylor's principles of scientific management, Weber's characteristics of bureaucracy, and Fayol's general principles of management all emphasized both **division of labor** and **specialization**. More than 230 years after Adam Smith introduced them, the process of organizing is still very much influenced by those two principles. How work is divided up and assigned to employees has a direct impact on other structural variables such as hierarchy and standardization.

HIERARCHY AND LINES OF AUTHORITY

A **hierarchy** is a system of ranking things according to relative importance, status, or authority. Organizations with many levels in the hierarchy are referred to as **tall organizations;** organizations with fewer levels in the hierarchy are referred to as **flat organizations.** The number of levels in an organization's hierarchy depends in part on the size of the organization, but it is also influenced by choices we make with respect to three efficiency principles related to **span of control, unity-of-command**, and **scalar chain**. In general, tall organizations tend to operate less efficiently than flat ones. Recent trends in both industry and government have been to reduce the number of levels in the hierarchy.

The principle of **span of control** states that a person can effectively manage only a limited number of employees. How many? The answer depends on a variety of variables, such as the nature of the task, the skill and motivation of the employees, the ability of the manager to delegate, and the amount of interaction between the employees and the manager. But the principle recognizes that as the number of individuals reporting to a manager increases, the more difficult it is to coordinate and control individual efforts. The size of the span of control is inversely related to the number of levels in the hierarchy. That is, for a given number of employees, as the span of control decreases (narrows), the number of levels in the hierarchy increases (the organization gets taller). More managers are needed and, hence, the greater the number of layers in the hierarchy. Conversely, the greater (wider) the span of control, the fewer the number of managers needed and, hence, the fewer the number of layers in the hierarchy (the organization becomes flatter).

A second key efficiency principle states that each person should report to one and only one manager. This is referred to as the **unity-of-command principle.** The principle ensures that employees know from whom they should expect job assignments and reduces the potential for conflicting job assignments. Building on the principle of unity of command, the **scalar principle (chain-of-command)** states that there should be a clear line of command linking each employee to the next-higher level of authority, up to and including the highest level of management. When the lines of authority are clear, it is easier to know who is responsible for the completion of each job.

STANDARDIZATION AND FORMALIZATION

Standardization and formalization refers to the extent to which there are specific standards, rules, and procedures established to direct behavior in the organization. In addition to helping create uniformity in products and services, standardization and formalization also provide benchmarks to make it easier to evaluate individuals on technical merit, rather than on personal preferences. Small organizations often remain informal with respect to rules and procedures. Standards can be communicated in person, and consistency can be maintained with regular feedback. In contrast, large organizations benefit from rules and procedures to ensure that performance is consistent across employees. Standardization can lead to major efficiencies when many people are doing the same basic job.

Just as standardized parts make a manufacturing process more efficient, standardized behavior on tasks can also increase efficiency. For example, having employees complete a standardized checklist when doing a financial audit not only ensures that all the relevant tasks will be completed, it also saves time for supervisors when reviewing the work that has been done. There is a cost of standardization, however, in terms of the autonomy of employees. Workers who have little discretion about how to do their jobs may feel less motivated.

DECISION-MAKING AUTHORITY

Where do decisions get made in the organization? The higher the level where decisions are made, the more ***centralized*** decision-making authority is said to be. Conversely, when decision-making authority is delegated to people at lower levels in the organization, then decision-making is considered to be ***decentralized***.

Centralization provides more consistency in decision-making, but also significantly slows down the decision-making process. Because the people with the most information about the situation are often on the front lines, decentralized decision-making can improve the speed of decision-making and the quality of the decisions. Employees who have decision-making authority are also likely to feel more empowered and motivated than employees who must always refer decisions up the chain of command.

STRUCTURAL TENSIONS

The principles of organizing related to specialization, division of labor, unity of command, scalar chain, and span of control—often contradict one another (Simon, 1976). There will always be situations in which adherence to one principle of efficiency will result in violation of a second principle. In these situations, trade-offs may be required across different types of efficiency. To decide which trade-offs to make, return to the overall mission of the organization and determine which principle of efficiency serves this mission most efficiently in the current environment. To help get a better sense of the tensions associated with designing and organizing, it is helpful to look at structural archetypes and the concepts of differentiation and integration.

MECHANISTIC AND ORGANIC ARCHETYPES

Organizations can combine the elements of structures in different ways, but it is often helpful to refer to archetypes or "ideal" types of structure to get a better sense of the tensions inherent in structural choices. To create a pair of archetypical structures, we need to recognize that all of the different elements of structure can be reflected on a continuum. For example an organization can have a very high degree of division of labor or a very low degree of division of labor. Two standard archetypical structures are "mechanistic" and "organic." Mechanistic organizations are more consistent with the internal process and rational goal models of management that emphasize control. In contrast, organic organizations are more consistent with the human relations and open systems models, which emphasize flexibility. Keep in mind, these are ideal types. In practice organizations rarely fit neatly into either category. Table M3.2 below provides a summary of the mechanistic and the organic structure archetypes.

Not surprisingly, organic organizations tend to be much more flexible than mechanistic organizations. New organizations and small organizations tend to be more organic, while older, larger organizations tend to be more mechanistic. If we look more closely at any particular organization, however, we are likely to discover that some parts of the organization look quite different from other parts. These differences emerge when the needs of particular departments differ from the needs of other departments, resulting in different degrees of differentiation and integration across the organization.

DIFFERENTIATION AND INTEGRATION

Organizations are needed to accomplish large, complex tasks, so it may seem paradoxical that the first thing we talk about in designing and organizing is how to break work up into small parts, which then creates a need to find mechanisms to put the parts back

TABLE M3.2 Comparison of Mechanistic and Organic Structures

Elements of Structure	Mechanistic	Organic
Division of labor & Specialization	High—jobs are narrowly defined and focus on small pieces of work	Low—jobs are broadly defined and may include a number of different tasks
Hierarchy	Tall (many layers)	Flat (few layers)
Span of Control	Narrow	Wide
Unity of Command & Scalar Chain	Strictly maintained	Less rigidly followed
Standardization & Formalization	High—specific, detailed rules and procedures are used to direct behavior; there are many formal rules that people are expected to follow	Low—values and general principles are used to guide behavior; there are few formal rules
Decision-making authority	Centralized	Decentralized

together. In fact, however, such differentiation and integration take place on a regular basis in organizations.

When the environments and technologies within a single organization differ, there is greater need for ***differentiation*** across departments. That is, departments should be structured differently so that they can approach their tasks differently. Departments can be differentiated according to time, goal, and interpersonal orientation.

1. *Time Orientation.* Some tasks, such as paper processing, require a shorter time orientation than others, such as planning or research.
2. *Goal Orientation.* Even when organizations have a single organizational mission, the goals of the individual work units will differ to some degree. For example, organizational units closely associated with the organization's mission pursue different goals from those of organizational units associated with maintaining the organization's structure (personnel, financial management, etc.).
3. *Interpersonal Orientation.* To the extent that the degree of interdependency among employees varies across organizational tasks, patterns and styles of interaction will differ across work units.

Thus, organizational subsystems that must be more responsive to their environments should be organized to allow for greater responsiveness. Organizational subsystems that have more uncertain environments must be organized to allow for greater flexibility and adaptability to sudden changes. Organizational subsystems that have more uncertain technologies should be organized to accommodate the greater need for interaction among people.

Returning for a moment to the organizational level, think about the organizational implications of maintaining a highly differentiated organization. If each subsystem is structured differently, the potential exists for the organization to become a "disorganization." In fact, the greater the differentiation across units, the greater the need for ***integration***, or coordination across units (Lawrence & Lorsh, 1967). Various mechanisms are available to the organization to achieve effective integration, ranging from basic tools (e.g., rules and procedures, referral of problems up the hierarchy, and planning) to more complex tools (e.g., liaison roles, task forces and inter-unit teams, and matrix organization designs).

In their research on multinational companies, for example, Hansen and Løvas (2004) looked at four different variables that influence integration with respect to the transfer of technological competencies: (1) whether the units have related competencies; (2) how geographically close the units are; (3) whether there are structures in place such as formal groups with a single supervisor, within-group communication channels, and/or group-based incentives; and (4) whether there is an established informal relationship between units. Although a more in-depth discussion of these variables is beyond the scope of this competency, suffice it to say that rules, procedures, and the referral of problems up the hierarchy tend to work best when the need for integration is low. Alternatively, when departments or units like those studied by Hansen and Løvas (2004) are highly differentiated and have high needs for integration, other types of mechanisms are needed including task forces, teams, and matrix structures, which we discuss in our next section on forms of departmentalization.

FORMS OF DEPARTMENTALIZATION

At the organizational level, dividing jobs among organizational members is called **departmentalization.** In addition to defining how the organization's work is to be divided, departmentalization also defines the organization's authority relationships—who reports to whom. As such, it relates to fundamental principles of hierarchy, span of control, unity of command, and scalar chain. Because departmentalization touches on so many key elements of structure, we will briefly describe some basic forms including grouping by function, by division, and departmentalization by matrix.

BY FUNCTION

Functional departments organize jobs based on the specific tasks that people perform. Common organizational functions include accounting, finance, marketing, sales and customer relations, and human resource management. Other more specific functions vary across organizations. For example, a manufacturing company might have functions for production operations, quality assurance, research and development, and engineering. Some organizations have departments to handle legal and regulatory issues and community relations.

Organizing by function is intended to increase organizational efficiency by having people with similar expertise working together to perform similar functions. Paradoxically, a functional structure can also decrease organizational efficiency because the structure creates barriers between departments that generally result in increased time to respond to cross-functional problems.

BY DIVISION

In a divisional organizational structure, divisions can be based on several different variables including product/service, process, customer, or geographic regions. As organizations change and grow over time, they may switch from one type of division to another. For example, a company that was originally organized with product divisions may seek to improve its efficiency as it expands into new areas by restructuring according to different geographic regions.

Organizing by division increases organizational efficiency because the departments can be more responsive to specific client or regional needs. Paradoxically, efficiency may be reduced because of duplication of effort and barriers to sharing ideas and learning from one another for people who are doing the same type of work in different departments.

BY MATRIX

A matrix organization attempts to reap the advantages and overcome the disadvantages of functional and divisional organizational forms by combining the two. In matrix organizations, employees are assigned (1) to a functional department and also (2) to a cross-functional team that focuses on specific projects or programs. They report to the heads of both the functional department and cross-functional team. For example, an engineer in a manufacturing firm that is organized in matrix form will report to the head of the engineering department and also to the product manager, who also manages marketing, production, and finance specialists assigned to that project or product. Such diverse service and manufacturing organizations as Prudential Insurance, General Mills, and Caterpillar Tractor are organized in matrix form.

Note that, by definition, matrix organizations violate the unity-of-command principle. This can create problems for employees who find themselves accountable to two bosses instead of one. Despite the added complexity of the matrix structure, there are some situations where the advantages of matrix organizations are considered to be sufficient to warrant this violation. Managers in matrix organizations, however, should monitor job assignments and communication patterns to ensure that employees are not receiving conflicting messages from their two bosses.

ORGANIZATIONAL FORMS IN PRACTICE

Because all of the basic forms of departmentalization have advantages and disadvantages, in practice organizations often use a mix of these forms. For example, because of the greater flexibility and ability to respond to client needs, many corporations are organized by division with respect to the specific products or services they provide, but they are organized by function with respect to personnel/human resources management, financial management, and legal offices. Similarly, some organizations are organized by division with respect to regions but by function within each region. Hospitals and psychiatric institutions may have matrix structures for providing services, but they maintain a functional structure for such activities as records management, building maintenance, and nutrition and dietary services.

LINKING STRATEGY, STRUCTURE, AND CULTURE

Traditional organization theory focuses on an organization's *strategy* and the *environment* in which it operates when determining the most effective way to design and organize. Structural contingency theory, for example, suggests that organizations be designed and structured along some continuum of "mechanistic" to "organic," depending on the complexity and turbulence of the environment within which they exist. The basic rule is that the more complex and turbulent the environment, the greater the need for a more organic structure and design.

Organizations today find themselves confronted with even more challenging environments. Customers are sophisticated and demanding; they want an incredible variety of options and expect instantaneous service. Organizations also must cope with an unprecedented breadth and depth of change in economic and political conditions and the very mixed blessing of ever-advancing information technology. These and other environmental circumstances have replaced the evolution of organizational structures suggested by structural contingency theory with the emergence and rapid mutations of organizational designs described as "lateral," "federated," "networked," "virtual," customer-centric (Galbraith, 2005) and human capital centric (Lawler, 2008).

Even with the ever-changing and morphing environments within which organizations must compete, designing and organizing is still driven ideally by the vision the organization has articulated as well as the strategy and super-ordinate goals articulated. No organization design is perfect, and each has relative strengths and weaknesses.

GALBRAITH'S STAR MODEL

The vision and strategy set the criteria for choosing among the many trade-offs posed by various designs. Galbraith (1995) has suggested the "star model" as a framework for approaching the design organizations. The star model identifies five categories or elements to consider in the design process: strategy, structure, processes, rewards, and people.

Strategy.   As defined by Galbraith, strategy is the organization's "formula for winning"—it specifies the goals and objectives to be achieved as well as the values and mission that will drive the organization. Strategy, as Galbraith frames it, includes two of the three competencies we have discussed already in the Compete quadrant—developing and communicating a vision and setting goals and objectives. For Galbraith, strategy in the design process is aimed at setting out the basic direction of the organization.

Structure.   In Galbraith's model, structure determines the placement of power and authority in the organization and incorporates the classic elements of structure that we addressed above. Discussions about organizational design often emphasize how the company is currently structured and how a "structural change" would impact effectiveness.

Processes.   Processes, in Galbraith's framework, broadly include information and decision processes that span the breadth and depth of the organization's structure. Management processes can be both vertical and horizontal. Examples of vertical processes include business planning and budgeting processes. Horizontal, or lateral, processes are designed around the work flow.

Rewards.   In any organizational setting, the outcome hoped for from reward systems is the alignment of the goals of individual employees with the goals of the organization. There has been much change in this area as the impact of lateral processes, increasingly team-based organizations, and the centrality of nonmonetary rewards has increased. This change has also been hurried along by the increasing presence of multiple generations of workers, several of whom are looking for noticeably different kinds of rewards from their roles in organizations, as we discussed in the competency Motivating Self and Others.

People.   Galbraith's definition of "people" in the context of his model includes the human resource policies that relate to the attraction, recruitment, selection, development, and rotation of employees. These policies, when combined and aligned appropriately, produce the talent pool that is necessary based on the strategy and structure of the organization.

ORGANIZATIONAL CULTURE AS A FRAME FOR DESIGNING AND ORGANIZING

Given the challenges of the new economy, the classical principles of organization structure almost seem too slow and cumbersome to reflect current organizational realities. Nadler and Tushman (2000) observed that in recent years it has become evident that "values, culture, and shared goals are replacing the formal structures as the glue that holds organizations together" (p. 58). With the increasing role that culture is playing in organizational life, it seems only logical that it should get more of our attention as we consider the design and organization of companies. A great deal of recent research suggests that initiatives aimed at organizational improvement often fail because of inattention to the role and impact of organizational culture. Studies of downsizing, total quality management, and reengineering have found that when they were implemented independent of a change in culture, they were often unsuccessful because when the organization's culture, values, orientations, definitions, and goals stay constant—even when procedures and strategies are altered—organizations return quickly to the status quo (Cameron, 1995; Cameron, Freeman & Mishra, 1993).

Galbraith (1995) suggests that the five elements of design that make up his star model are levers that leaders control that can affect organizational performance and culture, but only by acting "through" the design levers that affect behavior. We would like to suggest that today Galbraith's sequence of effects can be turned around (see Figure M3.3) and that culture can be used as a lead variable (i.e., lever) in understanding and leveraging (or changing) current organization design.

FIGURE M3.3
Framework for understanding and diagnosing organizational design.

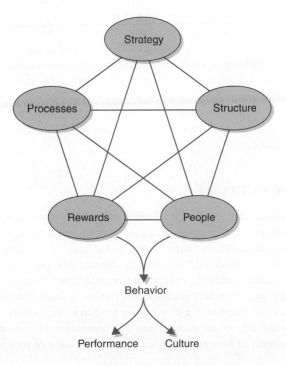

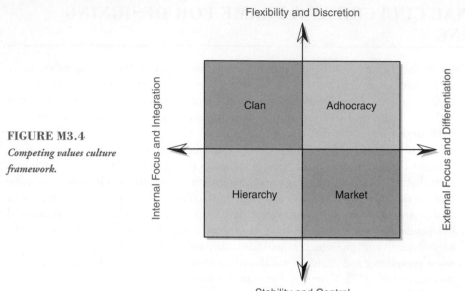

FIGURE M3.4

Competing values culture framework.

The competing values culture framework (Cameron & Quinn, 2006) emerges from the juxtaposition of the same two dimensions that make up the competing values leadership framework (see Figure M3.4). The horizontal dimension reflects the competing demands created by the internal organization and the external environment. One end represents a focus on buffering to sustain the existing organization, while the other represents a focus on adaptation, competition, and interaction with the environment. This dimension is analogous to our discussion of integration and differentiation. The vertical dimension reflects the competing demands of change and stability. One end represents an emphasis on flexibility and spontaneity, while the other represents a complementary focus on stability, control, and order. This dimension is analogous to the distinction we made above about structures varying from mechanistic to organic forms. The four culture types that result (see Figure M3.4) are reflections of the four competing values quadrants.

CLAN CULTURE

The clan culture mirrors the values of the human relations model and is represented by the color yellow. The clan has a primary concern with shared values and goals, cohesion, participativeness, individuality, and a sense of "we-ness"—more like an extended family than an economic vehicle. The ultimate purpose of organizations that emphasize a clan culture tends to be group maintenance. Core values include belonging, trust, and participation. Primary motivational factors include attachment, cohesiveness, and membership. Leaders in a clan culture tend to be supportive, considerate, participative, and facilitative of interaction through teamwork. Effectiveness criteria include the development of human capital and the commitment of individual members.

HIERARCHY CULTURE

The culture mirroring the values of the internal process model, the hierarchy (represented by the color red), has a primary concern with internal efficiency, uniformity, coordination, and evaluation. Typically, organizations with a strong hierarchical culture emphasize the execution of policies and regulations. Primary motivational factors include security, order, rules, and regulations. Leaders in a hierarchy culture tend to be conservative, cautious, and very attentive to technical issues. Effectiveness criteria include control, stability, and efficiency.

MARKET CULTURE

The culture mirroring the values of the rational goal model, the market culture, has a primary concern with productivity, performance, and goal achievement. The market culture (represented by the color blue) is oriented toward the external environment instead of internal affairs. It is primarily focused on transactions with external constituencies such as customers, suppliers, and so forth. Typically, the driving purpose of organizations with a market culture emphasis tends to be the pursuit and attainment of well-defined objectives. Primary motivating factors include competition and the successful achievement of predetermined ends. Leaders in a market culture tend to be directive, goal oriented, instrumental, and functional. These leaders are constantly vigilant about providing productivity and structure. Effectiveness criteria include planning, productivity, and efficiency.

ADHOCRACY CULTURE

The culture mirroring the values of the open systems model is the adhocracy culture (represented by the color green). The adhocracy culture is primarily concerned with flexibility and change, and maintains a primary focus on the external environment. Cultures that are strongly characterized by adhocracy emphasize growth, resource acquisition, creativity, and adapting and responding to the external environment. A central purpose is often to maximize individuality, risk taking, and anticipating the future. Primary motivating factors include growth, stimulation, creativity, and variety. Leaders in an adhocracy tend to be entrepreneurial and idealistic, with a willingness to take risks and an ability to develop a vision of the future. Effectiveness criteria include growth, the development of new markets, and resource acquisition.

DIAGNOSING AND ALIGNING ORGANIZATIONAL CULTURE

The Assessment that you completed at the beginning of this competency is based on the Organizational Culture Assessment Instrument (OCAI), which was developed to analyze organizational culture based on the competing values framework. Versions of the OCAI have been used in a variety of organizations. For example, Choi, Seo, Scott, and Martin (2010) recently translated a more detailed version of the OCAI for use with 133 members of the Korean Professional Baseball League. More detailed versions of the OCAI can provide a more fine-grained diagnosis of your organization culture, but for our purposes this broad-brush approach provides a starting point for thinking about the connection between organization culture and design.

The simplified OCAI you completed asked you to allocate 100 points across four descriptions of organizations. The first description is consistent with the clan culture, the second with the adhocracy, the third with the market culture, and the fourth with the hierarchy culture. Each of the four cultural types has a perceptual opposite. The "clan," concerned with cohesion, morale, and the development of human resources, starkly contrasts to the "market," with its pursuit of market share, goal achievement, and vanquishing competitors. The "hierarchy," with its passion for efficiency, timeliness, and smooth functioning, contrasts with the "adhocracy," looking for fulfillment in cutting-edge output, creativity, and growth. Yet while they exist as "polar opposites," they share a common focus—the clan and the adhocracy share an emphasis on flexibility, the adhocracy and the market share an external focus, the market and the hierarchy share the value of control, and the hierarchy and the clan share an internal focus.

Two key assumptions underlie the competing values culture framework. The first is that each of the four cultures should be viewed as ideal types defined by the competing values model. Organizations functioning in the real world are very unlikely to reflect only one of the four culture types. Typically, organizations reflect some level of all four, with one or two more dominant than the others. The second key assumption of the competing values culture framework is the critical importance of balance. When one of the four models is overused or overemphasized, an organization may become ineffective, and the positives of the quadrant may become weaknesses. The framework also stops short of the normative and prescriptive bias that the most effective culture is one that has incorporated the attributes of all four types because in practice, the most effective culture will depend upon environmental factors that are outside the control of the organization.

Cameron and Quinn (2006) have articulated a process involving the "profiling" of an organization's perceived current culture, identification of desired future states based on strategy and the current state of the organization, and necessary changes and actions aimed at altering the culture appropriately. Their process facilitates several types of comparisons important in understanding an organization's current culture and its impact on design and performance. Some comparisons that are useful in understanding the effectiveness of a given organizational design include the *type* of culture (i.e., market, adhocracy, etc.) that characterizes an organization, *discrepancies* between the current and the desired future culture, the *strength* of the culture type that seems to dominate, and the *congruence* of culture profiles generated on different attributes by different subsets of individuals in organizations.

Type of culture is critical since organizational effectiveness and success depend to a great extent on the match between an organization's culture and the various demands that the relevant competitive environment makes. If organization X is operating in a viciously competitive and aggressive industry within a rapidly changing and turbulent environment, it may not survive with a culture that is very strong on the group/clan aspect and relatively weak on market culture orientation. Discrepancies identify the disconnects between the state of the organization now and where the organization thinks it needs to be in order to be effective. These discrepancies help focus on the right elements of organizational design to use as levers to resolve the discrepancies. Strong cultures typically reflect homogeneity of energy, focus, efforts, and performance in environments where unity and shared vision are required. Depending on the nature of the challenge(s) the organization is facing, the desired culture may be stronger or weaker than the current culture. For example, a firm with a very strong and homogeneous culture may try to find opportunities to become more "flexible" and pliable when it needs to be heavily involved in alliances and multiorganizational partnerships. The notion of congruence implies that various aspects of an organization's culture are in fact aligned and consistent. That is, each of the five elements of Galbraith's star model—strategy, structure, processes, rewards, and people—would tend to emphasize the same set of cultural values.

In our discussion of this competency, we suggested that the nature, pace, and complexity of organizational life today requires a knowledge of the classic lessons about designing and organizing—derived mostly from work on organizational structure—as well as the ability to apply and leverage that knowledge in a way that makes it more usable working at Internet speed. The solution we have suggested is the use of organizational culture as a lens to help understand and diagnose the effectiveness of an organization's design as well as a lever to help improve an organization's effectiveness and performance.

Every organization is very much a function of its design. One student of organizations observed, "Every organization is perfectly designed to give us the results we are getting" (anonymous). The experience that key stakeholders have with an organization—be they customers, employees, suppliers, partners, shareholders, and so forth—will be enhanced or diminished by the appropriateness of the organization's design to its situation and environment.

ANALYSIS   Responding to Environmental Challenges

Objective This activity provides you with an opportunity to consider the dynamic relationship between an organization's environment and its strategy, design, and culture.

Background In January 2003, the U.S. Government Accounting Office designated the U.S. Postal Service's transformation efforts and long-term outlook as a "high-risk area." The USPS was experiencing serious financial difficulties and struggling to fulfill its mission of providing high-quality universal service while remaining self-supporting (GAO, 2003). One effort aimed at addressing these concerns was a review and analysis of the Postal Service's organization design and structure conducted by Unisys and Watson Wyatt under the auspices of the President's Commission on the USPS. Five highlights were identified in the Executive Summary of that study:

1. The fundamental management structure of the USPS—consisting of Headquarters, Functional Staff, and Operations—is appropriate for an organization that is committed to operational excellence.

2. The current management structure is appropriately lean, although there is a real opportunity to continue to rationalize the network.

3. Roles are generally clear.

4. Good line of sight exists.

5. Information is shared across management levels and boundaries.

The study suggested building on these existing strengths and made four recommendations:

1. Accelerate Rationalization of the Network

2. Provide Increased Decision-Making Role for Operations Managers

3. Improve Headquarters and Area Staff Coordination and Integration Operations

4. Adopt a Consistent Performance Cluster Model

Directions   1. Obtain a copy of the following documents:

   - U.S. Postal Service Organization Chart (check online for most current version available)

   - U.S. Postal Service Management Structure Study, July 8, 2003, Report to the President's Commission on the United States Postal Service (http://www.ustreas.gov/offices/domestic-finance/usps/pdf/project9.pdf)

2. In preparation for class discussion and a small group activity, please read the Management Structure Study report submitted to the President's Commission on the USPS in 2003 and answer the following questions.

Discussion Questions   1. Using Galbraith's Star Model, write a few sentences describing Strategy, Structure, Processes, Rewards, and People at the USPS. Draw on the study report as well as any other information and you can gather.

2. What kind of departmentalization currently exists in the USPS?

3. What part did the USPS' departmentalization play in the results of the 2003 study? Was the departmentalization appropriate and aligned with the USPS mission?

4. What culture types do you think characterize the USPS?

5. Do you believe the culture at the USPS was aligned with its mission at the time of the report?

6. What do you think of the report's four recommendations—are they primarily structural or cultural?

7. How effective do you believe the recommendations will be if implemented successfully?

Reflection   The mission of the U.S. Postal Service (below) focuses on public service, but the organization faces competition from a variety of for-profit companies and new technologies. Given the public service mission of the USPS, does it make sense to provide regulations to help protect the organization from for-profit competitors?

The Postal Service shall have as its basic function the obligation to provide postal services to bind the Nation together through the personal, educational, literary, and business correspondence of the people. It shall provide prompt, reliable, and efficient services to patrons in all areas and shall render postal services to all communities. http://www.usps.com/postalhistory/_pdf/MissionandMotto.pdf.

PRACTICE   USPS: Prescribe a Possible Future

Objective   The objective of this Practice activity is to provide a chance for you to try your hand at formulating a solution to an organizing and designing challenge.

Directions Read the Introduction/Context Setting below and building on your Analysis of the USPS, assume the role of organizational consultant and propose a course of action to the most senior leaders of the USPS. Draw on your Analysis and any and all information and experience that may be available.

1. Please ensure that your recommendations are consistent and aligned with the format and content of the 2003 study.

2. Please include mention of structural variables, departmentalization, and organizational culture in your work.

3. Please include two other organizations as benchmarks or examples in your recommendations.

INTRODUCTION/CONTEXT SETTING:

On July 30, 2009, an article appearing in the *New York Times* entitled "Increasing Postal Deficits Intensify Talks on Solution" predicted that the U.S. Congress would become increasingly focused on the USPS given the escalation of its record-breaking losses. Postmaster General John E. Potter stated that the USPS expected to run a record $7 billion deficit for 2009, up from an initially projected $6 billion deficit. Once again, the Government Accountability Office designated the USPS as a "high risk" federal program and urged it to work very closely with Congress to help solve its financial problems.

Postmaster General Potter proposed that Congress change the laws that mandated the USPS to deliver mail six days a week. That proposal was initially summarily rejected by congressional leaders. As finances worsen, this proposal may yet see the light of day. Another proposal to cut costs would allow the USPS to pay current health benefits from a pre-funded account for retirement health care benefits that is currently overfunded, potentially saving $2 billion a year from the operating budget. A hiring freeze has been in place at the USPS since the spring of 2008. Leaders of the two unions that represent various postal workers advocate the search for additional cost savings in lieu of considering what they see as extreme measures like cutting back on service delivery. Postmaster General Potter forecasted that the USPS would handle 27 billion fewer pieces of mail in 2009 than in the prior year, 2008. Many are questioning whether this is a temporary situation caused by the deep economic recession or a permanent change due to alternative communication technologies ("Increasing Postal Deficits Intensify Talks on Solutions," *New York Times*, July 30, 2009).

Reflection Consultants are often hired to analyze a situation in an organization and make recommendations, but their reports are not always welcome. As we'll discuss in Module 4, people and organizations tend to resist change, so clients may not want a report that recommends doing things differently, even when that was ostensibly the reason the consultant was hired in the first place!

APPLICATION Understanding the Design and Organization of Your Company

Objective The objective of this application activity is to improve your understanding of the design and organization of your company.

Directions Select an organization that you have extensive knowledge of. Ideally, this would be the organization you currently work in or very recently worked in. It could be a school-related organization or some other one that you have been extensively involved with. Using that organization as a focal point, complete the following:

1. Secure the formal organization chart (if available) of that organization. Review it and conduct an analysis of its use of efficiency as an organizing principle, its intended structural configuration, its line of authority, and any available information on the nature of differentiation and integration.

2. Review the discussions of cultural types and the competing values cultural framework. As best you can, try to "profile" the primary cultural type(s) reflected in your organization.

3. Consider the environment in which your organization is currently operating. Given your analyses from questions 1 and 2, decide whether the current structure and culture should be redesigned so the company could compete more effectively. Be sure that you can justify your claims regarding improvements to the organization design using grounds and warrants based on the principles of design and organization discussed in this competency.

4. Interview the leader of the organization and query that person as to his or her perceptions of the effectiveness of the organization relative to its current design. Ask what might make the organization more effective.

Reflection   Organization structure and culture can have an enormous impact on the atmosphere of an organization. So when considering job opportunities, it makes sense to try to learn as much about your prospective employer's structure and culture as possible. Doing this type of advance research will also prepare you to ask questions if you see things during your interview that appear to be inconsistent with published information about the organization.

Module 3 Competency 5   Managing Execution and Driving for Results

ASSESSMENT   Your Leadership Task-Orientation

Objective   This exercise is designed to give you an insight into your personal leadership style with respect to how you approach getting tasks completed.

Directions   Using the scale below, please complete the assessment focusing on how you typically behave when leading a work group, unit or team.

Does not describe me at all				Perfectly describes my behavior
1	2	3	4	5

_____   I establish ambitious goals that challenge people to achieve performance levels above the competition.

_____   Members of my work group perform at higher levels than members of other units.

_____   I monitor the strengths and weaknesses of the best competition and provide my unit with information on how they measure up.

_____ I have consistent and frequent contact with external and internal customers to gather information on their needs and level of satisfaction.

_____ I make sure that my unit is always aware of how well they are meeting customers' expectations.

_____ I ensure that everything the organization does is focused on better serving customers.

_____ I quickly address challenges and issues.

_____ I constantly push for faster performance in my unit.

_____ I encourage speed and timeliness in producing outcomes.

_____ I insist on intense, hard work and high productivity from my people.

_____ I push my unit to achieve world-class competitive performance.

_____ I facilitate a climate of intensity and high energy in my unit.

Reflection Being highly task-oriented may serve you well in terms of completing your individual tasks, but when leading others, too much emphasis on task issues can paradoxically undermine your efforts to get the task completed with good quality and on time.

LEARNING   Managing Execution and Driving for Results

Managing Execution and Driving for Results is a most appropriate capstone competency for this module. The vision and goals of the organization must be translated into results by the efforts of motivated people working within the organizational structures and culture that we have created. Simply put, managing execution and driving for results is about getting things done.

Much research has been done over the past 10 years on this topic, particularly at the organizational level. As academics undertook studies to improve our understanding of what is required for successfully executing a strategy and achieving the desired results, organizations were engaged in experiments, hiring "outsider" CEOs to improve upon disappointing results. Examples include Ford Motor Company and Hewlett-Packard, both companies with storied histories, that chose to hire leaders who emphasized execution and results to try to bring these organizations back to their former glory.

In Ford's case, William Clay Ford, Jr., the great-grandson of Henry Ford, stepped down as CEO after five years; at the time of his departure, the company was clearly in a crisis. The new CEO, Alan Mulally, had established his reputation by reviving Boeing's commercial airline business after 9/11 (Naughton, 2007), but "reaction inside the company ranged from suspicion to outrage. What did an airplane guy know about the car business?" (Kiley, 2009). Although top insiders questioned the decision, Bill Ford felt that the company needed a fresh perspective. Consistent with the rational goal quadrant and the internal process quadrant, one of Mulally's mantras is "Improve Focus, Simplify Operations." Results thus far suggest that its working—Ford is the only U.S. car company to avoid bankruptcy and has seen a return to profitability and impressive gains in its stock price since Mulally took the wheel in 2006 (Ingrassia, 2010).

At Hewlett-Packard, CEO Mark Hurd was hired in as CEO in early 2005, replacing Carleton S. (Carly) Fiorina who had served as HP's CEO since 2000. Hurd joined HP after spending 25 years at NCR Corp.; his last two years he held the CEO position. In a *Business Week* article entitled "HP says goodbye to drama," Hurd was quoted as saying:

> We need to temper the idea that this company has to have some earthshaking event every 15 minutes . . . . I'm not sure how it got that way—and to be very frank, I really don't care. Our job is to execute *(quoted in Burrows, 2005, p. 83)*.

Despite interest in the effective execution of strategy, actual organizational results to date leave much to be desired. For example, in a recent Conference Board study, 658 CEOs from multinational companies were asked to prioritize their most pressing management challenges. CEOs of organizations with revenues greater than $5 billion ranked "Consistent execution of strategy by top management" first. CEOs of smaller organizations ranked execution second, just after "Sustained and steady top line growth" (Barrington, Silvert & Ginsberg, 2005). Even more disturbing are claims by *Fortune* that approximately 70 percent of companies can't execute on strategy and that only 10 percent of organizations actually attain their strategic objectives. Research on the public sector by *Barron's* suggests that the results are no better there. In a study of nearly 800 federal programs, only 15 percent achieved their goals (Donlon, 2006).

In this competency, we will explore some of the challenges and dynamics associated with effective execution and attainment of desired results. We begin with the discussion of an integrative framework that helps us better understand the challenges and dynamics of execution at the organizational level. Then we will consider individual-level leader effectiveness and time management issues.

EXECUTION AND RESULTS AT THE ORGANIZATIONAL LEVEL

The roots of ideas about execution go back to early management theory focusing on the essential functions of management, namely, planning, organizing, staffing, directing, coordinating, reporting, and budgeting (Gulick & Urwick, 1937). Over time, as organizations became more adept at "getting things done," a new emphasis emerged on "getting things done better," with an emphasis on efficiency and effectiveness. During the last decade of the twentieth century in particular, business process reengineering (Hammer & Champy, 1993) emerged as a popular approach to improving execution and results.

The reengineering approach urged organizations to take a blank sheet of paper and reconsider how all processes might better serve the organization's goals and objectives. Although initially popular, it soon became clear that the technique put too much emphasis on efficiency and not enough emphasis on the well-being of employees who were affected by the layoffs and staff redeployments the technique called for. In retrospect, Michael Hammer, one of the founders of business process reengineering theory, admitted that there was a flaw in the theory. As reported in the *Wall Street Journal* by Joseph B. White (1996, p. A.1):

[Michael Hammer] and other leaders of the $4.7 billion re-engineering industry forgot about people. "I wasn't smart enough about that," he says. "I was reflecting my engineering background and was insufficiently appreciative of the human dimension. I've learned that's critical."

In contrast to the process-oriented focus of the reengineering approach to execution and results, other researchers have focused on the leader's role. For example, in their book, *Results-Based Leadership*, Ulrich, Zenger, and Smallwood (1999), argue that leadership skills must be deployed in alignment with the organization's vision to result in appropriate and purposeful action.

In this Learning section, we focus on a framework that incorporates elements of organizational processes and leadership behaviors for understanding the key aspects of execution that are required for achieving desired results. In 2002, Larry Bossidy and Ram Charan published the first edition of a book entitled *Execution: The Discipline of Getting Things Done.* In 2009, they released a second, updated edition devoting special attention to the colossal failures in the U.S. financial services industry. In *Execution*, which has sold over two million copies world-wide, Bossidy and Charan address what is often seen as the unglamorous, nitty-gritty nuts and bolts of getting things done within an organization. They ask, why are organizations so abysmal when it comes to execution? Their answer: a lack of discipline. As explained by Charan (2005),

Execution is not just tactics—it is a discipline and a system. It has to be built into a company's strategy, its goals, and its culture. No worthwhile strategy can be planned without taking into account the organization's ability to execute it. The heart of execution lies in three core processes: the people process, the strategy process, and the operations process.

THE PEOPLE PROCESS

According to Bossidy and Charan, the people process is the most important of the three—if the people process is not optimized, an organization is unlikely to reach its full potential. The people process must accomplish three things:

1. It should evaluate every individual in the organization in depth and with as much accuracy as possible.
2. It should provide a blueprint of the pipeline (selection, development, promotion, etc.) of leadership talent—all levels and all kinds—required by the organization in order to execute its strategy.
3. It should populate the leadership pipeline based on a strong and strategic succession plan.

Although the authors admit there is no single system for creating a robust people process, they do advocate certain characteristics the process should have, including: integrity, honesty, consistency, use of common language, and frequent feedback. Candor in providing timely and accurate feedback is seen as the hallmark of this process.

THE STRATEGY PROCESS

The strategy process that Bossidy and Charan advocate is not merely focused on formulating the strategy—***what*** should we do? The strategy process should also pay attention to the specific ways the strategy will be executed—***how*** should we do it? These execution details rely heavily on the involvement of the individuals closest to the customer and other people who have the best understanding of critical variables such as current opportunities and threats in the market; existing strengths and weaknesses of the organization; and the resources required to successfully implement alternative strategies.

In essence, the strategic plan should be a detailed action plan for achieving business objectives. Critical questions that must be raised include: How good are the assumptions we built the plan on? What are the pros and cons of the alternatives? Do we have the required organizational capabilities to be able to execute the plan? What must we do in the near and medium term to be successful in the long run? Will we be able to adapt the plan to rapid changes in the organizational environment?

THE OPERATIONS PROCESS

The operations process complements the strategy and people processes by outlining the path the people must follow to get to the results identified in the strategy. An operating plan is required to get from the long term to the short term. In many organizations, operations plans are prepared based on a budget, but Bossidy and Charan argue that this is backwards. They recognize that budgets often are detached from reality. To be realistic, the operations process must not simply build budgets around what top management desires, but must address the action programs that will make the outcomes a reality.

A related problem associated with typical budgets is that they are often political exercises in trying to protect personal interests, rather than thoughtful attempts to support the goals of the organization as a whole. Instead of being an opportunity to "game the system," budgeting should be an opportunity to debate the assumptions behind the organization's goals. Charan (2005) notes that only after those assumptions have been identified and examined should targets be set. In setting targets, consideration should be given to the action plans required to meet those targets and to any trade-offs that may be necessary between short-term and long-term goals. To ensure accountability, the participants in the process need to agree to the measures being used for targeted performance. As with any plan or budget, monitoring actual outcomes and taking corrective action if targets are not met is essential.

As important as the people, strategy, and operations processes are, just having them, is not enough, as Charan (2005) points out:

Every business and company uses these processes in one form or other. But more often than not, they stand apart from one another like silos. People perform them by rote and as quickly as possible, so they can get back to their perceived work. The key to successful execution is linking people, strategy, and operations together.

Bossidy and Charan argue that linking these processes together depends on three things: essential leader behaviors, an organizational culture focused on execution, and having the right people in the right places.

LEADER BEHAVIORS

Box M3.4 summarizes the seven leader behaviors that Bossidy and Charan identify as essential for integrating and aligning these three core processes. As you read through their list, you should recognize that many of these behaviors are competencies that we have covered in this text. From Module 1, which focuses on the Collaborate action imperative, the competencies of Understanding Self and Others, Communicating Honestly and Effectively, and Mentoring and Developing Others are reflected in behaviors 1, 2, 6, and 7. The Module 2 competencies related to Measuring and Monitoring Performance and Quality and Encouraging and Enabling Compliance relate to leader behaviors 4 and 5. In this module we've addressed Setting Goals and Objectives and Motivating Self and Others, which relate to behaviors 3 and 5.

BOX M3.4 ESSENTIAL LEADER BEHAVIORS FOR EFFECTIVE EXECUTION

In their research and writing about execution, Charan and Bossidy (2009) have identified seven leader behaviors that they consider essential for effective execution:

1. ***Know your people and your business.*** Stay in touch with the day-to-day activities in the organization.
2. ***Insist on realism.*** Confront the cold, hard truths and realities of the organization and its environments and insist that trouble be surfaced as soon as it's detected.
3. ***Set clear goals and priorities.*** Identify and focus on the few critical things that are essential for the organization to be successful.
4. ***Follow through.*** Take seriously each of the goals that are set for the organization and ensure closure around who needs to do what by when.
5. ***Reward the doers.*** Clearly distinguish across levels of performance and establish an unambiguous link between the performance required and the rewards that will be received for that performance.
6. ***Expand people's capabilities.*** Coach people so that the leader's collected experience and wisdom is passed on to the next generation of leaders.
7. ***Know yourself.*** Have the strength of character and intestinal fortitude to be honest with yourself and with the people you lead. Don't shy away from delivering difficult or uncomfortable messages and don't punish others when they bring you bad news.

A CULTURE OF EXECUTION

In addition to focusing on leader behaviors, Bossidy and Charan also recognize the importance of culture in understanding effectiveness. If an organization has not had a culture that emphasized execution in the past, then we cannot expect to achieve our desired results until we have changed the organizational culture. Conversely, Bossidy and Charan argue that attempts to change organizational culture often fail because those changes have not been linked to improving specific outcomes. To address that problem, they advocate focusing cultural change efforts on execution and making it clear what behaviors have to change in order for the organization to get the results it needs.

THE RIGHT PEOPLE IN THE RIGHT PLACES

Last, but certainly not least, Bossidy and Charan emphasize the importance of having the right people in the right place. This concept reinforces the role that the leader plays in connecting the people, strategy, and operations processes. Every leader must be personally committed to the importance of the people process and must be actively engaged in all aspects of it. There are several reasons why people are not in the right places. For example, managers may not have sufficient knowledge about the people they are appointing to positions, or they may be selecting individuals they feel comfortable with, rather than focusing on selecting the person with the most expertise. In some cases, managers may be too patient with weak performers or may lack the courage needed to distinguish aggressively between strong and weak performers and to take the actions required by those distinctions.

Throughout their entire framework, Bossidy and Charan (2009) make it clear that people are the most essential element of effective execution in organizations. We now turn out attention to execution at the individual level.

EXECUTION AND RESULTS AT THE INDIVIDUAL LEVEL

At the individual level, the topic of effective execution also has received a great deal of attention. For example, many executive education programs, consulting firms, and other organizations offer 360 degree feedback surveys to managers and leaders at all levels of the organization to help them evaluate their personal effectiveness. Often these feedback surveys include items specifically related to managing execution and driving results. For example, in their *Successful Manager's Handbook*, Personnel Decisions International (PDI), one of the originators of 360 degree feedback, includes two composite measures related to execution and results (Davis, 1992):

1. *Manage Execution* focuses on how managers delegate, coordinate, monitor, and track work assignments. It also includes items related to empowering others, being accessible for assistance and support, and coordinating work with other groups.

2. *Drive for Results* focuses on achieving results with and through others and includes items related to strengthening an individual leader's sense of mission and purpose, having results be a top priority, being able to communicate a sense of urgency when appropriate, being persistent in the face of obstacles and difficulties, displaying a personally high energy level, and being able to bring issues to closure.

As you probably noticed, many of the items included in the PDI measures for execution and results relate to competencies that are included in this text. This should come as no surprise, given the comprehensive nature of the competing values framework. Next we consider what may be the most important skill required for individual success—effective and efficient time management.

TIME MANAGEMENT

In his classic work on time management, *The Time Trap,* Alec Mackenzie asks the vexing question: "Why is time management still a problem?" Mackenzie (1997, pp. 4–5) observes:

. . . after all these years, and with all these innovations (e.g., books, magazine articles, seminars, workshops, paper and electronic organizers, etc.), we are still caught in the time trap. With this mountain of information, these dazzling new tools, we still groan and say, "There just isn't enough time!" Why is this? Why is it that we still find ourselves making some of the classic time management mistakes, even though we know better? The answer is simple—and very complex: human nature.

The knowing-doing gap is certainly alive and well when it comes to effective time management!

In this section, we use Peter Drucker's classic advice to "Know Your Time" as the foundation for our discussion. Although it was first published in 1966, Drucker's three-step process is reflected in many time management books and seminars today because the basic ideas of recording time, managing time, and consolidating time (Drucker, 2001, p. 225) provide a solid foundation for effective time management in any situation.

Record Your Time. If you don't keep a record, you can't know your time. Contemporaneous record keeping—recording what you are spending time on when you are actually doing a task—is the first essential step toward knowing your time. Drucker points out that people are notoriously bad at estimating how much time has gone by while working on a task. When we compound that problem by waiting until the end of the week to try to reconstruct our activities, any analysis of where our time went will be worse than useless, it will be misleading. Time management is one area where practice does not make us perfect. Although we do improve in our use of time with practice, most people discover that that they "drift" back into wasting time unless they remain vigilant and continue to keep a record of their time use, if not continuously, at least on a fairly regular basis.

Manage Your Time. Until you have a firm idea of where you are spending your time, it is impossible to effectively manage your time. Drucker (2001, p. 231) points out that although we have known this since the days of scientific management, we tend to apply this knowledge where it does the least good, rather than focusing on how highly paid knowledge workers and executives are spending their time. Managing your time requires prioritizing and eliminating activities that don't add value. Drucker begins with eliminating activities that are a complete waste of time, stating: "To find these time-wastes, one asks of *all* activities in the time records, What would happen if this were not done at all? And if the answer is, Nothing would happen, then obviously the conclusion is to stop doing it" (Drucker, 2001, p. 232). Although theoretically sound, this advice often is not quite so simple in practice. We may not know for certain if some of our activities really add value, and even if we are reasonably sure that they do not, not everyone has the courage to simply stop doing something that seems like a waste of time. In addition, cutting back on unproductive activities often means saying "no" to requests from others—something that many people find difficult, both in their work and personal lives. If you struggle with saying "no" to others, we recommend getting a copy of *The Power of Positive No: Save the Deal, Save the Relationship—and Still Say No* by William Ury (2007). Ury, a cofounder of Harvard's Program on Negotiation, provides valuable insights into how to say "no" in a positive way.

Once you have eliminated as many activities as you can, you can use the Time Management Matrix (Covey, 2004) that we introduced in Module 2 to prioritize your remaining tasks. Recall that the Time Management matrix is divided into four quadrants based on two dimensions, importance and urgency.

1. Important and Urgent

2. Important but Not Urgent (at the moment)

3. Not Important but Urgent

4. Not Important and Not Urgent

(Although if you have taken Drucker to heart, you should have only Important tasks remaining on your list at this point.) The final step in Drucker's time management process requires that you have an understanding of what blocks of time you have available for your work.

Consolidate Your Time. Drucker is adamant about the importance of having significant blocks of time to accomplish most tasks. For example, he writes:

The knowledge worker who thinks that he can discuss the plans, direction, and performance of one of his subordinates in fifteen minutes—and many managers believe this—is just deceiving himself. If one wants to get to the point of having an impact, one needs probably at least an hour and usually much more. And if one has to establish a human relationship, one needs infinitely more time *(Drucker, 2001, p. 229).*

Unfortunately, managers often do not feel that they can control their time to the extent that Drucker recommends. Managers are usually in the midst of transactions and operations. They need to be able to use their time efficiently, but they also need to allow time for unscheduled encounters. They need to be able to stop for an energy break when they recognize that the quality of their work is suffering. Most managers listen and talk far more than they read, and they share much more information through the spoken word, via plant tours, telephone and doorway conversations, and meetings, than they do through written reports, which require more consolidated blocks of time to prepare. Managers need to keep in touch with colleagues and customers so that they know what is going on within their organization, their industry, and the world. Much of their important work is accomplished in bursts of collaborative encounters with others, the average duration of which is about 11 minutes (Alesandrini, 1992).

The reality of a typical manager's day suggests that time management techniques need to accommodate a manager's need for a more fluid approach to time (Deutschman, 1992), one that focuses more on identifying priorities and concentrating on the critical tasks rather than on mapping out each minute of the day. Note that this all assumes two key elements of time management. First, you need to keep a calendar, preferably one calendar so that you don't "lose" appointments by failing to transfer them from one calendar to the other. Second, you need to keep a master list of things you need to do. From this list, you can make your daily to-do list or schedule, based on your priorities. Box M3.5 concludes this chapter with the story of a university professor whose own time management issues resulted in a legacy for the rest of us.

BOX M3.5 TIME MANAGEMENT ON A DEADLINE

What would you do if you knew you had a terminal disease and your doctors were talking about the rest of your life in terms of months, rather than years? When Randy Pausch, a professor of computer science, was diagnosed with terminal pancreatic cancer in September 2006, his response was to give an upbeat lecture entitled "The Last Lecture: Really Achieving Your Childhood Dreams" at Carnegie Mellon. What started out as a message for his children and a farewell to his colleagues ended up as a popular *You Tube* video and later a *New York Times* bestseller. Along with the core message of seizing every moment, Pausch's themes included the importance of overcoming obstacles for yourself as well as enabling the dreams of others.

Although he is better known for his Last Lecture, Pausch also gave an excellent presentation entitled "Time Management" at the University of Virginia in 2007. That presentation focuses on some nuts-and-bolts ideas about effective time management, and includes ideas that range from using multiple computer monitors to writing thank you notes. When we last checked, both these videos were still available on *You Tube*.

It is clear from his list of accomplishments that Randy Pausch took the idea of using time effectively and efficiently very seriously long before he learned he only had a few months to live. Randy Pausch died on July 25, 2008. His impact as a leader, however, lives on in all the people that he touched with his with his life and his message about the importance of time.

Sources: Pausch (2010) and "Randy Pausch" (2010, April 6).

ANALYSIS   Execution and Results in a Crisis Situation

Objective   This Analysis exercise provides you with the opportunity to consider a real event and examine how two of the leaders in the situation responded as the crisis unfolded. The event is the onslaught of Hurricane Katrina, which struck the city of New Orleans on August 29, 2005. Thousands of lives were lost, and the initial response to the catastrophe will go down in history as one of the poorest and most ineffectual ever.

Directions   Please read the following articles.

1. David D. Kirkpatrick and Scott Shane, "Ex-FEMA Chief Tells of Frustration and Chaos," *New York Times*, September 15, 2005.

2. "A Military General's Leadership Lessons" (Q & A with General Russel Honoré, former commander of Joint Task Force—Katrina who oversaw the military relief efforts after Hurricanes Karina and Rita), *Gallup Management Journal*, January 8, 2009.

After reading the two articles, please answer the following questions:

1. In the Kirkpatrick and Shane article, several leaders are mentioned including President George W. Bush, Homeland Security Chief Michael Chertoff, and FEMA Director Michael D. Brown. Briefly evaluate each of these leaders on their overall effectiveness at Managing Execution and Driving for Results.

2. We learn from the Kirkpatrick and Shane article that FEMA Director Brown was removed from his job one week after the Katrina struck New Orleans. What portion of this outcome for Mr. Brown would you attribute to organizational factors versus Mr. Brown's personal ability to manage execution and drive for results?

3. Compare your analysis of Mr. Brown with an analysis of General Honoré's overall effectiveness in terms of execution and results. Which of the two is more effective? Why? What part of the General's performance do you attribute to organizational factors? How much of his performance do you think relates to his personal skills?

4. In the Q & A with General Honoré, the interviewer describes the General as someone who knows quite a lot about bossing people and who stresses that above all, the last thing a leader should do is "boss" people! The general is quoted as saying, "A leader's job is strategic: to set people on the right path and to do the planning and then to motivate the execution." How do you interpret the general's call to "motivate the execution" and his advice NOT to boss people? Are these two ideas consistent with the frameworks we have discussed in this competency?

Reflection   No matter how much planning and preparation we do to prepare, when a crisis strikes, we often discover that many of our plans become irrelevant because the situation unfolds in ways that we failed to anticipate. That does not mean, however, that the time spent planning was wasted—it does mean that we need to be flexible in responding to crises, rather than trying to force the situation to fit our plans.

PRACTICE   Examining the Impact of a New CEO on Execution and Results

Objective   This exercise is intended to give you experience in analyzing changes in organizational leadership and evaluating the effectiveness of that change.

Directions   Please select one of the companies below, or one suggested by your instructor, and do a backward-looking research project focusing on that company's decision to replace the CEO. Was the decision to remove the prior CEO related to problems with managing execution and driving for results? To what extent did the company's problems stem from external forces rather than internal process problems? Was the new CEO selected based on his track record for execution and results? Since the new CEO took over, what changes have taken place? Do those changes align with the types of change you would anticipate if the core problem was in executing strategy rather than determining strategy?

- Hewlett Packard—Mark Hurd replaced Carly Fiorina in 2005.
- Ford Motor Company—Alan Mulally replaced William Clay Ford, Jr., in 2006.

- Procter & Gamble—Alan G. Lafley replaced Durk Jager in 2000 (Note: when Lafley stepped down in 2009, he was replaced by an insider, P&G COO Bob McDonald.)

Reflection The decision to bring in an "outsider" CEO to a company may result in a number of changes that can distract people from their work. Effective communication can help keep people focused on execution during the transition from one leadership team to another.

APPLICATION Know Your Time

Objective This exercise is intended to help you get started on developing good time management habits.

Directions Step 1: In the circle below, create a pie chart that shows where you think you currently spend your time during an average *24*-hour day. For example, if you usually get eight hours of sleep per night, then 1/3 of the circle would be labeled "sleep." Make as many categories as you think are appropriate.

Step 2: During the next week, keep a contemporaneous daily time log to track where you spend your time. If you have never done this in the past, you can use a simple format like the one below.

Start time	End time	Activity
7 a.m.	7:50	check emails
7:50	8:15	coffee with Fred
8:15	9:00	meeting with team leaders

Step 3: At the end of the week, calculate how much time you actually spent on the different categories that you identified in Step 1. You may need to add new categories at this point; that is fine.

Discussion Questions

1. How hard was it to keep track of your time? Did you often find gaps in your time log?

2. How accurate was your initial estimate of where your time was being spent?

3. Do you feel that you are allocating your time appropriately, based on the data that you collected? If not, what do you plan to do to improve your use of time?

Reflection   Managing time effectively requires that you get to know yourself. For example, after email became common in organizations, most time management experts began recommending that people turn off the "new message" feature on email to reduce distractions. If you check for electronic messages frequently, you may want to try identifying two or three times a day for dealing with your messages and letting people know when these times are. If you need to concentrate on a project in the morning, you may find it better not to look at your email until after you've completed the project (if it is short), or at least until you've made enough progress to create some momentum and motivation to come back to it even if you do need to check for important and urgent emails.

MODULE 3   Compete-Focused Competency Evaluation Matrix

Objective   The final exercise in each module is intended to give you a starting point for developing a comprehensive strategy for mastery that you can implement and monitor in the future. You will use these matrices at the end of this book for your long-term development plan.

Review   The first competency in the Compete quadrant focused on developing and communicating a vision and included exercises to help you connect your vision to your career goals. To help turn that vision into reality, our next competency was setting goals and objectives, where we emphasized the importance of creating SMART goals that are aligned with your overall vision. The third competency, Motivating Self and Others, provided insights into what is necessary to translate goals into actions and considered both what motivates people and how our beliefs and expectation influence our willingness to exert the effort needed to achieve specific goals. Our discussion of designing and organizing focused our attention on the organizational context and helped us understand how key structural variables and organizational culture can impact our ability to achieve the goals of the organization. Finally, we considered what kinds of systems and processes can help us be successful as we manage execution and drive for results.

Directions   Answer the questions in Table M3.3 for each of the competencies covered in this module based on the reading material, class discussions, and your personal work (e.g., Assessment exercises, Application exercises, etc.).

Reflection   Completing Table M3.3 below should give you some ideas about how you can continue to improve on competencies that focus on improving productivity and profitability, consistent with the goals of the rational goal quadrant.

TABLE M3.3 Module 3 Compete-Focused Competency Evaluation Matrix

With respect to this competency:	Developing and Communicating a Vision	Setting Goals and Objectives	Motivating Self and Others	Designing and Organizing	Managing Execution and Driving for Results
1. What do I know about my current performance?					
2. How could I be more effective?					
3. Who are some people I could observe?					
4. What books should I read?					
5. What objectives and deadlines should I set?					
6. With whom should I share my objectives?					
7. How will I evaluate my efforts?					

REFERENCES

Adams, S. J. (1963). Toward and understand of inequity. *Journal of Abnormal and Social* Psychology, 67, 422–436.

Alderfer, C. P. (1972). *Existence, relatedness, and growth*. New York: Free Press.

Alesandrini, K. (1992). *Survive information overload: The 7 best ways to manage your workload by seeing the big picture*. Homewood, IL: Business One Irwin.

Allen, P. (2010, April 19). H. Edward Roberts. *Time*, 19.

Barrington, L., Silvert, H., and Ginsberg, R. (2005, November 2005). *CEO challenge 2006: Top 10 challenges*. The Conference Board.

Bass, B. M., & Avolio, B. J. (1997). *Full range leadership development: Manual for the multifactor leadership questionnaire*. Palo Alto, CA: Midgarden.

Bennis, W., & Nanus, B. (1985). *Leaders: Strategies for taking charge*. New York: Harper & Row.

Black, J. S. (2005). *Motorola Penang*. A case study self-published by J. Stewart Black.

Bolt, J., McGrath, M. R., & Dulworth, M. (2005). *Strategic executive development: The five essential investments*. San Francisco: Wiley.

Booth, C., Jackson, D. S., & Marchant, V. (1997, August 18). Steve's job: Restart Apple. *Time* [On-line.]. Available: http://www.time.com/time/magazine/article/0,9171,986849,00.html.

Bossidy, L., & Charan R. (2002). *Execution: The discipline of getting things Done*. New York: Crown Business.

Bossidy, L., & Charan R. (2009). *Execution: The discipline of getting things done* (2nd ed.). New York: Crown Business.

Bowen, D. E., & Lawler, E. E. (1992, Spring). What, why, how, and when. *Sloan Management Review,* 31–39.

Burrows, P. (2005, September 12). HP says goodbye to drama. *Business Week,* 83.

Cameron, K. S. (1995) Downsizing, quality, and performance. In Robert E. Cole (ed.), *The fall and rise of the American quality movement*. New York: Oxford University Press.

Cameron, K. S., S. J. Freeman, & A. K. Mishra. (1993). Downsizing and Redesigning Organizations, in G. P. Huber, & W. H. Glick, (eds.), *Organizational Change and Redesign*. New York: Oxford University Press.

Cameron, K. S., & Quinn, R. E. (2006). *Diagnosing and changing organizational culture*. San Francisco: Jossey-Bass.

Cameron, K. S., Quinn, R. E., DeGraff, J., & Thakor, A. V. (2006). *Competing values leadership: Creating value in organizations*. Northampton, MA: Edward Elgar.

Charan, R. (2005). The discipline of execution. *Corporate EVENT, 1*(3) [On-line.] Available: http://www.exhibitoronline.com/corpevent/article.asp?ID=840&email=&s=375dc.

Choi, Y. S., Seo, M., Scott, D., & Martin, J. (2010). Validation of the organizational culture assessment instrument: An application of the Korean version. *Journal of Sport Management, 24,* 169–189.

Collins, J. C., & Porras, J. I. (1991). Organizational vision and visionary organizations. *California Management Review, 34*(1), 30–52.

Collins, J. C., & Porras, J. I. (1994). *Built to last*. New York: Harper Collins, 69.

Corporate Leadership Council. (2004). Employee engagement framework and survey. Available via subscription at: https://clc.executiveboard.com/Public/AboutUs.aspx.

Covey, S. R. (2004). *The 7 habits of highly effective people*. New York: Free Press.

Davis, B. L., Hellervik, L. W., & Sheard, J. L. (1992). *Successful manager's handbook*. Minneapolis: Personnel Decisions International.

de Luque, M. S., Washburn, N. T., Waldman, D. A., & House, R. J. (2008). Unrequited profit: How stakeholder and economic values relate to subordinates' perceptions of leadership and firm performance. *Administrative Science Quarterly, 53,* 626–654.

Deutschman, A. (1992, June 1). The CEO's secret of managing time. *Fortune,* 135–146.

Deutschman, A. (2004). Inside the mind of Jeff Bezos. *Fast Company* [On-line]. Available: http://www.fastcompany.com/magazine/85/bezos_1.html.

Donlan, T. G. (2006, March 6). Delusions of adequacy: How the federal government reviews the performance of its programs. *Barron's,* 50.

Doran, G. T. (1981). There's a S.M.A.R.T. Way to Write Management's Goals and Objectives. *Management Review,* November, 1981.

Drucker, P. F. (2001). *The essential Drucker*. New York: HarperCollins.

Drucker, P. F. (1954). *The practice of management*. New York: HarperCollins.

Ed Roberts (computer engineer). (2010, April 15). *Wikipedia, the free encyclopedia*. Available: http://en.wikipedia.org/wiki/Ed_Roberts_(computer_engineer).

Fry, S. (2010, April 11). On the mothership. A confessed Apple fanboy gets finger time with the iPad –and face time with Steve Jobs. *Time*, 40–43.

Fuller, Andrea. (2009, July 30). Increasing postal deficits intensify talks on solutions. *New York Times*. Available: http://www.nytimes.com/2009/07/30/business/30postal.htm.

Galbraith, J. R. (1995). *Designing organizations*. San Francisco: Jossey-Bass.

Galbraith, J. R. (2005). *Designing the customer-centric organization: A guide to strategy, structure and process*. San Francisco: Jossey-Bass.

Gallup Management Journal. (2006). Gallup study: Feeling good matters in the workplace. Available: http://gmj.gallup.com

Gallup Management Journal. (2009). A military general's leadership lessons. Available: http://gmj.gallup.com

Gallup Management Journal. (2010). Despite the downturn, employees remain engaged. Available: http://gmj.gallup.com

GAO. (2003). *Major management challenges and program risks: United States Postal Service*. Available: http://www.gao.gov/pas/2003/d03118.pdf.

Garvin, D. A., & Roberto, M. A. (2002). Paul Levy: Taking charge of the Beth Israel Deaconess Medical Center. Harvard Business School Case 303-008.

Garvin, D. A., & Roberto, M. A. (2005). Change through persuasion. *Harvard Business Review*, *83*(2), 104–112.

Gersick, C. J. G. (1991). Revolutionary change theories: A multilevel exploration of the punctuated equilibrium paradigm. *Academy of Management Review, 16*(1), 10–36.

Gittell, J. H. (2005). *The Southwest Airlines way: Using the power of relationships to achieve high performance*. New York: McGraw-Hill.

Gonzalez-Roma, V., Schaufeli, W. B., Bakker, A. B. & Lloret, S. (2006), Burnout and work engagement: Independent factors or opposite poles ? *Journal of Vocational Behavior, 68*, 165–174.

Gray, P. B. (2005, March). Rx for merger trauma. *CFO*, 35–38.

Gulick L. & Urwick, L. (1937). *Papers on the science of administration*. New York: Institute of Public Administration.

Hackman, J. R., & Oldham, G. R. (1980). *Work redesign*. Reading, MA: Addison-Wesley.

Hammer, M. M., & Champy, J. A. (1993) *Reengineering the corporation: A manifesto for business revolution*. New York: HarperCollins.

Hansen, M. T., & Løvas, B. (2004). How do multinational companies leverage technological competencies? Moving from single to interdependent explanations. *Strategic Management Journal, 25*, 801–822.

Hewlett-Packard Former CEOs. (2010). Hewlett-Packard webpage. Available: http://www.hp.com/hpinfo/execteam/formerceos.html.

Ingrassia, P. (2010, February 27). Ford's renaissance man. *Wall Street Journal*, A13.

Kahn, W. A. (1990). Psychological conditions of personal engagement and disengagement at work, *Academy of Management Journal, 33*, 692–724.

Kiley, D. (2009, March 5). Alan Mulally: The outsider at Ford. *Business Week*. Available: http://www.businessweek.com/magazine/content/09_11/b4123038630999.htm

Kirkpatrick, D. D., & Shane, S. (2005, September 15). Ex-FEMA chief tells of frustration and chaos. *New York Times*.

Kouzes, J. M., & Posner, B. Z. (1995) *The leadership challenge*. San Francisco: Jossey-Bass.

Latham, G. P., & Wexley, K. N. (1994). *Increasing productivity through performance appraisal* (2nd ed.). Reading, MA: Addison-Wesley.

Lau, J. B., & Shani, A. B. (1992). Don Smith's objection to objectives. In *Behavior in Organizations: An Experiential Approach* (5th ed., pp. 356–357). Homewood, IL: Richard Irwin.

Lawler, E. (2008). *Talent: Making people your competitive advantage*. San Francisco: Wiley.

Lawrence, P. R., & Lorsch, J. W. (1967). *Organization and environment: Managing differentiation and integration*. Boston: Division of Research, Graduate School of Business Administration, Harvard University.

Lawrence, P. R., & Nohria, N. (2002). *Driven: How human nature shapes our choices*. San Francisco: Jossey-Bass.

Livingston, J. S. (1969). Pygmalion in management. *Harvard Business Review, 47*(4), 81-89.

Locke, E. A., & Latham, G. (1990). *A theory of goal setting and task performance*. Englewood Cliffs, NJ: Prentice Hall.

Lohr, S. (2010, April 2). H. Edward Roberts, PC pioneer, dies at 68. *New York Times*. Available: http://www.nytimes.com/2010/04/03/business/03roberts.html.

Mackenzie, R. A. (1997). *The time trap* (3rd ed.). New York: American Management Association, 4–5.

Maslach, C., Schaufelli, W. B., & Leiter, M. P. (2001). Job burnout. *Annual Review of Psychology, 52*, 397–422.

"Manage" us? Puh-leeze... (2007, May 28). *Fortune* Available: http://money.cnn.com/magazines/fortune/fortune_archive/2007/05/28/toc.html.

Maslow, A. H. (1954). *Motivation and personality*. New York: Harper & Row.

McClelland, D. C. (1961). *The achieving society*. New York: Van Nostrand Reinhold.

Merton, R. K. (1968). *Social theory and social structure*. New York: Free Press.

Miller, G. W. (2009, May 11). Tomorrow's bosses: Open and accessible. *Providence Journal* [Online]. http://www.projo.com/news/content/boss_of_the_future_05-11-09_TAE3V14_v24.3998056.html#.

Morris, B. (2010, May 27). Chuck Schwab is worried about small investors. Should we worry too? *Bloomberg Business Week*, 58-64.

Morris, B. (2005, May 30). Charles Schwab's big challenge. *Fortune*. Available: http://money.cnn.com/magazines/fortune/fortune_archive/2005/05/30/8261246/index.htm.

Nadler, D. A., & Lawler, E. E. (Eds.). (1977). Motivation: A diagnostic approach. In J. R. Hackman, E. E. Lawler, & L. W. Porter (Eds.), *Perspectives in Behavior in Organizations*. New York: McGraw-Hill.

Nadler, D. S., & Tushman, M. L. (2000). The organization of the future: Strategic imperatives and core competencies for the 21st Century. *Organizational Dynamics, 27*, 45–60.

Nadler, D. M., Tushman, M. L., & Hatvany, N. (Eds.), (1982). Managing organizations. Boston: Little, Brown.

Nanus, B. (1992). *Visionary leadership*. San Francisco: Jossey-Bass.

Naughton, K. (2007). Excuse me, Mr. Ford; How to tell the man whose name is on the building that you're overhauling the family firm he once ran. *Newsweek, 150*(12), 42.

Nicholls, J. (1994). The "heart, head and hands" of transforming leadership. *Leadership & Organization Development Journal, 15*(6), 8–15.

Pausch, R. (n.d.) Fighting pancreatic cancer. Available: http://download.srv.cs.cmu.edu/~pausch/.

"Randy Pausch." (2010, April 6) *Wikipedia, the free encyclopedia*. Available: http://en.wikipedia.org/wiki/Randy_Pausch.

Pearce, T. (2003). *Leading out loud*. San Francisco: Wiley.

Quinn, R. E., & Spreitzer, G. M. (1997). The road to empowerment: Seven questions every leader should consider. *Organizational Dynamics*, *26*(2), 37–51.

Randolph, W. Alan. (1995). Navigating the journey to empowerment. *Organizational Dynamics*, *23*(4), 19–32.

Romanelli, E., & Tushman, M. L. (1994). Organizational transformation as punctuated equilibrium: An empirical test. *Academy of Management Journal*, *37*(5), 1141–1166.

Saks, A. M. (2006). Antecedents and consequences of employee engagement. *Journal of Managerial Psychology, 21*(7), 600–619.

Sashkin, M. (1989). The visionary leader. In J. Conger & R. N. Kanungo (Eds.), *Charismatic Leadership*. San Francisco: Jossey-Bass.

Schermerhorn, J. R., Hunt, J. G., & Osborn, R. N. (2008). *Organizational behavior* (10th ed.) Hoboken, NJ: John Wiley & Sons.

Shaw, K. N. (2004). Changing the goal-setting process at Microsoft. *Academy of Management Executive, 18*(4), 139–142.

Simon, H. A. (1976). *Administrative Behavior*. New York: Free Press.

Singer, N. (2010, January 15). Johnson & Johnson accused of drug kickbacks. *New York Times*. Available: http://www.nytimes.com/2010/01/16/business/16drug.html.

Smith, A. (1776/1937). *The wealth of nations*. New York: Random House.

Spreitzer, G. M. (2008). Taking Stock: A review of more than twenty years of research on empowerment at work. In C. Cooper & J. Barling (Eds.), *The handbook of organizational behavior*, pp. 54-72. London: Sage Publications.

Spreitzer, G. M. (1995). Psychological empowerment in the workplace: Dimensions, measurement, and validation. *Academy of Management Journal*, *38*(5), 1442–1465.

Thomas, K. W., & Velthouse, B. A. (1990). Cognitive elements of empowerment: An interpretive model of intrinsic task motivation. *Academy of Management Review*, 15, 666–681.

The tinkerer who helped spark the PC revolution. (2010, April 16). *The Week*, 38.

Ulrich, D., J. Zenger, & Smallwood, N. (1999). *Results based leadership*. Boston: Harvard Business School Press.

Ury, W. (2007). *The Power of positive no: Save the deal, save the relationship—and still say no*. New York: Bantam Books.

U.S. Postal Service Management Structure Study. (2003. July 8). Report to the President's Commission on the United States Postal Service.

Vroom, V. H. (1964). *Work and motivation*. New York: John Wiley & Sons.

White, J. B. (1996, November 26). "Next Big Thing": Re–engineering gurus take steps to remodel their stalling vehicles. *Wall Street Journal*, A1.

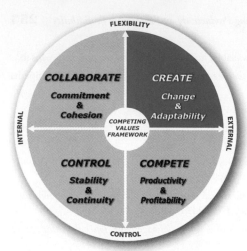

MODULE 4
PROMOTING CHANGE AND ENCOURAGING ADAPTABILITY

■ COMPETENCIES

Using Power Ethically and Effectively

Championing and Selling New Ideas

Fueling and Fostering Innovation

Negotiating Agreement and Commitment

Implementing and Sustaining Change

Organizations do not exist in a vacuum. They operate in a complex world that is constantly changing. In contrast to the internal process model, which seeks to buffer the organization from the environment by implementing a system of tight control, the open systems model accepts the need for flexibility and creativity.

Organizational Goals. The core assumption of the open systems model is that continual adaptation and innovation are necessary to acquire the external resources needed by the organization to be successful. As a result, the goals associated with the open systems model are focused on adapting to changes in the environment, rather than on resisting changes. Consistent with the Create action imperative, key activities associated with the open systems quadrant tend to focus on obtaining external support through political adaptation and creative problem solving.

Paradoxes. In our discussion of power and influence, we encounter a key leadership paradox: people yearn for powerful leaders and also distrust powerful leaders. We also consider how successful creative endeavors and innovations often depend more on habit than on spontaneity and why our efforts to implement changes often result in increased resistance to those changes.

254

Competencies. Our first competency, *using power ethically and effectively*, identifies different sources of power and describes influence tactics that managers can use. We continue with the theme of influencing others in *championing and selling new ideas,* where we provide two frameworks, one that identifies the characteristics associated with four basic types of managerial messages and another focused on the elements required for effective presentations. In *fueling and fostering innovation,* we explain the differences between creative and critical thinking, identify barriers to creative thinking, and describe some tools to encourage creativity. *Negotiating agreement and commitment*, the fourth competency in this module, discusses basic principles that managers can use to achieve win-win solutions. We conclude with *implementing and sustaining change.* After discussing forces for change and resistance to change, we conclude with a discussion of four different approaches to bringing change that are linked to the theoretical models that are the foundation of the competing values framework.

Module 4 Competency 1

Using Power
and Influence
Ethically and
Effectively

ASSESSMENT Who Is Powerful?

Objective One of the best ways to understand the concept of building and maintaining a power base is by thinking about the people who have had the greatest influence on your life. This exercise gives you the opportunity to assess your personal beliefs and expectations about power and influence.

Directions 1. Select someone who has greatly influenced your life. Who was this person? How did she influence you? What did this person specifically do, and how did it affect you? Did this person have formal authority over you? Write down 5 to 10 things that this person did to influence you.

2. Now consider your own personal power base. Who is within your circle of influence? Why are you able to influence them? What have you done recently to increase your ability to influence others? Have you done anything recently to add people to your circle of influence? Why or why not?

3. Finally, think about how your attempts to influence people compare with how you were influenced by the person you selected in the first part of this exercise. Are the tactics that you use to influence people similar or different? Can you think of ways to improve your ability to influence others by adopting some of the tactics that helped influence your life?

Reflection Sometimes the people who influence us the most are not those with formal authority over us. In fact, we may be greatly influenced by people whom we have never met. Perhaps we heard them speak at a conference or read their books. We may not think of these examples of influence as being related to power, but in fact they are—the power of ideas, the power to attract an audience, and the power of effective communication skills.

LEARNING Using Power Ethically and Effectively

POWER: WHY ARE WE AMBIVALENT?

Our perceptions of power are very revealing. They tell us as much about ourselves as they do about power. How do you feel about the role power plays in the organizations you have observed? When you think of power, what people, experiences, and memories come to mind?

All of us have power, and all of us are influenced by others who have it. Some of our most painful memories revolve around someone else's misuse of the power and influence they held over us. As teenagers, the authority of our parents may have collided with our need for freedom. As employees, we have all seen supervisors with authority but little ability to motivate followers. To handle power is to risk misusing it, often at the expense of others. But to be powerless is to be frustrated and defensive. Thus, most of us have mixed feelings about power.

Michael Maccoby, an expert on leadership, says, "At the same time that people yearn for protective and soothing leaders, they have become skeptical about leaders in general and distrustful of their motives and competence" (Maccoby, 2007, p. 2). He cites a study conducted by the University of Chicago in 2005 in which only 22 percent of the American public expressed a "great deal of confidence' in the executive branch of the U.S. federal government, 29 percent in banks and financial institutions (that percentage would probably be much lower now), and 25 percent in leaders of organized religion (Maccoby, 2007, p. 213). The problem this research exposes is one of mistrust. Effective leaders sustain their influence by building and maintaining trust and helping people perform at a higher level. In the long run, we grant power and influence only to people we trust.

In an organizational setting, the term "power" is most often defined as essentially "the capacity to mobilize people and resources to get things done" (Kanter, 1983, p. 213). People often say power is a "necessary evil" in organizations. That sentiment assumes that power, in all its manifestations, is negative. Power in organizational life is inescapable, but is it inherently bad? Organizations exist in order to get things done. Power concentrates around the most important things an organization has to do and around the people who have the greatest access to the resources required to do those things.

Working for an overbearing leader may be frustrating, but working for a weak leader can also be a liability. Working for a great leader, one who uses power positively, can be one of life's best experiences. The purpose of this chapter is to help you become the kind of leader you would like to have—one who uses power in a way that brings results while inspiring and lifting people. Leaders with little influence cannot represent the needs of their people, promote their ideas, or acquire the resources they need to do their jobs (Kotter, 2008, pp. 123–127). Leaders who know how to use power positively can do all these things. Box M4.1 highlights some misconceptions about power.

USING POWER AT THREE LEVELS

There are three levels from which to study power:

1. The macro or organizational level
2. The group or team level
3. The individual or personal level

On the organizational level, power can be viewed as the ability to influence the flow of available energy and resources toward certain goals. This kind of power shows up in activities such as legislating policies and laws, setting rules and procedures, bestowing rewards and punishments, and making goals and plans. On the group or team level, power can be seen as the ability to influence your peers through the strength of expertise and experience, and the ability to build coalitions of those who share your views and goals. On the personal level, power can be seen as person A's capacity to influence person B's behavior so that B does something he would not do otherwise. This focus on power and influence stresses interpersonal relationships and the resources we bring to bear in those relationships. In this module we will deal primarily with power and influence at the individual level, because it is the level managers can influence the most.

BOX M4.1 MISCONCEPTIONS ABOUT POWER

Myth: *I am the manager. I can do what I want.*

Authority and power are not the same thing. People do not do what you want simply because of the position you hold. It takes more than position to effectively influence people. When are you going to do a better job on a project: when your manager forces you to work overtime to finish ASAP or when you feel personally committed to the project out of respect for the manager?

Reality: ***You will be a better leader if you inspire commitment, rather than require compliance.***

Myth: *Power is something people in higher positions exercise upon people in lower positions.*

Managers exercise power and influence on subordinates, but subordinates also exercise power and influence on managers. Power is something that exists when people are dependent on each other. Some people have more power in organizations than others, but no one is completely powerless. Think, for example, of how an organization depends upon the discretionary effort of each employee. The discretionary effort is the difference between the level of effort required to hold down a particular job and the maximum level of effort the person is capable of putting out. In many jobs, the range of discretionary effort is immense. In most cases, people cannot be forced to exert this extra effort. They can only choose to do so.

Reality: ***You will be a better leader if you respect the concerns of others, rather than expect their blind obedience.***

Myth: *Supervisors and middle managers are powerless.*

This statement is partially true. Some are powerless. However, supervisors and managers are never powerless unless they choose to be. Often supervisors and middle managers claim to be powerless as a way to reduce responsibility. Because the organization is dependent on supervisors and managers, they do, in fact, have latent power.

Reality: ***You will be a better leader if you take responsibility, rather than make excuses.***

GOOD POWER, BAD POWER, AND NO POWER

When we commit ourselves to a cause or a project, we want strong, solid people in our corner. We don't want to entrust the things we cherish to weak and passive leaders or to overbearing leaders on a personal power trip. Managers who have no power base are not doing their jobs. Part of their job is to effectively and appropriately build a base of legitimacy, information, and influence from which to serve the needs of their unit and their organization (Cohen & Bradford, 2005).

FIVE SOURCES OF POWER

Where does power come from? Writer and consultant, Karl Albrecht, offers an acronym, POWER to list what he believes are the primary sources of social power and influence. These are:

P = Position

O = Opportunity

W = Wealth

E = Expertise

R = Relationships (Albrecht, 2006, p. 222)

Position power comes from formal roles and authority. If you are director of finance for a large firm or a state supreme court judge, you are likely to have considerable power by virtue of that position. In addition to the legitimate power associated with having a position of authority, formal positions in organizations may allow you to reward or punish by conferring or denying resources or opportunities to others.

Opportunity power relates to being in the right place at the right time. We have seen many people of equal ability and motivation who have not been equally successful, because some were in work units or organizations that offered more opportunity and challenge than others. Where you are, and when you are there, are sometimes as important as who you are. Malcolm Gladwell, in his best-selling book, *Outliers: The Story of Success,* describes the circumstances in people's lives that help foster success. In the world of hockey, a large percentage (about 40 percent) of the players in the best leagues in the world, amateur or professional, were born in January, February, or March, while only 10 percent were born in October, November or December. Behind this bizarre pattern is the simple explanation that the cutoff birthday for many hockey leagues in January 1. This means that the children born in the first three months of the year are slightly older, bigger, and stronger than most of their peers. The "advantaged" players make their way to the all-star teams, the special training camps, and the best coaches. Coupled with their own talent and determination, this advantage of birth date becomes a small difference that makes a big difference in their eventual success (Gladwell, 2008, pp. 15–34).

Of course, not all people in similar positions, or confronted with similar opportunities, do equally well. The differences can be explained by the other power sources listed below.

Wealth power. Obviously, people who possess great wealth can exert a lot of influence. In organizations, it is not necessarily the personal wealth of an individual that creates power. Rather, wealth as a source of power can also refer to the ability to control or manage money. For example, executives who control large sources of funds or public officials who can allocate financial resources to others are likely to have substantial power, regardless of their personal wealth. In many organizations, wealth power and position power are closely associated.

Expert power is based on the expertise or knowledge that you may have in a special field, or in a specific situation. Expert power plays a very important role in determining the influence people have in their organizations. For example, a young computer programmer who is proficient in writing code for a new software application may have as much power as the CEO or owner of that firm. As Karl Albrecht says, "If we're lost in the woods and you know the way out of the woods, then you're my leader—at least until we get out of the woods" (Albrecht, 2006, p. 223).

Relationship power can stem from two sources—your personal characteristics (who you are) and your social network (who you know). Sometimes a person has influence because of personal characteristics (e.g., charisma, trustworthiness, amiability). Simply put, when people like you, they are more likely to be influenced by you. Relationship power can also come from your social network and is sometimes referred to as "social capital," or network power. Your social network gives you power because it gives you access to the expertise and influence of people who know and trust you—and through all the people those people know. For example, an employee may be able to influence his supervisor's decision concerning what computer to purchase, not because of the employee's own expertise, but because the employee is friends with a well-known computer expert and can seek her advice about the purchase. Creating and maintaining a sizable network of people who know information and people we don't know is important because it provides us with access to crucial resources we could not otherwise tap. Box M4.2 describes how the actions of one person can lead to the creation of an extensive network that benefits thousands of people.

BOX M4.2 CREATING A POWERFUL NETWORK

When Jay Allen decided he was road-weary from his successful work in the corporate marketing world and wanted to spend time closer to home, he began to explore ways to get better connected with executives in the local community (Denver, Colorado). It became apparent quickly that there were few options available for high-level executive networking that didn't involve expensive dues, vendor and sponsor intrusion, or significant time commitments. Jay sat down with some of his executive friends who expressed similar difficulties in the area of networking. As a group, they decided to make a list of 10 influential business leaders they wanted to meet in town and invite them to lunch to meet each other. The rules would be: No vendors, sponsors, or speakers—and everyone would just pay for their own meal.

As Jay began to "cold call" the executives on the list and explain to them what he was doing, why, who was coming, and the rules of the lunch, the responses were all the same, "what a fantastic idea—count me

BOX M4.2 CREATING A POWERFUL NETWORK (*Cont'd*)

in!" The first lunch was so successful that they invited more the next month. Within 6 months, over 100 of the top local executives were participating in various lunches around town. When participation exceeded 400 executives, Jay formed CXO.org and hired some administrative support. The focus from the beginning was never financially motivated. Membership dues were optional, under $500, and went to support website functionality and administrative support. Members took turns hosting events and larger receptions were structured to be break-even.

Before long, over 1,500 influential leaders in seven major markets were leveraging CXO as a forum for simplifying the process of building, sharing, and leveraging influential relationships. In September 2009, CXO merged with Executives Network, growing the membership base to almost 5,000.

Members are asked to help each other, mentor students and entrepreneurs, and foster improved collaboration locally and regionally. The larger the network becomes, the more valuable it is to its members. Members often contact each other for advice and to foster deal flow. Since founding CXO.org, Jay Allen has created or been a part of a dozen new business ventures as a result of the high-trust relationships created through that network. But Jay says the greatest bonus is the personal satisfaction he gains from doing something he loves, and helping others thrive at what they love (from interview with Jay Allen, May 2009).

Networking is a vital skill not only because it helps you succeed professionally but also because it makes you a more effective resource in your personal life. Networking is a crucial skill, both for gathering information and for identifying contacts who can help you put your ideas into motion. An effective manager knows where to go for answers and whose support is necessary to carry the day. If you have a mission in life, you'll need help fulfilling it. Paradoxically, to be effective, networking must be other-focused. When we think of networking, we often think of social activities and gestures engaged in for self-serving reasons—and we assume that these activities are contrived and phony. Keith Ferrazzi, a marketing executive and best-selling author, says that we all want to avoid the "networking jerk." This is the "schmooze artist" who seems to have a pre-rehearsed elevator pitch ready for every person he or she meets. Ferrazi says,

I get emails all the time that read, "Dear Keith, I hear you're a good networker. I am too. Let's sit down for fifteen minutes and a cup of coffee. Why? I ask myself. Why in the world do people expect me to respond to a request like that? Have they appealed to me emotionally? Have they said they could help me? Have they sought some snippet of commonality between us? I'm sorry, but networking is not some secret society with some encoded handshake practiced for its own virtue. We must bring virtue to it" (Ferrazzi, 2005, pp. 58–59).

We hear about networking in the context of trying to get a job through friends, or doing lunch to get someone's attention, or asking for leads on new business. These are important activities, but, in a larger sense, effective networking is a process of helping other people who, over the long term, can also be a resource to us. Jay

Allen's approach to networking is an excellent example of this type of other-focused, long-term thinking.

Effective networking is really about being generous toward helping others, and being willing to ask for help from others. The concept of "lift" (Quinn & Quinn, 2009), which we introduced in Module 2 when talking about cross-functional teams, is also useful here. Recall that there are four key thoughts and feelings that are associated with lift: being purpose-centered, driven by internal values, other-focused, and externally open. These elements support the idea that people who feel uplifted and lift the people around them are likely to be particularly effective networkers. Box M4.3 offers some suggestions for creating a high-energy network based on the concept of "lift."

BOX M4.3 "LIFTING" YOUR NETWORK

Traditional advice on networking is plentiful and usually discusses core activities such as sharing information, making introductions and referrals, providing references, and offering ideas and advice (e.g., Harding, 1994). Although these types of activities are all appropriate, they are not likely to generate the type of energy and inspiration that can bring about profound change. In contrast, the questions below are based on the work of Quinn and Quinn (2009) and use the competing values framework for psychological states to think about our networks in terms of creating lift for others and for ourselves.

Compete by being Purpose-Centered: How can I create extraordinary results?

- What is it that I am authentically interested in accomplishing?
- How will the future be different after I have accomplished my mission?
- If I were starting with a blank page, whom would I include in my network to help me accomplish my mission?

Control by being Internally Directed: What integrity gaps do I have, and how can I close them?

- What are the values that are most important to me?
- Who are people who model the values that I want to live?
- Whom can I trust to help me make sure that I am living my values?

Collaborate by being Other-Focused: What can I do to help others satisfy their legitimate needs, feelings, and wants?

- How deeply do I understand the needs and interests of these people?
- In what ways am I striving to make their lives better?
- As I seek to serve them, do I let them know who I am and what my interests are?

Create by being Externally Open: How can I learn and change?

- What questions should I be asking to help me as I am pursuing my mission?
- What fears do I have that might be blocking me from learning and moving forward?
- Which of my previous experiences help remind me that I have overcome challenges in the past?

Daniel Goleman, a best-selling author on the importance of influence skills in the workplace has this to say about networking:

This talent for connecting [networking] epitomizes stars in almost every kind of job. For instance, studies of outstanding performers in fields like engineering, computer science, biotechnology, and other "knowledge work" fields find the building and maintenance of networks crucial for success. Even in fields like technology, the networks are linked the old-fashioned way, face-to-face and by phone, as well as through e-mail.

But what cements a connection is not physical proximity (though it helps) so much as psychological proximity. The people we get along with, trust, and feel simpatico with, are the strongest links in our networks. . . . People who work a network well have an immense time advantage over those who have to use broader, more general sources of information to find answers. One estimate indicates that for every hour a star puts into seeking answers through a network, an average person spends three to five hours gathering the same information *(Goleman 2000, pp. 206–207)*.

While they may differ in many ways, outstanding performers who are effective networkers are likely to share one valuable characteristic—the ability to energize people around them. As we mentioned in Module 2, research on network analysis by Baker, Cross, and Wooten (2003) demonstrates that the ability to develop energizing relationships is extremely important. Effective networkers don't merely save time gathering information, they also create energy for themselves and others.

INFLUENCE STRATEGIES AND TACTICS

Effective influence requires a broad base of approaches and tactics. Too many leaders are assertive or insistent when they need to be open and flexible. Others are passive and deferential when they need to be confrontational and firm.

Traditional research on power and influence has identified a number of different tactics that can be used to influence others (Falbe & Yukl, 1992). Different tactics may be appropriate in different situations, depending on the circumstances. Many common influence tactics depend on the elements of position power (legitimacy and the power to reward and/or punish). For example:

- ***Legitimate Authority**—*giving directives with the expectation that they will be carried out
- ***Upward Appeal**—*giving directions and indicating that they are what higher management wants done
- ***Co-optation**—*inviting a recalcitrant individual into a group to attempt to change their perspective (e.g., giving a union agitator a seat on the board of directors)
- ***Bargaining/Exchange**—*offering a reward or incentive for following a directive
- ***Pressure/Coercion**—*threatening a punitive action if the directive is not followed

Other influence tactics can be linked to relationship power:

- ***Inspirational Appeal**—*appealing to core values to encourage cooperation
- ***Personal Appeal**—*appealing to personal relationships to encourage cooperation

- *Ingratiation*—attempting to increase positive feelings as a way to increase personal relationship power and thus persuasiveness

For individuals with the appropriate expertise, rational persuasion can be an effective influence tactic.

- *Rational Persuasion*—using logical arguments as a justification for cooperation

Finally, individuals with a great deal of social capital and strong networks may find success by building coalitions, particularly if they are able to obtain support from a broad base of different constituent groups.

- *Coalition Formation*—gathering additional stakeholders to support a proposal

INFLUENCE VERSUS MANIPULATION AND CONTROL

There is often a fine line between perceptions of what is considered an acceptable influence tactic and what is seen as an inappropriate attempt to manipulate or control others. Winning a short-term concession with manipulative or coercive tactics but losing an important relationship in the process is not a good trade-off. Influence tactics that undermine trust should be avoided.

INCREASING POWER AND INFLUENCE WITH SUPERVISORS, PEERS, AND SUBORDINATES

If you consistently appeal, even in subtle ways, to the authority of your position in order to get people's cooperation, you should probably try strategies that will increase your interdependence on your subordinates or offer them more personal support by expressing appreciation or taking time to listen carefully to how things are really going for them. A common belief in U.S. management philosophy is that learning from subordinates is a sign of weakness. But learning from others is really a sign of being secure and authentic, and so is the habit of listening carefully. The master manager knows what other people need and how they feel. Most of that information comes from listening and observing, not from talking.

When we work as consultants with managers who are accused by peers and subordinates of being "over-controlling," these managers often defend their style by saying, "I'm results oriented more than people oriented." But that response assumes that there is only one way to get results: my way. Many of these managers are not results oriented as much as they are control oriented (Fisher, 2000, p. 109–110). They feel a great need to be in charge, and they assume that if they are not in control, the work unit is "out of control." Not surprisingly, they encounter immense resistance from the people they work with. The master managers we have observed focus on driving for results and the quality of relationships *simultaneously*. The literature on transformational leadership fully demonstrates that effective leaders are high on task and high on people (Bass & Avolio, 1994). To be effective you must learn to do both.

Here is a list of specific methods of increasing power and influence tailored to the role and level of the person you are trying to influence. These methods must, of course, be adapted to your situation.

SUPERVISORS

- Look for ways to solve problems that your superiors are facing.

- Show appreciation to superiors for things they do to help.

- Encourage superiors to discuss their problems. Ask them about their biggest worries or most important goals and how your role connects to those worries and goals. Listen carefully. Give understanding and support.

- Provide constructive feedback on things supervisors do. Be specific. Demonstrate how their efforts led to concrete outcomes. "Your training session on securing clear commitments from suppliers has helped us reduce our costs by over 10 percent."

- Point out new ways superiors can use your skills. "I've done a lot of work on web site design in my spare time. If I can help with this project, I'm available."

- Be loyal, even when it's difficult (unless some ethical principle or legal issue is at stake). Don't fall into the trap of bad-mouthing a boss. If the relationship is insupportable, get out of it.

- Take the initiative if you feel you are being used or exploited. Try bargaining and negotiating. "When you put restrictions on me as you did with the Fenlow project, I feel like I can't help the client and I can't help us avoid problems with the account. How do you see the situation?"

These are powerful and practical methods of increasing power and influence. However, there are roadblocks to using them. A major roadblock is the norms of the organization. As we discussed in the Module 1 competency, communicating honestly and effectively, norms are unwritten expectations about how work will be done, how people will act, and so on. Your work unit may have a "them and us" norm about relating to superiors. It may not be socially acceptable to show appreciation to your manager or to be loyal to or give encouragement to the people you manage. Suggesting new methods or solutions may be taboo. If so, you may want to consider how much these norms are costing you in your professional and personal development. You may not only need a new manager—you may also need a more positive work climate. Moreover, as a leader in your work unit, you may have to address those norms specifically and try to change them for everyone's benefit. Think about what methods of influence you could use in that effort. Here are some other methods of increasing power and influence for working effectively with peers.

PEERS

- Find ways to help peers reach their goals and look and feel successful.

- Try to understand their problems and share useful information.

- Look for common goals you can mutually pursue.

- Form informal problem-solving groups between units.

- Be sincere in how you present yourself. If you honestly seek to serve others, they will know. If you are self-serving in your efforts to help others, they will also know.

- If you are working with a large number of people, don't try to influence everyone at once. Identify the people you think are the most respected opinion leaders and recruit their support individually or in small groups. In most cases, wherever the opinion leaders go, others will follow.

Influencing peers is a tremendous challenge. Often organizations have norms that prohibit rocking the boat or going beyond the job description. Efforts to become more influential can be mistaken for power plays or a vote of nonconfidence toward your colleagues. Building power and influence with peers takes a long time and a lot of patience. But people ultimately respond when they see that you are determined to do good work and want to share the credit and stimulation with them. Remember, credit is not a zero-sum commodity. Stephen Covey, an author and management consultant, encourages people to create a "mentality of abundance," an attitude that there is plenty of credit, opportunity, and knowledge to go around (Covey, 1990, pp. 289–290).

This attitude is often self-fulfilling. When people are generous and encouraging, opportunities increase in an organization. The paradox of selfishness is that it usually results in a net *loss* of resources. When people start hoarding and hiding information, recognition, physical resources, and their own energy, the work unit begins to wither. If you have people reporting to you, here are some additional influence strategies for motivating good performance.

DIRECT REPORTS

- Consciously try to increase their trust in you by listening to their concerns and encouraging them to share ideas. Sometimes people "test" your patience and trustworthiness with little issues before coming to you with important ones.

- Make certain they know exactly what is expected of them in their role.

- Give them recognition for good performance, and point out how their performance has been helpful. For example, an orderly in a hospital works especially hard to prepare a patient's room. The supervising nurse can point out: "You got the patient's room ready in less than an hour. This usually takes two hours, and the patient often waits in the emergency room. This was a big help to him, and to the treatment team." There usually isn't enough recognition in the workplace, and when praise or recognition come, they are often too vague and indirect to be meaningful.

- Give them credit for their ideas when talking to your superiors. Good managers are generous in recognizing others' ideas and contributions.

- Do everything necessary to give them the tools and resources necessary to do their job.

- Help them solve problems that may be beyond their ability or experience. Keep current on new information and trends in your field. Good managers are good teachers. You don't have to know everything your subordinates know, but you need to be continuously learning.

- Provide training. Champion the cause of professional development; even if resources are scarce, you can do a lot informally.

- Never pretend to know something you don't know. The more you manage "knowledge workers," the greater the likelihood that they know a lot of things you don't know. That's to be expected.

- Hold regular performance appraisals, but go beyond the formal "rating sheet" that so many organizations require once a year. Hold candid, detailed conversations with your people on how they are doing and what they need. Take a personal interest in their development, not just in their productivity.

- Don't be afraid to talk about the ways you depend upon each other.

- Clarify your responsibilities to them and theirs to you. "Here's what I most need from you . . . What do you need from me to do your job effectively and feel good about your work?" Another question we've coached managers to ask frequently is: "Have I made any commitments to you that I haven't followed through on?"

ANALYSIS   "I Hope You Can Help Me Out": Don Lowell Case Study

Objective   For this exercise, you will practice identifying different sources of power and evaluating what types of influence tactics might be successful in the particular situation described in the case.

Directions   Read the following case study and answer the discussion questions.

Don Lowell is a mental hygiene therapy aide in a psychiatric center. He has been in his present position for 13 years, having worked his way up from the bottom. He thoroughly enjoys his job, but he missed being chosen for a promotion twice in the last two years. He was one of the top three on the list but was not able to get the promotions he wanted. He has been working very hard to make himself known in the right circles and has volunteered to serve on various county and private committees, boards, and task forces over the past few years.

Don also works three nights a week and weekends at the Rosewood Home, a well-known, highly rated nursing facility. Don serves as one of the two part-time activity coordinators. With his oldest daughter about to enter college, he can certainly use the money. He also enjoys the work and gets to meet a number of people in the community. He's been thinking for some time now that at some point in the future he would like to return to school and complete the degree, which he began years ago. Right now, however, he enjoys working with the patients and feels the added experience will help him in the future.

Last week Don received a phone call from Frank Calvin, the chief of service in his division at the psychiatric center. Frank's 79-year-old mother is in the hospital recovering from a broken hip. Frank has applied to the Rosewood Home primarily because of its reputation in the area of physical therapy and rehabilitation. The home, however, has a very long waiting list (from three to six months) and Frank understands that unless his mother receives physical therapy immediately upon release from the hospital, her chances of returning to her former mobility level are quite low. Moreover, Frank's sense of the situation, after meeting with the home's intake social worker, was that his mother was not going to be given priority consideration.

Frank discussed his situation with Sarah Anderson, his assistant. She reminded him that Don was still working as a part-time activity director at the Rosewood Home. Frank remembered Don's name from some paperwork that came across his desk. Frank called Don to see if there was any way around normal procedures and asked if Don could help.

During the conversation, Frank mentioned that if Don were able to assist him with this, he (Frank) would try to help him when he could. In addition, Frank said that he would put a note in Don's file mentioning the cooperation he had received from Don in placing his mother in the appropriate health facility. "I just don't know where to turn with this problem," said Frank, "and I really hope you can help me."

Don told Frank that he would see what he could do. He told Frank that he didn't know all that much about the admissions process and really didn't have that kind of "pull" at the facility but that he would give it his best shot.

Don made some informal inquiries around the home concerning the admissions procedures (of which he indeed knew very little). He found out that the director of the intake department, Sheila Hogan, was someone he knew slightly because he had worked with her on a couple of committees. He remembered her as being very focused and knowledgeable and someone who usually played everything by the book. However, he had found her to be accommodating when necessary.

He also remembered an item in the Rosewood newsletter stating that the intake department was severely short staffed and was looking for volunteers or other staff coverage. Don had some ideas that he thought would work very well at providing coverage at no additional cost to the home. He decided to arrange a meeting.

Discussion Questions

1. What sources of power and influence tactics does Don have available to him?

2. If you were Don, what action would you take?

    a. Would you decide not to try to influence the admission process? If not, why?

    b. Would you decide to help only by clarifying the mother's need for admission?

    c. Would you decide to do everything within your power to get the mother admitted?

3. Using the concepts and skills presented in the Learning activity, describe the possible consequences of how you would handle this situation. What do you think would happen?

4. What strategy and techniques is Frank using on Don?

5. What options or strategies should Don use with Frank?

6. What should Don's next steps be?

7. Have you ever encountered a similar situation? What strategies, if any, did you use? What steps did you take? Did these steps increase your power base? How do you know?

Reflection

It should come as no surprise that opportunities to exercise power and influence are sometimes linked to ethical dilemmas—situations where two values come into conflict. These types of situations are also complicated by cultural differences. For some people, helping a family member or friend would be the paramount value; people who view equity as the overriding value, however, might consider any attempt to influence the admission procedure to be unethical.

PRACTICE   The Big Move

Objective

This role-play will give you an opportunity to practice using and/or identifying different influence tactics.

Directions

Before class, read the situation background for this role-play.

Situation Background

Department X, a financial services unit of a large health care system, is currently located in Albany, New York. The department has come under pressure to move its headquarters from Albany to Westchester County, an area closer to New York City. Many of the hospitals and clients served by the unit are located around Westchester County, and the system has recently acquired a building large enough to house the entire financial services unit under one roof. The relocation would allow the system to cancel an expensive building lease in Albany. The current offices in Albany are now inadequate, and expansion would be very expensive and pose some legal difficulties with zoning. The board of directors has created an interunit task force to discuss the possibility of the move. This task force has to come up with a recommendation to the board. The department must move as a whole or not at all.

The task force consists of managers from the following areas:

1. Kim Ingo: Client Financial Services
2. Robyn Pinegar: Accounting
3. Carlos Armando: Stock and Bond Transfer
4. Lynn Stott: Personnel
5. Chris Jacobs: Facilitator

2. If your instructor provides you with a role description, read it carefully and develop a plan to try to influence the other members of the task force to agree with your position about the move. Come to class prepared to play a role if one has been assigned to you. If you have not been assigned a role, be prepared to analyze the power and influence attempts used by other students as they act out the role-play.

Each role description outlines an initial position or opinion as to the advisability of the move: for, against, neutral. This is only an initial position, however, and you should feel free to switch sides and/or be influenced by the others. Assume and display the power-personality characteristics outlined in your role description.

A secret-ballot vote will be taken at the end of the meeting, and the results will be announced. The board has asked for a recommendation from a task force of managers. You should assume that the recommendation of the group will strongly influence the board's final decision of whether or not to relocate. At the conclusion of the role-play, you will all be asked to complete a questionnaire on your assessment of each character's ability to persuade and influence the other managers.

3. In class, your instructor will provide directions for how the role-play will be performed. If you are assigned a role, you should attempt to influence the other members of the task force. If you are part of the audience, you will be observing the role-play and providing feedback after it is completed, so make notes on the influence attempts you observe. After the role-play is finished,

Observation Sheet: Assessing and Improving Influence Attempts

Task Force Member	Influence Tactics Attempted	Sources of Power	Degree of Power
Kim Ingo: Client Financial Services			
Robyn Pinegar: Accounting			
Carlos Armando: Stock and Bond Transfer			
Lynn Stott: Personnel			
Chris Jacobs: Facilitator			

identify the primary sources of power for each participant and evaluate the degree of power you felt each person had on a scale of 0 to 10, with 0 = No Power and 10 = Very Powerful.

Reflection   Each of the role descriptions provided for this exercise included information on the "power personality" of the character because individuals have different preferences in terms of using power and influence tactics. Effective managers recognize, however, that different situations may call for different influence tactics. Having a clear understanding of the interests of the people you are trying to influence as well as their preferences for using power and influence can be very helpful for selecting the most effective influence tactics.

APPLICATION   Building Your Power Base by Changing Your Influence Strategy

Objective   This activity is designed to help you further develop and maintain your own power base with your subordinates, colleagues, and superiors, if applicable, in your organization.

Directions   Think about the personal power analysis you did in the Assessment exercise at the beginning of this competency.

1. Identify someone that you would like to add to your circle of influence and consider how you could go about creating an interdependent relationship with that person. Be sure to have a clear idea of why adding them to your network would be helpful both to you and to them.

2. Identify someone who is currently in your circle of influence but who does not seem to value your abilities or contributions. What influence strategies have you used with that individual in the past? Why do you think they have been unsuccessful?

3. What are the similarities and differences between your strategies for expanding your circle of influence and your strategies for improving your power within your existing circle of influence?

4. Building on your responses from parts 1–3, write a brief memo to your instructor outlining a plan to help you expand and strengthen your power base. Be sure to identify the challenges you anticipate in implementing your strategy, and discuss the costs of trying to make these changes compared with the costs of just settling for the status quo.

Reflection   Expanding your circle of influence takes time and energy. But unlike typical investments, when investing in your circle of influence it is just as important to think about what you can contribute to others as it is to consider your potential gains.

Module 4 Competency 2   Championing and Selling New Ideas

ASSESSMENT   The Presenter's Touch: You May Have It but Not Know It

Objective   Teachers often encounter students who are talented oral presenters but who have little idea of how good they are. They also find students who can dramatically improve their presenting ability with minor adjustments in their approach. You may have the presenter's touch and not know it.

Directions Answer "yes" or "no" to the following questions, which are adapted from *I Can See You Naked* by Ron Hoff. Copyright © 1992 by Andrew & McMeel.

1. Do you enjoy helping people solve their problems?

2. Can you cut through a rambling, foggy conversation—dig out the main point and restate it so that everybody understands?

3. Do you have a high energy level? Do other people seem to you to be talking slowly?

4. Do you like to tell people what you've learned? Would you make a good teacher?

5. Do people ask you to retell a story or an experience you've shared before?

6. Can you deal with challenging questions in a public setting without flaring up?

7. Do you like to demonstrate what you're talking about? Do you tend to "act out" what you're describing?

8. Do you look people in the eye when you talk to them and when they talk to you?

9. Do people turn to you when it's time for a meeting to be summed up?

10. Do you notice specific things people do that make them effective or ineffective communicators—and then find yourself applying the effective ones?

Reflection If you answered "yes" to half of these questions, you already possess many of the qualities of an effective presenter. If you answered "yes" to fewer than half, don't be discouraged. Your honesty in self-assessment will be an important asset in improving your ability to communicate. Another important asset is your attitude. You need to believe you really can improve. Over the years we have coached many students, managers, and executives. Those with a desire to improve their presenting skills have all made significant progress. In this section we will share some tools and principles for improving your effectiveness at presenting ideas.

LEARNING   Championing and Selling New Ideas

All communication can be evaluated in terms of substance (what is communicated) and style (how it is communicated). Both of these elements are important when championing and selling ideas. In this competency, we discuss two different frameworks that can be used to help you improve the quality of your own communication and to coach others. The first framework is based on competing-values research and distinguishes among different types of messages based upon their purpose. The second framework is more general and provides a methodology for preparing effective presentations. We conclude this competency with a discussion of how you can find your own voice as a managerial leader.

COMPETING VALUES FRAMEWORK FOR MANAGERIAL COMMUNICATION

Traditionally, advice on business communication has emphasized the "seven C's," the idea that messages should be complete, concise, considerate, clear, concrete, courteous, and correct (Rogers & Hildebrandt, 1993). While these conventional guidelines are

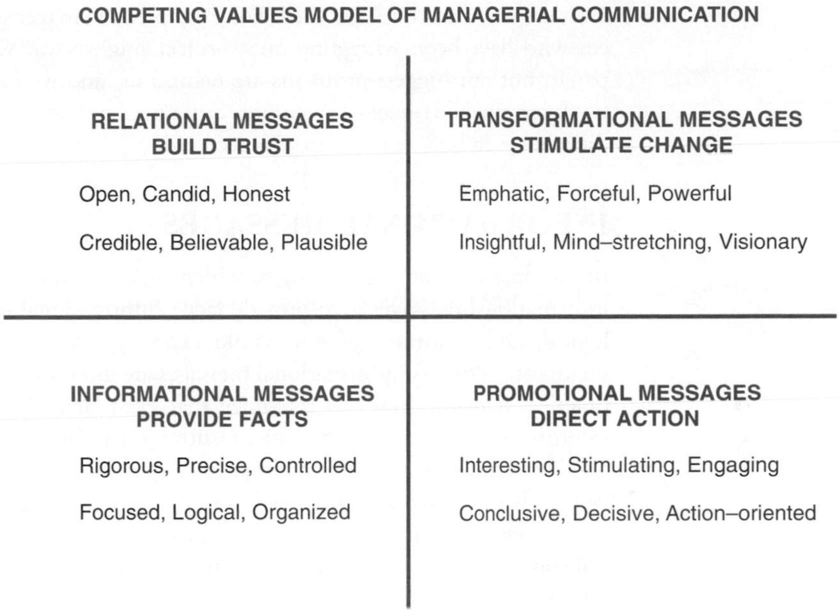

COMPETING VALUES MODEL OF MANAGERIAL COMMUNICATION

FIGURE M4.1

Competing values model of management communication (adapted from Quinn, Hildebrandt, Rogers & Thompson, 1991; and Rogers & Hildebrandt, 1993).

RELATIONAL MESSAGES BUILD TRUST	TRANSFORMATIONAL MESSAGES STIMULATE CHANGE
Open, Candid, Honest	Emphatic, Forceful, Powerful
Credible, Believable, Plausible	Insightful, Mind–stretching, Visionary
INFORMATIONAL MESSAGES PROVIDE FACTS	PROMOTIONAL MESSAGES DIRECT ACTION
Rigorous, Precise, Controlled	Interesting, Stimulating, Engaging
Focused, Logical, Organized	Conclusive, Decisive, Action–oriented

still important, they are limited for two reasons. First, they fail to address the need to communicate in different ways, depending on the purpose and context of the message. Second, they assume that the communicator has only a single goal related to the message. In reality, people frequently want to accomplish more than one thing with a single message and often have competing goals. For example, managers preparing performance evaluations want to both encourage employees and to document any performance problems to protect the organization (Rogers & Hildebrandt, 1993).

To address these concerns, Quinn and colleagues (Quinn, Hildebrandt, Rogers & Thompson, 1991; Rogers & Hildebrandt, 1993) developed a competing values framework for analyzing managerial communication. A simplified version of their framework is shown in Figure M4.1. The framework identifies four basic types of communication, along with several specific characteristics typically associated with each type. We address each of these basic types in turn.

RELATIONAL MESSAGES

The purpose of relational messages is to build trust by establishing credibility and building rapport. Consistent with the assumptions of the human relations model and the Collaborate quadrant, relational messages need to take into account the needs and interests of the receivers. Characteristics of effective relational messages include openness, candor, and honesty. If a relational message seems unbelievable or implausible in some way, its effectiveness will be greatly diminished.

In terms of style, relational messages tend to be more conversational than formal. To emphasize the connection between the sender and the receivers, inclusive pronouns such as "we" and "our" are used. For example, a manager giving a pep talk to employees who have been struggling on a project might say, "We've been through a rough patch, but our biggest problems are behind us, and we can hit our deadline if we all work together." It may seem minor, but even small choices in language can make big differences in how your message is received.

INFORMATIONAL MESSAGES

In contrast to relational messages, which seek to build trust, the primary purpose of informational messages is to provide facts. Informational messages tend to be focused, logical, and organized, as one would expect given their connection to the Control quadrant. In theory, informational messages are intended to provide neutral content. In practice, it is important to recognize that even factually accurate statements may be interpreted as reflecting a particular position on an issue.

In terms of style, informational messages are typically presented in conventional ways. They include cues, such as headings, to help people understand the structure of the message and use lists, tables, and charts to present information. Explanations of policies and procedures typically use an informational approach.

PROMOTIONAL MESSAGES

The messages most closely associated with the Compete quadrant are intended to promote action and are labeled promotional messages in the competing values managerial communication framework. Similar to informational messages, promotional messages also include facts and information, but promotional messages do not attempt to be neutral in their content. Because their goal is to persuade, promotional messages typically make specific recommendations and include decisive, action-oriented statements. Promotional messages also tend to be interesting, stimulating, and engaging. These characteristics help to convey energy, which is important when a message calls for action.

Promotional messages often include interesting, compelling examples; in contrast, an informational message might rely more on statistics than on stories. Action verbs are used to convey a sense of urgency and encourage the message recipient to act. Sales presentations, press releases, and letters of recommendation are common types of promotional messages.

TRANSFORMATIONAL MESSAGES

Similar to promotional messages, transformational messages also seek action, but because the action they seek requires change, these messages take on an even more emphatic, forceful character. Because change is being sought, the message must find ways to help others see the vision of the future that the manager is attempting to convey. In contrast to informational messages, transformational messages are not at all conventional.

Vivid language, colorful constructions, and symbolism are all found in transformational messages. Enthusiasm is essential if transformational messages are going to inspire and challenge organizational members. You might expect to see the characteristics of transformational messages in mission statements, executive summaries for strategic plans, and keynote speeches.

EVALUATING YOUR COMMUNICATION TENDENCIES

Many people have inaccurate perceptions of their communication skills. For example, we may think we are communicating in an informational way, but others may see our messages as being promotional. Rogers and Hildebrandt (1991, p. 135) describe a situation where a participant in an executive communication program discovered that while he viewed himself as high on Relational communication and low on Promotional communication, his subordinates rated him as being exactly the opposite. They go on to report:

Rob was shocked and disturbed by the discrepancy. "But, I'm constantly talking to my subordinates and asking them for suggestions," he said. "I don't understand why they rate me so low on candor and sensitivity. Part of my job is to hear employee concerns, but these scores indicate they don't feel comfortable talking with me." We discussed possible reasons for the widely different perceptions in our initial interview with Rob, and in conjunction with the written and oral presentations he completed as part of the communication program. Through this process, Rob discovered that his messages contained few personal pronouns and he never used personal examples. He had difficulty making eye contact even when explaining a simple technical process, and he spoke at a fast, clipped pace. His questions were largely rhetorical, and his statements were more often propositional (e.g., "This process must be instituted to meet the company quota") than informative and inclusive ("By instituting this process, I believe we can meet our quota"). These and other discoveries provided Rob with some concrete information on message features he could change when interacting with his subordinates.

This example is a good reminder that it is important to seek feedback to identify situations where your self-perceptions are inconsistent with the perceptions of others.

Regardless of the type of message you are attempting to convey, your effectiveness will be enhanced if you have prepared your message thoughtfully and thoroughly. The next section provides a tool that you can use to help make your presentations more effective.

THE SSSAP APPROACH TO EFFECTIVE PRESENTATIONS

Public speaking has been labeled the number-one phobia of Americans, but if a managerial role is in your plans, you must assume you will be giving a presentation or a talk often. In this competency, we will use SSSAP, a tool developed by Al Switzler and Vital Smarts (1994). The SSSAP (which stands for Set, Support, Sequence, Access, and Polish) approach for effective communications is shown in Figure M4.2.

Keep in mind that although the discussion below focuses primarily on giving effective stand-up presentations, most of the SSSAP principles apply to both written and oral management communication. So whether you are writing a proposal,

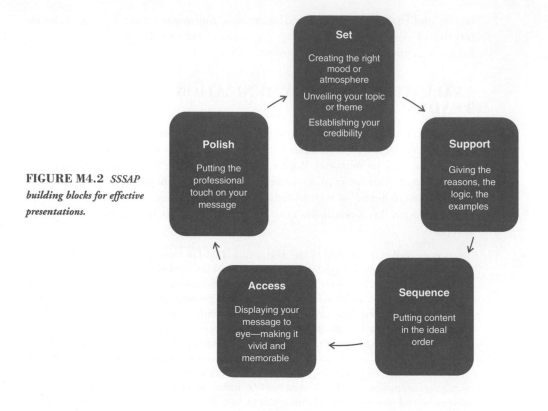

FIGURE M4.2 *SSSAP building blocks for effective presentations.*

planning a negotiation, interviewing a job candidate, or coaching an employee you can benefit from the principles below.

SET

Set deals with how you handle your audience's initial mood and expectations. When you "set" your audience, you help them get into the right position physically, emotionally, and mentally to hear, understand, and accept you and your message. Good communicators connect with their audiences early to prepare them for the journey they are about to take. Good presentations are audience centered, not speaker centered. Most poor presentations are built on a weak set. Set does three things: (1) It creates a mood and tone favorable to listening and acceptance; (2) it assures the listener that you are worth listening to; and (3) it maps the journey you are asking the listener to take with you. Switzler calls these three functions of set the climate set, credibility set, and content set.

Climate Set: What Mood Do You Want Them In?   **Climate set** is the effort you make to establish rapport with the audience and cue them to a mood or style appropriate to the presentation. The word "rapport" means having an accord or harmony with others, a feeling of sympathetic understanding. Your audience will encounter and assess *you* before they encounter your *message*.

Bert Decker is a successful author and communication coach. Decker tells his clients to address their audience's "First Brain" before addressing their "New Brain." Here's what he means. What he refers to as the New Brain is the cerebral cortex, the seat of conscious thought, memory, language, creativity, and decision-making. What Decker calls the First Brain is the nonreasoning, nonrational part of our brain. This is the seat of human emotion, composed of the brain stem and limbic system. Evolutionary biologists believe this part of the brain is millions of years older than the newer cerebral cortex. Decker says, "When people communicate by the spoken word, they almost invariably aim their message at the New Brain and completely overlook the First Brain" (Decker, 2008, p. 49).

The accuracy of Decker's anatomical description of the human brain is less important than the power of his advice: deal with the audience's First Brain first! *Engage their need to like and trust you before you deal with your need to have them understand and agree with you.* Your audience's First Brain wants to know one thing: Is it safe here? The First Brain wants to know, "Am I dealing with a friend or foe?" Once that part of the mind decides a situation is safe (and that may take only a few seconds) the logical, rational part of the mind can begin to hear your message. That's why it's so vital to establish rapport before you do anything else.

As a way of improving your ability at gaining rapport, try to apply some of the following principles at the next meeting you are required to conduct.

1. Be in the room first and greet each person if possible. At least make visual contact and acknowledge people with a smile or nod as they come into the room. We call this "taking roll" nonverbally—checking in with people as if to say, "Thanks for being here. I'll try to do my best to help you and keep things interesting."

2. Notice facial expressions and energy levels as people find a place to sit, engage in small talk (or say nothing), and generally situate themselves for the meeting. Try to get a reading on the general mood of the group.

3. Improve your "climate set" by being positive, even if you have unpleasant or difficult business to conduct. If you aren't positive, what is your justification for being in charge? When this advice is given to people, some react, "But this is just another boring meeting. Everybody knows that. I'd feel like a jerk trying to get people to enjoy it." That's the point. Routine events can be more challenging to our social-emotional skills than dramatic ones. We prefer to work with people who are professional and upbeat. There is a "market" for positive emotional energy. Every day we trade in that market. We are attracted to people who give us energy, and we tend to avoid (or limit our time) with people who drain our energy.

Credibility Set: Why Should They Listen to You? **Credibility set** is the assurance you provide the audience that you are an informed and legitimate speaker—that you know what you're talking about because of your experience, credentials, interest, special expertise, and so on. Often your credibility set is offered by the person who introduces you, but, in less formal settings, you may need to provide the credibility set yourself. Obviously, when speaking to a group you know very well, you may not need to provide a credibility set at all. Sometimes the briefest comment will suffice: "I had the opportunity last summer to spend three weeks at the FBI's National Training Academy in Virginia. Susan Grace, our bureau chief, asked me to share some of the things I learned at their forensic sciences lab." Here's another example of a simple credibility set from an executive in the accounting industry. She is speaking to a group of accounting majors at a university.

The pace of change continues to accelerate in our industry, and change is very intolerant of our need for comfort. I remember how hard I worked as a student at Penn State to understand the 1999 tax code, and how much I've wrestled to stay on top of changes in our industry since then, first when I was at Ernst and Young, and then when I started my own firm in Chicago.

This credibility set highlights relevant information about the speaker's background and gently tunes them in to her message. This is a modest but effective way for the speaker to establish credibility *before* sharing her message.

Don't assume people know why you are qualified to take their time. Without boasting, you need to think about your credibility set every time you address a group that doesn't know you well. Where possible, your credibility set should be specific to the needs of the audience and circumstance you're in.

Content Set: Where Are You Taking Them?   **Content set** is the roadmap you provide your audience. Most of us are uncomfortable with ambiguity. We want to know where we're going. When you talk to a group, let them know where you're about to take them and do it early in your presentation. "I want to talk for 10 minutes about why I think our record in work-related accidents is deteriorating and make some suggestions on how to turn the corner on our safety problems. When I've done that, I would like your questions and suggestions." With that content set, the audience can understand what's coming because you've given them a map to follow. Here's another example that combines a specific credibility set (a recent experience that has given the speaker valuable information) with a quick content set:

For the past two months I've been visiting all the branch offices in our company, interviewing customers and suppliers about how they experience the services we provide. I want to highlight the three most important issues that came out of those conversations, recommend two basic changes in our system, and then give you a chance to respond and ask questions.

Think about what people need to know up front so that they can relax and pay attention to you. How long will your presentation take? Will you give people a chance to ask questions? What major themes will you cover? How does your topic relate to people's jobs or their individual circumstances? Without the answers to these questions, people might interrupt just before you get to the point they are interested in. They might also stop listening because they assume you are not covering the topic they care most about. The roadmap you give your audience will keep their understanding and attention on track. In most cases, you will have a specific time frame in which to present. Never go beyond your time limit! If possible, take less than the allotted time. Of all the presentations you've listened to in your life, how many do you wish had been longer?

SUPPORT

Support is the substance of your presentation; the major reasons you offer for doing one thing rather than another. Without support, your claims or recommendations are just opinions (see Introduction, Thinking Critically). Support is the bones of your presentation. The support you provide in any presentation should be correct, concrete, complete, relevant, and logical. Al Switzler suggests you use these questions to determine how well supported your message is.

1. *What do I mean?* Do I define things adequately?

2. *Am I specific?* Do I use specific examples and illustrations that my audience will enjoy and understand? Do I wrap my message around a core story or experience that my audience can relate to?

3. *How do I know?* Do I draw on sources of evidence that my audience respects and understands?

4. *Do I answer the "so what?" question?* Do I demonstrate that my message makes a difference? Do I make my message relevant to this specific audience at this specific moment? Does my content focus on what I want my audience to understand, believe, or do as a result of my presentation—and does everything they hear and see contribute to that purpose (Vital Smarts, 1994, pp. 18–19).

Anticipate Objections and Counterarguments. Try, whenever possible, to anticipate objections and counterarguments to your position, and address them as you go. This strategy is especially effective when dealing with well-informed audiences. For example, the statement quoted below is part of a technical presentation given by a technician in a global construction company. Notice how the presenter anticipates two counterarguments or objections his audience might have to using a new product.

Our field tests have shown that this new compound forms a better bond for broken pipe joints than any we've used. Admittedly it's less effective in very cold temperatures, so we will be limited to three-season use, but new batches are being developed that promise to be effective year-round. Some of you pointed out in your field reports that the compound dries much slower—and it does by a factor of two; however, we know from tracking repair costs that we're saving at least 30 percent on repairing leaky joints, not to mention the savings from damage repairs.

The research on persuasion indicates that it's usually more effective to mix your responses to counterarguments with your own position rather than to isolate counterarguments in one section (O'Keefe, 2002).

Use the Magic Number Three. When you are presenting ideas, try to use the two or three reasons or sources of evidence you believe will have the greatest impact on the decision makers in the audience. Don't load too many reasons and angles into your message, or it will sound like a grocery list—with no one item having more value than another. A very helpful strategy is to use the magic number *three*. The number three is a very important number in most cultures. Suzette Hayden-Elgin, an expert on the psychology of human communication, says "People are comfortable with things that come in threes" (Hayden-Elgin, 1997). You can capitalize on that comfort by using three elements in your presentations, particularly if you have little time to prepare and little time to make the points you wish to make. Hayden-Elgin recommends this formula:

1. State or present the problem or situation [and frame that problem or situation through a story and key experience].
2. Provide three supporting items: *a, b,* and *c.*
3. Conclude with a summary.

For example, given the task of introducing a keynote speaker, this person uses a simple but effective three-element approach. It gives the speaker both a credibility set (which answers the question "Why should we listen to her?") and a warm climate set in very few words. Even the content set is at least implied in the introduction, and then left to the speaker to elaborate on.

I'm very pleased to introduce Fawn Ashton to you today because:

1. She is the person who organized the first Concerned Citizens for Clean Air chapter in the state.
2. As a pathologist specializing in pulmonary research, she is recognized as one of the best authorities in the country on air pollution and its effects on children with respiratory disorders.
3. She is a friend whose courage and integrity I have admired for over 20 years.

Fawn, thanks for sharing your valuable time with us today.

This three-element model will seem familiar and comfortable to your audience because they deal with this kind of structure all the time. Four or more items are often too many; fewer than three items may feel too limited, depending upon the complexity of your topic. When you think about support and sequencing, think about the number three, and then decide the best order in which to put those three items.

SEQUENCE

Sequence is the order or arrangement of your presentation. If you are conducting a meeting, it is the agenda you work from. Certain locations have more prominence in messages than others. For example, beginnings and endings are the most prominent locations. An audience is more likely to remember the opening and closing comments you make in a talk than the things that go in the middle.

While your content set gives the audience a map of the journey, the sequence of the content is more like the journey itself. Do you go to the drugstore first or the bank? Do you talk about the new security policy from the central office or the events that led to the policy? Do you give your recommendation upfront, or do you prepare your audience first with some background information?

Spill the Beans.   In most presentations or briefings, the best approach is to "spill the beans." Unveil your most important message first, and then support the point with

Managerial Presentations Begin with Recommendations

Managerial Style

R&D Style

1. Recommendations 7.
2. Conclusions 6.
3. Information 5.
4. Analysis 4.
5. Data 3.
6. Design of Experiment or Process 2.
7. Hypothesis or Questions 1.

FIGURE M4.3 *Sequence for managerial presentations.*

elaboration and details. This sequence of main point first, followed by details, is often called the "managerial sequence," for writing and presenting. Action-oriented people usually want the gist, or bottom line, of a message first. For example, a good memo tells the reader up front what its main point is. A good presentation spills the beans at the beginning and provides backup later. We love suspense when we're reading a detective novel or watching a film, but not when we're listening to a presentation at work. The Figure M4.3, developed by Roger McCarty (2010), illustrates two different approaches to ordering messages. The "managerial style" cuts to the chase: recommendations come first, with data and analysis following. In contrast, the "R&D style" begins by posing a question or a hypothesis, and then laying out what the data indicate, and ending with recommendations.

There are exceptions to the spill-the-beans rule. If you have bad news, you may need to "buffer" the jolt by verbally placing your arm on your listener's shoulder. In this example a manager has to give her staff some bad news about an upcoming move.

I think most of you know I've been meeting frequently with our director over office space. I've played all the chips I had to win a resource for what I think is the best staff in this agency. I appreciate your support and your patience. Unfortunately, we've lost this one. We won't be moving into the new wing when it's finished. We'll be staying here in the old facility. We need to talk about what that means, and how best to live with it.

The worse the news or the tougher the topic, the more the need for a buffer. However, don't overdo putting off the bad news. People don't want to be coddled. They usually just want to be treated civilly and professionally.

Deciding on Sequence. Sometimes it's hard to decide what sequence to use. Do you present things in the order in which they happened (chronologically)? Do you go from the known to the unknown, or the simple to the complex? Any of these approaches might work, but you have to decide in each particular case. Think about your purpose and the audience's needs. Think about a way to organize your material to give it the greatest punch and make it most memorable. Jeremy Weissman, an executive coach on presenting skills, teaches his clients some of the following methods for organizing the content of their presentations. He calls these organizing principles "flow structures." Listed below are seven flow structures that help organize a presentation or report.

1. *Chronological.* Organizes cluster of ideas along a timeline—the order of events in which they have occurred or might occur.

2. *Physical.* Orders ideas according to geographic or spatial location—as with market regions or the location of a firm's facilities.

3. *Problem solution.* Presents a high-stakes problem and then offers a solution to the problem.

4. *Issues-Actions.* Presents two or three core issues and recommends actions to take on each. (Note: Deciding the order in which to present these issues is another "sequencing" question.)

5. *Case study.* A specific narrative about an organizational experience. For example, a story about solving a problem for a customer, or one that represents how the organization is failing in customer service. Cases can be positive or negative, but they create an opportunity to persuade and inform a group with a single, memorable example.

6. *Argument/fallacy.* Presents your message by listing the major arguments against your own case or recommendation, and refuting them point by point. This approach can be persuasive, but beware of creating a negative tone.

7. *Features/benefits.* Organizes a message around the features and benefits of a specific product or service (Weissman, 2008, pp. 52–54.).

ACCESS

Access deals with making information visually and psychologically vivid to the listener or reader. When you write, you improve access by using boldface type, white space, headings, borders, numerals, and color. When you give a presentation, you can improve access by using visuals that stick in the audience's mind and by making clear transitions from one point to the next. You can also make things more concise by stating them in fewer words, or summarizing them. For this section on improving access in presentations, we have chosen to focus on ways to use Microsoft PowerPoint effectively.

Most of the presentations we see in the classroom and in organizations across the industrialized world are designed with Microsoft PowerPoint. This tool, which makes it easy to "compile" a message and display it to an audience, is both a benefit and a trap for most presenters. PowerPoint presentations are most often "data dumps," driven by the technology rather than the purpose of the presenter and the needs of the audience. Cliff Atkinson and Richard Mayer, experts on the architecture of information, describe how the easy-to-use features of PowerPoint make it easy to trip over ourselves in designing and giving a presentation.

Most PowerPoint presentations look a particular way because the PowerPoint tool has features that make particular tasks easy. PowerPoint makes it easy to use templates, so we use templates.

PowerPoint makes it easy to use bulleted lists, so we use bulleted lists. PowerPoint makes it easy to paste many items on the screen so we paste many items on the screen (Atkinson & Mayer, 2004, p. 5).

In short, we end up with a message that is too hard to follow and too easy to forget. A good presentation tells an interesting and memorable story—and, whenever possible, it puts the audience in the middle of the story as the lead protagonist, or actor. Atkinson and Mayer give us some basic advice on how to overcome "PowerPoint overload" and make every presentation more "accessible" visually and emotionally to the audience.

1. ***Write a clear headline that explains the main idea of every slide.*** Don't just put a generic title at the top each slide, such as "Marketing Objectives," or "Mission of Young Entrepreneurs Club." These vague headings provide a signpost for what the slide is about, but they don't direct the audience's attention and "set" them for the main message on that slide. Instead of writing a title, write a headline: "Capture 20% of the Hand Sanitizer Market!" Every slide should have a headline, one you can easily see when you open the "slide sorter" function of PowerPoint.

2. ***Break your story into digestible bites by using the slide sorter view.*** Most of us design PowerPoint slides while using only the "normal view" function. Atkinson and Myer recommend looking at your slides from time to time in the "slide sorter view" function. This will help you check to make sure that most, if not all, of your slides have a clear headline. As you move through your slides in a practice run, if you are taking much longer on one slide, consider breaking that slide in half and putting the information it contains on two slides instead of one.

3. ***Reduce visual load by moving text off-screen and narrating the content.*** Don't use PowerPoint as a word processor. Presentation slides are not MS Word documents. Most of the presentations we see have far too many bulleted lists on slides—too many words. A good way to avoid this problem is to use the "Notes Page" view in PowerPoint. Try writing a concise narrative of what you want to say for each slide in the Notes Page function. That way, you will be able to take some of the clutter off of the slide itself. Let your audience hear your message from what you say as you display each slide. The slide should not, and cannot, carry the whole message itself. By using the Notes Page function, you can also create a helpful handout to accompany your presentation. (For helpful tips on how to use the Notes Page view for creating handouts, see Cliff Atkinson's *Beyond Bullet Points: Using Microsoft PowerPoint to Create Presentations that Inform, Motivate, and Inspire*. Redmond, Washington: Microsoft Press, 2007).

4. ***Use visuals with your words instead of words alone.*** We understand why so many presentations are cluttered with bulleted lists. These lists are easy to create, and they remind the presenter what to say when she brings up a slide during the presentation. The bulleted lists of words serves as our "prompt book" for keeping us on track. Unfortunately, this can be deathly boring to the audience. Blend some visuals into your slides that add energy to the headline on the slide. In some cases, a good headline and a memorable visual are all you need on a slide. The rest of the message should come from what *you say* to the audience.

5. ***Remove every element on a slide that does not support the main idea.*** Atkinson and Mayer insist on this rule of thumb: If you're not sure you should include it, cut it! Cut all text from your slide that you are not explicitly going to narrate. Delete complex patterned backgrounds that have nothing to do with the content of your slide. The hardest thing about designing slides is getting them to the proper level of simplicity.

POLISH

Polish is the finish you put on anything that represents you or carries your reputation with it. It is the added attention to details and little things. It is having your notes in order, having clear and memorable visuals in an effective sequence, dressing in such a way that you do not draw too much attention to yourself but need not worry about your appearance. Polish also is arranging the environment for maximum effectiveness. People can hear you. They can see the screen. The room isn't stifling or chilly. You can't control all aspects of the environment, but you can do some things, and these make a huge difference. Polish tells the audience that the topic is important, they are worth the effort, and you are not wasting their time.

Practice, Practice, Practice. In many instances, practice is the difference between a great presentation and a mediocre one. Practice will allow you to discover your core message. Practice exposes the segments of a presentation that are unclear or redundant, or helps you come up with ways of fine turning your message. For a high stakes presentation, we strongly suggest having a small group of supportive but frank associates watch your presentation and give you candid feedback.

FINDING YOUR OWN VOICE

At the beginning of this competency we described four different types of managerial communications and suggested that, because they have different purposes, they will differ in substance and in style. It is also true, however, that each of us needs to find our own voice if we wish to become effective communicators. The following experience from communication coach Christopher Witt (2009, p. 34) illustrates what we believe is the fundamental principle of effective communication, whether talking one-on-one or speaking in public: find your own authentic voice, and use it to establish a connection with your audience and your subject.

I once met with an executive who was being groomed to replace the outgoing CEO, a truly charismatic speaker. When the CEO-in-waiting ushered me into his office, the place was abuzz with ringing phones and people scurrying around. He calmly shut his door and told his assistant to hold his calls and postpone any meetings.

Then he shook my hand, looked me in the eye and for the entire time we were together, gave me his full attention. I felt as if I were the only person who mattered to him at that moment.

Yet, when I saw a videotape of him speaking, he looked ill at ease and spoke in a strained, unnecessarily loud voice. When I asked him what his intention in his speech was, he said, "I was trying to channel my CEO."

"What works for him," I replied, "doesn't work for you." This man's gift was connection not charisma. And that's what I encouraged him to emphasize, because when you connect with yourself, with your audience, and with the moment, you are truly present. And that kind of presence, when you're standing in front of an audience, has a powerful effect all its own.

Witt's description of "presence" or what we call "voice," is the combination of your personal convictions, tastes, abilities, interests, and preoccupations. That voice can, and probably should, change over the years as you gain experience, but for any one point in time, you have an authentic voice through which you share ideas with others. Although you can, and should, tailor your communications based on your purpose and your audience, you must at the same time remain true to yourself and your values.

ANALYSIS   Applying Communication Tools to Evaluate a Presentation

Objective   One way to reinforce the ideas behind the competing values framework for managerial communication (CVFMC) and the SSSAP approach is to *analyze* other people's presentations to see how effectively they use these principles.

Directions   Within the next week, take special note of a presentation in which you are part of the audience. A live presentation would be better than a televised one. Use the CVFMC and SSSAP principles and your own experience and expertise as a communicator to evaluate the presentation. Consider these questions:

CVFMC Questions

1. What was the primary purpose of the presentation?
2. Did the presenter appear to have more than one goal for the presentation? If so, did the goals appear to be competing or complementary?
3. Did the characteristics of the communication match the purpose of the presentation?

SSSAP Questions

1. Did the presenter prepare the audience with climate, credibility, and content sets? Did the presenter seem to understand the audience?
2. Did the presenter provide the support necessary to make his stated claims?
3. Would you have organized the presentation in the same way, or do you think the presentation would have been more effective if the presenter had discussed certain things before others?
4. Did the presenter offer a clear and memorable summary?
5. Was the presenter's message accessible visually and psychologically? How effective were the visuals and why?

Overall Evaluation

1. Did you think the presentation was effective? Why or why not?
2. How could the presenter have improved his or her performance?

Reflection   Even great presenters occasionally have an off day—perhaps due to a late night trip to the emergency room with a child running a fever or a missed flight connection that results in getting in late for a meeting. Following the SSSAP principles when preparing for the presentation, however, should help to minimize the consequences of unexpected challenges. SSSAP ensures that the message has been prepared with care, and the practice sessions help ensure that it will be delivered effectively. As an added bonus, the confidence that comes from knowing you are well prepared can also mitigate the stress associated with last-minute problems.

PRACTICE   Improving A Memo Requesting Additional Personnel

Objective

The CVFMC and SSSAP principles can be applied to any message, not just to presentations. This exercise is intended to give you practice at applying those principles to a memo requesting authority to hire an additional employee.

Directions

Redesign the following document, or one suggested by your instructor, using the CVFMC and SSSAP principles. Use your editing and layout skills to make this document more user-friendly. Make any changes in wording, organization, tone, layout, or design that you think would make the document more effective.

TO: VP of Human Resources   DATE:

FROM: M. Petuous, Senior Mktg. Admin.   RE: Marketing Staffing Issues

The marketing department is struggling—we need to hire another person, if not two, very quickly. We currently have 12 full-time staff, but one person is on administrative duty with the strategic planning group, and three or four of our people just don't have the analytical and technological skills to do what needs to be done. I know that money is tight, but even if we can't fire the underachievers to free up some resources, we still need to hire someone who is willing to pick up their share of the work.

Another issue is related to the new performance evaluation system the board said we had to begin using by next quarter. We have to finalize the categories we will use to evaluate all employees, and then train every manager in the department on how to conduct the interviews and complete the forms. I get a knot in my stomach just thinking about how tough it will be to roll out this new system. Although we heard at the division meeting last week that performance assessment is important to the company, no one has time to work on developing the categories that are expected—and which will protect us from getting sued by a frustrated employee. Hiring an additional person or two would help us address that problem. It is no secret that the president is very enthusiastic about the new performance evaluation system, so it is not hard to imagine that failing to get this process on track in the next couple of months will result in a number of heads rolling, including mine and perhaps yours.

After ten years of service I am committed to this company, but I can't see how we can retain new employees who have less invested here if we don't do something to take the pressure off them. Expectations continue to climb, but there are no increases in pay or other benefits to make people feel that it's worth it, particularly when you've got people who've been here for 30 years refusing to learn the new technology and insisting on doing things "the way we've always done it."

The Board of Directors meeting is coming up in a few weeks, and I know that they like to micromanage things and may want to review any new authorizations to hire, so I hope that you agree that the marketing department should be given authorization to hire and that you are willing to present that case to the board. It is embarrassing when the chairman of the board's son is working as an intern in a department that is so understaffed that instead of giving him the typical copying and gophering jobs intended for interns but being done by the old-timers, he is getting stuck developing new marketing campaigns.

I'm sorry for dumping a load of problems on you, but someone has to speak up for our department and not just hope things will change.

Discussion Questions

1. What are the main flaws in the document as it was originally written? What do you think would happen if the vice president of human resources received the original memo? What would you do if you were in that position?

2. Do you think that anyone would ever write a memo like this one? Why or why not?

3. How does the tone of the memo affect your perception of the credibility of the writer?

Reflection All types of communication need to create some kind of climate set with the reader, establish the credibility of the communicator, and convey the content of the message. Information in memos and reports needs to be accessible visually through the use of white space, headings, italics, and other highlighting devices. Given the problems that everyone faces with information overload (recall Module 2, Competency 1), you can increase the chance that your message will be heard if you take the time to craft it using the SSSAP principles.

APPLICATION You Be the Speaker

Objective This exercise will give you practice in preparing and presenting an oral presentation.

Directions Prepare a six-minute presentation on a topic of your choice. It may involve a problem or project at work, but it may also be taken from another class or your personal experience. Based on the purpose of your presentation, make sure that it includes the appropriate characteristics based on the competing values framework for managerial communication. Apply the SSSAP principles as you design your presentation.

Focus on creating a coherent message with a crisp beginning, middle, and end. We suggest you deliver the presentation using presentation software, such as Microsoft PowerPoint. Each slide should contain a significant point. Don't spend a lot of time designing visuals. Use "primitive" visuals if you wish, using the chalkboard or overhead projector. Work less on visual polish and more on the "support" and "sequence" elements of your presentation. Primitive visuals can also be very accessible despite their lack of polish.

Here are some suggested topics to trigger your thinking:

- Talk about the organization you would most like to work for. What makes this organization a good employer?

- Present a "briefing" on a significant issue or trend in an industry or sector you are interested in. You can take examples from healthcare, high technology, retail, manufacturing, tourism, telecommunications, education, government, transportation, e-commerce, construction—any area in which you have a personal interest. Envision your audience as a group of people who are currently working in that industry and have an urgent need to understand the issue. or trend.

- Offer a consultant's proposal to one of your instructors on how a class you are taking (or have recently taken) could be improved. Be specific in your recommendations. Describe the benefits of implementing your ideas, and the costs of failing to make improvements. Assume that a group of faculty who teach sections of the course are your core audience.

- Design a brief training module on one of the competencies discussed in this textbook. Teach your classmates a specific skill that will help them be more competent managers.

Reflection In selecting a topic for your presentation, what influenced your choice? Did you choose something that you were interested in learning more about or a subject that you felt you could address without doing additional research? Was the topic something that you are passionate about, or did you choose something that wasn't especially important to you but would satisfy the requirements of the assignment? Why did you make the choices that you did? As we move to the concluding section on integration and the road to mastery, we have come full circle in the competing values framework, so it is appropriate to reflect back on the earlier competencies such as Understanding Self and Others. What does the choice you made about how to approach this assignment say about your interests, motivation, and dedication to becoming a master manager?

Module 4 Competency 3 Fueling and Fostering Innovation

ASSESSMENT   Are You a Creative Thinker?

Objective   What behaviors and attitudes do you think characterize creative people? This exercise is designed to help you understand how you think about creativity.

Directions   Read each of the statements below. If you think that the behavior or attitude characterizes what creative people are like, put a check in the first column. If you think that the behavior or attitude characterizes what you are like, put a check in the second column.

This assessment is from *How Creative Are You?* by Eugene Raudsepp (1981). Reprinted by permission of the Putnam Publishing Group.

Creative people do this	*I do this*	
_____	_____	1. In a group, voicing unconventional but thought-provoking opinions
_____	_____	2. Sticking with a problem over extended periods of time
_____	_____	3. Getting overly enthusiastic about things
_____	_____	4. Getting good ideas when doing nothing in particular
_____	_____	5. Occasionally relying on intuitive hunches and the feeling of "rightness" or "wrongness" when moving toward the solution of a problem
_____	_____	6. Having a high degree of aesthetic sensitivity
_____	_____	7. Occasionally beginning work on a problem that could only dimly be sensed and had not yet been expressed
_____	_____	8. Tending to forget details, such as names of people, streets, highways, small towns, and so on
_____	_____	9. Sometimes feeling that the trouble with many people is that they take things too seriously
_____	_____	10. Feeling attracted to the mystery of life

Reflection   In fact, all of the 10 statements above describe individual behaviors or attitudes that have been found to be related to creative thinking ability. Before completing this assessment, did you see yourself as a creative person? In looking at the "I do this" column, did you find that you checked a number of statements even though you never considered yourself a particularly creative? Sometimes, people fail to see their own creativity until they are encouraged to recognize it. That is the purpose of the following discussion, to convince you that everyone can become more creative and to give you some tools to develop your creative thinking skills.

LEARNING   Fueling and Fostering Innovation

In the organizational world, innovation goes a step beyond creative thinking. Creativity is, essentially, the development of an idea or object through unique combinations. Although creative ideas are necessary for innovation, not all creative ideas become innovations. An innovation is a product, service, or an improvement. Innovation is often about delivering value to customers and clients. Innovation is now recognized as "the single most important ingredient in any modern economy" (*The Economist,* 2007).

Today, most innovations are achieved by people working collaboratively. The complexity of the products and services we use every day are often beyond the ability of any one person to deliver. Innovation is a team sport, or at least a group sport. Perhaps the most crucial skill in the innovation process is the ability to bring people together and help them "harvest" their best thinking. The manager who can foster even modest improvements in innovation can add enormous value to an organization.

Managers are not required to come up with all the new ideas themselves. In fact, it's probably best that they don't attempt to be the creator of ideas as much as to develop a "space" in which coworkers can make innovative practices a habit.

Most of us think of innovation as the creation of brand new ideas—new things that have never been thought of before. Most often, however, an innovation is the result of "importing" an existing idea from one setting or context into another. A century ago, college students began playing catch with pie tins made by the Frisbie Baking Company. In the late 1940s, a World War II veteran, Walter Frederick Morrison, took out a patent for a plastic disc toy he called The Pluto Platter. This toy eventually came to be known as not at the Frisbee (Bellis, n.d. a). In 1895, an inventor named Jesse Reno featured an inclined conveyor belt as a novelty ride at Coney Island Amusement Park in New York State. Soon after, Charles Seeberger of the Otis Elevator Company saw how Reno's concept could be refined as a moving stairway that he called the "escalator" (Bellis, n.d. b). As these examples illustrate, innovation comes when one idea is taken from one context and applied in another. Innovation, as sociologist Ronald Burt says, is primarily an "import-export game," not a process of pure creation (Burt, 2005, p. 355).

In his book, *Borrowed Brilliance*, David Kord Murray claims, ". . . the farther away from your subject you borrow materials from, the more creative your solution becomes" (Murray, 2009, p. 69). Murray is fond of saying, "First you copy. Then you create." The key is freshness of perception and a willingness to tinker with our mind sets—the way we "normally" see things. One source of fresh perceptions is your social network. Being connected to a variety of people with different areas of expertise allows you to participate in an exchange of ideas that can benefit everyone in your network.

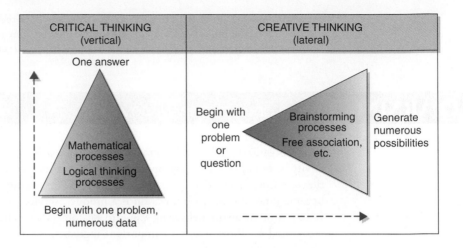

FIGURE M4.4 *Critical and creative thinking.*

How does creative thinking differ from critical thinking? Generally, critical thinking is analytical, logical, and results in one answer or just a few alternatives. Critical thinking is often described as vertical, logically moving upward until you arrive at a *correct* answer. By contrast, creative thinking is described as lateral, spreading out to find *many* possible solutions (de Bono, 1970). Figure M4.4. summarizes these differences.

For example, suppose that you, as a marketing specialist, have been assigned to join a special citizens' task force in your community. The task force is considering the problem of how to persuade families and tourists to take their vacations in your home state this year. Notice that there is not merely one answer to this; there are perhaps hundreds or thousands of ways to persuade people to take their vacations in your state. Notice, too, the need for imagination and the prospect of generating many ideas.

By contrast, consider any mathematical problem whose solution has a single answer. Such a problem involves critical thinking; information is analyzed to determine the one best or correct solution. If your task force has generated a large number of suggestions, it will need to use critical thinking in order to decide which ones would be best to implement. Further, critical thinking skills will be necessary in order to arrive at a viable plan of action.

The two modes of thinking are complementary; the findings of the creative thinking process can be analyzed for usefulness by critical thinking. Although Western culture has traditionally emphasized critical thinking skills, the value of creative thinking has become increasingly recognized within organizations and in society as a whole. Moreover, there is a growing assumption that both creative and critical thinking skills, reflecting the emphases of the Create and Control quadrants, respectively, will be needed to meet the challenges of the twenty-first century according to British expert on creativity and education, Sir Ken Robinson (2006).

DEVELOPING CREATIVE THINKING SKILLS IN YOURSELF AND OTHERS

People often underestimate their own creative ability. Research indicates, however, that there is one major difference between people who exhibit creative tendencies and people who don't: personal belief in their own creativity. That is, those who engage in creative thinking tend to regard themselves as creative; the others see themselves as noncreative.

Although many people simply do not see themselves as creative, the manager has an opportunity to affirm employees as individuals by recognizing their creative potential and encouraging the use of creative thinking. In this way subordinates are strengthened both on the job and as individuals. By empowering employees to think creatively, managers increase the probability that new and better ways will be found to do things.

INNOVATION AS A HABIT

There is growing evidence that people can improve their ability to think in innovative ways. Twyla Tharp is one of the best known choreographers in the world. Tharp contends that creative work is the result of habits that must be deliberately developed over time: ". . . there's a process that generates creativity," says Tharp, "and you can learn it. And you can make it habitual." We don't think of creative or innovative thinking as a habit, but more as a flash of insight, or an intermittent hunch. Tharp is a strong believer in the paradoxical nature of creative work. There's a paradox in the notion that creativity should be a habit. We think of creativity as a way of keeping everything fresh and new, while habit implies routine and repetition. That paradox intrigues us because it occupies the place where creativity and skill rub up against each other. Here again we see the need for an integration of the structure and routines of the Control quadrant with the willingness to change and innovate emphasized by the Create quadrant.

Tharp says that her creative habit begins each day when she gets out of bed at 5:30 A.M. puts on her work-out clothes, walks out of her Manhattan apartment, and takes a cab to the Pumping Iron Gym where she works out for two hours. This "ritual" is at the heart of her creative habit. "The ritual," she says,

is not the stretching and weight training I put my body through each morning at the gym; the ritual is the cab. The moment I tell the driver where to go I have completed the ritual. It's a simple act but doing it the same way each morning habitualizes it—makes it repeatable, easy to do. By the time I give the taxi driver directions, it's too late to wonder why I'm going to the gym and not snoozing under the warm covers of my bed *(Tharp, 2003, p. 14–15)*.

The confidence to do creative work increases as we practice creative habits. The creative space in which Tharp does her work is an empty "white room," a dance studio with eight-foot mirrors, and a bare hard-wood floor with thousands of scuff marks from dancers' shoes. But Tharp says that all of us have a white room we need to enter regularly—out of habit. The writer must come to the blank computer screen, the artist to her blank canvas, and the chef to a kitchen in which to create a new dish for customers in search of something novel. The key, says Tharp, is to go often into that room, into that space in which you practice and experiment with different combinations of ideas, tools, images, and experience. Notice that Twyla Tharp combines the discipline and routine of the Control quadrant in the competing values framework with the expansive and experimental behaviors of the Create Quadrant. Her contention, which is well-supported by research on creative productivity, is that creative work is best sustained by the momentum of discipline and habit. If we wait until we feel creative, or until we find ourselves in a situation that stimulates innovative thinking, we greatly reduce our creative output.

BARRIERS TO CREATIVE THINKING

One key to enhancing your own ability to think innovatively is to learn to break away from commonly held assumptions regarding the relationships between ideas and things, so that you are able to consider new relationships. It is especially important to recognize cultural barriers to creativity, those commonly held assumptions that are a part of our societal or organizational culture. For example, Western culture traditionally has embraced reason and logic to the exclusion of feeling and intuition. This emphasis on reason and logic has created several barriers to creative thinking, including the following:

1. A negative value on fantasy and reflection as a waste of time, a sign of laziness, or even a bit crazy.

2. The belief that only children should play and that adults should be serious.

3. The assumption that problem solving is serious and, therefore, humor is out of place.

4. A negative value on feeling and intuition, which are regarded as illogical and impractical.

Although we cannot change these socially based cultural barriers, we can guard ourselves against their influence. If we are able to diminish our cultural barriers to creative thinking, we enhance our abilities to think differently and develop skills for creativity.

We often make assumptions that hinder our attempts to become more creative. Like cultural barriers, individual barriers can be overcome if we consciously seek change. Individual barriers frequently have an emotional basis. These barriers result from personal beliefs and fears associated with taking risks, trying out a new idea, or trying to convince others of the value of our new ideas. The following are 10 of the most common individual barriers to creative thinking:

1. *Resistance to change.* It is natural to become secure in the way things are and to resist change.

2. *Fear of making a mistake and fear of failure.* To counter this fear, the Limited clothing stores encourage mistakes by evaluating buyers on their failures as well as on

their successes. They believe that if employees do not make mistakes, then they may not be taking initiatives and trying new ideas. Somerset Maugham once said, "You'll win some. You'll lose some. . . . Only mediocre people are always at their best" (quoted in Miller, 1987, p. 17).

3. *Inability to tolerate ambiguity.* Our need for predictability nurtures our inability to tolerate ambiguity. We like to know the way things are and to be able to categorize things, events, and people in our lives. Creativity requires flexibility in our thinking; inability to tolerate ambiguity is an inability to tolerate flexibility.

4. *The tendency to judge rather than to generate ideas.* This is an expression of the culturally based preference for critical thinking over creative thinking. Many of us are trained to be critical in our thinking and judgmental in our approach. To some extent, we may feel better about ourselves if we are able to critique another's work or choices.

5. *Inability to relax or to permit any new idea to incubate.* Many of us find a perverse comfort in having too much to do and, as a result, find relaxation uncomfortable and difficult. Some people report that they do not know how to relax. Others relax by engaging intensely in another demanding project. Research has shown, however, that freeing our conscious minds, through relaxation or repetitive activity (e.g., cutting the grass or cleaning the house), increases our ability to seek associations amid old ideas.

6. *The tendency toward excessive self-criticism.* Many of us are taught to be excessively self-critical. In this respect, some people are kinder to people they actively dislike than they are to themselves. Efforts to eradicate this self-defeating tendency can increase your creative abilities.

7. *Fear of looking foolish.* This is the biggest barrier of all and the hardest to remove. No one likes to appear foolish to others. We find, however, that often we think we appear foolish when we actually do not.

8. *Conformity or wanting to give the expected answer.* This is very apparent in groups and organizations. Individuals may not want to rock the boat or present an unpopular argument. Managers should actively encourage employees to present different ideas or perspectives (Murray, 2009).

9. *Stereotyping, or limiting the possibilities of objects and ideas to their "known" use.* The inability to see a problem from various viewpoints is a function of mental stereotyping (e.g., a chair is for sitting).

10. *Lack of information, or too much incorrect or irrelevant information.* Lack of information may limit the creative handling of data.

Are you tripped up by any of these barriers? The extent to which you are tripped up is an indicator of how much your creative ability is hampered. You can see from this list that many of the barriers to innovative thinking are social and emotional. Tom Kelly is managing director of the renowned product design firm, IDEO, and author of *The Ten Faces of Innovation*. IDEO is considered one of the most innovative product design companies in the world, but it has evolved into a firm that not only designs products for client firms, but as a consulting practice that coaches companies in what

Kelly calls "design thinking." Kelly contends that one of the greatest obstacles to innovative thinking is the tendency so many of us have to play the devil's advocate. "We've all been there," says Kelly (2005, p. 2):

The pivotal meeting where you push forward a new idea or proposal you're passionate about. A fast-past discussion leads to an upwelling of support that seems about to reach critical mass. And then, in one disastrous moment, your hopes are dashed when someone weighs in with those fateful words: 'Let me just play devil's advocate for a minute'.

This deflating experience occurs not just in formal meetings but in everyday conversations—anywhere where someone puts out an idea, and someone else quickly moves in to give the reasons why it can't work. Kelly says that the "persona" of the devil's advocate "encourages idea wreckers to assume the most negative possible perspective; one sees only the downside, the problems, the disasters in waiting. Once those floodgates open, they can drown an initiative in negativity" (Kelly, 2005, p. 5).

Kelly's caution about not allowing negativity to dampen the energy required to develop new ideas does not mean that the critical assessment of ideas and practices should always be avoided. At some point, all organizational practices and innovations must be evaluated in terms of risk, cost, and ethical soundness. For example, some critics of the social and business environment in the United States believe that a culture of blind optimism and "positive energy" has made it difficult for employees and leaders who are concerned about financial risks and other hazards to have their voices heard (Ehrenreich, 2009).

BUILDING A CREATIVE SPACE FOR PEOPLE

All individuals have the potential to be creative. The issues are (1) will they and (2) what can managers/innovators do to increase the opportunities for their employees to use their creative thinking abilities? Individual and cultural barriers often decrease our ability to create such environments. Managers must be aware of these barriers as they strive to enhance creativity in the workplace.

Table M4.1 is a checklist that may help you to assist yourself and your coworkers to foster innovative thinking and not cave in too easily to the devil's advocate. Review this checklist and assess yourself on each item. Ask yourself: (1) To what extent is change needed to help my unit be more creative? (2) To what extent is this within my control?

BRAINSTORMING AND THE NOMINAL GROUP TECHNIQUE

One of the most effective strategies for finding and encouraging collective innovation is **brainstorming.** Marshaling the skills, thinking, and knowledge of employees, brainstorming is a technique used for generating new ideas. Most of us have had at least some experience with brainstorming, but the process is often practiced with insufficient

TABLE M4.1 Checklist for Managers to Build Creative Spaces for People

1. Do not overdirect, overobserve, or overreport.

2. Recognize differences in individuals. Have a keen appreciation of each person's unique characteristics.

3. Help subordinates see problems as challenges.

4. Ask your employees about ways in which they think they are most creative—or would like to be most creative—and what sort of creative contribution they would most like to make.

5. Allow more freedom for individuals to guide their own work.

6. Train yourself and others to respond to the positive parts of proposed ideas rather than react to the often easier-to-spot negative ones.

7. Develop greater tolerance for mistakes and errors.

8. Provide a safe atmosphere for failures.

9. Be a resource person rather than a controller, a facilitator rather than a boss.

10. Act as a buffer between employees and outside problems or higher-up demands.

11. Enhance your own creative ability through special workshops and seminars, specialized reading, and practice of creative exercises and games. This sets an excellent example employees will want to emulate and makes it easier for you to recognize and relate to the creative ability of others.

12. Make sure that innovative ideas are transmitted to your boss with your support and backing; then insist on a feedback mechanism. Without feedback, the flow of creative ideas dries up because innovators feel that their ideas are not given a fair hearing or taken seriously.

Adapted from Eugene Raudsepp, President, Princeton Creative Research, Inc., in R. L. Kuhn, *Handbook for Creative Managers* (New York: McGraw-Hill, 1987), 173–182. Used with permission.

discipline on the principles that make it effective: generate as many ideas as possible; no evaluation or criticism allowed until the group agrees the generation process is done; everyone participates; let your mind stretch—don't be too conservative. Tom Kelly of IDEO believes that brainstorming is the best place to begin jumpstarting innovation in your organization. Brainstorming is high-energy, and it helps people disconnect from routine. Kelly recommends that you start with organizational problems or challenges that you think you can "make a dent in right away"—questions like, "How can we reduce our customers' waiting time?" or "What's the best use of our empty office space?" (Kelly 2005, pp. 148–149). Kelly also recommends you appoint a "master of ceremonies" for the event, someone with plenty of positive energy and optimism. Don't be discouraged by rough spots and obstacles. Some coworkers may resist, but our experience is that groups and teams become more effective with brainstorming the more they do it.

Nominal group technique (Delbecq, Van de Ven & Gustafson, 1975) is a process that uses brainstorming to generate new ideas and then uses group discussion and systematic voting to choose from among the ideas generated by the group. It is often used when the problem has a large number of potential alternative solutions.

Assume that 10 professional employees who depend very heavily on secretarial and clerical support report to you. Two secretaries have just left for higher-paying jobs, and one clerk will be out for several weeks for surgery. As time progresses, it is apparent that conflicts are about to develop over the need for support staff time. You have several options: you may devise a plan and issue memoranda to your employees regulating the use of the available secretarial and clerical resources (and hope they are pleased enough with your solution to happily go about their work in order to finish before the deadline); you may go to your boss for direction (risking, perhaps, the judgment that you cannot handle this yourself); or you can plan a nominal group technique session during which you will get ideas from your employees and, with them, arrive at a workable solution.

Before you hold a brainstorming session, you must first settle in your own mind that you genuinely want the ideas from your employees. Brainstorming sessions can be inadvertently sabotaged by well-meaning managers who have hidden agendas and use the session as a way to manipulate employees to accept an already formulated plan. You must resolve that all ideas should be heard; you must provide a safe environment for the free flow of ideas from employees. You have to be able to accept good ideas from employees and not feel that you have to be the one to generate all of the good ideas at work.

Use the following steps for conducting a nominal group technique session.

1. *Make sure that everyone agrees on the problem definition.* If there is not agreement on the problem definition, you may find that different members of the group are solving different problems.

2. *Have participants write down all their ideas.* Even ideas that do not seem feasible may give other people ideas. During this time no one should talk, except to ask questions about the problem definition. This step may take anywhere from 10 minutes to half an hour.

3. *Use a round-robin procedure to allow participants to share their ideas.* Have each participant give one idea at a time. Record the ideas on a flip chart so that all ideas are visible to all participants. Again, do not allow discussion as the ideas are being recorded.

4 *After all ideas are recorded, review each idea one at a time.* Allow participants to ask questions and share reactions regarding the feasibility and merits of the idea. Use your meeting management skills to ensure that you stay on track and that people are contributing appropriately.

5. *Have participants vote on their preferred alternative solution.* Generally, the voting should be secret, and a rank vote should be used. That is, have participants individually identify their top five ideas, and then assign a score of 5 to their first-ranked idea, 4 to their second-ranked idea, and so forth. Then sum the scores.

6. *Review the voting pattern.* If one alternative stands out as the obvious preferred choice, then you are ready to decide how to implement that choice. If not, choose the top five to 10 alternatives and return to step 4, this time rank-ordering only the top three choices.

THE IMPORTANCE OF CREATIVE THINKING IN ORGANIZATIONS

The use of creative thinking in problem solving allows organizations to access human resources that often go untapped. In comparing Japanese and American organizations, Deming (1986) has argued that "the greatest waste in America is failure to use the abilities of people." Managers should recognize that employees' abilities are a free resource. Although most resources have extra cost factors involved, creative thinking does not. From this perspective, one could argue that no organization—public or private—can afford to waste this resource.

Beyond the overall organizational benefits, managers should recognize the personal benefits of encouraging creative thinking among their employees. Creative thinking can increase the effectiveness of the unit through better problem solving. In addition, creative thinking can be used as a motivational tool. In the work environment of large organizations, it is sometimes easy for employees to see themselves as a replaceable cog in the giant wheel and to become unmotivated. When individuals are encouraged to be creative in their thinking and problem solving, they are more likely to feel unique, valued, and affirmed as important employees of the organization. Thus, not only are there benefits from the employees' good ideas, but individuals feel better about themselves as employees. In sum, the encouragement of employees' creative thinking can result in substantial benefits to the organization, to the work unit, and to the individuals who exercise their creative skills.

ANALYSIS   Creativity and Managerial Style

Objective   Creative problem-solving skills are not always tied only to your own thought processes. Often creativity involves knowing how to work with other people who are creative and using techniques that will maximize the probability that those people will generate creative solutions. Managers can either encourage or discourage employee creativity. This exercise is designed to examine how you have responded to different managerial styles in the past.

Directions   Reflect on the managers with whom you have worked. If you have not yet been employed, use this exercise to reflect on the skills of a parent, teacher, or anyone else who has evaluated your work. Choose one person for this exercise and analyze whether that person's style helped or hindered the tapping of your creativity. Check any of the following that applied to your situation:

_____ 1. Were you instructed to do things according to a set pattern?

_____ 2. Did this person seek your opinion regarding matters that affected you?

_____ 3. Did this person ever reconsider a decision in light of your input?

_____ 4. Did you have a tendency to fear that you might appear foolish to this person?

_____ 5. Did this person value your ideas and your thinking?

_____ 6. Did you ever feel that there was a better way to do something but not bring it to the attention of this person?

_____ 7. Did you feel that it was important for this person to like you?

_____ 8. Did you feel that this person would like you more if you tended to agree with him?

_____ 9. Did you feel as if this person was always evaluating you?

Discussion Questions
1. How did you feel about yourself in that situation?

2. From your responses, identify specific behaviors that helped you feel affirmed as a valued person and those that did not.

3. How would you answer Question 2 focusing on two other persons: one with whom you had a very positive experience and one with whom you had a negative experience?

Reflection
Our creativity in organizations can be encouraged or stifled by the people around us. Think about your own managerial style—does your behavior encourage creativity in others? There is little argument that providing too much structure and direction can inhibit creativity. It is also true, however, that too little structure can also be a problem.

PRACTICE   Encouraging Creative Thinking

Objective
The activities in this practice are intended to encourage you to move out of traditional ways of thinking.

Directions
Breaking Established Thinking Barriers

1. *The paper clip.* To assist in thinking differently about objects and concepts, list on a separate piece of paper as many uses as you can think of for a paper clip.

2. *The restaurant.* A new restaurant is opening adjacent to your campus. It will feature vegetarian food. Think of as many possible names for this restaurant as you can.

Using Analogies
Identify three pressing problems that you currently have at school or work. Describe each one briefly in writing. Then review the following list of analogies. Try to apply an analogy from this list, or from your own thinking, to each problem.

1. A snowball rolling downhill, gathering speed, and growing rapidly

2. Finding your way in the fog

3. Trying to start a car on a cold winter morning

4. Taking a bath

5. Frying potatoes

6. Sending a letter

7. Trying to untangle a ball of string

8. Cutting the grass with a pair of scissors

9. A child playing with a new toy

10. A fish out of water

Identify the feelings you have associated with each problem, and describe them with an analogy. The use of analogies should help you to see the problems differently. Describe the different perspectives that you now have on each problem. Use the perspectives to generate possible solutions to the problems.

Reflection   Some people initially respond somewhat negatively to the practice activities above. What is the point of thinking of new uses for paper clips or comparing problems at work to untangling a ball of string? The point is to practice changing your perspective. Sometimes when you need a long piece of string you need to patiently untangle the entire ball. If you only need a short piece of string, however, you may find that you can simply cut the string to meet your objective. Perhaps your problem at work can be solved if you are willing to give up something that you initially thought was important but now realize is beyond what you actually need.

APPLICATION 1   Import an Idea

Objective   There are many ways to be creative or innovative as an individual. Generally, new ideas can emerge in two ways: (1) people see new things, or (2) people see things anew. For this assignment, we want you to see new things.

Directions   Listen in on a "conversation" taking place outside your circle of experience; watch other people going about their work within some other community of practice. We recommend the following steps.

Step 1   Locate a "conversation" that is new to you. Think about conversations in a broad sense: For example, every magazine or website is a kind of conversation that brings together people who share an interest or concern.

Step 2   Listen and watch. What's new and different? How are they going about their work? Do you see practices, ideas, or tools that might be appropriated and applied in another situation? Do their conversations spark any ideas for your organization and its needs? Are they using tools that could help improve the work at your "shop"? And so forth.

Step 3   Describe what you have found (ideas, practices, tools, etc.). Write about the source of what you discovered and how you propose to use it within your work or organization. Your paper should be approximately 300 words.

Reflection   Sometimes we have difficulty seeing how new ideas could be applied to our situation because we focus too much on specific details that differ and not enough on more abstract concepts that are applicable to many different situations. Creativity and innovation can benefit from looking at both the forest and the trees.

APPLICATION 2   New Approaches to the Same Old Problem

Objective   Now that you have had a chance to warm up your creative thinking muscles, you can apply them to a problem that you are currently facing.

Directions   Develop a plan to approach an old problem in a new way.

1. Start by writing a description of the problem.
2. Restate the problem in several ways.
3. Write down as many facts related to the problem as possible.
4. Identify advantages to this problem—try to see it as an opportunity.

5. Identify as many new ways as possible to approach this problem.

6. Identify people who might be able to help you with this problem.

7. Determine which action you will take first in arriving at a solution to this problem and write down on your calendar the date and time that you will take that action.

Reflection   Identifying something as a "problem" immediately sets up a series of assumptions that may inhibit our ability to be creative. Problems suggest something that is "bad" and needs to be "solved." By reframing problems as opportunities and considering any potential advantages that they may offer, it may be possible to come up with more creative ways of responding. As you go forward, try to remember to use your creative thinking skills when you face a situation that seems to require a problem-solving response. Practice exercising your mind by stretching for alternatives, rather than jumping to conclusions.

Module 4 Competency 4   Negotiating Agreement and Commitment

ASSESSMENT   How Effective Are You at Negotiating Agreement?

Objective   Some people approach bargaining with a sense of dread, others with confident anticipation. This exercise will help you assess your own feelings about negotiating.

Directions   Think about some experiences you've had with negotiating—as a consumer, an employee, or a partner in a relationship you value. Ask yourself questions such as those listed, and add any you think are significant.

1. How well are you able to communicate with others? Do you easily understand what others are thinking and feeling? Do you express yourself clearly? How well are you able to deliver arguments and counterarguments?

2. Have you ever bargained for a shift change, a raise, or an adjustment in working conditions with a manager or employer?

3. Do you press for more information or clarification when listening to a sales pitch, a lecture, or another person's explanation, or do you hesitate to ask questions for fear of appearing uninformed or unsophisticated?

4. In a personal relationship, do you ever tolerate negative behavior in the other person because

    (a) you feel incapable of broaching the issue effectively?

    (b) you fear being misunderstood?

    (c) you don't want to hurt the other person's feelings, even though the behavior is causing you serious problems?

5. As a rule, do you feel you have a reputation among your peers and family members for being a tough bargainer or as someone who is easygoing and deferential in presenting your needs and conditions?

Based upon your responses to these questions, indicate your comfort level with negotiating agreement and commitment.

Very Uncomfortable	Uncomfortable	Somewhat Uncomfortable	Comfortable	Very Comfortable

Reflection Even people who dread negotiating can become more effective negotiators. Sometimes simply reframing the situation can help. For example, Courtney may feel that asking for a day off is selfish, and she does not want people to think of her as a selfish person. If, however, she recognizes that she is getting burned out from working too many hours and that taking some time off will improve her productivity, she may find it easier to assert herself when negotiating with her supervisor for that day off.

LEARNING Negotiating Agreement and Commitment

Negotiation is not limited to formal sessions across the desk with "the other party." We negotiate anytime we need something from someone else. William Ury, an associate at Harvard Law School's Program on Negotiation, reminds us that most of the important decisions we make in life are not made unilaterally. Most are negotiated. "Negotiation," says Ury, "is the preeminent form of decision-making in personal and professional life" (Ury, 1993, p. 5).

HOW IS YOUR SOCIAL CREDIT RATING?

The first competency in this module dealt with building and maintaining a power base. However, we can't exert influence in an organization or a group without knowing what kinds of influence people are ready to accept. This competency will deal with negotiating agreement and commitment. Successful negotiators know that trying to use power to force people into an agreement rarely results in optimal outcomes and can seriously damage relationships in the long run.

All members of an organization or group have a social credit rating. That rating goes up or down depending on how supportive, cooperative, and competent people perceive us to be. We do a balancing act. We have to be concerned about the needs of others, and we have to get our jobs done as well. Support is not automatic. We earn it moment by moment, turn by turn as we interact with other people. Ineffective negotiators believe that their assigned duties guarantee them support. Expert negotiators never take such support for granted.

THE VITAL ROLE OF DIALOGUE

An important preliminary dimension to effective negotiation is "dialogue," a process of working things out through a thoughtful sharing of viewpoints. Our colleagues at the management consulting firm, Vital Smarts, define dialogue as "the free flow of meaning in an atmosphere of mutual trust and respect." We don't learn from people we don't respect, and we seldom make commitments to people we don't trust. Our colleagues focus on improving the ability of clients to establish and maintain the conditions of dialogue. These conditions include three elements: mutual purpose, mutual meaning, and mutual respect. If one or more of these elements are not present, dialogue will elude us (Patterson, Grenny, McMillan & Switzler, 2002).

THE CONDITIONS OF DIALOGUE: MUTUAL PURPOSE, MEANING, AND RESPECT

The first condition, mutual purpose, is an "entrance condition" for dialogue. Without a clear and agreed-upon purpose, there is little point in investing in dialogue to begin with. When people and groups disagree, the disagreements are often about means or strategies, not about fundamental purposes; however, the purposes must be spelled out clearly from the beginning.

We once saw a group of environmentalists and real estate developers (two groups who seldom engage in dialogue) come together effectively because they had found a common purpose. Several people in each group had mentioned that as children they had learned to fish with parents and friends in a wilderness area whose future was now being hotly debated. They wanted to preserve that experience for their own children. With that mutual purpose established, the group effectively moved to a constructive dialogue on how to achieve it while still meeting other needs.

Mutual meaning involves each party knowing what the other is actually saying. Do we share the same definitions of terms, words, and expressions? Do I feel, as a participant in this dialogue, that my interests and opinions have been heard? "People never change without first feeling understood" (Stone, Patton & Heen 1999, p. 29). But how do we know we really have mutual meaning? When we can describe the other person's opinions, position, and feelings to his satisfaction. Another way to say this is, "To get anywhere in a disagreement, we have to understand the other person's story well enough to see how *their* conclusions make sense within it" (Stone et al., 1999, p. 30).

Mutual respect is also essential but fragile, especially if two parties have already had a disagreement or conflict. At least one party has to have the courage and wisdom to not resort to name-calling and blaming. When you watch two people in a heated argument, you're usually seeing a game of "tit-for-tat." I call you a name, you call me one; I threaten you, you threaten me. To create and maintain mutual respect, someone has to swallow hard and break the cycle of tit-for-tat. Nor can two parties move to silence, or even partial withdrawal, and hope to reach a constructive agreement. We demonstrate respect by listening respectfully, speaking candidly, and focusing more on solving problems than on placing blame. Box M4.5 provides an example of successful dialogue and negotiation in the field.

BOX M4.4 TOUGH-MINDED, SOFT-HEARTED LEADERSHIP

William Peace, a former executive with Westinghouse and United Technologies, does not apologize for being a tough-minded, soft-hearted leader. For Peace, soft leadership does not imply weak leadership, and a desire to consider many sides of an issue and listen to the recommendations of others does not imply indecisiveness. He learned a lot about establishing mutual respect from a manager named Gene Cattabiani, a vice president in the Steam Turbine Division of Westinghouse. Cattabiani faced a huge challenge with labor-management relations. The hourly employees in the division were fiercely loyal to their union leaders and convinced that management was out to get them. Managers, on the other hand, were equally convinced that the union leaders were turning employees against management at the expense of the company and even the employees themselves. "Most of these people are just plain damn lazy" was a comment often heard in management team meetings. "We need discipline more than we need negotiation," was another popular comment.

Cattabiani knew things had to change. The division was losing money, costs were climbing, and other companies were eating up market share. But how could he push for improvements and better performance when there was so much anger in the air? He came to the conclusion that he had to communicate with everyone in the plant. If dialogue were going to begin, he would have to step out and make the first move.

Because of the size of the plant and the presence of three shifts for each working day, he would have to give the same presentation several times on the huge shop floor to hostile audiences. His management team tried to dissuade him. "You don't have to submit to bad treatment," they said, "we'll give people the news in smaller groups." Another, stronger argument was that the risk was too great: "This will become a massive gripe session that may get out of control." But Cattabiani insisted and the meetings were held. Here's how Bill Peace describes what happened.

The initial presentation was a nightmare. Gene wanted the workforce to see that the business was in trouble, real trouble, and that their jobs depended on a different kind of relationship with management. But the workers assumed that management was up to its usual self-serving tricks, and there, on stage, for the first time, they had the enemy in person. They heckled him mercilessly all through the slide show. Then, during the question-and-answer period, they shouted abuse and threats.

At this point, Bill Peace was convinced that Cattabiani had made a serious strategic error. The management team worried that this "weakened" leader had lost all credibility and would now be bulldozed by employees who were really flexing their muscles. But Peace and others began to notice some subtle changes in the days that followed the meetings.

When Gene went out on the factory floor for a look around (which his predecessors never did unless they were giving customers a tour) people began to offer a nod of recognition—a radical change from the way they used to spit on the floor as he walked by. Even more remarkable was his interaction with the people who had heckled him at the meetings. Whenever he spotted one, be would walk over and say something like, "You really gave me a hard time last week," to which the response was usually something like, "Well, you deserved it, trying to pass off all that bullshit." Such exchanges usually led to brief but very open dialogues, and I noticed that the lathe operators and blading mechanics he talked to would listen to what Gene said, really listen (Peace, 1991, p. 46).

BOX M4.4 TOUGH-MINDED, SOFT-HEARTED LEADERSHIP (*Cont'd*)

As months, and even years passed, this division made steady progress, and Gene Cattabiani was largely responsible for it. Not every person came "on board" and supported the changes Cattabiani proposed. Some were moved to another job, and a few were let go. Others were put in leadership positions and were given more authority to make changes. Throughout the process, Cattabiani had a purpose greater than protecting his ego. He knew that people needed some opportunity to ventilate, and they needed to be convinced that he meant what he said about wanting their input and suggestions. He was willing to put himself on the line and not return insult for insult. With mutual respect in place, people could build the other conditions of dialogue: mutual meaning and purpose. Without respect, meaning and purpose don't really matter.

Cattabiani also understood that leadership can be a lonely spot. He did not expect the plant employees to love him or admire him. He knew that his position required tough choices at times. His goal was to build the overall capability of the organization, not to gain the personal approval of everyone in it. He wasn't seeking popularity or personal approval. He was trying to improve performance so his division could live to fight another day. He eventually gained the approval of most people, and the organization's performance improved significantly, but that gain was a by-product of being a reasonable, consistent leader who was willing to listen and learn as well as teach.

Cattabiani's experience helps us learn another important principle about dialogue: Dialogue is usually a separate process from decision-making. Dialogue is an excellent preliminary process to actually making decisions because (1) it enlarges the pool of information available to decision makers and (2) it builds a great sense of mutual respect and understanding among those who have to implement and live with the decision.

NEGOTIATING TO BUILD TRUST AND GET TO "YES"

In many cases trust is destroyed not by bad motives but by ineffective strategies. We may have needs and goals very similar to those of a roommate, spouse, colleague, or team member; however, an ineffective approach to filling those needs could trigger distrust in the other person. Once distrust or defensiveness sets in, confrontation or withdrawal follows. Once we're in either of those boxes, it's very tough to get out.

In this section we will present some principles that we have found very helpful in avoiding the traps of confrontation. The negotiation style recommended in this book is somewhat on the soft and "reasonable" side, but it also recognizes the need for tough-mindedness. This reasonable approach tries to be tough on principles and gentle on people.

Roger Fisher and William Ury, in their influential book *Getting to Yes* (2002), offer four basic principles they believe should guide any negotiation. These are:

1. Separate the people from the problem.
2. Focus on interests, not positions.

3. Generate a variety of possibilities before deciding what to do.

4. Insist that the result be based on some objective standard.

SEPARATE THE PEOPLE FROM THE PROBLEM

The natural tendency when there are misunderstandings or bruised egos, or struggles over credit or blame, is to focus on personalities. This is a mistake. The problem is the thing that needs solving. The tougher we have to be on the problem, the softer we need to be on people.

Once people feel personally threatened or embarrassed, their energy goes into saving face, not into solving the problem. Keep the focus on the problem, even if you feel another person is at fault. All relational conflict is destructive. On the other hand, as we discussed in Module 1, a healthy level of task conflict can help generate diverse ideas.

Remember, the other person may be mentally constructing the situation in a totally different way. Ask yourself, "How does the other party see the situation?" A good way to find out is to ask questions and then lean forward and really listen. Don't assume anything. Talk to the other person about her perceptions, and then feed them back to be certain you have heard correctly. Your paraphrase of the other person's position must be accurate in her judgment. If it fails, talk some more until you arrive at mutual meaning.

When you focus on problems, not personalities, you are better able to let people blow off steam without your taking it personally. There's an old German proverb that says, "Let anger fly out the windows." It's good advice because it saves both parties from that chain reaction of one person's anger feeding off the other's. All professional negotiators seem to agree: Don't react too quickly to emotional outbursts.

FOCUS ON INTERESTS, NOT POSITIONS

When we negotiate, we often begin by taking a "position." We believe that in the final outcome we can feel good if we have defended that position and not "given too much away." For years, during the Cold War, the Soviets and Americans argued from different positions on limiting strategic weapons. The U.S. team was committed to a position of allowing for at least six missile base inspections per year by each side. The Soviets dug in for a maximum of three. Negotiations were stalemated for weeks over the magic numbers six and three.

The problem was that no one had really thought through the needs and concerns behind the positions they had taken. Both parties had dug into their positions. Someone needed to ask, "What is an inspection? One person walking around a missile site for one day, or a team of eight people spending a week?" The United States was apparently concerned about sufficient frequency and thoroughness in inspections, and the Soviet Union was anxious about how intrusive the inspections would be. But on reflection, it became obvious that the number of inspections was not the major issue. A bigger issue was how much authority the inspection teams would have and how disruptive inspections would be to the military sites where they were conducted (Fisher, Kopelman & Kupfer-Scheider, 1994).

When we coach executives, we challenge them to put their purpose before their initial position. "You are not your position," we tell them, "so don't become too invested in that position." Focus on the goals and principles behind your position, and separate those goals from your own ego (as best you can). There may be other ways of reaching your goal than those offered by the first position you develop. Thus, the next rule: Generate other possibilities.

GENERATE OTHER POSSIBILITIES: MAKE THE PIE BIGGER

When people are arguing over how to divide a pie, most of them never consider the possibility that the pie could be made bigger. Often it can. Good negotiators try to think of options that are of low cost to them but of high benefit to the other party. This strategy is often called "dovetailing" or collaborating. In order to dovetail your needs with the needs of the other party, you have to probe what those needs are and not take the other party's position at face value. When a coworker says that she must have control of the training rooms in your facility every Friday afternoon, that position may be based more on a need for power and control than on a practical need for those rooms at that time. It may also be that she needs guaranteed space over time, but not necessarily every Friday afternoon. The trap is in reacting to that person's position before uncovering her real needs. That act of questioning and probing will usually enable you to come up with alternatives.

For example, in negotiating over price with a box supplier, a purchasing agent from a small company saw an opportunity. The agent learned from the discussion that the supplier was in a cash-flow squeeze after buying a very expensive fabrication machine. The supplier had taken a rigid position on price, and now the purchasing agent knew why. Seizing the opportunity, the agent offered to prepay the supplier for the entire job in exchange for a faster turnaround time *and a major price reduction.*

These opportunities for win-win agreements are too often overlooked because negotiators fail to solve the other side's problems first. Dovetailing your needs with those of the other party requires you to separate your needs from your position, but also to separate the other party's needs from its position.

If alternatives don't come to mind right away, don't give up. Take some time. Huddle with a few associates and friends you trust and do some brainstorming. Come up with creative alternatives based on everything you know about your needs, the needs of the other party, and the facts of the situation at hand. Finally, be sure you create agreements and commitments in such a way that both parties "win." Negotiating is not about who can walk away with the best deal. Negotiating is not a zero-sum game. Short-term negotiating will create win-lose agreements and commitments that will actually erode long-term power.

As a manager, you may need to use your negotiating skills in helping others resolve problems or reach compromises. This process is called *mediation.* Expert managers think twice before intervening in a dispute or disagreement between colleagues or subordinates. It's usually best to wait to be invited, but this is not always possible. For example, if two people have to work together and a disagreement is making it impossible for them to work effectively, their manager may need to become involved. As their manager, you would have to decide whether you want to deal with the people individually or together and determine how willing they are to solve the problem. For cases in which you decide it's necessary to function as mediator, here are some principles to help you develop a strategy:

1. Acknowledge to your people that you know a conflict exists, and propose an approach for resolving it.

2. In studying the positions of both parties, maintain a neutral position regarding the disputants—if not the issues.

3. Keep the discussion issue oriented, not personality oriented. Focus on the impact the conflict is having on performance.

4. Help your people put things in perspective by focusing first on areas on which they might agree. Try to deal with one issue at a time.

5. Remember, you are a facilitator, not a judge. If you assume the role of judge, each person will focus his energy on trying to persuade you rather than on solving the problem and learning something about negotiation. Judges deal with problems; facilitators deal with solutions.

6. Make sure your people fully support the solution they've agreed upon. Don't stop until both parties have a specific plan, and if you sense hesitancy on anyone's part, push for clarification: "Tom, I sense you're less enthusiastic than Carol about this approach. Is there something about it that bothers you?"

INSIST ON USING OBJECTIVE CRITERIA

Fisher and Ury (2002) advise us to make negotiated decisions based on principles, not pressure. Often negotiators make the process a contest of wills: It's my stubbornness and assertiveness against yours. Some people call this yes-we-will-no-we-won't cycle "inefficient disagreement." A way around this trap is to find some objective standards or criteria that will help the parties test the reasonableness of a position. For example, your car is totaled in an accident, and you refuse to argue with the insurance adjuster over a price based upon sentimental value: "My father gave me that car!" or "I've owned that car since I was in high school!" You would have to refer to some standard, such as market value as indicated in the "blue book," or some other objective that both parties could consider reasonable.

It's smart to look for the theories and assumptions behind the position. Fisher and Ury use the following example from a colleague whose parked car was totaled by a dump truck. It was time to settle with the insurance company through an adjuster:

Adjuster:	We have studied your case and have decided the policy applies. That means you are entitled to a settlement of $6,600.
Tom:	I see. How did you reach that figure?
Adjuster:	That was how much we decided the car was worth.
Tom:	I understand, but what standard did you use to determine that amount? Do you know where I can buy a comparable care comparable car for that much?

Adjuster:	How much are you asking?
Tom:	Whatever I'm entitled to under that policy. I found a second-hand car just like mine for about $7,700. Adding sales and excise tax it would come to about $8,000.
Adjuster:	$8,000! That's too much!
Tom:	I'm not asking for $8,000, or $6,000 or $10,000, but for fair compensation. Do you agree that it's only fair I get enough to replace the car?
Adjuster:	Okay, I'll offer you $7,000. That's the highest I can go. Company policy.
Tom:	How does the company figure that?
Adjuster:	Look, $7,000 is all you get. Take it or leave it.
Tom:	$7,000 may be fair. I don't know. I certainly understand your position if you're bound to company policy, but unless you can state objectively why that amount is what I'm entitled to, I think I'll do better in court. Why don't we study the matter and talk again? Is Wednesday at eleven a good time to talk?
Adjuster:	Okay Mr. Griffith, I've got an ad here in today's paper offering an '89 Taurus for $6,800
Tom:	I see, what does it say about the mileage?
Adjuster:	49,000. Why?
Tom:	Because mine had only 25,000 miles. How many dollars does that increase the worth in your book?
Adjuster:	Let me see . . . $450.
Tom:	Assuming the $6,800 as possible base, that brings the figure to $7,250. Does the ad say anything about a radio?
Adjuster:	No.
Tom:	How much extra in your book?
Adjuster:	That's $125.
Tom:	What about air conditioning? (Fisher & Ury, 2002, pp. 92–94).

Half an hour later, Tom walked out with a check for $8,024. Notice how unemotional Tom was. He was working from a need to ground the discussion of price on objective criteria acceptable to both parties. He didn't lose control, and he didn't cave in to personal pressure. He knew his appeal to objective criteria was fair and reasonable. Negotiating can be an emotional ordeal, but good negotiators don't lose control. They keep dragging an emotional discussion back to the issue at hand.

ANALYSIS Your Effectiveness as a Negotiator

Objective To help gauge your skill as a negotiator, this exercise asks you to focus on a specific example of a past negotiation in which you participated and to evaluate your performance in light of the information provided in the Learning section for this competency.

Directions Take an issue or event from your life in which you needed to engage in some negotiation or secure a commitment from another person or party. You can use any situation you found challenging, for example, buying a product you later wanted to return or needing to lodge a complaint about a service. You may have needed to negotiate a change in your shift during a summer job, or perhaps you had to solve a problem in a personal or work relationship.

Prepare a brief memo concerning your experience. Describe the issue in terms of the negotiating techniques you have learned in this competency and perhaps others that you have found helpful. Evaluate your negotiating performance. How could you now improve it?

Reflection Sometimes our perceptions of our abilities are inaccurate, we base them on flawed recollections or beliefs that don't match up with reality. Identifying a specific example as grounds for a claim makes the argument more persuasive, as noted in the discussion of critical thinking in the introductory chapter of this text. Successful negotiators do their homework to make sure that they have as much credible evidence as possible to support their claims and further their interests.

PRACTICE Standing on the Firing Line

Objective An important aspect of negotiating is the ability to communicate your own position and views on an issue, but also to understand the other party's position—including the strong emotions and feelings that often accompany that position. Emotions are the footprints of values, values that people feel are under some kind of threat. The purpose of the following exercise is to help you manage the emotional side of a public discussion about a difficult issue.

Directions In the two cases described below, you read about two people who are in a position that requires them to manage some difficult and negative emotions in a public setting. In groups of six to eight people, count off 1–2, 1–2 . . . so that each person will have the responsibility of playing one of the two roles, either Boyd Sterling or Karen Williams. (The gender of the person playing the role is not important. You can change the name of characters as needed.)

Your instructor can select a couple of you to take a turn standing on the firing line and playing the role of the person in the case. The rest of you will function as highly engaged audience members who have a deep interest in the issues at hand. Each of you will prepare to be on the firing line in one role and to be an audience member in the other role. Take 10 minutes to study the role before your instructor calls on someone to take the firing line.

We have included some sample questions and comments that audience members can use, but, as an audience member, feel free to go beyond these to comments of your own. The idea is not to "destroy" the person on the firing line but to create a realistic and challenging level of pressure.

The person on the firing line should try his or her best to apply the principles in the section on "negotiating agreements and commitments" to this situation. Give the person some feedback after each performance and discuss as a group what you're learning about handling such situations effectively. Where are the traps to avoid, and what kinds of responses seem to be most effective?

Role 1: Boyd Sterling, Chief of Police, Roseville

You are the Chief of Police in Roseville, a Midwestern community of 36,000 people. Two of your officers have been accused of brutality by a homeless man, David Oakeson. Oakeson came into the area about six months ago. He lives out of his car most of the time but occasionally spends a night in a local shelter provided by the Coalition for the Homeless, a local charity organization.

Oakeson claims that officers Wilson and Ortega pulled him over on a Saturday evening and ordered him out of his car. When Oakeson insisted he had not been speeding, they allegedly began threatening him if he didn't leave town. Oakeson said that an argument ensued and that the officers clubbed him with their flashlights. He claims they threatened his life if he didn't leave.

The incident became more visible when two other homeless people said they were willing to testify that Wilson and Ortega had used unnecessary force with them as well on separate occasions. Consistent with policy in handling investigations into officer behavior, you have suspended the officers, with pay, while you conduct the investigation.

You are meeting at this moment with two members of the Roseville City Council and several local leaders from public interest groups, such as the Coalition for the Homeless. People at the meeting are quite upset and are directing most of their questions and comments at you.

Questions/Comments

1. I think I see a pattern here, and it really has me concerned. I hear people at the shelter complain about the police. They say they are handled roughly. They are sometimes cuffed and pushed, and they are verbally abused. I'm sick of hearing about tough, mean cops. You must know this kind of thing goes on.

2. Last night the article in the paper said these guys had been suspended, but with pay. What kind of a statement is that to the community—that you can manhandle citizens and then get a free vacation?

3. What do you think is the problem here, Chief? What's the cause of this kind of thing really?

4. What kind of training are officers getting about dealing with the homeless or the indigent? I get the impression they aren't getting any kind of training in this area at all.

Role 2: Karen Williams, Executive Director, Cold Harbor Research Center

You are Karen Williams, executive director of the Cold Harbor Cancer Research Institute. With a staff of 47 people, most of them with advanced degrees in microbiology or chemistry, the Center is a significant and prestigious employer in the town of Cold Harbor (population 56,000). The Center has struggled, since its founding 12 years ago, to secure funding from private and public sources. You have been director for only one year, having come to Cold Harbor from Boston, where you worked in hospital administration. It has been an especially difficult year, because both state and federal grants, for which the Center has historically qualified, have been cut.

Last month, you received a visit from the attorney of Robert Knowles, a wealthy entrepreneur who has recently moved into the community. Knowles, now retired, made his fortune in the southeastern part of the country, developing harvesting and processing equipment for tobacco farmers. He has, for over a decade, been an active force in the tobacco industry's lobbying efforts in Washington.

During a brief visit in your office, the attorney informed you that Knowles has decided to offer the Center a $10.8 million endowment to be used for any purpose its board of directors deems appropriate. There is only one stipulation: The Center would have to change its name to The Robert Knowles Cancer Research Institute.

Fearing that the Center is facing financial demise, you made a verbal agreement with the attorney that you would make every effort to secure the approval of the board of directors to change the name and accept the funding.

That evening, you called Knowles and asked him to have lunch with you to discuss the issues. You became more convinced, as you listened to him describe his motives and interests, that it would be appropriate to accept the funding and change the name of the Center. Knowles claimed that he is trying to "give something back" to the country that has made him wealthy. He has a niece who has been diagnosed with a rare form of cancer, and he himself has been diagnosed with prostate cancer.

One week later, having met with a quorum of the board and gaining their approval, you announced the board's approval and held a brief press conference attended by Knowles and several members of the board.

Within hours, members of the Cold Harbor City Council were denouncing the decision through the local press. Citizens have written angry letters to the city newspapers, and the television stations in the state are beginning to carry the story. Under pressure, you have agreed to hold a press conference to discuss the decision.

Be prepared to respond to questions from the press, members of the city council, and local citizens.

Questions/Comments

1. How can the Center justify accepting money from a person who has so aggressively championed the cause of the tobacco industry? The moral inconsistency seems too obvious to consider, but apparently it needs some more considering.

2. What exactly is Mr. Knowles hoping to accomplish by having the Center carry his name?

3. This Center was created by donations from about half a dozen donors, all of whom were local citizens or at least attached to this community in some significant way. What do you have to say to the citizens of this community who feel that their memory and contribution are being undermined by this decision?

4. What will you do if the community insists that the name of the Center not be changed? Surely you've considered this possibility.

Reflection   Situations that require negotiation often are linked to fundamental values and thus may have ethical implications. Going beneath surface positions to identify any values that may be in conflict can be an important step toward finding an effective solution.

APPLICATION   Negotiating at Work

Objective   This exercise is designed to help you think about restructuring negotiations in ways that increase the possibility of "win-win" outcomes.

Directions   Think of a fairly small change that you would like to see made in your organization or in one of your classes. For example, you might want to convince a coworker to help you out on a project or get a professor to extend the deadline for a paper. Write up a plan to help you successfully negotiate to make that change happen. We recommend using the following steps:

1. Describe the change you would like and explain why you want that change (identify your interests).

2. Describe what you think are the reasons your proposal might be rejected. Try to think in terms of both the positions your negotiation partner might take as well as the true interests behind those positions.

3. Identify some options to help make the pie bigger. What would you be willing to give up in exchange for a negotiated agreement? What would your negotiation partner be interested in getting in exchange for their agreement?

4. Given the interests that you have identified, estimate how likely it is that you will be successful in negotiating your proposed change.

5. If appropriate, use your plan to start a negotiation and then write about your experience. Be sure to reflect on how the negotiation process unfolded as well as on the actual outcome.

Reflection   It is easy to become myopic in negotiation situations; negotiations that are narrowly focused are often the most difficult to resolve in a "win-win" fashion. Learning how to expand negotiations by including multiple interests can help to "make the pie bigger" and can also identify other areas where changes would be beneficial.

Module 4 Competency 5   Implementing and Sustaining Change

ASSESSMENT   Changes in My Organization

Objective   For this assessment you are asked to consider how changes are implemented in your organization. This task will help you obtain insights into the differences between successful and unsuccessful approaches to managing change.

Directions   Think about two changes that have taken place in an organization with which you have been involved. The organization may be a work organization, a school-related organization, or a community group. On a separate piece of paper, carefully describe the following:

1. An implemented change that, from your perspective, was needed, was implemented, and was successful long after implementation.

2. A change that was attempted but was not successfully implemented .

3. From what you have observed, why was the first change implemented successfully but not the second one? If you can distinguish the content of the idea from the methods for implementation, identify the extent to which the success (or lack of success) of the proposed changes was due to content versus the implementation strategies.

4. Write down one change that you would like to make in that organization. If you received approval to make that change, what is the most important thing you would do in your efforts to implement that change? Why?

Reflection   Successfully managing change in organizations is difficult. Although much can be learned by studying how other organizations have managed change, observing successful and unsuccessful change initiatives in your own organization is also important because some roadblocks to change are specific to a particular organization's culture.

LEARNING   Implementing and Sustaining Change

Our society is currently experiencing change at an exponential rate. Change comes from many different sources including political and governmental initiatives, economic conditions, consumer preferences, social values, and advances in technology and knowledge. Although any of these sources of change can impact the way we work and live, for many of us, changes in technology have the most obvious impact on how we work. For example, today we can use our GPS to find a coffee shop near the beach where we can use our cell phones and laptops to keep working on our PowerPoint presentations even when we are on vacation!

These common tools look quite different today from what they did when they were invented, as described by Acohido and his colleagues (2007). For example, the first hand-held cell phone weighed nearly 2 pounds and cost $4,000, when it was introduced in 1983. Also in 1983, the first portable IBM-compatible computer was launched by Compaq—with a $3,000 price tag and weighing in at 28 pounds. Power-Point became available in a Windows version in 1990 and with the invention of WiFi in 1991, we found ourselves in a world where coffee shops could become workplaces. Of course until 2000, when the quality of satellite signals improved (James, 2009), most of us relied on maps, rather than a GPS system to find the coffee shop (and some of us still do!). As technology continues to advance, we soon may even be able to recharge our wireless batteries using WiFi—if Airnergy, an invention that debuted at the 2010 CES Tech Expo, lives up to its marketing (Long, 2010).

This brief history lesson serves as a reminder that how we do things today may be totally unlike how we do things tomorrow. But making the transition from one way of working to another is rarely easy. To successfully implement and sustain change, managers first must understand the forces for change as well as reasons for resistance to change.

UNDERSTANDING THE FORCES FOR CHANGE AND RESISTANCE TO PLANNED CHANGE

Changes are necessary in order to accomplish goals and objectives, such as improving efficiency, improving cost effectiveness, competing for money and resources, or improving services to clients. However, it has become fashionable to describe all "planned change" efforts as necessary, and to describe people who resist proposed change as "unwilling to leave their comfort zones," or simply, "resistant." We need to make the point at the outset of this section that not all proposed changes are beneficial. Many organizations have been run into the ground from too many changes being imposed too quickly. Some changes *should* be resisted because they are bad for the organization and the people in it.

When a change is being considered, the manager must ask whether a change is truly necessary and, if so, what specifically should be changed. More than 60 years ago, Kurt Lewin (1951) proposed a model called **force field analysis** that can be used to help managers understand whether a change is needed and whether that change is likely to be successful. Lewin's model is an analogy based on laws of physics: An object at rest will remain at rest unless the forces on the object to move are greater than the forces on it to remain stable. For example, when your car is parked in the driveway with the emergency brake on, it will remain there, in a stable condition, even if your neighbor's nine-year-old son decides to push on the car to try to move it. The emergency brake is a stronger stabilizing force than is the boy's force. If the car is put into the neutral gear with the emergency brake off, however, the forces for its stability are diminished, and it becomes more possible that the young boy could disrupt the equilibrium.

Similarly, there are forces outside as well as within organizations that are pressures for change and forces that are resistances to change. When the forces for change are stronger than the resistant forces, change will occur; likewise, when the forces against change are stronger than the pressures for change, change will not occur.

FORCES FOR CHANGE—SHOULD WE CHANGE?

Many of the forces for change affecting organizations are the result of changes that have occurred in the external environment. For example, changes in government regulations, technology, economic conditions, and social values can all create pressure on organizations to change.

Some forces for change are driven by internal initiatives that may or may not be related to external forces for change. For example if a company makes a strategic decision to pursue a low cost strategy, there will be pressure to improve efficiency and cost-effectiveness. In contrast, a strategy that focuses on differentiation might create pressure to improve product quality and customer satisfaction.

A key assumption of the open systems quadrant of the competing values framework is that organizations need to align their strategies with the external environment. Internal initiatives that are not aligned with external pressures can be highly risky.

RESISTANCE TO CHANGE—CAN WE CHANGE?

Even necessary and beneficial changes may encounter resistance. In some cases resistance is based on structural factors such as limited resources, standardized routines, or an organizational culture that values tradition. Sometimes changes are resisted for interpersonal reasons—for example, some people may resist any idea that they did not come up with themselves or may resist ideas from certain people but not from others.

In many cases, however, employees have legitimate reasons to be resistant to change. Often fear of change relates to the possibility of economic loss, such as when a reorganization is being considered that may result in demotions or job losses. Employees also are likely to resist changes such as automation or new software programs that make their skills seem outdated or unnecessary. Similarly, changes that require employees to take more risks are likely to encounter resistance, particularly in organizations that have not traditionally rewarded risk taking. Although some employees may appreciate being given new responsibilities, others may feel overwhelmed by changes in their job requirements.

Non-economic changes may also face resistance if they affect employee status or relationships. Although organizations have public missions and purposes, they also provide a social environment in which people associate and form friendships. For many people, their work organization is a primary source of social interaction. When these patterns of interaction are likely to be disrupted, people often resist change.

Leading change effectively requires that managers understand the reasons and emotions behind the resistance just as thoroughly as they understand the reason for implementing the change. Change must be carefully planned, and the impact of the change must be carefully evaluated so that ill-advised changes may be avoided. Once the decision has been made that a change in the work processes, procedures, or structure should occur, the manager must determine: (1) the design of the specific change that needs to occur, and (2) how the change will be implemented.

DESIGNING CHANGE

Designing change involves considering various alternative courses of action, anticipating consequences of such actions, and choosing which specific course of action is appropriate. For example, assume an expensive private college is concerned about falling enrollments due to economic conditions. You have been asked to come up with a proposal for a faculty initiative to help increase the percentage of accepted students who decide to attend the school. In the past, the faculty have not been involved with students until they arrive on campus to take classes. You might begin by brainstorming about different ways faculty can encourage prospective students to enroll. For example, faculty could contact prospective students by telephone, email, or a hand-written letter. Alternatively, faculty could arrange for dinners with groups of prospective students in different locations in the areas where the college recruits. Once you have generated a number of different options, you can then prepare a force field analysis to help you decide which option is the most likely to be accepted by the faculty. The following steps are necessary to set up a force field analysis:

1. List the driving forces and the resisting forces.
2. Examine each force and assess its strength—not all forces are equal. Note the possible consequences of each force and its value. You may wish to assign a numerical value to each force.
3. Identify those forces over which you have some influence or control.
4. Analyze the list to determine how to implement the change. Your analysis will reveal several natural choices for action:
   - Increase the strength of driving forces
   - Add new driving forces
   - Decrease the strength of resisting forces
   - Remove some of the resisting forces
   - Determine whether any of the resisting forces can be changed into driving forces

As a change leader, you need to consider more than the length of the list. Think also about the importance or relative force of the individual items. Some items may have more impact on a situation than others. To make the list more useful, you would need to assign weights or values to each item.

You should also be aware that research has shown that the last three strategies, which involve diminishing the effect of resisting forces, are more effective than the first two strategies. Paradoxically, increasing the driving forces often serves only to increase the resistance. Once you have worked through this process, you have a chart of the driving and resisting forces to the proposed change, the relative weight of each force, and an assessment of which forces you can influence. Identifying the items over which you have some influence should tell you where to direct your efforts and planning when implementing your changes.

To go back to our college admissions example, the primary driving force is the same for each option—falling enrollments result in reduced budgets and possible faculty layoffs. There may be some additional driving forces that could be used to encourage faculty cooperation, however. For example, are faculty evaluated on their service to the college? If so, that can serve as a force that will help move faculty to participate in the admissions program. It might seem in this example that getting faculty to participate would be a "no brainer." After all, they have a vested interest in making sure that the college recruits a strong incoming group of students. It is only logical to help with that effort. But leading change, even on a modest scale, is not reducible to logic alone.

Change is a social-emotional process, and people must be willingly recruited and engaged in the effort. Change leadership is not coercion. Bradford and Cohen (1984) describe the work of change leadership as having three vital components: (1) creating a shared vision of the future, (2) sharing responsibility and ownership for achieving the vision, and (3) focusing on developing the capacity of the people involved to perform at their best. This view of change draws on the theme of transformational change, as opposed to transactional change. In transformational change, as described in the pioneering work of James McGregor Burns (1978, 1984), the function of leadership is to engage followers, not merely to activate them. Transformational leaders combine the hopes and talents of people with a focus on a common goal. To combine needs and aspirations and goals in a common enterprise, and in the process make better citizens of both leaders and followers" (quoted in Rost, 1993, p. 122). Transactional changes are made on the surface and are usually short-lived. Transformational changes are rooted in the growth of a common purpose. A purpose is more than a goal. Box M4.5 describes an example of implementing change in practice by a leader who succeeded in constructing a sense of purpose against the odds.

BOX M4.5 CHANGING THE WORST TO THE BEST

When U.S. Navy Captain, Michael Abrashoff, took command of the USS *Benfold*, a destroyer armed with state-of-the-art missile detection systems, he was shocked when the 330 crew members cheered in derision as the out-going captain left the ship. As indicated by this event, morale on the *Benfold* was dangerously low, and cynicism and anger sky-high. The cost of recruiting one sailor and sending him through boot camp is over $35,000. Training throughout a first tour of duty averages more than $100,000 per sailor. Only 30 percent of those recruited sign up for a second term of enlistment, but crew members on the *Benfold* were leaving the ship, and the Navy itself, in even larger numbers. The performance of the ship was terrible by every standard used by the Navy to measure performance: low number of crew members becoming qualified in technical specialties through training; crew performance on battle-readiness; number of grievances filed for harassment, racial discrimination and other charges of mistreatment, and so forth. Captain Abrashoff realized that the rumors he had heard about the *Benfold* were apparently true: he had accepted command of what was possibly the worst ship in the U.S. Navy.

When Abrashoff left the *Benfold* after a 20-month tour in the Gulf, the *Benfold* was the best-performing ship in the Pacific fleet. This transformation was accomplished with largely the same crew members who were in place when Abrashoff took command. The vast majority had re-enlisted, and the list of names of personnel requesting a spot on the *Benfold* was pages long. In one year, the reduction in turnover alone saved the Navy $1.6 million in personnel-related costs, but the benefits of building a high-performance crew far exceeded the money saved. Sailors spending time on the *Benfold* went on to other assignments with superb training and motivation. The *Benfold* had become an incubator of high-performing technicians and team players. How had Abrashoff done what many of his peers believed was impossible?

First, Captain Abrashoff decided he would not go into telling mode, but into "asking" mode. He determined to interview every member of the crew individually. From the moment he took command, Abrashoff promised himself he would "treat every encounter with every person on the ship as the most important thing in my world at that moment" (Abrashoff, 2001). In the first month of almost non-stop interviews, Abrashoff would ask questions such as, "What do you like most about the *Benfold*? What do you like least? If you could change one thing around here, what would it be?" "Tell me about one thing you've done on this ship that you're proud of?" "What led you to join the Navy in the first place?" (LeBarre, 1999, p. 114). This kind of patient, relentless listening was a daunting task, and Abrashoff initially faced cynicism and resistance from some crew members. Every time his own energy or patience started to sag, he would feel renewed when a crew member offered an idea on how to improve the ship's performance. As the weeks passed, the energy level aboard ship gained momentum, and the *Benfold* became a seedbed of innovation and hard work. The crew realized they had a leader who was willing to listen and wanted to learn, but who also had high expectations of them. His focus was on purpose, not command. Abrashoff says he learned aboard that ship, "The most important thing that a captain can do is to see the ship through the eyes of the crew" (LeBarre, 1999, p. 114).

But Abrashoff began to see that *he* also had to change. He had to unlearn some of the traditions he had been taught, such as the tendency to "command and control to the max." He had to become less concerned about his own career and looking good in front of his leaders, and more concerned about the growth of his people. If he wanted to retain his crew, he had to help "redeem" them. Most of these young recruits were trying to get a foothold in their lives and in the world. Many were from difficult backgrounds, surrounded by drugs and violence. These sailors knew what they were trying to get away from, but not always sure what they were pursuing. Abrashoff decided that he and his crew would have to learn a different way of thinking and acting. Everyone would assume responsibility for making the *Benfold* the best it could be. In the process, everyone would achieve important personal goals and get a better purchase on their own lives.

His interviews were a powerful tool for building trust, but he also set stretch goals for performance. The *Benfold* was no country club under his leadership. He pushed the crew to think of ways to stop doing mindless, non-value-added work—like scraping and repainting endlessly—and do work that was more important and interesting. These sailors thought of literally hundreds of ways to save time, money, and effort, and use those resources to become better at their jobs. Michael Abrashoff and his crew created a tradition of constant growth and high performance that still thrives aboard the USS *Benfold*.

Michael Abrashoff took the risk of not hiding behind his formal authority as ship's captain and began to learn from his crew. He applied a different theory of change to his role, believing that fear and deference to authority are less motivating in the long term than the excitement of learning and being part of a successful team.

FOUR APPROACHES TO IMPLEMENTING CHANGE

Here we will examine some approaches to implementing change that are used in day-to-day life. The first three approaches were identified some years ago by Chin and Benne (1976). For simplicity, we have given them straightforward titles. The first strategy, Telling, uses logical arguments to implement change and is most consistent with the rational goal quadrant of the competing values framework. The second strategy, Forcing, uses forms of leverage such as the threat of being fired or being ostracized, consistent with the more control-oriented approach of the internal process quadrant. The Participating strategy fits with the human relations quadrant and emphasizes using open dialogue to pursuing win-win strategies. The fourth strategy, Transforming, comes from work by Quinn (2000) and fits best with the open systems quadrant and its focus on the external environment.

It is important to note that all four of these strategies may be appropriate, depending on the specific circumstances facing the manager in a change situation. Table M4.2 locates all four strategies within the competing values framework and presents questions that a person who wants to bring about change might ask of herself to help decide which strategy is the most appropriate for a particular circumstance.

TELLING

The telling strategy assumes that people are guided by reason. If they decide it is in their best interest to change, they'll gladly do so. It is further reasoned that any resistance to change could only be the product of ignorance and superstition. To counter that resistance, the change agent just needs to educate the people to the truth and their resistance will dissolve.

The telling strategy is most effective for normal situations. Someone tells me my tire is going flat and that I need to get it changed. I can verify this by looking at the tire. I can make a clear cost-benefit assessment; I must have a good tire to drive my car. I am not emotionally tied to not getting the work done, and I am quite certain that when it is done I can drive safely again. I know what to do, and no learning is required. That is normal or "in-the-box" change. It is relatively easy. But what if someone were to tell me that I must change the way I drive because it is causing undue wear and tear on my car? It will be a good investment, I am told, and all I have to do is attend a weekend conference. Now I am out-of-the-box. I have no way of assessing immediately if that person is right or wrong. Besides, I would have to attend classes and learn a whole new way of driving. It does not sound like a good idea for me.

Telling is not as effective in out-of-the box contexts because it has a narrow, cognitive view of human systems. It fails to incorporate values, attitudes, and feelings. Thus, while people may understand why they should change, they are often not willing to make the painful changes inherent in more complex situations. They simply want and expect to get conformity.

FORCING

The forcing strategy persuades people to change or face some kind of punishment or sanction. This strategy often involves money and politics. Political power is exerted by

TABLE M4.2 Four Strategies for Changing Human Systems and the Questions Change Agents Should Ask Themselves

Human Relations Quadrant—Collaborate	*Open Systems Quadrant—Create*
The Participative Strategy	*The Transformational Strategy*
Method: Engaging others in conceptualizing change	Method: Modeling change for others
Objective: Alignment of the actors in a win-win dialogue	Objective: Alignment with changing reality
Is there a focus on human process?	Am I aware of the realities of the emergent system?
Is everyone included in an open dialogue?	What are my patterns of self-deception?
Do I model supportive communication?	Are my values and behaviors aligned?
Is everyone's position being clarified?	Am I freed from external sanctions?
Are decisions being made through participation?	Do I have a vision of the common good?
Is there commitment to a win-win strategy?	Do I operate at the edge of chaos?
Are the people cohesive?	Do I maintain reverence for others?
	Do I inspire others to enact their best self?
	Am I engaging in unconventional or paradoxical ways?
	Have I changed myself as a model for the system to change?
Internal Process Quadrant—Control	*Rational Goal Quadrant—Compete*
The Forcing Strategy	*The Telling Strategy*
Method: Leveraging others to change	Method: Telling others to change
Objective: Align the change target with established authority	Objective: Align change target with established facts
Is my authority firmly established?	Am I within my expertise?
Is the legitimacy of my directives clear?	Have I gathered all the facts?
Am I capable and willing to impose sanctions?	Have I done a rigorous analysis?
Is there a clear performance-reward linkage?	Will my conclusions withstand criticism?
Am I controlling the information flow?	Are my arguments logical?
Am I controlling the design of the context?	Do I have a forum for instruction?
Are the people complying?	Do the people understand my argument?

Adapted from Robert Quinn, *Change the World: How Ordinary People Can Accomplish Extraordinary Results.* San Francisco: Jossey-Bass, 2000. Used with permission.

applying sanctions when others fail to align themselves with the change agent. Economic power is exerted by controlling the flow of resources, either within an organization or in terms of salary increases to the person who is resisting change. When political power comes to bear, those with more power apply sanctions upon those with less power. Hence, the strategy is: Identify and apply levers of power, thus forcing the change target to comply.

The forcing strategy tends to work in the short term, but it usually evokes anger, resistance, and damage to the fundamental relationship. Thus, it is not likely to result in the kind of voluntary commitment that is necessary for healthy and enthusiastic change that will sustain the system.

The way for the normal person, acting as a change agent, to behave is to engage in the following two step process:

1. Tell the target why he needs to change.
2. If telling fails, figure out a way to force the person to change.

This two-step process is so normalized that most of us do it over and over again, especially in relationships in which we think we are in "control." Since we are seldom interested in changing ourselves, we repeat this process while refusing to recognize that in using force we damage the relationship and seldom obtain our desired long-term outcome. The fact that we seldom obtain our desired end seems to make no difference, however. We refuse to learn. For this reason, the reader might find hope in our third strategy.

PARTICIPATING

The participating strategy involves a more collaborative change process and thus is consistent with the human relations quadrant of the competing values framework. Change targets are still guided by a rational calculus; however, this calculus extends beyond self-interest to incorporate the meanings, habits, norms, and institutional policies that contribute to the formation of human culture. The participative change agent welcomes the input of others as equals in the change process. Change does not come by simply providing information, as in the telling strategy. Rather, it requires the change agent to focus on clarifying and reconstructing values. In this model, the change agent attempts to bring to light all values, working through conflicts embedded in the larger collective. The emphasis is on communication and cooperation with the change target. The motto might be: Involve the change target in an honest dialogue, while mutually learning the way to win–win solutions. Yet this strategy is difficult to understand and implement. Consider the following illustration from Bob Quinn.

As an undergraduate, I took a rigorous course entirely devoted to learning a single skill. The skill was active listening, whereby the listener is not just passive as another person speaks but actively watches his or her own behavior so that he or she can accurately hear what the other person is trying to communicate. The supporting philosophy was the essence of the Participating strategy.

For the rest of my life, that course had provided me with a source of power for both myself and others. I have been able to use the Participating strategy to move through many seemingly impossible situations. Yet I know that not everyone left that course with the same abilities. During the last week of classes a student raised his hand and asked, "Professor, what if I do all these listening things, and the person still will not do what I want?" The deeply disappointed professor shrank behind his podium. After all we had been through, this student could not comprehend the most basic point of the Participating strategy; he could not comprehend the notion of reducing control enough to join with another human being in learning and mutual creation of a win–win solution. This notion remains a mystery to many people, even those who claim to be experts at active listening.

There is still another mystery associated with the participating strategy. Here we are reminded of a story told by Steven Covey. A skeptical CEO told Covey, "Every time I try win-win, I lose." Covey replied, "Then you did not do win-win." The paradox is that this strategy calls for the reduction of control while remaining clear and strong about one's underlying values and intent. It is not a strategy of weakness, but of strength—the kind of strength that many people lack. Participatory strategies and active listening both require that each person allow others to express their truth while insisting that his own truth be heard.

Because participating strategies and active listening are so difficult to understand and implement, they are seldom used as they are intended, but are used instead to manipulate. The change agent determines a solution and then asks a group to join in a discussion. Any answer they come up with is acceptable, as long as it is the "right" one. Because so many people experience the participating strategy as a manipulative technique, they become deeply cynical. Some crew members of the *Benfold* probably believed their new captain was just manipulating them when he began interviewing each crew member individually. Eventually, when they saw him listening carefully to their ideas—and encouraging them to implement their ideas—resistance morphed into support.

TRANSFORMING

Quinn (2000) has suggested a fourth strategy that complements the above three. It is called the transforming strategy, and it is a part of something he calls Advanced Change Theory, a set of action principles for effectively introducing change. It is rooted in the teachings of such people as Jesus, Thoreau, Gandhi, and Martin Luther King Jr. Although it fits most closely with the open systems quadrant because of its emphasis on flexibility and its focus on external reality, the transforming strategy also assumes that a deeply held set of core values are driving the manager's behavior. As explained in more detail below, this may result in the leader acting in ways that attempt to alter the external environment, rather than adapt to it.

One of the formative voices of the nineteenth century was that of Henry David Thoreau, a friend of Ralph Waldo Emerson. Both men were concerned about transcending the pressures for conformity in an industrialized society. Thoreau was born in 1817 and entered Harvard at 16 years of age. After his graduation, he briefly taught school, but after some time he gave up teaching and other professional pursuits. For a time, he lived alone in a simple cabin he built on Walden Pond. His writing about this experiment in solitude would later become renowned. In his essay, *Civil Disobedience,* he wrote:

Action from principle, the perception and the performance of right, changes things and relations; it is essentially revolutionary, and does not consist wholly with anything which was. It not only divides states and churches, it divides families; aye, it divides the individual, separating the diabolical in him from the divine.

Reflecting on this statement, Quinn (2000) suggests that altering our behavior to reflect what we really value is revolutionary because principle-driven actions tend to be outside the normal boundaries of exchange and transaction. When someone engages in a new behavior based on principle, it challenges the norms. The person with a moral purpose is usually willing to endure punishment in order to pursue the purpose. Such principled behavior sends the dreaded signal that perhaps "the emperor has no clothes." It questions whether the present system is moving toward stagnation and decay or toward new levels of life and complexity and productivity. People in the system split into camps, one embracing the new behavior and the other condemning it—hence, the division of humanity into states, churches, and families.

Yet Thoreau's statement suggests that even the individual is split. In the face of principled behavior, the individual observer is constantly required to choose between preservation of the current self and the creation of the new self. When we discipline the self in the pursuit of higher purpose, a new self emerges. This process is exhilarating because it makes us aware of the profound power we each hold within us. On the other hand, when we know that we should be walking a higher road and we do not, we acknowledge the diabolical that also lurks within. We become divided. We lose psychic energy. We become flat, dull, and without enthusiasm, easy prey for those who would dominate or manipulate us.

Thoreau's statement about principle suggests that moral power plays a major role in the transformational process. All change theories are rooted in assumptions of morality, but the assumptions differ greatly. Before we take any action, we ask ourselves: What is the right thing to do in this situation? The name for this process is "moral reasoning." There are different levels of moral reasoning. The moral reasoning we see most frequently is based on the assumption that people are externally driven and self-interested. Quinn argues that the transformational strategy only works when we become internally driven and focused on others. It is thus at a higher level of moral reasoning. It is based in principle, not in situational pressures.

So most of the time most of us witness and enact change strategies that reflect and support the norms and expectations of the group. We are driven by the external conditions in which we find ourselves. Very few theories include the role of internalized principles; few theories suggest the need for a transformational change agent who is willing to sacrifice self in the pursuit of the collective good.

To observe transformational ability, we cannot observe normal people doing normal things. We must observe people who are outside the box. In order to develop transformational capability, we cannot be normal people doing normal things. We must stand outside the box. To do that, we need to go inside ourselves and ask who we are, what we stand for, and what impact we really want to have. Within ourselves we find principle, purpose, and courage. There we find the capacity not only to withstand the pressures of the external system but to actually transform the external system. We change the world by changing ourselves.

ANALYSIS   Reorganizing the Legal Division

Objective   This exercise asks you to analyze a change process in a series of steps. It is important to take time to respond to the questions as you read through the scenario, as each set has a different purpose. For example, the first set of questions gives you an opportunity to practice some of your creative-thinking skills.

Directions	Read the following case study and answer the questions that follow each section.
The Relocation and Reorganization Begins	As part of a new relocation and reorganization plan for the legal division of a large corporation, the director, Paul Lindford, decided to set up a central paralegal pool. This pool would handle all of the research reports for the entire office, which consisted of 20 attorneys. In the old location, the paralegals had been located in offices adjoining those occupied by the attorneys for whom they worked. Several paralegals even had their own small private offices.
	The nature of the firm was such that many of the attorneys traveled a considerable amount and consequently were away from their offices for extended periods. During these absences the paralegal assistants had little to do.
Stop Reading	Respond to the following questions.

1. Based on the limited information, what advantages of the change approved by Paul Lindford can you identify?
2. What might be the response of the paralegal assistants to this change?
3. What might be the response of the attorneys to this change?
4. If you were Paul, what problems would you anticipate at this point?

The Case Continues	For some time, Paul had felt that establishing a central paralegal pool would result in a saving of personnel as well as more efficient use of the paralegal staff. Paul had been reluctant to make this change in the old location, where the attorneys and paralegal assistants were accustomed to working in adjoining offices. But now, with the new office, he felt the time was right to try out the new arrangement.
	Two weeks before the move, Paul asked Ashley Ricci to coordinate the move for the paralegal assistants, even though she was not the most senior paralegal. There were two others of higher rank, with more experience than Ashley, but Paul felt good about his choice. Ashley had a lot of energy and was well liked by her coworkers. She seemed to best fulfill the requirements for the job as he saw it. She had worked on some special projects for Paul in the past, and she had been exceptional. At this point, Paul had not really given any thought to who would be directing the paralegal assistants when the move was complete.
Stop Reading	Respond to the following questions.

1. Paul has chosen to implement this change when the general office moves into a new location. Why does he see this timing as advantageous? Do you agree?
2. If you were Paul, would you have chosen Ashley to coordinate the move? Why or why not?
3. What mistakes do you believe Paul has made so far in the implementation process?

The Case Continues	Paul announced his plans for the new central paralegal pool one week before the move. It was received with little enthusiasm. Several assistants objected and threatened to leave rather than accept the change. Some insisted they could not work for more than one person; others complained they would be unable to work in a small cubicle office in a large room. Many of the attorneys affected by the new policy were resentful as well. They believed that a personal paralegal assistant was essential for efficient conduct of their business.
	Although Paul knew this change was unpopular, he believed the feelings of the attorneys would change as the benefits of the more efficient service became apparent. Although many of the attorneys probably felt the loss of a personal paralegal assistant as something in the nature of a "demotion," Paul felt they should understand and help make the new plan work. He felt that the few diehards should not be pampered.
	During the first few weeks after the move, Ashley did everything she could to maintain the workload at a high level and hoped that, as a result, the complaints from the attorneys would decrease. Their complaints centered around (1) errors made by paralegal assistants who were

unfamiliar with the attorneys' caseloads, (2) the slowness of the paralegal staff in bringing back final drafts of the reports that had been assigned to them, and (3) the excessive time they themselves had to spend in minor research efforts that had previously been handled by their personal paralegal assistants.

Stop Reading   Respond to the following questions.

1. What are the specific sources of resistance from the paralegal assistants and the attorneys? Do you see these resisting forces as unreasonable or legitimate?

2. Do you think that Paul is correct in his prediction that the complaints will decrease after the change has been in operation for a while and its benefits are noted? Why or why not?

3. What type of change strategy is Paul using? How well is it working? What should Paul do at this time?

The Case Continues   Ashley also listened to complaints from the paralegals. They felt very strongly that (1) the work they were getting was neither challenging nor generally very interesting; (2) they were not able to consistently work on a particular caseload, and, therefore, the quality of their work was decreasing; and (3) they were tired of taking abuse for the changes they themselves had not instituted.

After the new system had been in operation for six months, Ashley suggested to Paul that perhaps some of these complaints might be eliminated if each attorney were allowed to have priority claim on the time of one paralegal assistant. This arrangement would allow the paralegal to become familiar with the particular work of one attorney, including the issues and current caseload of that attorney.

The paralegal could then be asked to work elsewhere when not busy with the work of the attorney. Paul, however, felt that such a move would defeat the very purpose for which the central paralegal pool had been established.

Stop Reading   Respond to the following questions.

1. What are Paul's sources of resistance? Are they legitimate?

2. If you were Paul, what would you do at this point? Why?

The Case Continues   After much prodding by Ashley, Paul finally agreed that something had to be done to make things run more smoothly. Paul admitted that he shared some of her doubts about the success of the new arrangement and wondered whether perhaps the change had not been managed well. More important, he wondered whether something could be done to regain the full support and cooperation of the attorneys and paralegals. He even considered returning the office to its old method of operation, allowing each attorney to work solely with one paralegal assistant.

Discussion Questions   1. What do you think Paul may have learned about this experience regarding implementation of change?

2. Do you think the change was well designed? Why or why not?

3. What strategies could Paul have used in the beginning to help him sort out the aspects of the proposed change and to help him plan?

4. If you were a consultant and Paul commissioned your professional expertise, what advice would you give him about what he should do now and how to do it?

Reflection   Although this case has focused on resistance to change, using some of the other competencies that we have discussed can be useful for understanding and overcoming resistance to change. For example, once complaints began, how could Paul have used some of the ideas and tools related to communicating honestly and effectively (Module 1, Competency 2), motivating self and others (Module 3, Competency 3), and negotiating agreement and commitment (Module 4, Competency 4)?

PRACTICE　Understanding Your Own Influence Attempts

Objective　This exercise is designed to help you integrate what you have learned from multiple competencies in relationship to your own ability to influence others to make some type of change.

Directions　Evaluate your least successful interpersonal influence attempt over the past year or so. You can go back in time further than a year, but try to use an example that is still pretty fresh in your mind. This example should involve a conscious effort on your part to influence someone else directly, yet failing in the attempt.

　　As you reflect on that incident, answer the following questions:

1. What did you want this person to change? Why did you think that change would be beneficial? Did you concider the benefits to the other person?

2. What is your most compelling explanation of why your influence attempt was unsuccessful?

3. What would a force field analysis have suggested about your likelihood of being successful in that situation?

4. How might you approach similar situations differently in the future?

Reflection　Performing a force field analysis can be a valuable way to identify potential unintended consequences of an action because it requires that you look at the proposed change from the perspective of all of the impacted parties. This type of creative thinking exercise, sometimes referred to as "perspective taking," may also help you identify innovative approaches that had not previously occurred to you.

APPLICATION　Planning a Change

Objective　Hindsight, it is said, is always 20/20. This exercise asks you to plan a change of your own, without the benefit of hindsight.

Directions　In the assessment activity at the beginning of this competency you were asked to write down one change that you would like to make in an organization in which you have been involved.

1. Do a force field analysis for this situation, listing the driving and resisting forces for the change you would like to see made. Estimate the strength of the driving and resisting forces, as well as your level of influence over those forces.

2. On a separate sheet of paper, write today's date. Then describe the change you wish to make. Determine when you would like to begin implementing the change. The format should be as follows:

　Today's Date:　　　　　　　　　　　　　　　　Implementation Target Date:

　Description of a change you wish to make:

　Design of the change:

　Strategies for implementing the change:

Discussion Questions　1. How did you feel once you identified the change and the implementation date? Many people feel vaguely dissatisfied with themselves when they want to change something and often think the dissatisfaction will remain until the change is completed. However, as you probably experienced in this activity, when we take action toward change, the dissatisfaction with ourselves often diminishes, and we are thereby encouraged to continue our plans.

2. What difference did you note in writing down your proposed change, with its accompanying dates, rather than merely having these ideas in your head? Writing down the proposed change is a clarifying effort, and by so doing you tend to increase your belief that it will happen.

Reflection   As you were writing up your change plan, did you think about how to use what you have learned from other competencies such as setting goals and objectives (Module 3, Competency 2)? If not, go back and review your plan to see if it can be improved by including "SMART" goals or applying other tools we have covered throughout the text.

MODULE 4   Create-Focused Competency Evaluation Matrix

Objective   After completing this evaluation matrix, you will have four matrices, one for each quadrant of the competing values framework.

Review   The first competency in the Create quadrant focused on using power ethically and effectively. In addition to identifying different sources of power and influence tactics, we also discussed the importance of networking effectively to build your power base. Next, we addressed the competency of championing and selling new ideas. After describing four different types of managerial communication, we discussed how the building blocks of Set, Support, Sequence, Access, and Polish can improve the quality and impact of presentations and other types of communication. Our third competency, fueling and fostering innovation, described the characteristics of creative thinking and provided suggestions for encouraging creativity in the workplace. Negotiating agreement and commitment, the fourth competency in this module, provided suggestions for how to achieve win-win solutions by focusing on the problem and the interests of the parties, generating multiple possibilities, and using objective standards rather than emotional arguments. Finally, we considered implementing and sustaining change and described how to conduct a force field analysis. We also identified four approaches to bringing change, discussed how they are related to the four quadrants of the competing values framework, and explained how different approaches may be appropriate for different situations.

Directions   Answer the questions in Table M4.3 for each of the competencies covered in this module based on the reading material, class discussions, and your personal work (e.g., Assessment exercises, Application exercises, etc.).

Reflection   Now that you have completed evaluation matrices for each of the four modules, take some time to go back over your earlier work and select the three or four competencies that you think are most critical for you to focus on now. As your skills in these areas improve, you can return to these matrices to identify new areas for development.

TABLE M4.3 Module 4 Create-Focused Competency Evaluation Matrix

With respect to this competency:	*Using Power Ethically and Effectively*	*Championing and Selling New Ideas*	*Fueling and Fostering Innovation*	*Negotiating Agreement and Commitment*	*Implementing and Sustaining Change*
1. What do I know about my current performance?					
2. How could I be more effective?					
3. Who are some people I could observe?					
4. What books should I read?					
5. What objectives and deadlines should I set?					
6. With whom should I share my objectives?					
7. How will I evaluate my efforts?					

REFERENCES

Abrashoff, D. Michael. (2001). Retention through redemption. *Harvard Business Review, 79* (2), 136–141.

Acohido, B., Hopkins, J., Graham, J., & M. Kessler. (2007). 25 years of "eureka" moments. *USA Today.* [On-line.] Available: http://www.usatoday.com/news/top25-inventions.htm.

Albrecht, K. (2006). *Social intelligence: The new science of success.* San Francisco: Jossey-Bass.

Atkinson, C. (*2007*). *Beyond bullet points: Using Microsoft PowerPoint to create presentations that inform, motivate, and inspire.* Redmond, Washington: Microsoft Press.

Atkinson, C., & Mayer, R. E.. (2004). Five ways to reduce PowerPoint overload. Available: http://www.sociablemedia.com/PDF/atkinson_mayer_powerpoint_4_23_04.pdf.

Bass, B. M., & Avolio, B. J. (Eds.). (1994). *Improving organizational effectiveness through transformational leadership.* Thousand Oaks, CA: Sage.

Bellis, M. (n.d., a). The history of the Frisbee. About.com: Inventors. Available: http://inventors.about.com/library/weekly/aa980218.htm.

Bellis, M. (n.d., b). The history of the escalator. About.com: Inventors. Available: http://inventors.about.com/library/inventors/blescalator.htm).

Bradford, D. L., & Cohen, A. R. (1984). *Managing for excellence.* New York: John Wiley & Sons.

Burns, J. M. (1978). *Leadership.* New York: Harper & Row.

Burns, J. M. (1984). *The power to lead*. New York: Simon & Schuster.

Burt, Ronald S. (2005, September). Structural holes and good ideas. *American Journal of Sociology, 10*(2), 349–399.

Chin, R., & Benne, K. D. (1976). General strategies for effecting changes in human systems. In W. G. Bennis, K. D. Benne, R. Chin, & K. E. Corey (Eds.), *The planning of change* (3rd ed.). New York: Holt, Rinehart & Winston.

Cohen, A. R., & Bradford, D. L. (2005). *Influence without authority*. New York: John Wiley & Sons.

Covey, S. R. (1990). *The seven habits of highly effective people*. New York: Simon and Schuster.

de Bono, E. (1970). *Lateral thinking: Creativity step-by-step*. New York: Harper & Row.

Decker, B.. (2008). *You've got to be believed to be heard*. New York: St. Martin's Press.

Delbecq, A., Van de Ven, A., & Gustafson, D. (1975). *Group techniques for program planning: A guide to nominal group technique and Delphi Processes*. Glenview, Il: Scott, Foresman.

Deming, W. E. (1986). *Out of the crisis*. Boston: Massachusetts Institute of Technology Center for Advanced Engineering Study.

The Economist. (2007, October 13). Something new under the sun: A special report on innovation, 3–20.

Ehrenreich, Barbara. (2009). *Bright-sided: How the relentless promotion of positive thinking has undermined America*. New York: Henry Holt & Company.

Falbe, C. M., & Yukl, G. (1992). Consequences for managers of using single influence tactics and combinations of tactics. *Academy of Management Review*, 35(3), 638–652.

Ferrazzi, K. (with T. Raz). (2005). *Never eat alone: And other secrets to success, one relationship at a time*. New York: Doubleday.

Fisher, K. (2000). *Leading self-directed work teams: A guide to developing new team leadership skills*. New York: McGraw-Hill.

Fisher, R., Kopelman, E., & Kupfer-Schneider, A. (1994). *Beyond Machiavelli: Tools for coping with conflict*. Cambridge, MA: Harvard University Press.

Fisher, R., & Ury, W. (2002). *Getting to yes: Negotiating agreement without giving in*. New York: Penguin.

Gladwell, M. (2008). *Outliers: The story of success*. New York: Little Brown and Company.

Goleman, D. (2000). *Working with emotional intelligence*. New York: Bantam.

Granovetter, M. (1973). The strength of weak ties. *American Journal of Sociology*, *78*(6), 1360–1380.

Harding, F. (1994). *Rain making: A professional's guide to attracting new clients*. Holbrook, MA: Bob Adams.

Hayden-Elgin, S. (1997). *More on the gentle art of verbal self-defense*. New York: Prentice-Hall.

Hoff, R. (1992). *I can see you naked—A fearless guide to making great presentations*. Kansas City: Andrews & McMeel.

James, R. (2009, May 26). A brief history of GPS. *Time* [On-line]. Available: http://www.time.com/time/nation/article/0,8599,1900862,00.html.

Kanter, R. M. (1983). *The change masters: Innovation for productivity in the American corporation*. New York: Simon & Schuster.

Kelly, T. (2005). *The ten faces of innovation: IDEO's strategies for defeating the devil's advocate and driving creativity throughout your organization.* New York: DoubleDay.

Kotter, J. P. (2008). *A sense of urgency.* Cambridge, Mass.: Harvard Business School Press.

Kuhn, R. L. (1987). *Handbook for creative managers.* New York: McGraw-Hill.

LaBarre, P. (1999, March 1). Grassroots leadership. *Fast Company Magazine,* no. 23 [On-line]. http://www.fastcompany.com/magazine/23/grassroots.html.

Lewin, K. (1951). *Field theory in social science.* New York: Harper & Row.

Long, D. (2010). CES 2010: Inventions promises to harness WiFi signals for wireless battery charging. Australian PC Authority [On-line]. Available: http://www.pcauthority.com.au/News/164385,ces-2010-invention-promises-to-harness-wifi-signals-for-wireless-battery-charging.aspx.

Maccoby, M. (2007). *The leaders we need, and what makes us follow.* Boston: Harvard Business School Press.

McCarty, R. (2010). Presenting to decision makers: Guidelines for student consulting teams. Unpublished manuscript, Marriott School, Brigham Young University.

Miller, W. C. (1987). *The creative edge: Fostering innovation where you work.* Reading, MA: Addison-Wesley.

Murray, D. K. (2009). *Borrowed brilliance: The six steps to business innovation by building on the ideas of others.* New York: Gotham Books.

O'Keefe, D. (2002). *Persuasion, theory and research.* Newbury Park, CA: Sage Publications.

Patterson, K., Grenny, J., McMillan, R., and Switzler, A. (2002). *Crucial conversations: Tools for talking when stakes are high.* New York: McGraw-Hill.

Peace, W. H. (1991). The hard work of being a soft manager. *Harvard Business Review, 69*(6), 40–47.

Quinn, R. E. (2000). *Change the world: How ordinary people can accomplish extraordinary results.* San Francisco: Jossey-Bass.

Quinn, R. E. (2005). Moments of greatness: Entering the fundamental state of leadership. *Harvard Business Review, 83*(7/8), 73–83.

Quinn, R. E., Hildebrandt, H. W., Rogers, P. S. Thompson, M. P. (1991). A competing values framework for analyzing presentational communication in management contexts. *Journal of Business Communication, 28*(3), 213–232.

Quinn, R. W., and Quinn, R. E. (2009). *Lift: Becoming a positive force in any situation.* San Francisco: Berrett-Koehler.

Raudsepp, E. (1981). *How creative are you?* Putnam Publishing Group.

Robinson, K. (2006). Schools kill creativity. Presentation at TED Conference. Available: http://www.ted.com/talks/lang/eng/ken_robinson_says_schools_kill_creativity.html.

Rogers, P. S., and Hildebrandt, H. W. (1993). Competing values instruments for analyzing written and spoken management messages. *Human Resource Management, 32*(1), 121–142.

Rost, J. C. (1993). *Leadership for the twenty-first century.* Westport, Connecticut: Praeger.

Stone, D., Patton, B., and Heen, S. (1999). *Difficult conversations: How to discuss what matters most.* New York: Viking.

Tharp, T. (with M. Reiter). (2003). *The creative habit: Learn it and use it for life.* New York: Simon & Schuster.

Thoreau, H. D. (1993). *Civil Disobedience and Other Essays*. New York: Dover Publications.

Ury, W. (1993). *Getting past no: Negotiating your way from confrontation to cooperation*. New York: Bantam Books.

Vital Smarts. (1994). *Presenting with power: A guidebook* (training manual published by Vital Smarts, formerly called The Praxis Group). Provo, UT.

Weissman, J. (2008). *Presenting to win: The art of telling your story*. Upper Saddle River, N.J.: FT Prentice Hall.

Witt, C. (with D. Fetherling). (2009). *Real leaders don't do PowerPoint: How to sell yourself and your ideas*. New York: Crown Publishing.

INTEGRATION
AND THE ROAD
TO MASTERY

■ CONCLUSION*

Integration and Behavioral Complexity

How Master Managers See the World

The Leveraging Power of Lift

The Never-ending Road to Mastery

In the introductory chapter to this text, we argue that to be successful, organizations and their managers must move away from the traditional either/or thinking of the past and embrace the both/and thinking required for success in dynamic, complex environments. Rather than seeing collaboration and competition as being diametrically opposed, master managers must be able to harness the power of both these approaches. Similarly, the need for control cannot be allowed to overwhelm the need for creativity and change. This reflects the essence of the competing values framework.

Each of the four main modules of the text takes the perspective of a different theoretical management model. The five core competencies in each module were identified based on research with mid- and senior-level managers and support the action imperatives associated with the four management models. You have had the opportunity to learn about 21 competencies and see that many of them reinforce one another. For example, Thinking Critically, which appeared in the introductory chapter, played an important part in other competencies such as Managing and Encouraging Constructive Conflict in Module 1 and Championing and Selling New Ideas in Module 4. Similarly, what you learned about Organizing Information Flows in Module 2 was reinforced in the Module 3 competency, Managing Execution and Driving for Results.

*[Portions of this chapter are adapted from Robert E. Quinn, *Beyond Rational Management* (San Francisco: Jossey-Bass, 1988. Used with permission.) and Ryan W. Quinn and Robert E. Quinn, *Lift: Becoming a Positive Force in Any Situation* (San Francisco: Berrett-Koehler Publishers, 2009.)]

This concluding section begins by emphasizing the importance of integration and behavioral complexity. It explains how systems thinking and paradoxical thinking help managers see the world differently. Master managers are not simply technically adept at using different competencies at different times. Rather, master managers see the world differently, think about possible courses of action in more sophisticated ways, and then integrate and blend apparently competing competencies in innovative ways that meet the needs of the situation at hand. We also discuss the concept of "lift" and how you can use it to raise your performance and the performance of others to an even higher level. We conclude with a discussion of the developmental process and the need for life-long learning.

ASSESSMENT   Reexamining Your Personal Competencies

Objective   At the end of each module, you were asked to complete an evaluation matrix to help you organize your thoughts about your personal competencies. In this exercise you will update and integrate these earlier matrices and identify specific areas of focus for the next steps on your developmental journey.

Directions—Part 1   First, review the four evaluation matrices that you prepared at the end of each module, and then respond to the questions that follow.

1. Please evaluate your **comfort with**, **use of**, and **future need for** each competency listed below.

2. Sum your scores for each quadrant of the competing values framework and write the sum in the appropriate box on the rows labeled for each of the four action imperatives.

In the left hand column, indicate your current comfort-level with each competency below using the following scale:

In the right hand columns, indicate how much you use each competency today (in the first column) and how much you expect to need each competency within the next three years (in the second column). Please use the following scale:.

Very low	Low	Moderate	High	Very high	Rarely	Seldom	Sometimes	Often	Very often
1	2	3	4	5	1	2	3	4	5

Right now, my comfort-level with this competency is ...	Competing Values Framework Managerial Competencies by Quadrant	For my job today, I need to use this competency . . .	Within the next three years, I will need to use this competency . . .
_____	Understanding self and others	_____	_____
_____	Communicating honestly and effectively	_____	_____
_____	Mentoring and developing others	_____	_____
_____	Managing groups and leading teams	_____	_____
_____	Managing and encouraging constructive conflict	_____	_____
_____	**COLLABORATE**	_____	_____

Very low 1	Low 2	Moderate 3	High 4	Very high 5	Rarely 1	Seldom 2	Sometimes 3	Often 4	Very often 5
Right now, my comfort-level with this competency is ...		Competing Values Framework Managerial Competencies by Quadrant			For my job today, I need to use this competency . . .			Within the next three years, I will need to use this competency . . .	
_____		Organizing information flows			_____			_____	
_____		Working and managing across functions			_____			_____	
_____		Planning and coordinating projects			_____			_____	
_____		Measuring and monitoring performance and quality			_____			_____	
_____		Encouraging and enabling compliance			_____			_____	
_____		**CONTROL**			_____			_____	
_____		Developing and communicating a vision			_____			_____	
_____		Setting goals and objectives			_____			_____	
_____		Motivating self and others			_____			_____	
_____		Designing and organizing			_____			_____	
_____		Managing execution and driving for results			_____			_____	
_____		**COMPETE**			_____			_____	
_____		Using power ethically and effectively			_____			_____	
_____		Championing and selling new ideas			_____			_____	
_____		Fueling and fostering innovation			_____			_____	
_____		Negotiating agreement and commitment			_____			_____	
_____		Implementing and sustaining change			_____			_____	
_____		**CREATE**			_____			_____	

Directions—Part 2   Complete the Summary Evaluation Matrix below to see if any of the action imperatives stand out as particularly important to focus on now. For example, if a competency ranks number one in terms of your use now and number one in terms of your need for that competency in the future, but ranks fourth in terms of your comfort level, that is probably a good place to focus your attention. Note that there is no simple mathematical formula for determining the overall ranking in the last line of the table. You will need to use your own best judgment to determine the most appropriate path to take on your journey toward mastery.

Please keep this Assessment to use for the Application exercise at the end of this concluding chapter.

Summary Evaluation Matrix

Based on your summary scores for each quadrant, rank the four action imperatives from 1 to 4, as explained below:	*Collaborate*	*Control*	*Compete*	*Create*
Comfort level. (1 = I am **most** comfortable with the competencies associated with this action imperative.)	_____	_____	_____	_____
Use in job today (1 = I use the competencies associated with this action imperative the **most** today, so this action imperative is very important to my short-term success.)	_____	_____	_____	_____
Need for in the next three years (1 = I expect to need to use the competencies associated with this action imperative the **most** in the near future, so this action imperative is very important to my long-term success.)	_____	_____	_____	_____
Overall ranking for development plan (1 = I think that I should focus on developing the competencies associated with this action imperative **first** in my strategy for mastery.)	_____	_____	_____	_____

Reflection   It is natural to want to spend time doing things that you enjoy and are good at; it is also natural to want to challenge yourself and learn new things. In fact, we are often more motivated by challenging goals than by easy goals, as long as we believe that our goals are achievable.

LEARNING   Integration and the Road to Mastery

Using this book, you have had the opportunity to develop skills associated with four different approaches to management that are reflected in the action imperatives Collaborate, Control, Compete, and Create. Although some of the competencies that we addressed may seem slightly more challenging than others, applying any one competency at a given point in time is not that difficult. The mastery of management, however, requires more than just the development of different competencies. It requires the ability to enter a situation, to see it from multiple perspectives, to determine what actions are needed, and then to use and blend contrasting competencies without appearing inconsistent or hypocritical. This is not easy. But it is possible.

We begin this final section with a discussion of the importance of integrating the four action imperatives and their related competencies to achieve behavioral complexity and to avoid slipping into negative management styles. We discuss how master managers see the world and then describe how the concept of lift, which we refer to briefly earlier in the book, can be used to help leverage the power of the competing values approach to management. We conclude with a discussion of the importance of continuous learning, because mastery is a journey, not a destination.

INTEGRATION AND BEHAVIORAL COMPLEXITY

Throughout this text we have tended to use the terms "managers" and "managerial leaders" interchangeably. In this concluding chapter, however, we want to distinguish between individuals who happen to have management positions and individuals who truly display leadership in their management of others. Learning to perform well as a managerial leader requires a different approach from learning to perform well in a single quadrant of the competing values framework. In the same way that none of the early management models we covered in the introductory chapter was sufficient for ensuring organizational effectiveness, leadership effectiveness cannot be achieved by individuals who use a management approach based on a limited number of competencies or a single action imperative.

Becoming a master manager requires not only the ability to use competencies associated with all four quadrants of the competing values framework, at least at a competent level; it also requires the ability to blend and balance the use of different competencies in support of all four action imperatives in an appropriate way. Recall from the introductory chapter the notion of behavioral complexity, "the ability to act out a cognitively complex strategy by playing multiple, even competing, roles in a highly integrated and complementary way" (Hooijberg & Quinn, 1992, p. 164). This ability involves two components—behavioral repertoire (the number of leadership approaches and skills a manager can use effectively) and behavioral differentiation, the ability to use the skills they have in their behavioral repertoire differently, depending on the situation (Hooijberg, Hunt & Dodge, 1997). In the future, behavioral complexity will become increasingly important for global leaders whose ability to "generate superior corporate performance . . . [will require them to balance] (1) profitability and productivity, (2) continuity and efficiency, (3) commitment and morale, and (4) adaptability and innovation" (Petrick, Scherer, Brodzinski, Quinn & Ainina, 1999, p. 60). When managers fail to demonstrate behavioral complexity, their actions are likely to result in negative outcomes, as explained below.

THE NEGATIVE ZONE

Individuals who emphasize a single approach to management may become very skilled in that approach and may even find that their strengths in that single approach carry them a long way in their careers, but this does not mean that these individuals are effective managerial leaders. Effective managerial leaders are behaviorally complex and are able to integrate all the approaches to management identified in the competing values framework. The paradox of being successful using a single approach is that, sooner or later, continuing to rely on that approach will likely lead to a serious career setback.

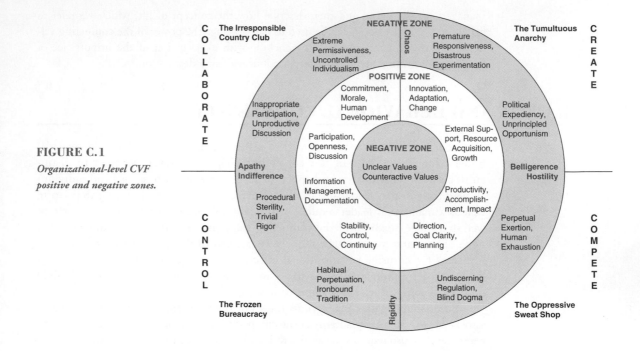

FIGURE C.1

Organizational-level CVF positive and negative zones.

Without behavioral complexity, one's strengths can become the source of one's failure. Low behavioral complexity on the part of a manager can lead to unfortunate organizational outcomes. To illustrate this, Faerman and Quinn (1985) developed the concept of the "negative zone," which can be seen in Figures C.1 (organizational-level effectiveness) and Figure C.2 (leader effectiveness).

In each of the two figures, three circles are superimposed over the four quadrants of the competing values framework. In the middle circle are the positively stated values that we have been focusing on throughout this book. The inner and outer circles are considered negative zones. The inner circle is well understood. At the organizational level it represents unclear or counteractive values that result in the loss of direction. At the individual level, the inner negative zone represents a lack of awareness or ability to perform the skills associated with different management models.

In contrast to the inner circle, the outer circle reflects what happens when each set of positive values is "pushed" until it becomes a negative. For example, in the Create quadrant, when the quest for change and adaptability is pushed too far, organizations act prematurely and expend too many resources on experimentation, turning a responsive adhocracy into a tumultuous anarchy. When pushed too far at the individual level, the individual becomes an impractical dreamer who wastes energy and disrupts the continuity in the organization. This type of negative transformation happens in each quadrant of the model when the emphasis on that approach to management gets too far out of balance with the management approach of the opposing quadrant.

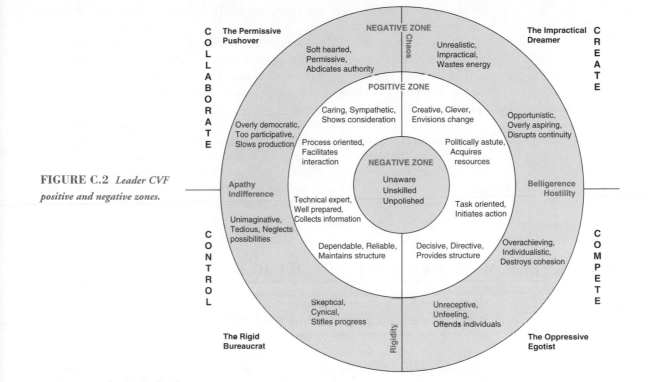

FIGURE C.2 *Leader CVF positive and negative zones.*

BEHAVIORAL COMPLEXITY AND PERFORMANCE

Many managers perform well in some situations, but have difficulty or feel uncomfortable in others. As a result, they tend to favor certain styles of managing relative to others. Theory suggests that these managers should be less effective than managers who are comfortable using a variety of different management approaches. But what really happens in the world of practice? How do these managers fare in terms of effectiveness in their organizations?

Early research on the competing values framework by Quinn, Faerman, and Dixit (1987) found that ineffective managers tended to have profiles that were badly out of balance. Those individuals might be above average on the top two action imperatives (Collaborate and Create) and then be well below average on the bottom two (Control and Compete). Such managers were seen by associates as impulsive and chaotic, spreading disorder everywhere. Some had the opposite profile. They were seen as narrowly focused on control and abrasive toward people. All of the profiles of ineffective managers were badly out of balance.

Interestingly, when looking at the profiles of effective managers, Quinn et al. (1987) also found that most of these profiles had some imbalance in them. However, the profiles of effective managers tended to be larger. Although most of these effective managers still tended to emphasize some areas more than others, they did use all four of the approaches to management that are included in the competing values framework to some extent.

Finally, some of the effective managers had profiles that seem to have transcended style. These "master managers" seem to appreciate the underlying values in each quadrant in the competing values framework. They are able to use competencies that support all four action imperatives and appear to be adept at integrating competencies in complementary ways.

More recent research by Lawrence, Lenk, and Quinn (2009) supports earlier findings that managers who have more extensive behavioral repertoires are rated higher in terms of overall performance and the ability to lead change. How do these individuals come to round out their profiles? Part of the answer lies in experience. Masters tend to be in upper-middle and top-level positions. It is unlikely that these managers began their careers as masters. Experience alone, however, is not enough. Master managers behave differently because they see the world differently.

HOW MASTER MANAGERS SEE THE WORLD

Why are some individuals more successful than others on their journey to mastery? What characteristics differentiate these managerial leaders from other managers? Why are some people better able to integrate seemingly opposite modes of behavior? Although we cannot say for certain, our experience has suggested that the answer begins with an understanding of how master managers see (and think about) the world. People who become masters of management do not see their work environment only in structured, analytic ways. Instead, they also have the capacity to see it as a complex, dynamic system that is constantly evolving. To interact effectively with their work environment, they employ a variety of different, sometimes contradictory, perspectives or modes. In other words, they employ different modes of thinking. Here we will briefly discuss two modes of thinking that appear to be related to behavioral complexity: systems (dynamic) thinking and paradoxical thinking.

SYSTEMS THINKING

Peter Senge describes *systems thinking* as "a discipline for seeing wholes. It is a framework for seeing interrelationships rather than things, for seeing patterns of change rather than static 'snapshots.'. . . [It is] a discipline for seeing the 'structures' that underlie complex situations, and for discerning high from low leverage change" (1990, pp. 68–69). One of the key elements of systems thinking is the concept of *feedback*, or the "reciprocal flow of influence" (1990, p. 75). In a situation where there is feedback behavior, if A influences B, and B influences C, C (or something that is influenced by C) will ultimately influence A. Often, when C and A are separated in time, it is difficult to recognize the feedback.

Most of us learn to think about organizations in a very static and purposeful way. We see the world in terms of simple one-way cause-and-effect reasoning, believing that events will cause (or are caused by) other events—if you cut expenditures, profits will rise; if you send employees to training, their performance will improve. We tend not to notice that actions taken today can result in new problems that we will need to deal with several months (or years) down the line. We tend to believe that a problem addressed in one area of the organization has no consequences for other areas. As noted by Senge, this type of simple cause-and-effect thinking "distract[s] us from seeing the longer-term patterns of change that lie behind the events and from understanding the causes of those patterns" (1990, p. 21).

When organizations exist in stable, predictable environments, this type of cause-and-effect thinking may be acceptable, but few, if any, organizations exist in stable, predictable environments today. Instead, organizations exist in dynamic, changing environments, where small changes in the social, political, economic, and technological environment can have a major impact on the organization's future. That means we need to be far more aware of interrelationships. Master managers and other expert decision makers use holistic recognition in a way that allows them to deeply understand the situation. The ability to see the underlying structures, to see the interrelationships, and to understand that actions have a long-term impact is essentially the basis of systems thinking.

PARADOXICAL THINKING

Both paradoxical thinking and systems thinking help us deal with apparent contradictions. In the introductory chapter we discussed the fact that organizational leaders spend much of their time living in fields of perceived tensions. They are constantly forced to make trade-offs; there are often no right answers. Moreover, the higher one goes in an organization, the more exaggerated these tensions become. Because one-dimensional guidelines (care for people OR maintain control OR work harder OR be innovative) represent only a single perspective, they are similar to partial-truths—they don't tell the whole story. The truth is that organizations and their leaders exist in an environment of competing pressures. Often the choice is not between good and bad, but between good and good—or bad and bad. In such cases there is sometimes a need for paradoxical thinking, thinking that transcends the contradictions and recognizes that two seemingly opposite conditions can simultaneously be true.

To engage in paradoxical thinking, one must be willing to engage in contradiction. This does not simply mean that managers are willing or able to act in different ways at different times. It means that they must be willing to try to resolve the contradiction and to integrate seemingly opposite ideas or behaviors. It means maintaining standards and retaining control at the same time you are being flexible and creative. It means being collaborative and open to new ideas at the same time you are providing a vision that makes sense in the current environment. It means making the impossible possible (e.g., Cameron & Lavine, 2006). To do this, managers must be willing to move outside their current level of thinking and attempt to see things from a new perspective. Albert Einstein is often quoted as saying, "No problem can be solved from the same consciousness that produced it" (quoted in Wheatley, 1992, p. 5).

As you have seen, the competing values framework is built around the notion of paradox. It assumes that organizations need to be simultaneously adaptable/flexible and stable/controlled. It assumes that to perform effectively, organizations need to focus simultaneously on their external environments and competitive position and on their internal environments, their people, and work processes. As a conceptual model, the framework itself suggests that we tend to think of activities on opposite sides of the axes as antithetical. In addition, throughout this book we have identified paradoxes that require managers to act in unconventional ways, such as creating conflict to reduce conflict. Implicitly, the model suggests that managers who are most capable of thinking paradoxically would also be most capable of acting in seemingly opposite ways.

One of the most effective ways to increase your ability to engage in paradoxical thinking is to challenge yourself to see the value in areas that are not your strengths—to move outside of your comfort zone. What kinds of challenges take you outside your comfort zone? First, you can look at different points of view. Rather than listening only to people you think are right, try listening to people you think are wrong. Here we can learn from the words of Martin Luther King Jr.:

Help us to see the enemy's point of view, to hear his questions, to know his assessment of ourselves. From his view we may indeed see the basic weakness of our condition, and if we are mature, we may learn and grow and profit from the wisdom of our brothers who are called the opposition (*quoted in Phillips, 1999, p. 85*).

Second, you can stretch yourself. You can take on new tasks and responsibilities in your current job, or you can take the advice of Ira Chaleff in his book *The Courageous Follower:* "We also need external growth opportunities. There is often ample room for growth within our current position if we assertively seek it. . . . At some point, however, it may be desirable to move away from the comfort of our current role to test ourselves in a new, unproven role" (Chaleff, 1995, p. 39). Finally, you can look for the many interdependencies that exist between what you value and are drawn to and what you devalue and tend to ignore or reject. For example, most people see art and science as very different and are drawn to one or the other. People often ask whether leadership is an art or a science. Leonardo da Vinci, one of the world's greatest geniuses, whose work embraced uncertainty, ambiguity, and paradox (Gelb, 1998), saw the connections between art and science. As Gelb notes:

For Leonardo, art and science were indivisible. In his *Treatise on Painting* he cautions potential adepts: "Those who become enamoured of the art, without having previously applied to the diligent study of the scientific part of it, may be compared to mariners who put to sea in a ship without a rudder or compass and therefore cannot be certain of arriving at the wished for port" (p. 166).

Leonardo da Vinci had the ability and willingness to see the world in new and unconventional ways. He embraced creative as well as critical thinking, and his curiosity led him to many different fields of study. One of his many interests was the phenomenon of flight. He wrote about the flight of birds and developed plans for flying machines. Although not all of his ideas were practical, a hang glider he designed had the necessary elements to harness the aerodynamic force of lift, as demonstrated in the PBS program, *Leonardo's Dream Machines* (2005). Recently, Quinn and Quinn (2009) used the concept of lift to explain how individuals can be a positive force in any situation.

THE LEVERAGING POWER OF LIFT

In our discussion of cross-functional teams in Module 2, we introduced Quinn and Quinn's (2009) concept of "lift" to explain why some people seem to have a positive influence on everyone around them, no matter what the situation. We believe that by creating the psychological conditions necessary for lift, managers can multiply the impact of the competing values approach to management.

ACCENTUATING THE POSITIVE

The theoretical roots of lift reach back to research on positive psychology (Seligman, 2002) and positive organizational studies (Cameron, Dutton & Quinn, 2003). In contrast to more traditional approaches in psychology and organizational studies that focus on finding problems (and, ideally, solving them), both these schools of thought focus on studying positive behaviors and outcomes (e.g., learned optimism, optimal experiences, authentic leadership, high-reliability organizations) and identifying their causes. Research on the concepts of positive influence and psychological states provide key insights that led to the development of the concept of lift.

Positive Influence.   Building on both research and observations from practice, Quinn and Quinn (2009, p. 8) offer the following description of positive influence. "Influence is positive when it (1) invites people toward purposes that (2) meet the needs of the people involved (3) in ways that increasingly reflect their highest personal and social values and (4) adapt to changing circumstances over time." Research suggests that the ability to be a positive influence depends upon the psychological state of the individuals involved.

Psychological States.   The term "psychological state" refers to a pattern of thoughts and feelings that we currently are experiencing. Psychological states are temporary, rather than permanent, they can be simple or complex. For example, when given an opportunity to work on an assignment in another country, an employee might experience a number of different emotions and thoughts that will influence her decision. She may be excited and proud to know she was selected. She may feel guilty because she knows that another colleague really wants that assignment. She may feel concern about how her partner will feel about the opportunity. She may feel anxious about her ability to learn a new language and fit into a new culture. All these feelings and thoughts contribute to that employee's current psychological state, and are likely to influence the psychological state of her partner when they talk about this new opportunity.

MAKING CONNECTIONS

Research in several disciplines helps us understand how our own psychological states influence others. First, our nonverbal cues such as facial expressions, body language, and tone of voice send cues that other people interpret and react to (Lishner, Cooter & Zald, 2008). Second, emotions are contagious (Hatfield, Cacioppo & Rapson, 1992).

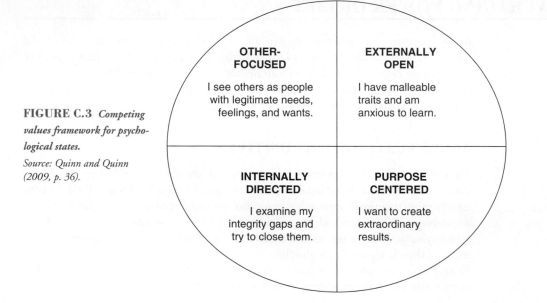

FIGURE C.3 *Competing values framework for psychological states.*

Source: Quinn and Quinn (2009, p. 36).

Third, our own psychological states influence our decisions and actions, which may in turn influence other people's decision and actions (Schön, 1983; Isen, 1999). Fourth, different actions performed in different ways generate different results. When our results are more effective, more creative, of higher quality, or more beneficial to others, people are likely to notice and try to make sense of how we achieved those results (Collins, 2001; Weick, 1984).

Quinn and Quinn (2009) noticed that the types of psychological states that were being described in both the positive psychology and the positive organizational studies literatures as being linked to positive influence seemed consistent with the quadrants of the competing values framework, as shown in Figure C.3.

LIFTING OTHERS

Each of the psychological states associated with the competing values quadrants has a positive aspect and may lead to positive results. However, just as using one management approach exclusively can have negative impacts, experiencing only one of these psychological states is also likely to lead to negative zone types of outcomes.

According to Quinn and Quinn (2009), all four of the psychological states identified in Figure C.3 must be in place for lift to occur. Because these psychological states are related in a multiplicative fashion, if any of these characteristics are missing, the positive power of lift will not be generated. When all four characteristics are in place, we experience lift personally and, through the processes described above, our own state of lift becomes contagious and serves to lift the people around us. Table C.1 provides some guiding questions that you can use to help generate lift in yourself and in others.

TABLE C.1 Guiding Questions for Generating Lift

- What values serve as my anchors, regardless of the situation?
- What specific results do I want to achieve in this particular situation?
- What are a few strategies I could use to accomplish my purpose in this situation?
- How would I feel if I were experiencing this situation from other people's points of view?

Managerial leaders who have developed the competencies and behavioral complexity associated with the competing values framework and who also experience the psychological state of lift are able to increase their positive impact. Keep in mind, however, that lift is a temporary psychological state. It is easy to get distracted from being other-focused, internally directed, purpose-centered, and externally open. Therefore it is important that we continually remind ourselves of these critical conditions as we continue on our journey toward mastery.

THE NEVER-ENDING ROAD TO MASTERY

Is it appropriate to apply the notion of mastery to the tasks of management? Certainly managerial leaders progress through stages and can become increasingly effective in their performance. In addition, we can point to examples of individuals who have demonstrated exceptionally skillful management in the past. So it would seem that those individuals have reached the state of mastery. At the same time, the world keeps changing, so that what was called for yesterday may not be what is needed today. In that sense, mastery is a journey of life-long learning, rather than a destination. The notion of *becoming* a master manager recognizes that there are always more things to learn and new ideas that will challenge you to enhance your abilities. As you near mastery at one level, you will likely be promoted or moved into a new area where you will be faced with new responsibilities and new challenges, and therefore you will return to the process of *becoming*. As you go through the different stages of your career, you will always need to develop new competencies. The earlier you understand the need for continuous learning—the earlier you learn to value the process of *becoming*—the more effective you will be as a manager and a managerial leader.

MILESTONES ALONG THE ROAD

As you consider the different management models, action imperatives, and competencies presented in this book, you may question whether it is possible for you to do it all—to become, even briefly, a master manager. As you worked through the readings and exercises, you may have found that you felt very comfortable performing some competencies and uncomfortable with others. You may have questioned whether it truly was possible to link the demands of one action imperative with the demands of the action imperative in the opposite area of the competing values framework. In the previous section, we described profiles of effective managers and managerial leaders who transcended the paradoxes associated with competing values in management. We are confident that you are just as capable of expanding and balancing your own management profile, if you commit yourself to that goal and commit yourself to life-long learning.

Although learning sometimes takes place when you are not consciously aware of it, learning generally requires a focused effort at understanding new concepts and practicing new skills. Just as you cannot become an expert swimmer by jumping into the deep end of the pool, you are unlikely to become a master manager by taking charge of a large organization. You need to start at a level at which you are comfortable and consciously work at developing your competencies, always challenging yourself to perform at a higher level. Dreyfus and Dreyfus (1986) provide a five-stage model that describes the journey from novice to expert (see Figure C.4).

Stage 1: The Novice.   As a novice, you learn facts and rules. The rules are learned as absolutes, which are never to be violated. For example, a beginning chess player learns the names of the pieces, how they are moved, and their value. She is told to exchange pieces of lower value for pieces of higher value. In management this might be the equivalent of learning the principles of negotiating and being told that effective negotiations require attention to all of these principles.

Stage 2: The Advanced Beginner.   In this stage, experience becomes critical. As real situations are encountered, performance improves and you are able to put into practice the stated facts and rules. As you observe certain basic patterns, you begin to recognize factors that were not stated in the rules. A chess player, for example, begins to recognize certain basic board positions that should be pursued. The new manager

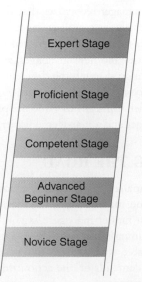

FIGURE C.4 *Five steps to mastery.*

discovers the importance of understanding the basic norms, values, and culture of the organization. Technical procedures, types of relationships, appropriate dress, and typical career paths are among the things that may vary dramatically from what the novice learned in textbooks and what he experiences in the workplace.

Stage 3: Competence.   As you gain competence, you gain a better appreciation of the complexity of the task and recognize a much larger set of cues. You develop the ability to select and concentrate on the most important cues. You are no longer aware of the absolute rules; they are assumed. As your competence increases at this stage, you develop some personal "rules of thumb" that guide, but do not direct, your actions. You engage in calculated risks and complex trade-offs. A chess player may, for example, weaken her board position in order to attack the opposing king. This plan may or may not follow any rules that the person was ever taught. The manager may experiment with going beyond the basic tools and techniques taught in school as he tries out new behaviors. Here the manager is more willing to trust his intuition and take risks or suggest new approaches. This may occasionally result in successful outcomes; many times it will not. In this stage, the trial-and-error process is critical to continued development.

Stage 4: Proficiency.   Here, calculation and rational analysis seem to disappear. Unconscious, fluid, and effortless performance begins to emerge, and no one plan is held sacred. You learn to unconsciously "read" the evolving situation. You notice and respond to new cues as the importance of the old ones recedes. New plans are triggered as emerging patterns call to mind plans that worked previously. Your grasp of the situation is holistic and intuitive. Probably only professional chess players achieve the level of play at which they have the ability to recognize and respond to changes in board positions intuitively. Managers who reach this stage are seen as highly effective because they are capable of performing in a wide variety of situations and dealing with seemingly contradictory demands.

Proficiency does not come easily. It requires practice and an ability to develop one's senses to a point where patterns can be recognized intuitively. Gary Klein studies individuals who make life-and-death decisions to learn about "how people perceive and observe, think and reason, act and react" (Breen, 2000). He has worked with Duke Power Company, several airline companies, the U.S. Army, and the U.S. Air Force to help these organizations develop faster and better decision makers. What he has found is that individuals who must make critical decisions quickly develop their intuition to draw on previous experiences. In Klein's study of firefighters, Air Force pilots, intensive care nurses, and others, he has found that although novices tend to follow classic decision-making models, these individuals abandon these models as their skills and experience grow. Klein talks about a fighter pilot who initially followed all the "rules and checklists in order to fly the plane correctly." At one point, however, the pilot reported that he had a profound breakthrough and that "it felt as if he wasn't flying the plane—it felt as if he was flying. He had internalized all the procedures for flying until the plane had felt as if it was a part of him. He no longer needed any rules."

Stage 5: Expertise. At this level optimal performance becomes second nature. People at this stage are not consciously aware of the details; rather they use a holistic perspective that gives them a deep understanding of the situation. They have programmed into their heads multidimensional maps of the territory of which the rest of us are not aware. They see and know things intuitively that the rest of us do not know or see. They frame and reframe strategies as they read changing cues. Klein notes that this runs counter to what most people believe. "We used to think that experts carefully deliberate the merits of each course of action, whereas novices impulsively jump at the first option." Thus, many people believe that experts make decisions slowly because they are "weighed down by information, by facts, by memories." Instead, Klein argues, "the accumulation of experience does not weigh them down—it lightens them up. It makes them fast" (quoted in Breen, 2000). This ability facilitates their engagement of the natural flow of events. Here the manager fully transcends any natural blind spots and is able to shift roles as needed. The expert seems to effortlessly meet the contradictions of organizational life.

THE POSSIBILITY OF SELF-IMPROVEMENT

When a person is willing to put forth the effort required to make a change and is determined to make a change, that person is likely to succeed. Many managers, however, excuse themselves from this responsibility. The number of excuses for not making the effort to improve is unlimited; a few examples include:

- "Conflict is just too stressful for me; I'd rather just go along than risk causing trouble."
- "I'm a 'big picture' person; you can't expect me to keep track of all the details."
- "There's no way I'll ever be good at meeting deadlines; I was even born late!"
- "I'm simply not creative; there's no way to change that."

In each case the statement is an excuse for not making changes. In each case the statement is untrue. Some people have years of experience and are still not effective managers. In contrast, managerial leaders tend to focus consciously on personal and professional development. They recognize the need to constantly grow; they welcome even the most challenging transitions. Most important, managerial leaders come out of each transition with a wider array of competencies and less tied to a particular managerial style.

Although you will no doubt encounter challenges along your road to mastery, you now have some major advantages that will help you on your journey. First, you have a framework to help you understand the value of different approaches to management and appreciate the necessity of performing more effectively in areas that may not come naturally to you. Second, you have had the opportunity to practice using different competencies, and thus should have greater confidence in your ability to perform them effectively. Finally, your experiences in this course should have given you an understanding of the necessity of using systems thinking and paradoxical thinking to understand the complexity of situations and to help you determine how best to integrate diverse and even competing competencies. Thus, you have both cognitive and behavioral performance tools that will help you continue developing as a managerial leader.

To encourage you to move forward, we conclude with an agenda you can use on your journey toward mastery.

AGENDA FOR SELF-IMPROVEMENT

Table C.2 provides an agenda for self-improvement that involves three general steps: Learn about yourself, develop a change strategy, and implement the strategy. Within each of these steps are some key subpoints. This process has been used with many practicing managers and students. In the beginning of the process, many participants are cynical, and some make only half-hearted efforts. Needless to say, they show little achievement. But others attack the process with zeal, and they naturally achieve considerably more. Interestingly, people who put in the effort make progress in whichever quadrant they choose. It is possible to learn and to improve in any area of the competing values framework, regardless of your initial strengths and weaknesses.

The actions included in this agenda are straightforward, and many relate directly to competencies that you have already begun to develop, such as Understanding Self and Others and Setting Goals and Objectives. You know what to do. Now you just need to start doing it. Although it may seem daunting at first, the improvement process is sometimes easier than one thinks it is going to be. Although change takes time and perseverance, if you have the patience and the will, you can be successful. For example, one manager's competing values profile suggested that she was very strong in all the

---

TABLE C.2 Agenda for Self-Improvement

---

1. Learn About Yourself
   * Complete the competing values self-assessment instrument.
   * Do a written self-evaluation of your competencies in each quadrant of the competing values framework.
   * Have others evaluate you.
   * Discuss your skills with people who will be honest.
   * Keep a journal.
2. Develop a Change Strategy
   * Identify specific areas in need of improvement and set SMART goals.
   * Consider how you can use your strengths to help you develop in your weak areas.
   * Identify positive role models for your weak areas.
   * Identify courses or workshops that you can take to help you develop new competencies.
   * Identify new job assignments or a new job consistent with your goals.
   * Read relevant books.
3. Implement the Change Strategy
   * Be honest about the costs of improvement.
   * Develop a social support system.
   * Evaluate your progress on a regular basis, and modify your strategy, if necessary.

---

competencies except those associated with the control quadrant. She saw herself as a visionary, and she thought that being detail-oriented and emphasizing control was simply "not her style." Hence, it was with some dread that she began to implement the change strategy she had outlined for herself with respect to that approach to management. Here is her report:

I picked a role model, read some books, made some notes, and designed a change program. It was really very simple. Basically it boiled down to setting times to do a whole raft of tasks that I normally ignored. That was all there was to it. I was amazed. It was not a matter of ability; it was actually quite easy. It is now hard to believe that I once thought I was incapable of doing the[se] things . . . .

We close this section by encouraging you to believe in yourself. It is possible to become a better manager and a managerial leader. It is possible to improve in areas that seem far from your natural style. If you are willing to follow the steps outlined herein, they can be very helpful in moving you forward along the road to mastery.

ANALYSIS   Looking for Behavioral Complexity and Lift

Objective   This exercise will give you the opportunity to analyze an individual's behavioral complexity and ability to generate lift.

Directions   Identify a leader you admire and with whom you are familiar. You may select someone that you know personally or someone you have read about enough to familiarize yourself with her history as a leader.

1. What actions has this person engaged in that suggest she is comfortable using each of the following approaches when working with and/or managing others? Try to identify as many different types of behaviors as you can.

   - A human relations approach that emphasizes collaboration, commitment, and cohesion?
   - An internal process approach that emphasizes control and stability?
   - A rational goal approach that emphasizes competition and productivity?
   - An open systems approach that emphasizes creativity, change, and adaptability?

2. Based on your answers above, does it appear that this person has a large behavioral repertoire and a high level of behavioral complexity?

3. Does working with or reading about this person leave you feeling inspired and energized? If so, can you identify some examples of her actions that are consistent with the four psychological states required to achieve lift? That is, what does this person do to suggest that she is:

   - Internally directed by a set of core values?
   - Purpose-centered and intent on achieving extraordinary results?
   - Externally open, interested in learning, and willing to change?
   - Other-focused and respectful of people's needs, feelings, and wants?

Reflection   Although you may have found that the leader you selected tends to rely on behaviors associated with one of the quadrants of the competing values framework more than others, that does not necessarily mean that this person has a small behavioral repertoire or lacks behavioral complexity. Why not? Because the behaviors that you observed may have been the most appropriate behaviors for the situation at hand. A more comprehensive analysis of that person's behaviors using 360 degree feedback (Lepsinger & Lucia, 1997) might reflect a much more balanced profile.

PRACTICE   Generating Lift to Support a Planned Change

Objective   This exercise is intended to give you a chance to use lift to increase your ability to create positive change.

Directions   The last Application exercise in Module 4 asked you to plan a change. Please refer to that plan, and answer the questions below to see if your plan as originally written was consistent with the four psychological states associated with lift.

1. What values does this change reflect? Are these the same values that serve as my anchors, or does the change I am proposing suggest an integrity gap?

2. What specific result do I want to achieve by making this change?

3. Were the strategies that I originally identified for implementing this change flexible, suggesting that I am open to learning and willing to change my approach?

4. How would I feel if I were experiencing this proposed change from other people's points of view?

Reflection   Did you discover during this exercise that one or more of the psychological states required for generating lift was not present? If so, why do you think that was the case? How could you revise your plan so that it will lift you and create lift for others?

APPLICATION   Your Strategy for Mastery

Objective   This final exercise gives you a chance to begin taking action on your own agenda for self-improvement.

Directions   Based on the Assessment that you completed at the beginning of this concluding section, write a long-term development plan that addresses:

- Developing the competencies that you have identified as top priorities
- Using systems and paradoxical thinking to expand the way that you see the world
- Enhancing your behavioral complexity and integrating multiple competencies
- Lifting yourself and others
- Maintaining an active personal development program in the future

Reflection   With your Summary Evaluation Matrix as a starting point, you should be well on your way to developing a comprehensive strategy for mastery. Rather than organizing your personal strategy in the order that the competencies appear in the text, you may find it helpful to focus first on those competencies that you have identified as most important to you at this point in your career. Keep in mind that for strategic planning to be worthwhile, the strategy must be implemented and the results must be evaluated relative to the original goals. There will undoubtedly be modifications that you will need to make to your strategy for mastery as time goes by, so the sooner you get started, the better!

REFERENCES

Breen, Bill. (2000). What's your intuition? *Fast Company*, no. 38 [On-line]. Available: http://www.fastcompany.com/online/38/klein.html.

Cameron, K. S., Dutton, J. E., & Quinn, R. E.. (2003). *Positive organizational scholarship: foundations for a new discipline.* San Francisco: Berrett-Koehler.

Cameron, K. S., & Lavine, M. (2006). *Making the impossible possible: Leading extraordinary performance—the Rocky Flats story.* San Francisco: Berrett-Koehler.

Chaleff, I. (1995). *The courageous follower: Standing up to and for our leaders.* San Francisco: Berrett-Koehler.

Collins, J. (2001). *Good to great: Why some companies make the leap . . . and others don't.* New York: HarperBusiness.

Dreyfus, H., L., & Dreyfus, S. E., with T. Athanasiou. (1986). *Mind over machine: The power of human intuition and expertise in the era of the computer.* New York: Free Press.

Faerman, S. R., & Quinn, R. E.. (1985). Effectiveness: The perspective from organizational theory. *Review of Higher Education, 9*, 83–100.

Gelb, M. J. (1998). *How to think like Leonardo da Vinci: Seven steps to genius every day.* New York: Delacorte Press.

Hatfield, E., Cacioppo, J. T., & Rapson, R. L. (1992). Primitive emotional contagion. In M. S. Clark (Ed.), *Emotion and Social Behavior:* Vol. 14. *Review of Personality and Social Psychology* (pp. 151–177). Newbury Park, CA: Sage.

Hooijberg, R., Hunt, J. G., & Dodge, G. E. (1997). Leadership complexity and development of the Leaderplex model. *Journal of Management, 23*(3), 375–408.

Hooijberg, R., & Quinn, R. E. (1992). Behavioral complexity and the development of effective managers. In R. L. Phillips and J. G. Hunt (Eds.), *Strategic leadership: A Multiorganizational perspective* (pp. 161–176). Westport, CT: Quorum Books.

Isen, A. M. (1999). Positive affect and creativity. In S. Russ (Ed.), *Affect, creative experience, and psychological adjustment* (pp. 3–7). Philadelphia: Bruner/Masel.

Lawrence, K. A., Lenk, P., & Quinn, R. E. (2009). Behavioral complexity in leadership: The psychometric properties of a new instrument to measure behavioral repertoire. *Leadership Quarterly,* 20, 87–102.

Leonardo's Dream Machines. (2005) DVD available from the U.S. Public Broadcasting Service.

Lepsinger, R. & Lucia, A. D. (1997). *The art and science of 360° feedback.* San Francisco: Pfeiffer.

Lishner, D. A., Cooter, A. B., & Zald, D. H. (2008). Rapid emotional contagion and expressive congruence under strong test conditions. *Journal of Nonverbal Behavior, 32*, 225–239.

Petrick, J. A., Scherer, R. F., Brodzinski, J. D., Quinn, J. F., & Ainina M. F. (1999). Global leadership skills and reputational capital: Intangible resources for sustainable competitive advantage. *Academy of Management Executive, 13*(1), 58–69.

Phillips, D. T. (1999). *Martin Luther King, Jr. on leadership: Inspiration & wisdom for challenging times.* New York: Warner Books.

Quinn, Robert E. (1988). *Beyond rational management: Mastering the paradoxes and competing demands of high performance.* San Francisco: Jossey-Bass.

Quinn, R. E., Faerman, S. R., & Dixit, N. (1987). Perceived performance: Some archetypes of managerial effectiveness and ineffectiveness. Working paper, Institute for Government and Policy Studies, Department of Public Administration, State University of New York at Albany.

Quinn, R. W., & Quinn, R. E. (2009). *Lift: Becoming a positive force in any situation.* San Francisco: Berrett-Koehler.

Senge, Peter. (1990). *The Fifth discipline: The art & practice of the learning organization.* New York: Currency Doubleday.

Schön, D. A. (1983). *The reflective practitioner: How professionals think in action.* New York: Basic Books.

Seligman, M. E. P. (2002). *Authentic happiness: Using the new positive psychology to realize your potential for lasting fulfillment.* New York: Free Press.

Weick, K. (1984). Small Wins: Redefining the scale of social problems. *American Psychologist, 39*, 40–49.

Wheatley, Margaret J. (1992). *Leadership and the new science.* San Francisco: Berrett-Koehler.